W9-CZO-042

SOCIAL STUDIES
and the elementary/middle school student

SOCIAL STUDIES
and the elementary/middle school student

CYNTHIA SZYMANSKI SUNAL

University of Alabama, Tuscaloosa

MARY E. HAAS

West Virginia University

Harcourt Brace Jovanovich College Publishers

Fort Worth   Philadelphia   San Diego   New York   Orlando   Austin   San Antonio
Toronto   Montreal   London   Sydney   Tokyo

Editor in chief **Ted Buchholz**
Acquisitions Editor **Jo-Anne Weaver**
Developmental Editor **Tracy Napper**
Project Editor **Kelly Riche**
Production Manager **Monty Shaw**
Book Designer **Burl Sloan**
Compositor **York Graphic Services, Inc.**

Copyright © 1993 by Holt, Rinehart and Winston, Inc.

All rights reserved. No part of this publication may be reproduced or transmitted in any form or by any means, electronic or mechanical, including photocopy, recording, or any information storage and retrieval system, without permission in writing from the publisher.

Requests for permission to make copies of any part of the work should be mailed to: Permissions Department, Harcourt Brace Jovanovich, Publishers, Orlando, FL 32887.

Address for Editorial Correspondence
Harcourt Brace Jovanovich, 301 Commerce Street, Suite 3700, Fort Worth, TX 76102

Address for Orders
Harcourt Brace Jovanovich, 6277 Sea Harbor Drive, Orlando, FL 32887
1-800-782-4479, or 1-800-433-0001 (in Florida)

ISBN: 0-03-055042-4

Library of Congress Catalog Card Number: 92-81849
Printed in the United States of America
2 3 4 5 6 7 8 9 0 1   039   9 8 7 6 5 4 3 2 1

Acknowledgments
Table 13-1   Reprinted with permission from *Master Curriculum Guide in Economics, A Framework for Teaching the Basic Concepts.* Copyright © 1977, Joint Council on Economic Education, New York, New York.
Table 14-1   Used by permission of David R. Procter.
Table 14-3   Reprinted by permission from National Council for the Social Studies, *Social Education.*
Table 14-4   D. Procter & M. E. Haas. *A Handbook of School-Based Projects for Student Participation.* Eric Document ED 326 467. Reprinted by permission of the authors.

Photo Credits
Dennis W. Sunal: Photos on pages 24, 25, 26, 45, 163, 200, and 272.
Mary E. Haas: Photos on pages 11, 89, 110, 134, 149, 181, 195, 221, 267, 269, 271, 295, 296, 300, 328, and 355.
Nancy Swanek Szymanski: Photos on pages 6 and 67.
Barbara Gibson Warash: Photos on pages 228 and 327.

To Dennis, who has always given me constant support,
encouragement, and patience.
To Alisa and Paul, who have grown up
to be concerned, active citizens.
To Joseph and Sophie Bartnik Szymanski,
who involved me in active citizenship.
To my grandparents, John and Anna Kacala Szymanski,
and Frank and Veronica Michalska Bartnik,
who struggled to attain citizenship.

Cynthia Szymanski Sunal

To my parents, Gladys and Marvin,
and my grandmothers, Leah and Elida,
all role models of concerned citizens,
and to Maxine, Anna, and Cynthia for encouraging
my interest in social studies for elementary students.

Mary E. Haas

Preface

Social Studies and the Elementary/Middle School Student demonstrates a firm conviction that children should begin social studies in the kindergarten and continue that study throughout their schooling. We also believe social studies is best learned by stressing meaningful learning of content, skills, and values that promote democratic behavior in and among citizens.

Drawing upon the combined teaching experience of more than 25 years in the public schools and an equal number of years in higher education teaching, supervising, and reading and contributing to the research literature, we have written a textbook designed to illustrate the following: 1) the processes (strategies) for teaching social studies, 2) the structure of the knowledge to be learned, and 3) the theory and research that explain learning in social studies. This book focuses on *meaningful learning,* recognizing that students construct knowledge in their own minds so that it has meaning for them. The research literature on constructivism and information processing has contributed heavily to the approach taken in this book. As we have worked with the research literature, conducted our own research, and developed and taught social studies lessons, we have practiced what we preach. We are convinced that the learning cycle approach to structuring lessons provides teachers and learners with flexibility and assures the inclusion of the best aspects of the major theories describing how students learn. We have applied the learning cycle in teaching social studies concepts, generalizations, skills, and values.

This book is rich in examples and illustrations of how to teach social studies. Examples of learning cycles are provided for all grade levels, from kindergarten to grade eight, and are drawn from many social science disciplines and history. These examples begin in Chapter 1 and are distributed throughout the book. Several chapters are designed as a learning cycle to help the reader work through the ideas being presented as these chapters are read. Integral to many of the chapters are "Time for Reflection: What Do YOU Think?" exercises. Students will benefit most from these sections if they are used when encountered in the text, and if students can share their thoughts with others. Single, correct answers are not always appropriate. Students are invited to use these exercises to enter into dialogue with the authors, their instructor, and their peers. Instructors may want to use these as starters for discussions. Chapters also contain an element entitled "A Practice Activity." These are designed to review the content of the chapter or to provide additional practice for key ideas.

The major curriculum movements, such as multicultural education and global education, discussed throughout the book, demonstrate their impact on many social studies topics. Because of the important role of history, geography, economics, values, and political science in the social studies curriculum, chapters are devoted to each of these disciplines. These chapters identify content and appropriate strategies that can be utilized in teaching information from each of these disciplines. Computers, electronic technology, and other media in social studies are discussed in a chapter that describes their implementation in the classroom.

This textbook guides the user in planning and teaching successful lessons and units. It also elaborates on the steps for teaching a wide range of specific strategies and provides guidance in selecting appropriate content. Therefore, it is a very comprehensive reference for those who are teaching and developing the social studies curriculum.

To complement the textbook there is an extensive Instructor's Manual. It highlights topics to stress, suggests activities, and provides a variety of test questions for each chapter. Nine learning cycles for methods students are also presented. Masters for many tables from the textbook and suggested activities are reproduced for easy use.

Many thanks to Donna Buckhalter and Karen Skoglund for their secretarial expertise, willing assistance, and patience. Thanks also to Barbara Warash Gibson, Dennis W. Sunal, and Nancy Swanek Szymanski for their help with photography. Their excellent photographs are a most important part of this book. We also wish to thank our developmental editor, Tracy Napper, for her encouragement and for keeping us on task.

The suggestions and comments of the reviewers were very helpful and challenged us to think in new directions. The extensive amount of time each devoted to reviewing the manuscript for this book is much appreciated. We would like to thank:

John Anfin, Winthrop College; Joanne Bernstein, Brooklyn College; Thomas Bibler, University of Tennessee at Chattanooga; Steven P. Brochinsky, Southern Connecticut State University; Helen Carlson, University of Minnesota; Kenneth Craycraft, Sam Houston State University; Sr. Barbara Gould, R.S.M., University of Massachusetts at Boston; Phyllis Huff, University of Tennessee; Ann Lockledge, University of North Carolina at Wilmington; Patricia Mosley, University of North Texas; Dick Needham, University of Northern Colorado; Lynn Nielsen, University of Northern Iowa; Anna Ochoa, Indiana University at Bloomington; Ron Pahl, California State University at Fullerton; Joan Livingston Prouty, Sam Houston State University; Carrie Sorensen, Saginaw Valley State University; Dennis Strasser, Kutztown University; Scott Waters, Emporia State University

Table of Contents

Chapter Seven
Instructional Strategies and Materials for Teaching Social Studies   126

Chapter Eight
Using Audio-Visual and Electronic Media in Social Studies   156

CHAPTER 1

OVERVIEW

This chapter begins by asking you what you remember about social studies during your elementary and middle school years. You are encouraged to use your past experience with social studies to consider several questions: What is social studies? What is the purpose of social studies? Where does the content of social studies come from? What are its characteristics? What methods are most often used to teach it? This chapter will try to demonstrate the diversity of responses that can be expected when these questions are asked. It is also a chapter that will ask you to think about your own response to these questions.

Introducing Social Studies

OBJECTIVES

1. *Identify the content of the current social studies curriculum for grades K–8.*
2. *Name the instructional strategies most frequently used to teach social studies.*
3. *Give examples of different views of the purposes of the social studies.*
4. *Define social studies.*
5. *Describe how the authors' definition of social studies combines and expands on others' views of social studies.*
6. *Describe the characteristics of social studies.*

REMEMBERING SOCIAL STUDIES

Think back to your elementary and middle school years. What memories surface when you think of "social studies"? Some preservice and inservice elementary and middle school teachers have said:

- *Units on a country.* Every month, we would study a different country. We would arrange our desks in the shape of that country. We would be responsible for knowing all about that part of the country our desk was located in, its culture, occupations, natural resources, and so on. At the end of the month, we would share what we had found out. During the month, we would all sample food from our country, sing songs, and listen to stories. I loved it and was always excited about which country would be next.

- *Memorizing states and their capitals.* I don't remember ever looking at a map to try to find a state capital, although probably I did do so. It was such a chore memorizing those state capitals because we took quizzes on them until we got 100% on a quiz.

- *Field trips.* I can remember two really great field trips. One was to a local doughnut store. The kitchen smelled wonderful. We were impressed at how mechanized doughnut making was. At the end of the field trip, we each got to pick out six doughnuts and take them with us. The other field trip was to a state park with mounds built by Native Americans long ago. They were huge. I wanted so much to know what had happened to the people who built these mounds. Why didn't they have villages around these mounds now? After the trip, I read everything I could find about these people.

- *Writing reports.* We had to write a report on somebody or something related to each unit we studied. At first, I enjoyed the reports but, after a while, I got so tired of them. It was really boring listening to each student read his or her report.

- *Worksheets and questions.* There were always so many questions to answer at the end of the chapters. As if there were not enough to answer, we would also be given worksheets to fill in. The teacher called them "funsheets" but we knew they were no fun.

- *Discussions.* One year my teacher really encouraged us to say what we thought about things. We brought up a lot of issues that were important to us, such as why we were the last stop on the school bus route and got home later than anyone at the other schools. We had not considered the fact that we also started school later. After some discussion, we decided this did not make up for our long afternoons and petitioned the school board for a change.

- *Role playing.* I was shy but I did enjoy role playing. Because I could think of it as a school assignment, I would make myself put aside my shyness. I really got involved in it. It seemed to make me understand situations much better. My teacher did some economics-related role playing that I enjoyed most of all. Suddenly, economics was interesting!

Some of the memories described above are positive and some are negative. Would you rate your memories as mostly positive, mostly negative, or a mixture of both?

Social studies should involve students so deeply that in 10, 20, or 30 years from now, students will be able to reminisce about fondly remembered social studies activities. Notice that the positive memories occurred when students were actively involved. Their minds were constructing new knowledge or revising knowledge they had. They were thinking and enjoying it.

SOCIAL STUDIES TODAY

What is social studies usually like for today's students? Is it composed of the enjoyable activities remembered by the preservice and inservice teachers above? Do the negative aspects dominate the program? If negative aspects are there, can we eliminate them by doing it differently when we teach? Let's examine what the professional literature can tell us about the answers to these questions.

SOCIAL STUDIES CURRICULUM

One curriculum pattern is frequently used in social studies. This is the "expanding environments" approach (Superka, Hawke, & Morrissett, 1980). In this approach, kindergarten students focus on themselves and their families. As they progress through the grades, they "expand out" from their personal world to explore a wide range of cultures and governments in the seventh grade. There is a different movement in the eighth grade as students move from the worldwide view of seventh grade to studying American History. This expanding environments approach generally includes the topics given in Table 1–1.

For how long has this pattern been commonly followed? It has been typical of many kindergarten through grade-6 programs since 1955. Seventh and eighth

Table 1–1

Topics in the Expanding Environments Approach to Social Studies

Kindergarten	*Third Grade*	*Sixth Grade*
Self	Communities	World Cultures
School		Western Hemisphere Studies
Community	*Fourth Grade*	
Home	State History	*Seventh Grade*
	Geographic Regions	World Geography or History
First Grade		
Families	*Fifth Grade*	*Eighth Grade*
	History of the United States	American History
Second Grade		
Neighborhoods		

Source: Superka, D., Hawke, S., & Morrissett, I. (1980). The current and future status of the social studies, Social Education, 44 (May), 362–369.

graders have studied virtually the same topics since 1916 (Superka et al., 1980; Morrissett, 1981).

Recently, this pattern has been questioned. Some critics question the underlying assumption that children are most familiar with their immediate environment and that their frames of reference are confined to it (Naylor & Diem, 1987). Others have criticized it for being too age/grade level oriented (Baskerville & Sesow, 1976). Others point out that it does not make provision for teaching issues of immediate concern to children (Joyce & Alleman-Brooks, 1982).

Numerous curriculum development projects tried to change the pattern, particularly in the 1960s and 1970s. Among these were the Minnesota Social Studies Project (Capron, 1972) and the Social Roles Model (Superka & Hawke, 1982). The sequence followed in the Minnesota project was: Kindergarten—the earth as the home of man; Grades 1, 2—families around the world; Grades 3, 4—communities around the world; Grade 5—regional studies; Grade 6—our economic system; Grade 7—man and society; and Grade 8—our political system. The Social Roles Model stressed social participation by students. Seven social roles were stressed: citizen, worker, consumer, family member, friend, member of various social groups, and self. Research studies with the Minnesota project in grades 1–5 led to the conclusion that the program achieved better results than other social studies programs that were not as well-defined or structured (Mitsakos, 1978). Little research has been done with the Social Roles Model so that it is not possible to make conclusions about its effects. Despite efforts to develop alternative patterns and approaches to the social studies curriculum, the expanding environments approach has continued to be the most popular approach used. Major support has not developed for an alternative to it.

SOCIAL STUDIES INSTRUCTIONAL STRATEGIES

What about instructional strategies? Teachers use lecture and discussion as the main strategies for teaching social studies. Discussion is used almost daily by 60% of K–6 teachers while lecture is used almost daily by 20% (Superka et al., 1980). Teaching occurs in a large-group situation with little individualization or small-group work (Shaver, Davis, & Helburn, 1979). Students usually listen, read a textbook, complete workbooks and worksheets, and take quizzes (Goodlad, 1984). The textbook is the main tool in teaching, used daily by 90% of grades 4–8, and 65% of grades K–3 teachers (Superka et al., 1980). When teachers teach, they want students to learn facts. They do not focus on thinking about those facts, analyzing, or questioning them (Shaver et al., 1979).

Time for Reflection: What Do YOU Think?

Think back on your memories of social studies. Then, think back again to your elementary and middle school years. What instructional strategies were used in social studies? What instructional strategies do you think elementary and middle school students might find interesting and stimulating?

What instructional strategies do students want to see used in social studies? They want: group projects, field trips, independent work, less reading, discussions, clear examples, student planning, challenging learning experiences, class activities, role playing, and simulations (Schug, Todd, & Beery, 1984). The professional literature suggests that there doesn't seem to be a match between what teachers do in social studies and what students want to do.

THE PURPOSE OF SOCIAL STUDIES

The National Council for the Social Studies (1979) has said the purpose of social studies ". . . is to prepare young people to be humane, rational, participating citizens in a world that is becoming increasingly interdependent." This statement represents the dominant view of social studies. It defines the overall goal of social studies as citizenship education. *Citizenship* means active participation in community and national decision making (Goodman & Adler, 1985, p. 1; Barr, Barth, & Shermis, 1977).

While agreeing with the overall goal of citizenship education, some people place a greater emphasis on any one of the following six viewpoints:

1. teaching history and geography
2. understanding social science
3. facilitating cultural transmission
4. supporting personal development
5. developing reflective thinking skills
6. encouraging rational problem solving, decision making, and social action

Each of these supports the dominant view of citizenship education as an overall goal in social studies.

Social studies has been called "the great connection" by Goodman and Adler (1985). It is seen as the core to which all parts of the elementary and middle school curriculum can be tied. Social studies can integrate mathematics, science, art, music, physical education, health, reading, language arts, and all the other content areas. Such integration is important. The school curriculum often splits knowledge into many separate areas of study, but the real world in which citizens live and work is not so divided. Social studies can serve as the connector that brings the curriculum and the world together. Other chapters in this book will discuss developing units that incorporate several content areas. Social studies is an interdisciplinary approach relying heavily on the content of the social sciences and history to achieve its goal of preparing people to be citizens of a democracy.

THE DEFINITION OF SOCIAL STUDIES

The professional literature gives teachers several definitions of social studies just as it gives several purposes. When people view the purpose of social studies from different perspectives, they can be expected to have differing definitions. Yet, there are some common elements that can be identified.

Social studies field trips are a way to make the "great connection" integrating social studies with the other content areas.

In definitions of social studies, citizenship education is identified as an over-all goal. The "social" focus is also recognized. Social studies deals with our social lives by investigating the ways we adapt to each other and come to understand ourselves (Sunal, 1990). Many educators define social studies as incorporating in-quiry, active participation in society, and an understanding of social science (Goodman & Adler, 1985, p. 15).

The definition of social studies continues to undergo changes as the world in which its citizens live undergoes changes. In 1984, the Task Force on Scope and Sequence of the National Council for the Social Studies (NCSS) formed this defi-nition:

> The social studies may be defined as an area of the curriculum that derives goals from the nature of citizenship in a democratic society and links to other soci-eties, draws content from the social sciences and other disciplines, and reflects personal, social, and cultural experiences of students.

This definition clearly incorporates several of the purposes described above. It re-flects cultural transmission as a purpose but does go beyond it when it states that social studies goals are derived from the nature of citizenship in a democratic so-ciety. It also stresses links to other societies so that the emphasis is not on a cul-tural heritage of a single group but rather on a heritage which comes from all of the world's societies. The definition then describes the social science disciplines as the major source of content in social studies. Although much social studies con-tent comes from the social sciences and history, the definition does note that it also comes from other disciplines. These include the humanities, the arts, and the biological and physical sciences. Finally, the definition includes students them-selves and says that social studies is personal. It reflects each student's personal, social, and cultural experiences. This is compatible with the view of social stud-ies that focuses on helping students develop personally to their fullest. It also touches upon the view that stresses the development of reflective thinking skills. The definition, however, does not incorporate the social action view. It does not describe social studies as encouraging students to actively work to improve their social world.

THIS TEXT'S DEFINITION OF THE SOCIAL STUDIES

This text uses a definition of social studies that builds on the 1984 NCSS defini-tion. It views learners as individuals who will develop over time into active citi-zens of a democracy. It reflects the belief that teachers can best assist the student's development through the use of a curriculum and instructional strategies that sys-tematically incorporate appropriate skills, content, values, and participation.

Social studies is an area of the curriculum deriving its goals from the nature of citizenship in a democratic society with links to other societies. Drawing its content from the social sciences and other disciplines, it also incorporates the personal and social experiences of students and their cultural heritage. It links

> factors outside the individual, such as cultural heritage, with factors inside the
> individual, particularly the development and use of reflective thinking, problem
> solving, and rational decision-making skills, for the purpose of creating in-
> volvement in social action.

Social action is a continuum of possible activities ranging from single efforts
requiring small commitments of time and talent to long-term projects requiring a
regular commitment of time and multiple intellectual and social skills. These possible activities can involve regularly picking up litter on the playground, reading
stories to children in younger grades during rainy lunchtimes, making Valentine's
Day cards for nursing home residents, washing dishes at a soup kitchen for home-
less people, or working to have a stop sign installed at a busy intersection that
school children cross. Social action is undertaken after careful study and preparation by students so that they understand why they are involved in a project and
how to carry it to completion. Social action is the final step in problem solving
and decision making for citizens in a democracy. Its end goal is to make our social world a better place for each person.

Social studies has been defined above in order to clarify for the reader how
the authors view it. This definition is not the final definition nor is it one that
everyone must agree on. There has been a continuing controversy over how social studies is defined. As you work with this book, your definition may or may
not be revised. We do hope that it will be enriched.

SOCIAL STUDIES, SOCIAL SCIENCES, AND SOCIAL LIVING EDUCATION

Social studies, social sciences, and social living education are all terms used in
education. They are related, yet different. The discussion above has focused on
social studies. Social sciences were also discussed as the content areas (such as
political science and geography) that contribute heavily to the social studies. They
have also been discussed in relation to their methodology. In social studies, students should be encouraged to investigate the content they study as social scientists do, using processes that analyze and critically evaluate the information
they work with. Social living education refers to the assistance children and young
adolescents receive in learning how to socially interact with others. This assistance comes from various institutions in the society such as family, church, and
school. Many people help educate each child and young adolescent in the skills
and knowledge needed in social living. The school and its social studies program
are one of many contributors to the social living education of the individual. Most
evident in the primary grades, social living education is perhaps also needed
when students move from their primary or elementary school to a middle or junior high school, where they must adjust to a new school emphasis and new
friends at a time in their lives when they are rapidly changing intellectually and
physically.

CHARACTERISTICS OF THE SOCIAL STUDIES

Thus far, the discussion has focused on content, that is, on what to teach students and whether that is history or reflective decision making or any of a number of other things. Now, the discussion will turn to what occurs when a learner is involved in social studies. The following characteristics describe the study of social studies:

- involves a search for patterns in our lives
- involves both the content and processes of learning
- requires information processing
- requires problem solving and decision making
- involves the development and analysis of one's own values and the application of these values in social action (Sunal, 1990, pp. 3–4)

SEARCHING FOR PATTERNS

A pattern is a regular activity that has occurred in the past and can be expected to occur again in the future. The world is full of patterns, for example:

- People wear fewer, and lighter, clothes in summer.
- Every group of people has a complex set of social relationships.
- Past events influence current events.
- People want things they do not need.

Students are inundated by information about their social world from the media, peers, and family members. They try to make sense out of such things as family relationships, what money means, what people do when they work, why people are happy or sad. These are but a few of the patterns they construct out of the information they gather from their experiences. These patterns are constructed, challenged, redefined, or accepted many times in life as people gather more information through their experiences (Osborne & Freyberg, 1985; Taba, 1967). Later chapters are devoted to areas contributing in great degree to social studies, including economics, geography, history, psychology, sociology, and political science. In each chapter is a discussion of patterns identified in this area. These patterns become the concepts and generalizations of the area.

Social studies helps students identify patterns and develop their own mental construction of the social world. The patterns that are developed are the concepts and generalizations of social studies. It also helps students develop thinking and decision-making skills. These skills enable them to construct or modify a concept or generalization. Once students have constructed a pattern, social studies helps them respond to it through social action.

INVOLVING CONTENT AND LEARNING PROCESSES

The search for patterns in our social world occurs naturally and continually in everyday life. People try to make sense out of what they experience.

In searching for patterns, people use processes, such as observing and inferring (Michaelis, 1992). Chapter 3 discusses the range of processes used. Social studies involves both content and process. Neither can exist without the other. Process involves "doing." For example, students are looking at a set of slides of public buildings in Thailand. They find Thai temples particularly interesting. They observe that temples are tall buildings, always at least two stories high. They also notice a high ceiling inside. All of the temples are ornate. The temples have a lot of windows yet the inside seems dark and there is little furniture. The temples always seem to be located near a market square or along a busy street. The students look at another slide set, one of European cathedrals. They identify many similar characteristics: height, little furniture, busy location, ornateness. A small group of students hypothesize that people build places of worship in a similar way no matter what their culture. They decide to check it out further and scour architecture books for examples of churches and temples from other cultures. They also go on a field trip and visit several places of worship in their own town. Their search supports their hypothesis as they find similar characteristics in their local places of worship as well as in Mexican churches, Japanese temples, and Syrian mosques. The group next begins to ponder why these characteristics are evident in places of worship.

Several processes are occurring during the students' activity. They are *observing;* they notice various characteristics of the style and location of the Thai temples, and later of the European cathedrals. They are *hypothesizing* that people build places of worship in similar ways no matter what their culture. They are *inferring* that places of worship are more ornate than are other buildings.

Content is being acquired during this activity as a product of the processes occurring. The students have learned many facts, such as, "this building has a high roof-line and a high ceiling inside." They develop a generalization after a search for information supporting their hypothesis: People do build places of worship in similar ways across cultures.

The facts and generalization developed during this activity are part of the content of the social studies. The actual forming of a pattern involves the process side of the social studies. The pattern, once formed, is the product, part of the content of the social studies.

Students discover the content of the social studies through their search for patterns in the social world. The content of the social studies is tremendous and comes from many sources. Only when students have acquired some content in the social studies through many experiences with the processes used to discover patterns among facts, concepts, and generalizations will they become able to understand the abstract verbal presentations of content found in social studies textbooks.

PROCESSING AND USING INFORMATION

Social studies is characterized by a search for patterns based on information. Single items of information are gathered, organized, and summarized. Through this

What patterns might these children have discovered on their visit to Prickett's Fort, West Virginia?

process, called information processing, single items of information are transformed into concepts and generalizations that are more usable than are the isolated pieces themselves (Dworetzky, 1990; Fabricius & Wellman, 1983).

People learn to process information efficiently through practice. Requiring students to learn concepts and generalizations through rote memorization rather than allowing them to form the patterns through their own processing limits understanding (Ryan, 1977). Students who develop their ability to process information are better able to work with the mass of information that comes to them from their social world and can become more competent citizens of it (see also chapter 3).

DECISION MAKING AND PROBLEM SOLVING

Recognizing patterns in their lives helps people make decisions based on information. It also helps them process information. The ability to recognize patterns and to process information in turn helps solve the problems that confront citizens. Solving problems requires refusing to avoid them and refusing to jump to a partial solution. It requires waiting to reach a conclusion until people have information that helps them choose the best solution. The problems studied in school may be economics related, may have historical roots, or may involve using the political support of interest groups. In any case, social studies prepares students to make decisions and solve problems arising in their social world.

INVOLVEMENT WITH THE DEVELOPMENT AND ANALYSIS OF VALUES AND THE APPLICATION OF VALUES IN SOCIAL ACTION

Decision making, problem solving, and other major characteristics of the social studies (Sunal, 1990) lead toward the development and analysis of what one believes to be the important things in life. These values shape people's responses to the social world in which they live. Students today have, and must confront, many more choices than did previous generations. Communication between people on a personal level through telephones, facsimile ("fax") machines, and other technology is possible in much of the world. Communication on a less personal level through radio, tape recordings, and television is widespread even in many developing nations. Transportation enables people in most of the world to travel farther and more frequently than did their grandparents. As people come in direct contact with more and more people and have indirect contact through the media with many other people, they are exposed to a wide range of ideas. Such exposure requires them to make choices, to accept or reject or simply not acknowledge an idea they come into contact with. The alternatives are varied and can be overwhelming. Each choice affects many other aspects of their lives and the lives of other people. Social studies helps students learn how to exert some control over their lives as they define and clarify their values (Banks, 1985; Sunal, 1981). When students consider the implications of their values and then act on them, they further extend the control they have over their lives (Banks, 1985).

Students need to analyze their values, to be consciously aware of them, and to recognize alternative values. The teacher models some values and helps students think about their own values. The right answer is not automatically dispensed. Instead, the teacher may ask questions that encourage students to examine the consequences of their choices for themselves, others, and their community (Banks & Clegg, 1985; Fraenkel, 1977).

Personal and public policy decisions are based on criteria that require reflection on facts, generalizations, consequences, and feelings toward people. All the characteristics of social studies mentioned above are incorporated and used when a value decision is made and social action is taken.

Students need to be encouraged and taught to use all the characteristics of social studies that have been described. This will enable them to gain the expertise needed to eventually become people who are conscious of the reasoning needed to make better decisions. It should also translate into social action that demands reflective and careful decision making from individuals and from society's leaders.

▣ PLANNING FOR TEACHING

Students have definite ideas about many of the things around them. These ideas come from past experience with other similar objects, from adult comments that may be interpreted differently than adults would expect, and from the media and other educational experiences (Dykstra, 1985; Stepans, 1985). Many of these conceptions are different from accepted explanations (Osborne & Cosgrove, 1985). The lesson plan in Table 1–2 models a strategy—the learning cycle—supported by research as effective and used by many educators to help students restructure personal ideas (Karplus, 1977; Osborne & Freyberg, 1985). This text will describe the creation and use of learning cycles that help students develop their role as citizens who participate in social action. A learning cycle takes into account the abilities of students and uses instructional strategies that are appropriate to a student's level of development.

Table 1–2

LEARNING CYCLE: Making Good Rules

*Theme: **Making Good Rules** (For Primary Grades)*

OBJECTIVES	PROCEDURES	EVALUATIONS
	Exploration	
Students will discuss the need for rules in a game.	Arrange students in relay teams of 8–10 for an eraser relay. Teacher starts game but does not give any rules. Stop students for not playing correctly and give one or two directions and restart game only to stop it again. Repeat this 3–6 times. Game rules include:	Students' participation in discussion recorded on a checklist.
	1. Pass the eraser down the row and then back up. Winning team is first to complete this.	
	2. Players must hold eraser with both hands.	
	3. First player bends down and passes eraser to the next player by reaching through his or her legs.	
	4. Next player passes the eraser over his or her head, etc.	
	5. Players turn around after passing eraser.	
	6. When the eraser gets back to the first player, everyone on the team sits down on the floor.	
	After the game is played correctly, repeat it several times. Teacher asks: "How did you like playing this relay?" "How important to playing the game was it that everyone knew all of the rules?" "How do rules help us?" "Does everyone have to obey rules?" "What would happen if there were no rules?"	

Invention

Students will analyze a good and a poor rule and develop a list of characteristics of a good rule.

Display two statements and read them to the students: "When the stoplight is red, stop and wait until it is green before going on;" "When the stoplight is red, stop and wait until it is green before going on—except if you are wearing red shoes."

Teacher asks: "Could both of these statements be rules?" "How are they different?" "Is one a better rule than the other?" "Why?" Have students work with a partner to develop a list of characteristics of a good rule. Share ideas. List their ideas. "What are the characteristics that make a rule a good rule?" Develop a statement together that answers this question. Expect some of the following:

It is needed for a good reason.
It is clearly worded.
It applies fairly and equally to all.
It is easy to use or follow.
It is agreed to by all.

"Besides playing games, when do you have to obey rules?" "Who makes rules?" "What are some of the rules (laws) that people have to obey?" Check answers against criteria and summarize statement.

Criteria listed by pairs of students.

Expansion

Students will write rules using characteristics of a good rule, then apply them and evaluate them.

Students examine the rules for a fire drill or the bus rules. They practice them and compare them with their criteria.

Students practice writing rules by making one or more for a specific classroom activity such as free reading time, science lab, or art class. Use the rule(s) during the day. Discuss how well they worked. Rewrite, if needed. Post rules for later use. As the year progresses and new activities such as field trips and parties occur, have the students write, practice, and use appropriate rules for the class.

Record of student participation in developing, applying, and rewriting

When teaching with this model, the teacher is a motivator and a guide as well as a provider of information. The teacher's role in helping students restructure their ideas is particularly important. Three main lesson phases are suggested in learning cycles. The first part of the lesson begins with "exploration" activity, during which students attempt to learn the new idea or skill through their own actions and thinking, with minimal guidance from the teacher. Students start with their own ideas, connecting them to the experiences at hand. If constructed well, the experiences confront their personal conceptions. They also require a review of existing ideas and result in questions being asked. Next, in phase two, the lesson continues with "invention," where students are helped to invent the new idea or skill being introduced and explained through more teacher-guided activities. Finally, in phase three, the lesson finishes with "expansion," where the new idea or skill is practiced and applied in new situations. If only one part of the lesson is taught, students will be unlikely to modify their personal conceptions and will continue to interpret the world using inadequate ideas (Osborne & Freyberg, 1985).

Other chapters will describe the process of translating the purpose and definition of social studies a teacher uses into curriculum and instruction. The lesson plan presented here represents the major decisions a teacher must make. The model is flexible and involves teachers in making several decisions, beginning with: "What content should this lesson teach?" Then they must decide: "What content are my students developmentally able to learn?" Finally, they must decide: "What instructional strategies will most appropriately teach this content to these students?" This chapter has focused on some of the issues related to the first question. Other chapters will guide you further in considerations that will help you make these decisions and plan effective and stimulating social studies lessons.

SUMMARY

The current social studies curriculum is dominated by the expanding environments approach. Instructional strategies focused on lecture and discussion are often used. Students have indicated that they prefer more active teaching approaches that incorporate group projects, field trips, and other challenging learning experiences.

Social studies has been defined and viewed in various ways. A focus on citizenship is seen as an overarching goal of social studies despite the diversity of definitions and purposes given for it. Social studies can be learned only through experiences that provide the opportunity to gather information and form it into abstract ideas concerning how people interact. The naturally occurring search for patterns throughout our lives leads to the processing of information, which helps us solve problems, make decisions, and develop and analyze values. Since all people must interact with others in groups, communities, and nations, the goal of social studies is to produce a person who is reflectively and actively involved in society.

Students need to be encouraged to use all the characteristics of the social studies. A strategy for teaching, the learning cycle, is suggested as a means of involving students in using the characteristics of the social studies in order to restructure their ideas.

REFERENCES

Banks, J. & Clegg, A. (1985). *Teaching strategies for the social studies: Inquiry, valuing, and decision making* (3rd ed.). White Plains, NY: Longman.

Barr, R., Barth, J., & Shermis, S. (1977). *Defining the social studies* (NCSS Bulletin 51). Arlington, VA: National Council of the Social Studies.

Baskerville, R. & Sesow, F. (1976). In defense of Hanna and the "expanding environments" approach to social studies. *Theory and Research in Social Education, 4*(1), 20–32.

Bloom, A. (1987). *The closing of the American mind.* New York: Simon & Schuster.

Bradley Commission on History in Schools. (1988). *Building a history curriculum: Guidelines for teaching history in schools.* Washington, DC: Educational Excellence Network.

Capron, B. (1972). University of Minnesota Social Studies Project, *Social Education, 36,* 758–759.

Crabtree, C. (1989). Returning history to the elementary school. *Historical literacy: The case for history in American education* (eds. P. Gagnon and the Bradley Commission on History in Schools). New York: Macmillan.

Curriculum Task Force of the National Commission on Social Studies in the Schools (1989). *Charting a course: Social studies for the 21st century.* Washington, DC: National Commission on Social Studies in the Schools.

Dykstra, D. (1985). Science education in the elementary school: Some observations. *Journal of Research in Science Teaching, 23,* 853–855.

Dworetzky, J. (1990). *Introduction to child development* (4th ed.). St. Paul, MN: West Publishing Co.

Fabricius, W. & Wellman, H. (1983). Children's understanding of retrieval cue utilization. *Developmental Psychology, 19,* 15–21.

Fraenkel, J. (1977). *How to teach about values: An analytic approach.* Englewood Cliffs, NJ: Prentice-Hall.

Goodlad, J. (1984). *A place called school: Prospects for the future.* New York: McGraw-Hill.

Goodman, J. & Adler, S. (1985). Becoming an elementary social studies teacher: A study of perspectives. *Theory and Research in Social Education. 13*(2), 1–20.

Jarolimek, J. (1973). In pursuit of the elusive new social studies. *Educational Leadership, 30,* 596–599.

Joyce, W. & Alleman-Brooks, J. (1982). The child's world. *Social Education, 46,* 538–541.

Karplus, R. (1977). *Science teaching and the development of reasoning.* Berkeley, CA: University of California.

Michaelis, J. (1992). *Social studies for children: A guide to basic instruction* (10th ed.). Boston: Allyn & Bacon.

Mitsakos, C. (1978). A global education program can make a difference. *Theory and Research in Social Education, 6*(1), 1–15.

Morrissett, I. (1981). The needs of the future and the constraints of the past. In H. D. Mehlinger and O. L. Davis, Jr. (eds.), *The social studies* (80th Yearbook of the National Society for the Study of Education). Chicago: University of Chicago Press.

National Council for the Social Studies (1979). Revision of the NCSS curriculum guidelines. *Social Education, 43*(4), 262.

Naylor, D. & Diem, R. (1987). *Elementary and middle school social studies.* New York: Random House.

Oliner, P. (1976). *Teaching elementary social studies: A rational and humanistic approach.* New York: Harcourt Brace Jovanovich.

Osborne, R. & Cosgrove, M. (1985). Children's conceptions of changes of state of water. *Journal of Research in Science Teaching, 20,* 825–838.

Osborne, R. & Freyberg, P. (1985). *Learning in science.* London: Heinemann, 91–111.

Ryan, F. L. (1977). Implementing the hidden curriculum of the social studies. In B. Joyce & F. Ryan (eds.), *Social studies and the elementary teacher: Promises and practices* (Bulletin 53). Washington, DC: National Council for the Social Studies, 152–156.

Schug, M., Todd, R., & Beery, R. (1984). Why kids don't like social studies. *Social Education, 48,* 382–387.

Shaver, J., Davis, O. L., Jr., & Helburn, S. W. (1979). The status of social studies education: Impressions from three NSF studies. *Social Education, 43,* 150–153.

Stepans, J. (1985). Biology in elementary schools: Children's conceptions of life. *American Biology Teacher, 47*(4), 222–225.

Sunal, C. S. (1981). The child and the concept of change. *Social Education, 45,* 438–441.

Sunal, C. S. (1990). *Early childhood social studies.* Columbus, OH: Merrill.

Superka, D. & Hawke, S. (1982). *Social roles: A focus for social studies in the 1980's.* Boulder, CO: Social Science Education Consortium.

Superka, D., Hawke, S., & Morrissett, I. (1980). The current and future status of the social studies. *Social Education, 44*(May), 362–369.

Taba, H. (1967). *Teacher's handbook for elementary social studies* (Introductory Edition). Menlo Park, CA: Addison-Wesley.

CHAPTER 2

OVERVIEW

How does a teacher help students learn social studies content so that it is meaningful to them? This chapter considers an instructional approach that has been developed to facilitate students' construction of meaningful learning. This research-based approach is called the learning cycle (Dillon & Sternberg, 1986; Clarke, 1990; Lawson, Abraham, & Renner, 1989).

The learning cycle approach suggested in this chapter is designed for teaching the content of social studies, which includes concepts and generalizations and the thinking skills necessary for understanding them. It also includes the skills needed if students are to explore and define their attitudes and values. The learning cycle approach can best be used as part of an instructional program that also stresses creativity, development of self-worth, self-reliance, and respect for the opinions of others. It is compatible with knowledge gained from developmental studies involving children, the results of information-processing studies examining the functioning of the brain, and information gained from cognitive science research (Dillon & Sternberg, 1986; Clarke, 1990; and Lawson, Abraham, & Renner, 1989).

The first part of this chapter discusses the learning cycle approach and uses a lesson plan to illustrate it. The second part of the chapter involves the reader in practice activities using the learning cycle approach.

The Learning Cycle: A Framework for Teaching Social Studies

OBJECTIVES

1. *Identify the three phases of the learning cycle.*
2. *Describe five prerequisites for meaningful learning.*
3. *Describe the goals of an exploration activity that initiate a lesson.*
4. *Identify the goals of the teacher-guided portion of a lesson where students construct or "invent" new knowledge.*
5. *Describe three types of activities that need to be considered if new learning is to be expanded and stabilized in long-term memory.*
6. *Plan activities that will encourage meaningful learning in a social studies lesson.*

TEACHING FOR MEANINGFUL LEARNING

The learning cycle is an approach supported by research studies as effective and is used by many educators to help students restructure personal ideas so that their misconceptions are reduced (Karplus, 1977; Osborne & Freyberg, 1985). Three main lesson phases are used:

1. beginning with *exploration* of the idea or skill
2. leading to a more guided *invention* of the idea or skill
3. culminating in *expansion* of the idea or skill through additional practice and trials with new data or in new settings.

The underlying principle of the learning cycle focuses on helping the student generate personal knowledge and form accurate ideas that are based on the student's own investigations of materials and events. The teacher provides materials and sets up events and situations that are appropriate to students' cognitive, social, and psychomotor development. With the teacher's guidance, students compare their ideas and skills with those of experts (teacher, textbook, guest speaker, literature, etc.). The teacher continually monitors students' progress and gives feedback as necessary to prevent students from forming misconceptions. Meaningful learning follows a sequence where the learner:

* *begins* with an established idea or skill (an approach used with a group of problems)
* *tries to interpret* the new experience with an old idea or skill
* *realizes* the existence of a problem, confronts it, pauses, and reflects; emotional responses at this time can include confusion, disorientation, and some discomfort
* *uses* trial and error strategies, gains feedback, and develops a partially correct idea or skill
* *recognizes* the need for a different strategy, observes others, listens, then tries again to restructure ideas or skills
* *begins to form* a new idea or skill by modifying old ones or by creating new ones
* *applies* the new idea or skill to a variety of tasks, thereby *stabilizing* it

This sequence of development is usually found in lessons producing meaningful learning. There are, however, prerequisites which must be met if the sequence is to occur and result in meaningful learning. One prerequisite is that the change in reasoning should not be too great (Karplus, 1979). Students should be challenged but not overwhelmed. The gap between what a student already knows and where the lesson hopes to take him should not be large. A second prerequisite for learning is that what is taught must be related to the prior knowledge of the students (Seiger-Ehrenberg, 1991). A third prerequisite is that many concrete examples must be used in situations requiring active mental and physical involvement by the students. Since the vast majority of elementary and middle school students are concrete operational, a concept or generalization whose existence can only be imagined will not be useful in developing understanding in social studies for these students (Piaget, 1969). A fourth prerequisite is that practice must be provided (Costa, 1991). Students need to practice using real or simulated activities. Without practice, meaningful learning does not occur, because the learning is not stabilized in the student's mind. A fifth prerequisite is that students must be given time to reflect, make mistakes, revise, and form new ideas or skills (Barell, 1991). Other prerequisites may exist in various situations but these five are always essential.

The lesson plan in Table 2–1, "National Memorials and the Display of Power," incorporates the five prerequisites. The approach to working through the problem is similar to the sequence described above. Look at Figures 2–1, 2–2, and 2–3 (pages 24–26), then take a few minutes to read through the lesson plan.

Table 2–1

LEARNING CYCLE: National Memorials and the Display of Power
Theme: Political Power *(For Middle School/Intermediate Grade Levels)*

OBJECTIVES	PROCEDURES	EVALUATIONS
	Exploration	
Students will make inferences about an unfamiliar artifact.	Give each student copies of Figures 2–1 and 2–2. Tell students these are pictures of different views of the same memorial. Divide the class into groups of 3–5 students. Have each group discuss the pictures using the following questions: "Which details in the picture are familiar to you?" "Which are unfamiliar or unusual?" "Who do you think this person is?" "From what culture do you think this person comes?" Write the questions on a transparency for all to see. Following the discussion ask students to write a short paragraph describing what they see in the picture, using the four questions as a guide.	Completeness of paragraph. Has the student responded to all 4 questions?
	Invention	
Students will share ideas about what the artifact represents.	Have a representative from each group read their paragraph to the class. Discuss or speculate on the following, recording student responses: "What were the first things noticed?" "What specific details stand out?" "Possible reasons for making this memorial include: The face on the memorial is probably the face of . . ."	Participation is recorded on a checklist.
Students will identify characteristics of the artifact and of coins that suggest a person's political power.	Read the following statement written by a fifth grader: *"It seems like it's carved. It's a strong face, quiet and powerful. When people have a powerful ruler, they honor him by making a statue like this."* Ask: "Does this student agree with your conclusions?" "What evidence did the student use in making his conclusions?" Discuss ideas. Read further writing by the student: *"I looked at the memorial some more to check if my ideas about it were right. It looks like it's wearing a lot of*	Participation is recorded on a checklist.

crowns. The face looks calm. It's smiling a little. You see the same thing on all sides." Ask: "Did you notice the same details?" "What role do you think this person had in the society?" "What do you think the people thought about or felt when they looked at the statue?" "Has anyone personally seen a big memorial like this one?" "Have you seen any pictures from another culture similar to this memorial?" Discuss responses.

Read more of what the fifth grader wrote: "This memorial reminds me of pictures I've seen of kings. Lots of times they are wearing a crown and have a calm face. This memorial has the face looking in all directions; this shows he rules over all places he can see. I think that when a ruler is powerful, people honor him by making statues that show his power." Ask: "Do you think this student's ideas are logical?" "Why?" Discuss responses. Ask: "How do we Americans show that a president was important, had a lot of power?" "What different ways do Americans use to honor an important president or leader?" Examine a picture of Mount Rushmore or the Lincoln Memorial or the presidential faces on coins or paper money. Ask: "Do these faces show any of the characteristics we have discussed?"

Give students an explanation about the memorial in Figures 2–1 and 2–2. The memorial is in Kampuchea (Cambodia), in the old capital city of Angkor. Locate these on a world map. The memorial is of Jayavaraman VII, ruler of the Khmers (who lived in what is now Kampuchea) from 1181–1220 A.D. It is 50 ft. tall and is made of stone. It tops the towers in the buildings of what was the capital city near the temple complex of Angkor Wat. Jayavaraman VII was a powerful king whose people also thought he was a god. He was a general, a conqueror of new lands, and a masterful builder of cities. Show students copies of Figure 2–3, another view of Jayavaraman VII's head topping a tower. Discuss Figure 2–3.

Students will summarize 3 characteristics used in depicting political power: size, frequency, and calmness of attitude.

To bring closure to the lesson, show the students a couple of political cartoons. Use a cartoon that clearly shows an emotion on the face of the leaders. The more quickly the cartoon will get a response such as a laugh from the students the better. Ask: "Do these cartoons give you the same impression of the political leaders that the memorial gave you? Why? or why not?" Ask the students to discuss for a few minutes with a partner their ideas about: "How is a person's political power demonstrated to the public?" Then ask the students to list their conclusions on the board.

Participation is recorded on a checklist.

Students will form a hypothesis that suggests where they find likenesses that convey political power.	Explain that authorities have identified three major ways to convey political power: 1) bigger than life images with strong and powerful features, 2) a wide distribution of the person's image, 3) a calm face that shows the leaders are secure in their power and goals. Ask students to examine the class list to see if their ideas reflect what the experts say. Ask them to talk about these findings with their partner. Do they think the experts' three categories are correct? Ask each pair to develop a summary statement that incorporates all three of these ideas, beginning with the phrase: "In any culture you can identify which of its leaders were the most powerful because . . ." These should be shared in the class.	Participation is recorded on a checklist. Participation is recorded on a checklist.

Expansion

Students will identify the level of support each hypothesis has, based on the evidence collected.	Ask: "Where are you likely to find likenesses of famous political leaders?" (Answers: statues, money, stamps, paintings, TV public service announcements). Record answers on a chart or transparency. Divide students into small groups of 3–4. Have each group select one location from the list and develop an investigation plan to test the statement they wrote at the end of the invention phase. If possible, the students should find data from several different nations. (Note: TV public service announcements will be difficult for students to document. You may wish to have a discussion about an announcement students have seen instead of a group report.) Have students carry out their investigations.	Presence of supported hypotheses in students' summaries.
Students will summarize their conclusions regarding where likenesses conveying political power may be found.	Have each group make a presentation to the class that includes: 1) an explanation of where they looked for information and how successful they were in finding the information, and 2) several examples of representative evidence to support or disprove the hypothesis. Return to the list of locations and place one star next to the categories that provide some support for the hypothesis, two stars next to those that supply much support, and cross out any that do not support the hypothesis. Conclude the cycle by having students write a paragraph summarizing the findings of their individual groups. If possible the students should use a computer to word process their report and a drawing program to illustrate it. Reports and illustrations can be printed and displayed on a bulletin board titled: "Ways Political Heroes Are Honored."	

Figure 2–1   Front and left side view.

Figure 2–2   Back and right side view.

Figure 2–3   A view of the original artifact.

At first, students use visual feedback from Figures 2–1 and 2–2, as well as their remembrances of objects that were similar in some way. Their first responses to the visual information received from the figures often will be awkward. Students interpret the figures by accounting for the unusual characteristics of the artifact: the four faces, the shape of the features on the face, and the carving above the faces, in terms of existing ideas already present in their long-term memory.

These initial difficulties prompt students to pause and reflect. They may try to find details that look like religious symbols, or details that would identify what material the artifact was made of. Or they may search their memory to find something that looked a lot like it. Students often wish they had the actual artifact in front of them to touch and to examine in three dimensions. They realize that the more senses they are able to use, the more information they can gather.

Some students decide to examine the pictures of the artifact really closely, looking for flaws in the artifact or the signature of its maker, introducing elements that were not obvious parts of the situation. They might examine a world map, thinking it might jog their memory and suggest something that would be similar to the artifact. Some students discuss the artifact with another person or watch someone else trying to decide what this artifact is in order to get ideas on how to proceed. There are many ways to help a student restructure existing ideas and skills. Teachers need to plan lessons that enable students to be helped in a variety of ways. The learning cycle is an approach that enables teachers to do this.

THE LEARNING CYCLE

The learning cycle is designed to adapt instruction to help students construct their own knowledge and restructure knowledge, connect new knowledge to what they already know, and apply the new knowledge in ways that are different from the situation in which it was learned.

The learning cycle has been effectively used with students at all levels to accomplish this purpose (Karplus, 1979; Osborne & Freyberg, 1985; Dillon & Sternberg, 1986; Lawson, Abraham, & Renner, 1989). If appropriate exploration activities are provided, the learning cycle helps students self-correct inaccurate conceptions and develop more appropriate conceptions. The advantage in using this approach is that the student is more likely to apply knowledge gained in the classroom to new areas or new settings. This is because the student is more aware of his or her own reasoning, can recognize its shortcomings, can apply procedures successful in other areas, and can search more effectively for new patterns. An instructional sequence must strengthen these tendencies in all students and discourage unquestioning acceptance of poorly understood principles and procedures.

The learning cycle incorporates into an instructional approach our understanding of how students learn. When a teacher does not use this approach, an understanding of how students learn is not often incorporated into instruction. What the teacher usually does is tell students what they are to know, show students examples of the social studies content to be memorized, and use tricks and motivational techniques to keep them on task long enough to be able to pass the next test. The result of this type of teaching may be somewhat effective in memorizing facts. However, in classroom testing it consistently gives inadequate results when the objective is understanding of a concept, generalization, or process skill (Karplus, 1979). When a teacher has a theory or framework that describes student learning and bases a sequence of instructional activities on that framework, meaningful learning takes place for more students.

EXPLORATION

A teacher makes several important decisions when beginning to plan a lesson. An objective is selected that is relevant to the curriculum, to the students' level of development, and to their past experience in the area. Next, the teacher decides how the initial part of the lesson can best be used to prepare students for the intended learning outcomes. To do this, the teacher looks at three components necessary in planning an effective learning sequence. Which activities will:
- diagnose what the students now know
- help focus their attention
- relate previous learning to new learning (Seiger-Ehrenberg, 1991)

DIAGNOSING STUDENT LEARNING

An important function that should be accomplished during the first part of instruction is determining students' present understanding of the new idea and/or skill being taught (Clarke, 1980). By observing students' actions in discussions, activities, or experiences the teacher can obtain valuable information about their retention of content previously learned. The teacher can also help students review and can focus them on the new learning to be introduced.

FOCUSING STUDENTS' ATTENTION

As a lesson begins, students' minds are in different places. By focusing students' attention on the intended lesson objective, greater learning is likely to occur. The first few minutes of any lesson are important since new sensory information is held in memory for less than one second before the mind decides what to hold and what to forget (Steinberg, Belsky, & Meyer, 1991). If the teacher does not help a student focus, the student will provide his or her own focus, which may not be relevant to the topic of the lesson.

Student attention can be focused in many ways. For example, to focus students' attention on ways of dealing with scarcity, the teacher can ask students to develop a list of items there are never enough of in the classroom, such as scissors. To introduce a lesson on perspective in map making the teacher might take students outside and ask them to stand at various points on the playground and describe how a specific tree looks from each point. The teacher might also use a game, demonstration, or a problem-solving activity to focus students' attention. Such activities can be omitted if students are already focused on the intended objectives and are ready to begin learning. This is often the case when a lesson is taught over several days. In this case the teacher asks students to describe activities completed in recent days.

RELATING PREVIOUS LEARNING TO NEW LEARNING

In order to help students more readily remember what they have learned or trans-fer it to other things they know, it is important to help students use their long-term memory. The teacher should help students retrieve as many related items of knowledge or skill from long-term memory as possible. This can increase the rate at which students learn (Steinberg, Belsky, & Meyer, 1991). The retrieval of rele-vant information provides a knowledge structure for new material. For example, asking second grade students to recall what happens when they look at things in the distance is not sufficient to relate previous learning of perspective to new learn-ing. A more effective approach involves second graders in: first, playing with an object; second, making drawings predicting how the object will look to them when it is 10 feet away and 30 feet away; third, observing the object when it is 10 feet and 30 feet away and drawing what they see; and fourth, comparing the two sets of drawings. Frequently, one activity can accomplish all three purposes of explo-ration: diagnosing, focusing attention, and relating old learning to new learning.

The learning cycle, although based primarily on developmental concepts of learning and construction of knowledge, takes advantage of a variety of infor-mation-processing methods. Thus, the exploration phase encourages learning by:

1. allowing students to recall previous knowledge from long-term memory
2. confronting students with the inadequacies of their knowledge while trying to connect it with new data being gathered by the sensory memory
3. helping some students construct their own new knowledge by processing taking place in the short-term memory

INVENTION

When planning this second, teacher-guided phase of the lesson, teachers make de-cisions for the following questions:

- What is the key idea or skill to be learned?
- How is this idea or skill best explained?
- How should the idea or skill be modeled or demonstrated?
- What strategies or techniques should be used to make certain students under-stand the idea or skill being taught?

PROVIDING EXPLANATIONS

Explanation may be accomplished in a variety of ways, including: teacher expla-nations, guided student activities, discussion of findings resulting from the ex-ploration activities, viewing a videotape, or reading from trade or textbooks. Since short-term memory has a limited capacity, teachers must make certain that im-portant information is provided in small sequential steps (Steinberg, Belsky, & Meyer, 1991). Use of events, pictures, graphs, and demonstrations can accompany verbal explanations and enable students to store more information. All informa-tion should be presented in an organized way in order to demonstrate concretely its basic structure. This will help facilitate long-term memory storage and retrieval at a later time (Perkins, 1986). Notetaking guides are often helpful in making the organizational structure concrete when provided at the beginning of the invention phase.

PROVIDING EXAMPLES

In addition to knowing what they are to learn, students need to see clear examples of what the new learning represents. One or more examples demonstrating the information should be presented. Sometimes this consists of demonstrating a completed product or skill. It also could involve taking the students through the process to show them the complete idea. The more ways in which an idea or skill can be modeled for students the better they will be able to learn it. Teachers should tell students what to look for when ideas are modeled (Costa, 1991). For many students it may make the difference in their understanding of the main idea or skill.

CLOSURE

It is important to plan activities to quickly assess student understanding. One procedure involves the use of signaled responses, obtaining answers from every member of the group by means of a flashcard or signal (such as "Put your thumbs up if you think the answer is 'yes' or put your thumbs down if you think the answer is 'no.' Think about your idea for a few moments then be ready to vote with your thumbs when I say 'vote.'"). Another procedure is to ask the entire group a question and get responses from representative members of the group. A third way to obtain closure is to observe students during the invention phase of the lesson in their group discussions, their work with activities, when sharing their answers, or when quizzing each other on the main idea of the lesson. The information gained from these activities allows a teacher to decide whether to move on, to stop and clarify, or to recycle students through another explanation set of activities. The different elements found in the invention phase of a lesson—providing explanations, giving examples and modeling, and checking for closure—may be repeated over and over as each objective is taught. These procedures may also be repeated if an objective is abstract or contains several pieces of information.

EXPANSION

It is important to help students transfer information gained in the invention, or explanation, part of the lesson into their long-term memory (Lawson, Abraham, & Renner, 1989). The teacher must decide how to provide the necessary practice. Neither an idea nor a skill is learned until it is stored in the long-term memory.

HELPING STUDENTS PRACTICE

The teacher must guide students at first, using an activity in which they can be successful if they have some understanding of the idea or skill. Without guidance, students might practice errors. This may create alternative conceptions that take a great amount of effort to unlearn. When students first practice new learning, they should work with examples that are as concrete as possible. For example, during the expansion in the lesson in Table 2–1, students were asked to identify and then examine items such as stamps. They used concrete items to determine whether they had the characteristics associated with how political power is displayed. Another activity might have been to examine the official portraits of presidents, like those displayed in the White House, and to identify the characteristics found in them. These behaviors let the teacher know how accurately the students understand the lesson objective. The teacher can decide whether students need more work to understand the lesson's material or whether they can move on. An important part of this practice includes asking students to explain their answers, whether correct or incorrect.

FINAL PRACTICE

The teacher must decide at some point during the practice whether the students have met the lesson objective. This part of the lesson should include a way of evaluating information about each student's progress. Students should demonstrate orally or through an activity their achievement of the lesson objective. This final practice enables the teacher to decide whether the students are ready to move on to independent activity, where they apply their new knowledge in different situations. The teacher can also determine which students need more help. Types of activities for this final practice include manipulative activities, role playing, paper and pencil exercises, and question and answer discussions.

INDEPENDENT ACTIVITY

In order for an idea or skill to be used automatically from the long-term memory, intensive practice is needed followed by further practice spaced out over time (Steinberg, Belsky, & Meyer, 1991). After students perform the new skill or use the new idea appropriately, they are ready to demonstrate it in another situation. It is critical that practice activities at first match the learning objective in context but later are transferred to situations different from that given in the lesson. Examples of this type of practice, which could have been used in the lesson in Table 2–1, include asking students to find out the namesakes of their school building, local streets, football stadium, or other important public constructions; to investigate pictures of European royalty; or to look at the school office to describe how they know a certain room is the principal's office and not a classroom or teacher's office.

INVENTING YOUR OWN IDEA
OF THE LEARNING CYCLE

An important part of the invention phase of the learning cycle is having students begin to work with, or practice, the idea or skill being taught. To help you construct a meaningful understanding of the learning cycle, you will now have an opportunity to begin to work with it. An example set of activities to be used in a lesson on latitude and longitude is given below. Identify which activity you would start with as the exploration part of your lesson. Then identify those you would use as an invention and an expansion activity. Activities for both the elementary and middle childhood lessons are described. Complete the elementary lesson first, then make decisions about activities for the middle childhood lesson.

A Practice Activity

Elementary Lesson Activities

1. Describe where you are sitting. (For example, "I am sitting in front of Ellen and next to the sink.") Ask students to tell the class where they are sitting in the room. Then ask each student to pick out another student's name from a jar and describe where that student is sitting. Discuss any problems as they arise.

2. Create a grid on all or much of the classroom floor. Have each student place his or her chair in a square. Tape cards to the floor to identify the rows with numerals and the columns with letters. Ask students to identify their "address" with the numeral and letter representing the square their chair is in. Have them put their address on any drawings or other papers they do. Select one student to act as mail carrier each day and use the addresses to deliver finished papers and drawings for students to take home.

3. Using masking tape, make two columns on the floor, then divide them by another tape strip so that there are four squares. Label each row with a picture of a bird (e.g., robin and cardinal) and each column with a picture of an article of clothing (e.g., pants and sweatshirt). Ask a student to stand in a square. Ask the other students to tell you what square the student is standing in. Repeat with students standing in different squares. They should soon discover that each square has two names (it can be robin-pants, robin-sweatshirt, cardinal-pants or cardinal-sweatshirt). Encourage them to use both names. Repeat on another day with six squares, later with eight squares. Eventually introduce letters

and numerals so the squares will be identified as A1, A2, B1, and so on.

4. Introduce students to the game Bingo. Use cards that have letters and numerals identifying rows and columns. Play the game several times over a few weeks.

Middle Childhood Lesson Activities

1. Provide students with travel magazines and other magazines with pictures of interesting places to visit. Have them select one they would most like to visit, but keep it a secret. Help them find it on a world map. Ask them to plan a one- or two-minute presentation for the class describing the place they would most like to visit, their "mystery place," without naming it. Then, tell them to give the other students clues by describing where it is located using two neighboring places. Have the other students try to guess what the mystery place is. Discuss problems that arose as they tried to guess each mystery place.

2. Ask groups of three students to plan a treasure hunt through five cities. Each city can be identified only by its location using latitude and longitude. Students should do some library research to identify an item that is made in each city. They should draw the item or find a picture of it, then place it in an envelope identified with the name of the city.

   Each team will go on a treasure hunt designed by another team. Using a world map, they will find each city by using its latitude and longitude coordinates. When all five cities have been located, each team will make a list of the names of the cities found at particular sets of coordinates. Then they will claim the envelopes printed with the names of these cities. They will glue the items found in the envelopes onto a map, identify the city that goes with each item, and display the map on a "Treasure Hunt" bulletin board.

3. Tape yarn onto a world map, forming a grid with ten rows and ten columns. Ask students to suggest a way of labeling the grid. (They might suggest, for example, letters and numerals.) Label the ends of each row and column with the system suggested. Then, have pairs of students pull a card out of a box and try to find the city named on the card. After finding it, ask the students to identify its location as closely as possible using the grid. Talk about problems they encounter, such as not being able to pinpoint a location well if it is in the center of a square or not directly on a grid line.

Ask if anyone can tell the class what the equator is and where it is on the grid. Identify the equator for the students, if necessary, and label it. Ask them to identify whether their city is above (north) or below (south) of the equator on this map. Repeat this procedure with the prime meridian. Discuss whether these designations help students identify the location of their city or make it more confusing. Ask if anybody can share something about latitude and longitude. Discuss. Then describe how the grid system currently on the map relates to latitude and longitude. Introduce finding locations with latitude and longitude. Introduce a globe and find latitude and longitude lines on it. Is it easier to understand with the globe? Practice finding their cities on the globe.

4. Ask students to find a city of their choice on the globe and then write down only its latitude and longitude on a strip of paper and place it in a jar. Ask each student to select a strip out of the jar, use the coordinates given to find a city, and write the name of the city on the strip of paper. Offer to assist any student who is having difficulty. Then, have the class generate a list of cities they have heard of in the news. Ask students to choose five cities, find their coordinates, and write them on a sheet of paper. Check papers for accuracy.

In both the elementary and middle childhood lessons, the approach best representing an exploration activity upon which meaningful learning can be built is activity #1. It represents the exploration phase of a lesson.

In this activity students have a chance to ask their own questions, try out their own ideas, and learn from their own mistakes as they gain background experience with ideas they will use to invent a new understanding for latitude and longitude during the invention phase that follows. As students are involved in the exploration activity, the teacher should note the types of reasoning patterns students are using and the alternative ideas they hold.

During exploration, students must learn through their own actions and reactions in a new situation. In this phase they explore new materials and ideas with minimal guidance or expectations for specific accomplishments. The new experience should raise questions that they cannot answer with their usual reasoning patterns. For many students, having made an effort that was not completely successful will help ready them for the more guided explanation activity in the invention phase that follows.

The second phase of a lesson built on the learning cycle, the invention, formally introduces the new idea or skill that leads the students to construct new knowledge from their experiences (as compared to the idea the students started the lesson with). The idea may be introduced by the teacher, the textbook, a game, a film, or another medium. This phase should always follow the exploration. Students should be encouraged to construct as much of the new idea as possible by themselves in the exploration before it is explained to the class. However, expecting students to form all complex ideas themselves is not always realistic. Invention activities should relate to the questions students were asking themselves at the conclusion of the exploration. The students' own questions are now being answered. A combination of discussion and a floor grid, found in elementary lesson activity #3, would form an effective invention for defining a grid system, a concept essential to eventually understanding latitude and longitude. In the middle childhood lesson, activity #3 starts with a map and a simple grid system and uses it as a beginning point for helping students invent for themselves an appropriate understanding of latitude and longitude.

In the expansion phase, the last part of any effective lesson designed to teach ideas and skills meaningfully, students should apply the new idea in additional situations. The expansion part of any lesson plan is necessary to extend the range of applicability of the new idea or skill. Expansion provides additional time and experiences that help stabilize the new idea or skill in the mind. Without a number and variety of applications, the meaning will remain restricted to the examples used during its construction. Many students may fail to abstract it from its concrete examples or to generalize it to other situations. Asking students to construct their own situations, as in the treasure hunt in the middle childhood lesson, or to examine other examples of the main lesson idea and interpret their meaning, as in the mail-carrier strategy in the elementary lesson, are effective expansion activities with which to conclude the lesson. In both lessons, activities 2 and 4 could be used as expansion activities. These activities involve students in demonstrating and practicing their own construction of the idea just explained in the invention phase of the lesson.

Expansion activities also help students whose knowledge construction takes place more slowly than average, or who did not adequately relate the teacher's explanation to their own experiences. Talking to individual students with these difficulties during expansion activities can help identify and resolve their problems.

Learning is based on connections made to previous knowledge during the exploration part of the learning cycle. The invention phase builds on connections made during the exploration and encourages learning from guided experience. The expansion phase provides needed practice and experience in applying the idea or skills in new situations. These situations help stabilize the thought process by which knowledge enters long-term memory and is stored so that it can be easily retrieved. All of these methods contribute to knowledge construction if students are allowed to fully complete the learning cycle. If a phase is eliminated or if all students are expected to demonstrate specified uniform accomplishments after the first or second phase, then the overall effectiveness of the learning cycle will be compromised. A summary of the criteria used to determine the effectiveness of a learning cycle appears in Table 2–2.

Table 2–2

Sequencing Instruction—The Learning Cycle

EXPLORATION PHASE

Purposes

To provide background experience and learning through students' own actions and reactions

To introduce aspects of a new idea or skill

To allow students to confront and make evident their own thinking/representation of the idea or skill to be taught

Characteristics

1. Encourages learning through student's own inquiry
2. Requires minimal guidance or expectation on the teacher's part
3. Confronts students' old way of thinking
4. Raises questions for students
5. Involves students in physical and mental activity
6. Provides adequate time to get acquainted with that idea or skill
7. Helps students become familiar with the purpose and objective of the lesson
8. Enables teacher to determine students' existing ideas and skill levels in the area the lesson will focus on

INVENTION PHASE

Purpose

To build on the exploration by more directly guiding students to experience and develop the idea or skill being taught.

Characteristics

1. Follows exploration where some development of an idea or skill may have occurred
2. Encourages learning from explanations, which include an interesting variety of teaching methods and student activities
3. Introduces an idea or skill in a structured manner through additional experiences that involve a variety of the senses, teacher explanation, film, textbook readings, computer programs, video, guest speakers, or other mediums
4. Encourages students to construct as much of the new idea or skill as possible through providing one or more complete cycles of explanation, giving clear examples and modeling, and checking for understanding
5. Provides a closure on the new idea or skill

EXPANSION PHASE

Purpose

To apply the new idea or skill to additional examples to help stabilize it.

Characteristics

1. Provides for learning by repetition in different situations
2. Provides additional time and experiences for the idea or skill to become part of the student's thought processes
3. Extends the range of applicability of the new idea or skill by having students use it in other contexts

EXPANDING YOUR UNDERSTANDING OF THE LEARNING CYCLE

The final part of this chapter will provide opportunities for practicing the ideas it presents. There will also be an opportunity to apply your knowledge of the learning cycle to new situations. This is the expansion phase of this chapter.

A first part of the expansion phase of a lesson is guided practice. To guide your practice in your work with the learning cycle, examine the lesson plan in Table 2–1 (page 21). Quickly skim through it, looking at the activities following each heading.

You will note that the lesson does not begin with a statement of the idea focused on in the lesson. Instead, students are asked to describe their own ideas related to an artifact. That serves as the exploration. Next, the lesson activities involve students in concrete explanations of the artifact and its purpose as given by a fifth grader, and in considering other examples—the coins in their pockets. These activities are found in the invention phase of the lesson. The expansion phase of the lesson allows students to practice the lesson's ideas and skills in similar and in different contexts. To get an overall view of the lesson format when the learning cycle is used, look at the outline in Table 2–3.

Table 2–3

Lesson Format

TOPIC
GOAL

EXPLORATION PHASE

Materials
Objective(s)
Activities
    Focus Student Attention
    Diagnose Student Learning
    Relate Previous Learning to New Learning

INVENTION PHASE

Materials
Objective(s)
Activities
    Provide Explanations
    Provide Examples
    Provide Closure

EXPANSION PHASE
Materials
Objective(s)
Activities
Guide Practice
Give Final Practice
Provide Independent Activity

As a final practice activity you will be involved in suggesting activities for the three phases of a learning cycle.

A Practice Activity

1. Design an exploration activity for a learning cycle introducing the concept of an *assembly line.* Among the attributes this concept should have are "speed," "efficiency," and "use of division of labor."

2. Design an invention activity to follow the exploration above.

3. Describe an expansion activity for this lesson on the concept of an assembly line.

☛ *Use Table 2–2 to evaluate your activities. Will each activity enable you to carry out the purpose of the phase of the learning cycle in which it is used? (If not, try to restructure it so that it will enable you to accomplish this purpose.)*

Now that you have had some practice with the learning cycle, let's go a step further and involve you in some independent activity.

A Practice Activity

1. Examine an elementary or middle school social studies textbook. Briefly examine a chapter or section of a chapter related to economics. What is the major topic? What process skill(s) are required of students? What concepts, generalizations, attitudes, and/or values are students expected to learn by the end of the chapter or chapter section?

2. Identify areas in the chapter or chapter section where difficulties in learning might occur because effective conditions for meaningful learning are not being provided.

3. Consider modifications that would help minimize the possible learning difficulties you have identified. What activity could you use to involve your students in meaningful learning in the areas where you think learning difficulties might occur?

Research studies suggest that children develop thinking and social abilities over time and with experience. Students at different ages can be expected to have different levels of development. The range within any particular group of students will also be wide. As students develop their ability to work with different aspects of the social studies, the curriculum changes. Very young students in the preschool and primary grades need to learn many thinking and social skills. They need to learn how to learn. By the third grade, students have a skill level and a range of experiences that enable them to focus on learning concepts. In the middle school, students have more-developed thinking and social skills. They also have a broad foundation of concepts and can begin to focus on relating the concepts they know to form generalizations.

The learning cycle is an instructional approach that focuses on helping students of all ages and developmental levels construct meaningful learning. It can be used to teach skills, concepts, or generalizations. It can also be used to explore and define attitudes and values. The content of the social studies curriculum involves all of these: skills, concepts, generalizations, attitudes, and values.

SUMMARY

A teacher can help students learn social studies content so that it is meaningful to them. The learning cycle is an instructional approach that has been developed to facilitate students' construction of meaningful learning. There are three phases in a learning cycle. The first phase of the learning cycle involves students in exploring the idea or skill the lesson develops. It focuses their attention on the idea or skill, allows teachers to diagnose students' current conceptions of it, and relates those conceptions to the new learning. During the second phase, invention, teachers guide students in constructing the new idea or skill. The third phase, expansion, involves students in practicing the idea or skill as they apply it in new situations. Through their application activities, students stabilize the new idea or skill in their long-term memory. Later chapters will discuss how teachers can use learning cycles to help students construct skills, concepts, generalizations, attitudes, and values.

REFERENCES

Barell, J. (1991). Reflective teaching for thoughtfulness. In A. Costa (ed.), *Developing minds: A resource book for teaching thinking,* Vol. 1. Alexandria, VA: Association for Supervision and Curriculum Development, 207–210.

Clarke, J. (1980). The learning cycle: Frame of discourse for paragraph development. *Leaflet* (New England Association of Teachers of English) *79,* 3, 3–11.

Clarke, J. (1990). *Patterns of thinking, integrating learning skills in content teaching.* Boston: Allyn & Bacon.

Costa, A. (1991). Teacher behaviors that enable student thinking. In A. Costa (ed.), *Developing minds: A resource book for teaching thinking,* Vol. 1. Alexandria, VA: Association for Supervision and Curriculum Development, 194–206.

Dillon, R. & Sternberg, R. (1986). *Cognition and instruction.* Boston: Academic Press.

Dykstra, D. (1985). Science education in the elementary school: Some observations. *Journal of Research in Science Teaching, 23,* 853–855.

Harlen, W. (1985). *Teaching and learning primary science.* New York: Teachers College Press.

Karplus, R. (1979). Teaching for the development of reasoning. In A. Lawson (ed.), *1980 AETS Yearbook: The psychology of teaching for thinking and creativity.* Columbus, OH: ERIC/SMEAC, 150–173.

Lawson, A., Abraham, M., & Renner, J. (1989). *A theory of instruction: Using the learning cycle to teach concepts and thinking skills.* Atlanta: National Association for Research in Science Teaching, Monograph #1.

Osborne, R. & Cosgrove, M. (1985). Children's conceptions of changes of state of water. *Journal of Research in Science Teaching, 20,* 825–838.

Osborne, R. & Freyberg, P. (1985). *Learning in science.* London: Heinemann, 91–111.

Perkins, D. (1986). Thinking frames. *Educational Leadership, 43*(8), 4–10.

Piaget, J. Forward to Hans G. Furth. (1969). *Piaget and knowledge: Theoretical foundations.* Englewood Cliffs, NJ: Prentice-Hall.

Seiger-Ehrenberg, S. (1991). Concept development. In A. Costa (ed.), *Developing minds: A resource book for teaching thinking,* Vol. 1, Alexandria, VA: Association for Supervision and Curriculum Development, 290–294.

Steinberg, L., Belsky, J., & Meyer, R. (1991). *Infancy, childhood, & adolescence: Development in context.* New York: McGraw-Hill.

Stepans, J. (1985). Biology in elementary schools: Children's conceptions of life. *American Biology Teacher, 47*(4), 222–225.

CHAPTER 3

OVERVIEW

Can you think of anything you have learned when you didn't use some intellectual processing skills? Can you think of any time you learned a skill apart from any knowledge? Can you think of any time you've learned and not experienced feelings and emotions? Social studies involves students in experiences that help them construct an understanding of their social world. These experiences are focused on achieving three major goals:

- developing intellectual process skills
- learning content
- assisting in developing attitudes and values and in judging the correctness of our actions

This chapter discusses the first goal, helping students develop intellectual process skills. Each of the other two components is described in detail in later chapters. Chapters 4 and 5 discuss teaching content: concepts and generalizations. Other chapters discuss teaching the content specific to different areas in social studies. Chapter 9 discusses assisting students in developing attitudes and values and in judging the correctness of their actions.

How do we teach social studies process skills to students? A skill is learned through working with it, learning when and how it is used, and practicing it until it is stabilized. Meaningful learning of content involves the use of process skills (Prawat, 1991).

Learning a skill in one subject does not necessarily mean that the skill will be transferred and used elsewhere. Research by Carey (1985) suggests that skills may not transfer but must be retaught in each area of content. Therefore, each unit must include lessons that focus on teaching the process skills used in that unit. Without those skills, concepts and generalizations in the unit will not become part of the student's knowledge structure. This chapter discusses how to help students construct new process skills and reconstruct existing ones so that they are more widely usable.

Teaching Process Skills in Social Studies

OBJECTIVES

1. *Identify the wide range of skills used in social studies learning.*
2. *Explain the contributions of the various skills to social studies learning.*
3. *List three major characteristics of a process skills lesson.*
4. *Explain the role of content in a process skills lesson.*
5. *Work through a sample process skill learning cycle.*
6. *List the teacher activities used in planning a process skill lesson.*
7. *Describe the types of activities students must be involved in during a process skills lesson.*
8. *Identify three key questions that guide the evaluation of process skill learning.*

EXPLORATION IN SKILLS TEACHING

Here is an activity in a lesson teaching a skill.

Time for Reflection: What Do <u>YOU</u> Think?

Look at Figure 3–1. Then answer the following questions without looking back at the picture.

- What is your first impression of where this picture was taken?
- What do you think the people in this picture are doing?

Now look at Figure 3–1 again.

- What details do you notice on a second look that you did not notice when you first looked at it?
- Do these details support your first impression of where this picture was taken? If not, where do you now think it was taken?
- What information can you recall to support your idea of where this picture was taken?
- Do the details you noticed on a second look support your first impression of what these people are doing? If not, what do you now think they are doing?
- What can you remember seeing, experiencing, or reading that supports your idea of what these people are doing?

This activity asked you to look at a picture without telling you anything about it. Then it asked you to make some inferences regarding where it was taken and what is happening in it. After having a second opportunity to make observations about the picture, it asked you to recall anything you might have seen that would support your ideas. These questions incorporated the three characteristics that should exist in an exploration activity beginning a skills lesson: diagnosing what students now know, focusing their attention, and relating prior knowledge to new learning. Through asking you what your first impression was and what you remembered that might be related to the picture, the activity was diagnosing prior knowledge and relating prior knowledge to new learning. The activity focused your attention by asking you to look at the picture and make some inferences about it. By reflecting on your responses to the questions above, you should be able to evaluate how appropriate your inferences were about the picture.

Figure 3–1   What are these people doing?

■ INVENTION IN SKILLS TEACHING

You have been involved in an exploration activity that was used as a beginning point for a lesson on a process skill. We can assume that you already have some ideas about skills teaching. So, let's move on to invention as we try to help you reconstruct your ideas about teaching skills.

The content of the social studies—facts, concepts, and generalizations—is mentally constructed by each person. It is constructed through using *social studies learning process skills* that enable us to **gather, organize, process,** and **communicate data.** These social studies learning process skills are indicated in Table 3–1.

As a group these skills define the process of investigating problems and learning content. They are not necessarily used in the sequence given. (Observing, for example, may lead to hypothesizing, but sometimes hypothesizing leads to observing.) Nor are all of these skills used in a particular instance of learning.

This chapter gives an overview of the skills used in social studies. This overview should serve as an introduction and a quick guide. Later chapters describe these skills in greater detail and discuss the teacher's role in helping students develop them.

Table 3–1

Social Studies Learning Process Skills

DATA GATHERING	DATA ORGANIZING	DATA PROCESSING	COMMUNI-CATING	OVERALL THINKING SKILLS
observing	classifying	finding patterns	reporting	critical thinking
reading skills	ordering observations	predicting	writing	reflective thinking
library or research skills	interpreting observations	finding relationships	formal discussing	decision making
questioning		inferring	informal discussing	
interviewing and surveying		hypothesizing		
interpreting charts, graphs, and maps		raising questions		

AN OVERVIEW OF THE SKILLS USED IN SOCIAL STUDIES TEACHING

DATA-GATHERING SKILLS

Data gathering is where learning begins. When students gather data they begin the process of working with it and turning it into something that has meaning to them. There are a number of skills used to gather data in social studies. These skills are: *observing, reading, library or research skills, questioning, interviewing, surveying, and interpreting charts, graphs, and maps.* Students need to become proficient at each of these skills. To do so they will need many opportunities to practice using these skills and lots of constructive feedback when problems develop as they use them.

DATA-ORGANIZING SKILLS

As important as data gathering is to social studies education, it is only the beginning point. The information gathered has little meaning to students unless students are helped organize it into usable form. Three skills are important in organizing data: *classifying, ordering observations, and interpreting observations.* These skills enable us to take individual pieces of information and make some sense of them. We do this by putting together pieces that show some similar characteristics. A set of data that hasn't been organized is like a closet into which all sorts of items have been thrown. We cannot really know what is in there nor can we easily use the items until we organize them.

DATA-PROCESSING SKILLS

Once data is organized, it can be processed into concepts and generalizations. Several skills are utilized in this processing of data. They are: *finding patterns, predicting, finding relationships, inferring, hypothesizing, and raising questions.*

COMMUNICATING

Communicating is central to social studies. It is part of what defines us as social beings. Communicating is essential to the thinking process enabling us to share the questions we formulate, the hypotheses we develop, and the answers we find. Language in written, spoken, or signed form involves us in verbal communication. Social studies not only provides the opportunity to use communication skills from language arts but requires the use of these skills to share information, viewpoints, and values. Nonverbal communication uses conventional symbols and means of representation through drawings and diagrams, tables, graphs, and maps. Communication is a large part of our lives and takes place both formally and informally. The communication skills include *formal communicating through reporting, discussing, and writing, and informal discussing.*

OVERALL THINKING SKILLS

Critical thinking, reflective thinking, and decision making are overall thinking skills that utilize the other social studies learning process skills. Because they are complex and involve a number of other skills, they develop over a long period of time. Many social studies educators consider decision making as an end product of the other overall thinking skills. While students begin making decisions early in life, these are often not logical and might be described as "jumping to conclusions." The decisions citizens make should be based on critical and reflective thinking. The steps included in a citizen's decision making are:

1. Clearly define the problem.
2. Generate alternatives.
3. Establish criteria for the solution.
4. Judge the alternatives based upon whether they meet the criteria and reflect values and democratic principles.

TEACHING SOCIAL STUDIES PROCESS SKILLS

Teachers have a multifaceted role. They: 1) listen empathically; 2) model thinking; 3) collaborate with students; 4) design learning as problem solving and experimentation; 5) plan, monitor, and evaluate progress; and 6) empower students toward self-direction (Barell, 1991). In an example suggested by Barell, a teacher, Ms. Mulcahy, talks with her first and second graders about how she thinks through life's dilemmas. The students then pose and resolve problems related to real situations they encounter such as graffiti on school walls. Eventually her students reflect on their thinking processes to decide that a good problem solver does four things:

1. discards the parts of the problem that are not needed and gets to the main problem *(defines the problem)*
2. looks at the problem from different angles *(interprets facts and viewpoints)*
3. adds onto someone else's thinking *(listens, infers, and questions)*
4. works problem out on paper *(uses the decision-making model)*

The teacher is assisting students in becoming able to design experiences that will help them pose a wide variety of "what if" questions throughout their lives. Human life involves continual experimentation, acting "in order to see what follows" (Schon, 1987), if we are to control our own destinies (Barell, 1991) through responsible decision making.

An overview of the process skills used by students in social studies has been given above and presented in Table 3–1. The skills were organized into five major areas. Such an overview identifies the skills used in social studies (*what is taught*) but does not really address *how to teach*. The rest of this chapter will focus on how to teach social studies process skills. In particular, it will focus on guiding you through the reconstruction of your ideas about skills teaching. To begin, here is a reflection activity.

Time for Reflection: What Do YOU Think?

· If you were to design a lesson plan and use the exploration activity based on Figure 3–1 and discussed earlier in this chapter, what might be an objective for the activity?

· Can you identify specific content that was being taught in the exploration?

☞ *A possible objective for the exploration activity could be: "Students will **infer** where an event pictured is occurring and what is happening."*

You will note that the objective given above focuses on a process skill, that of inferring. The exploration activity above asked you to make inferences from a small piece of data contained in the picture. Afterwards, you were asked to recall any information you might have that would help you refine your initial inferences.

No specific content was being taught in the exploration activity. However, it is not content-free. As you may have inferred, this picture was taken in Africa. Specifically, it was taken in the town of Daura in northern Nigeria, during a Moslem festival celebrating the end of Ramadan, the annual fasting period. These people are passing through a gate leading to the palace of the Emir of Daura, a cultural and religious leader. In examining the picture, you have an opportunity to add to your information regarding another culture. You may have noted the clothing people are wearing, architectural details, or any number of other items. The questions above and the discussion here should help you review your original observations, think about your inferences, and enter any content you noted into your long-term memory.

Any activity focused on developing a process skill must use some content. In the lesson using Figure 3–1, there may be additional objectives that focus on content.

However, to teach a process skill well, it is important to make the skill the focus of the lesson. The lesson should be integrated with content but priority should be given to the skill (Eggen, Kauchak, & Harder, 1979).

A skill lesson has four major characteristics:
- primary focus on a process skill
- concrete and/or manipulative experiences
- utilization of content in an organized fashion
- extensive practice of the skill (Sunal, 1990)

Concrete experiences are those that use materials students can experience with their own senses. Such experiences might involve students in activities that feature: a guest speaker dressed in Vietnam War military clothing, a 1910 glass bottle, or a copy of the Declaration of Independence. Manipulative experiences provide students with the chance to handle the materials to some extent. They might try on a Vietnam War era helmet, pick up a 1910 glass bottle, or handle the copy of the Declaration of Independence and try to trace an original signature with their finger. Students need time to explore the materials or information available in order to make observations for use in later parts of the lesson.

Processing unfamiliar information is a difficult task made easier when concrete materials are available (Ginsburg & Opper, 1988). There is evidence that children have limited space in their sensory memories (Sylvester, 1985). They can address just a few items coming in through their senses. When all the sensory memory space is being used items simply are not addressed; no attention is paid to them. Having concrete examples in front of them allows students to work with greater amounts of new information. They do not have to hold it all in their sensory memory at once. Having an item present in concrete form enables a student to refer to it and makes it possible for the student to work with a greater variety of information at the same time. When concrete materials are not available the teacher should decide whether to defer the topic until students can more adequately deal with it in the absence of examples, or whether photographs, slides, pictures, computer software, or other less concrete materials can be used.

In the lesson, many different activities encourage and emphasize process skill development. Observations can be classified into a wide range of categories. Inferential activities can follow considering how and why observations are similar and dissimilar. The focus may be on the development of any of several process skills, including observing, classifying, or inferring. The teacher does not explicitly focus on concepts and generalizations but on the processes and steps that direct thinking in identifying or applying the concept or generalization. However, as opportunities to teach content occur during the activity, the teacher takes advantage of them.

PLANNING ACTIVITIES TO TEACH SKILLS

Planning includes everything a teacher considers and does in getting ready for classroom activities. Planning for skills activities involves:
- identifying the skill(s) to be developed
- writing objective(s)
- deciding which activities will be used and sequencing them

- obtaining the materials that will be used during the activity
- setting up the grouping arrangement for the activity (Sunal, 1990)

GOALS AND OBJECTIVES

Effective planning begins with setting goals. A skills lesson has two goals for students: developing process skills and gathering an unspecified body of information (Eggen, Kauchak, & Harder, 1979). Objectives for a skills lesson are developed from its goals. They identify the specific skill(s) students will be constructing (Sardo, 1982).

A Practice Activity

Consider the objectives below. Which ones focus on teaching skills?

1. Sort old Valentine's Day cards into groups.
2. State the differences between a political and topographic map.
3. Observe apple butter being made and list all the items used in the process.
4. Display a time line by dressing in costumes from different time periods and standing in a line chronologically.
5. Watch adults as they attempt to find solutions to pushing heavily loaded grocery carts through supermarket doors that are sticking and difficult to push open.

☞ *Objective 1 focuses on teaching skills because its emphasis is on the processes of observing and classifying. Objective 2 is oriented toward the acquisition of the concepts of a political map and a topographic map rather than teaching skills. Students would need to have constructed the skill of observation in order to accomplish this objective. The construction of skill in observation is not the primary focus of this objective. A skill is being used to construct a concept. Objective 3 is oriented toward helping students construct the process skill of observation. Objective 4 is focused on constructing the concept of a time line. To achieve this objective, however, students would have to be able to put costumes in order, so they would be using a process skill. Objective 5 is a skills activity objective where students are observing and inferring.*

MATERIALS

In order to develop skills, students need information to process. The teacher provides students with materials that will give them access to the information needed.

If possible, each student or pair of students should have a set of materials with which to work. This will enable students to experience personally the information on which the activity is based. When it is not possible to provide enough materials the following alternatives can be considered:

- Ask the students to bring in materials.
- When just a few items are available, set up a learning station.
- When just one object is available, organize opportunities for each student to explore the object with the teacher and/or the person providing the object.
- When no materials are available, use media or electronic technology such as computer software.

GROUPING

The availability of materials is one factor to consider in deciding the grouping arrangement for an activity. Skills activities should use grouping arrangements that give students maximum opportunity to work with materials. Unless students can actively use the skill and practice it until it is stabilized in their minds, the skill will not be learned. Large groups, small groups, learning stations, or one-on-one interaction can be used equally well with careful planning.

IMPLEMENTING ACTIVITIES THAT TEACH SKILLS

Skills activities are implemented after the objectives of the activity have been selected, the materials gathered, and the grouping arrangement decided. Implementation involves the three steps of the learning cycle: exploration, invention, and expansion.

EXPLORATION

Skills activities typically begin with observation. For example, census rolls are visually observed, music from another culture is auditorily observed, an indigo blue-dyed hand-woven cloth from Niger is tactually observed by rubbing it between our fingers and visually observed as we notice that some of the blue dye has come off on our fingers. All the information we have came to us through our senses, so observation is a part of all exploration activities (Renner & Marek, 1988). The exploration also challenges students' existing ability and creates a need for development of the process skill that is the objective of the lesson. Once students have become aware of a need to reconstruct the process skill, the teacher can move to the teacher-guided, or invention, phase of the lesson and assist students in further development of the skill. The activity using Figure 3–1 was focused on inferring. After examining the picture, students may find that they are able to make inferences about it but they may feel unsure about the inferences they make. They are beginning to realize that inferences can be made with little information but that they may very well be inaccurate or inappropriate. They should be receptive to a teacher's introduction of additional pictures or other materials providing them with information they can use to be more sure of the inferences they make.

INVENTION

During the second phase of a skills learning cycle, the teacher guides students more directly as construction of a new process skill or reconstruction of an existing one is fostered (Eggen, Kauchak, & Harder, 1979). The teacher may ask leading questions, give explanations, and provide examples of the use of the process skill. The teacher will often guide students to recognize that they may have used the skill in a limited fashion, for example, making just a few observations of something that has the potential for many observations. Or, as with Figure 3–1, they may have made inferences based on very little information. The teacher helps students define the use of the skill. While the teacher may not be focusing on the acquisition of specific facts, concepts, or generalizations, he or she takes advantage of opportunities to foster their acquisition during the invention phase. For example, in an invention activity following up the exploration activity using Figure 3–1, the teacher may help students find Nigeria on a world map. They might also examine pictures of adobe buildings typically built in this area and compare them to adobe buildings in the southwestern United States. Students might note that most of the people are wearing light-colored clothing, then look at a graph of average monthly temperatures in this part of Nigeria and make inferences about how the preferred color of clothing might be related to temperature. The students will be acquiring a variety of content.

The invention phase of the process skill learning cycle must end with a closure activity. This enables the teacher to assess how well students have developed the skill. If the skill being invented is observation, for example, the teacher might set an item down in a central location in the room, ask each student to make observations of it, and then compile a class list of observations of the item, encouraging students to contribute something not previously mentioned. Such a closure activity enables teachers to determine whether the students are ready to move on to the expansion phase of the skill or whether they need more guided activities to develop the skill systematically. If the skill were inferring, the teacher might provide some additional pictures from Nigeria and ask students to make inferences about them. The teacher can talk with students to determine what information they are using and whether they recognize limitations of the information used to make the inferences. During the invention phase, a teacher can use guided inquiry or direct instruction techniques. Teacher behaviors during the invention phase include: 1) asking guiding questions that stimulate the use of the skill and its prerequisite skills, if any, 2) modeling procedural steps used in the skill, 3) asking students to explain or describe how they attained their answers, and 4) providing opportunities for students to use the skill.

EXPANSION

After students have initially acquired a skill, they need to practice it and use it in situations different from the one in which they acquired it. This practice will enable them to stabilize the skill and make it a permanent part of their thought processes.

GUIDING PRACTICE

In the first part of the expansion, students practice using the skill under teacher guidance. The teacher asks students to explain why they have decided something is or is not an observation. As the teacher guides the practice, students take some responsibility for their own learning. By asking students to explain their response, the teacher is enabling them to discover for themselves whether they are correctly using the skill.

As an example, in a lesson focusing on the skill of inferring, the teacher might follow up some of the exploration and invention activities related to Figure 3–1 by providing students with pictures of fast food restaurants in the United States and asking questions that require them to make inferences about the pictures. For example, "What food is served here?" and "How big is the restaurant?" By asking "Which of the questions we have answered here could be directly answered by observation of the picture and which require making inferences?" students practice identifying and making inferences.

GIVING FINAL PRACTICE

The second part of the expansion phase is final practice. Eventually, it will appear to the teacher that the students have developed the process skill being taught. The teacher then involves each student in a quick practice activity to demonstrate their achievement of the lesson's objective. For example, the teacher may give each student a list of five observations about an item such as the classroom chalkboard and ask students to circle those observations that can be directly verified. Or the teacher may give students a new picture, provide them with a list of inferences about it, and ask them to identify the inference they would be most unsure of based on the information they have in the picture. These types of activities serve as an opportunity to determine which students can move on to independent activity and which students may need more guided practice or even reteaching.

PROVIDING INDEPENDENT ACTIVITY

The last part of the expansion involves intensive independent activity. An example of independent activity with the process skill of observation is giving students a simple map and asking them to list observations they can make about it.

Independent activity with the skill of making inferences might involve students in examining a map of Nigeria that shows its river systems and making inferences regarding: 1) where agriculture might be expected because of the location of rivers and 2) where large cities might have begun as a market for farm products from the local area. Students could check their inferences by using library resources. Or students might invite a guest speaker into the classroom and ask questions to help them find out whether their inferences about Nigeria were accurate.

In order for a skill to be used automatically from the long-term memory, students will need to practice the skill over a long period of time. Opportunities to use a skill should be a part of lessons that follow the learning cycle in which the skill was first introduced. These later lessons do not have to focus primarily on the skill but may use it to teach a concept or as part of activities that lead to the construction of a different skill.

TEACHING SKILL ACTIVITIES

Activities that teach skills require the teacher to provide materials, to manage the creative use of the materials, and to be flexible and responsive to students. This is teaching that is demanding and tiring. It is also teaching in which students will be busy, enthusiastic, and talkative. The teacher provides students with an opportunity to construct and master a process skill through using it. The teacher also uses every opportunity to ask questions, probe, and encourage students to verbalize their ideas and develop their language skills.

EVALUATION

Students should be evaluated to assess how well the process skill taught has been constructed. As indicated in the discussion above, evaluation should be occurring in all three phases of a learning cycle that teaches a skill (see Table 3–2). During the exploration phase a teacher asks: *Do the students know what the skill is?* During the invention phase a teacher asks: *Do the students comprehend how the skill is used in social studies activities?* During the expansion phase a teacher asks: *Can the students apply the skill in a new situation?* (Bloom, 1956)

Table 3–2
Evaluation of a Skills Lesson

LEARNING CYCLE PHASE	KEY EVALUATION QUESTION	APPROPRIATE STUDENT RESPONSE TO EVALUATION QUESTION	TEACHING STRATEGY WHEN STUDENT RESPONSE IS INACCURATE/ INAPPROPRIATE
Exploration	Do students know what the skill is?	Students define a skill being taught or recognize a correct definition of it.	Teacher guides students to construct skill during invention activity.
Invention	Do students comprehend how the skill is used in social studies activities?	Students discriminate between appropriate and nonappropriate times to use the skill.	Teacher helps students discriminate during invention.
Expansion	Can students apply the skill in a new situation?	Students use skill in a variety of situations.	Teacher determines if students can define and comprehend skill. Teacher reteaches skill at level students are having difficulty with.

As a response to the first question, students should be able to define the skill being taught or recognize a correct definition of it. If the teacher has found that they cannot do this during the exploration activity, the teacher needs to guide students to construct a definition of the skill during the invention activity.

Stating a definition doesn't necessarily mean that the student understands it or can recognize when it occurs in a situation (Anderson, 1972). If students are able to comprehend the skill they will be able to discriminate between instances and noninstances of the skill being performed. This is a critical point, since without comprehension of the skill, students are unlikely to be able to apply it in a variety of social studies activities. During the invention activity the teacher helps students identify examples and nonexamples of the skill.

Eventually, the teacher will move into the expansion phase and give students an opportunity to apply the skill in new situations. When students are having difficulty doing this, it may mean that they are still at an early point in learning it—they may not be able to define it or to recognize a definition of it. Not knowing what it is will make it impossible for them to use it. If students are unable to apply a skill in a new situation, teachers should first evaluate their knowledge of the skill. For example, if the skill is observation, the teacher may ask: "What are their senses telling them about it?" "Are they using their eyes to look at it?" "Are they tapping it to find out what sort of sound it makes?" "Are they smelling it?" "Are they running their fingers over it to see what it feels like?" After measuring students' understanding of the skill, and finding they do understand it, the teacher can then begin to evaluate their ability to apply it in a new situation. Evaluating its use in a situation very similar to that in which it was first developed is not an appropriate measurement of it. Students may have memorized the use of the skill in the situation. Its use in a new situation will demonstrate whether they are able to apply it elsewhere.

EXPANSION IN SKILLS TEACHING

The discussion thus far has attempted to guide you in reconstructing your idea of skills teaching. This part of the chapter will involve you in practice as you apply your idea in several situations.

A Practice Activity

Read the following activities in a lesson for primary grade students. Then answer the questions that follow.

- *Exploration.* Arrange students in a circle around a set of foods including sweet potatoes, peanuts, tomatoes, squash, pumpkins, Indian corn, yellow corn, and sunflower seeds. Encourage them to examine the items. Tell them that these were all foods that European immigrants acquired from Native Americans.

· *Invention.* Discuss students' observations of the food items. Are they familiar with this food? Do they enjoy eating it? Do they eat it cooked or raw? Ask groups of three students to sort samples of the foods. Talk about how they are sorting them using questions such as "Why did you put these together?" and "What is the same about the foods in this pile?" Have each student choose three items that go together and tell why. Ask the students, "What do people do when they put things into groups?" or "How do people decide that some things should go together in one pile and other things belong together in another pile?"

· *Expansion.* Encourage the students to taste small samples, both raw and cooked, of each food. Then have them use taste to sort the items into groups. Ask students to decide which is their favorite among the foods. Ask them to think of another food that tastes somewhat like their favorite. If they have difficulty, ask them to think of another food, not currently in the selection before them, that is similar in some way to their favorite food (i.e., color, texture). Then ask them to describe how it is similar. Finally, ask students to use magazines to find pictures of foods they like that are the same in some way, cut them out, paste them on a piece of paper shaped like a dinner plate, and write a description of how these foods are similar.

Which process skill is being taught in this lesson?

Is the *primary focus* of this lesson on having students further develop their skill at classification?

What unit might this process skill lesson be a part of?

What lesson might follow next in this unit?

☞ *This is a lesson in which the primary focus is on the process skill of classification using Native American foods acquired by European immigrants as the content classified. The lesson could be part of several different units, including a unit on Native Americans or a unit on European settlement of North America. The next lesson in either of these units could focus on recognizing how these foods became part of the North American diet.*

FINAL PRACTICE

What other materials might the teacher have used as part of a unit on Native Americans to teach the skill of classification?

What are three characteristics that might be used to classify these materials?

INDEPENDENT ACTIVITY

Use the materials you suggested in the final practice above in a learning cycle teaching the process skill of classification. Briefly describe an exploration, an invention, and an expansion activity.

You have developed a set of activities for a skills lesson. Now, examine a lesson plan someone else has developed, the one in chapter 14. The focus of the lesson in chapter 14 is an idea. What is this idea? What process skill(s) will students need in this lesson?

☞ *This lesson focuses on teaching a generalization, the idea that "the United States is a nation ruled by a body of laws, not any one person or group." It expresses the relationship between several concepts including: "United States," "nation," "rule," "body of laws," "person," and "group." The process skills used in the lesson include:*

· *inferring ("What do you think the president can't do?")*
· *ordering observations (for example, identifying the steps a person follows to become president)*
· *finding relationships (for example, determining the relationships of the Constitution to the duties of the president)*
· *hypothesizing (for example, predicting which other occupations might require an oath to protect and defend the U.S. Constitution).*

You may have found additional skills utilized in the lesson. Lessons for older students often incorporate several process skills. A teacher needs to analyze a lesson to determine which skills are needed. If students have not developed a skill to the level needed in the lesson, the teacher will have to help students reconstruct it.

SUMMARY

Process skill development needs careful planning and implementation of activities challenging students to identify, define, understand, and practice the skill. It is dependent upon the use of concrete activities that enable students to develop the skill in real-life situations. The learning cycle is effective in teaching process skills to students since it involves them in exploring the skill, inventing it for themselves, and finally expanding its use to new situations.

Process skills are an important part of the social studies program. Students use process skills to construct meaningful learning. While content and skills cannot really be separated, and are often integrated in lessons, skills must have attention focused on them if they are to be learned. In the earliest grades, many skills lessons are needed in units as students lay a foundation for further learning. Older students are learning some new skills and reconstructing existing ones so that they are extended and further developed. Units should contain a mix of lessons, some focusing on helping students construct a new skill or reconstruct an existing one, and some focusing on teaching ideas and examining attitudes and values.

REFERENCES

Anderson, R. (1972). How to construct achievement tests to assess comprehension. *Review of Educational Research, 42,* 145–170.

Barell, J. (1991). Reflective teaching for thoughtfulness. In A. Costa (ed.), *Developing minds: A resource book for teaching thinking,* Revised edition, Vol. 1, Alexandria, VA: Association for Supervision and Curriculum Development, 207–210.

Bloom, B. (ed.). (1956). *Taxonomy of educational objectives. Handbook 1: cognitive domain.* New York: David McKay.

Carey, S. (1985). *Conceptual change in childhood.* Cambridge, MA: MIT Press.

Eggen, P., Kauchak, D., & Harder, R. (1979). *Strategies for teachers.* Englewood Cliffs, NJ: Prentice-Hall.

Ginsburg, H. & Opper, S. (1988). *Piaget's theory of intellectual development.* (3rd ed). Englewood Cliffs, NJ: Prentice-Hall.

O'Reilly, K. (1991). Infusing critical thinking into United States history courses. In A. Costa (ed.), *Developing minds: A resource book for teaching thinking,* Revised edition, Vol. 1, Alexandria, VA: Association for Supervision and Curriculum Development, 164–168.

Prawat, R. (1991). Why embed thinking skills instruction in subject matter instruction? In A. Costa (ed.), *Developing minds: a resource book for teaching thinking,* Vol. 1. Alexandria, VA: Association for Supervision and Curriculum Development, 185–187.

Renner, J. & Marek, E. (1988). *The learning cycle and elementary school science teaching.* Portsmouth, NH: Heinemann.

Sardo, D. (Oct. 1982). *Teacher planning styles in the middle school.* Paper presented to the Eastern Educational Research Association. Ellenville, NY.

Schon, D. (1987). *The reflective practitioner.* New York: Basic Books.

Sunal, C. (1990). *Early childhood social studies.* Columbus, OH: Merrill.

Steinberg, L., Belsky, J., & Meyer, R. (1991). *Infancy, childhood & adolescence: Development in context.* New York: McGraw-Hill.

Sylvester, R. (April, 1985). Research on memory: Major discoveries, major educational challenges. *Educational Leadership 42*(7), 69–75.

CHAPTER 4

OVERVIEW

This chapter is based on research indicating that students usually come to us with concepts already formed (Harlen, 1985). These concepts are typically incomplete or, in some cases, misconceptions. Teachers must help students reconstruct their concepts so that they are a better approximation of reality. In some cases, the teacher helps students construct new knowledge, concepts about which the students had no previous ideas. This chapter involves the reader in activities designed to provide a more concrete experience with the material presented than simply reading would do. In order to accomplish its goal, this chapter is organized as a learning cycle with integral exercises to complete while studying the chapter.

Developing Social Studies Concepts

OBJECTIVES

1. Describe why teaching might have little effect on the concepts students have formed prior to instruction.
2. Describe five ways through which teachers can influence students' concepts.
3. List the teacher activities used in planning a lesson in which students will construct a new concept or reconstruct an existing one.
4. Describe strategies used by teachers to help students explore a concept, invent it, and expand its use.
5. Work through a sample concept learning cycle.

EXPLORATION IN DEVELOPING CONCEPTS

Here is an activity that involves you in exploring a concept.

A Practice Activity

Think about who sits next to you in one of your classes.

If someone sits on your left, is it a man or woman? If you know this person's name, what is it?

If someone sits on your right, is it a man or woman? If you know his or her name, what is it?

If someone sits directly behind you, is it a man or woman? If you know this person's name, what is it?

If someone sits directly in front of you, is it a man or woman? If you know this person's name, what is it?

Draw a simple map that shows you and those people who sit near you.

Do you know the people who sit near you better than those who sit farther away from you?

In this exploration activity, you were asked about some people in your class and then you were asked to draw a map including them. Think about what characteristic you used in selecting the people. What attribute did they share?

INVENTION IN DEVELOPING CONCEPTS

During the invention phase of a lesson, the teacher guides students in the construction of the concept on which the lesson focuses. This part of the chapter will guide you in reconstructing your ideas regarding how to help students learn concepts.

To begin the invention phase of this chapter some further consideration needs to be given to the exploration activity just completed. The attribute that was the focus of this exploration activity was location. All of the people you were asked to think about were sitting in class in a location near you. You were not asked about others who were located farther away from you, perhaps on the other side of the room. Now, to build on the exploration activity here is an invention activity on a concept.

A Practice Activity

Suppose the classroom walls expanded so that the classroom became twice its current size. When this happened, each of the students' chairs would be farther away from you. Now, the distance would be twice what it was between your chairs. Is the person who was on your left still on your left? Is the person who was directly in front of you still in front of you?

☞ *The only thing that has changed is the distance between your chairs. Distance has not really affected the location of other people relative to your position.*

What might we call someone who sits next to us in class or who lives next door to us at home?

☞ *This person is often called a "neighbor".*

Using the characteristic of location, how would you define "neighbor"? Brian, a fourth grader, defined neighbor as "someone who is in a place close to you." Is this an appropriate definition of the word neighbor?

If the person sitting on your left were to switch seats with someone else at the other side of the room, would that person still be your neighbor?

☞ *Using Brian's definition, he or she would no longer be your neighbor. The concept of neighbor then, can be defined in terms of location and specifically in terms of closeness in location.*

In lessons that focus on helping students construct a new concept or reconstruct an existing one, the teacher's role involves:
• providing students with information to work with
• asking questions to focus their attention on important aspects of the
    information
While the teacher serves as a guide during the invention phase of a lesson, the activities are centered on interactions between students and their social environment. Activities enable students to work with examples of the concept. Eventually,

students are able to invent a definition of the concept using the information they have worked with during the invention activities.

DEVELOPMENT OF CONCEPTS

FACTS ARE USED TO BUILD CONCEPTS

Content is acquired through the five senses in the form of facts. They are gathered as observations are made of people and events. They come out of our direct, sensory experiences or indirectly through the experiences of others—we can hear or read about facts others have acquired. For example, we might explore a map of Pennsylvania and identify towns such as "California" and "Indiana" that bear the same name as a state. We have acquired some facts directly through our exploration of a map. Or, we might read an article in a newspaper that identifies towns in Pennsylvania with the same names as states. In this second instance, we indirectly acquire facts others have identified because we have not explored the map of the state of Pennsylvania ourselves.

Facts are forms of content that are single occurrences, taking place in the past or present. They do not allow us to predict an event or action (Eggen & Kauchak, 1988, p. 44). Using the example given above, we could not predict that we would find towns having a state name in Maine or in any other state although we have identified two such towns in Pennsylvania. Facts provide us with the information needed to construct the concepts and generalizations that make up the core of social studies content. If few facts are available to us, we may not be able to form a pattern from them. Instead we may memorize strings of words having little connection to each other, and therefore, little meaning to us because the experiential background they are tied to is narrow or scattered. Without an adequate background of facts based on concrete experiences, a student's understanding of a concept such as "Middle Ages" remains vague. Facts provide reference points for the concepts and generalizations formed from them.

A Practice Activity

Which of the following are facts?
1. Martin Luther King, Jr., was a minister.
2. All governors are the chief executives of their states.
3. Freedom of press is guaranteed by the Bill of Rights.
4. Volcanoes can be divided into two groups: explosive and free flowing.

☞ *Of the four items above, numbers one and three are facts. Number one describes a specific person. Number three identifies a specific piece of content in the Bill of Rights.*

In the example given above, number two is a concept statement describing a group of people—governors. Number four is another concept statement since it describes and categorizes volcanoes. Both numbers two and four describe sets of similarities we have found between the facts from which they were formed.

Don't be concerned if you are finding it difficult to identify facts and concepts. It takes some practice before you can quickly and easily do this. The discussion of concepts that follows should help you better identify both facts and concepts.

CONCEPTS

Ideas that people form to help them better understand their social world are called concepts (Beyer & Penna, 1971). Concepts are formed by finding similarities between two or more facts and temporarily emphasizing those similarities. For example, "house" is a concept we form by focusing on its structure of walls and a roof and its usefulness in protecting us from rain, sun, and snow. We emphasize similarities between structures that are houses and ignore such differences as size, color, and the material from which they are constructed. A *concept* can be defined as the set of characteristics common to any and all instances of a given type or the characteristics that make certain items examples of a type of thing and that distinguish any and all examples from nonexamples. Some of the many concepts that social studies helps students form are "mother," "neighborhood," "war," "socialism," "internal conflict," "honesty," "culture," and "holiday."

CONCEPTS DIFFER IN COMPLEXITY AND ABSTRACTNESS

Concepts range widely in their *complexity* and *level of abstractness* (Klausmeier, Ghatala, & Frayer, 1974). Of the concepts listed above, "holiday" and "mother" are understood by very young children. Both are closely tied to concrete items in the child's world. Mother is a real person with whom most children have frequent contact. She performs many services the child needs, like providing food and playing with the child. A holiday is a time when the child eats favorite foods, plays games, and hears music and laughter. While each of these concepts is complex, each is also tied to a number of concrete experiences the child has. As a result, children having these experiences typically form the concepts "mother" and "holiday" before they enter kindergarten.

Among the most complex and abstract of the concepts listed above is "socialism." This is a concept that is typically learned in high school or later. Socialism is complex, as is the concept of mother. Socialism, however, has fewer concrete characteristics. Because its characteristics are complex and more abstract

students have greater difficulty in learning it. How easily a concept can be learned is dependent on:
- the number of characteristics it has
- how concrete these characteristics are (Stanley & Mathews, 1985; Tennyson & Cocchiarella, 1986)

FORMING CONCEPTS

As concepts are formed, a number of examples and nonexamples of the concept are usually examined (Eggen, Kauchak, & Harder, 1979). *Examples* are any and all individual items that have the characteristics of a given concept. If a class were working with the concept of "lake," a teacher might use examples such as Lake Erie, the Great Salt Lake, Lake Baikal, and a local lake. Students might find these lakes on maps and look at slides and pictures of them. (See also Figure 4–1 for an example that could be used in teaching a concept.) *Nonexamples* are any and all individual items that may have some but not all the characteristics that make items examples of a given concept (Seiger-Ehrenberg, 1991, p. 291). As part of the process of constructing the concept of "lake," students might examine nonexamples such as ponds and oceans. While these have some characteristics similar to those of a lake, they are not similar enough to be considered a lake.

In this process it is important to identify characteristics *essential* to the concept. For example, in learning the concept "holiday," very young children may consider a birthday cake an essential characteristic of a holiday. With help they can learn that a birthday cake, fireworks, bunnies, hearts, and other similar items are associated with specific holidays but are not an essential characteristic of all holidays. The teacher plays an important role in helping students identify those characteristics that are essential. The teacher might, for example, use a monthly calendar on which students' birthdays are identified with a picture of a birthday cake. Other holidays are identified with other symbols, perhaps a heart for Valentine's Day and a silhouette of Abraham Lincoln for Lincoln's birthday.

CONCEPTS DIFFER FROM FACTS

Concepts differ from facts in two major ways:
- First, facts are isolated bits of information acquired directly through seeing, hearing, tasting, feeling, or smelling. Concepts go beyond this initial contact and involve more than simple observation.
- Second, concepts summarize two or more observations into categories. Similarities are identified and summarized. For example, "A voter can be male or female, of any race or any religion, but has to be at least 18 years old."

The summarizing capability of a concept is very important. Without it we would find it difficult to use all the facts we learn. For example, people ride in many kinds of vehicles: big and small, with room for two or six, with and without air conditioning. To remember each of these with a name takes up a lot of mental capacity; so we form concepts, grouping together similar vehicles by shared characteristics, such as: pick-up truck, van, station wagon, and limousine.

Figure 4–1 A child's grandparents can be used as an example of the concept "family."

INACCURATE CONCEPTS

Sometimes a concept may be inaccurate. A young child may, for example, decide a voter cannot be a police officer or a member of the military because she has never seen anyone in a uniform at the voting booths when she accompanies her parents to the building where they cast their votes. The child has formed the concept on the basis of the limited facts available to her. A narrow range of facts can result in an inaccurate concept. Or the individual may not have abstracted essential characteristics. For example, the child may have noted that everyone waiting in line to vote was talking about how angry he or she was with a recent raise state legislators had voted for themselves. The child may decide that you can't vote unless you are angry about an issue. Although the concept is inaccurate, it does represent an effort by the individual to abstract similarities. As more facts are acquired, or when the individual reviews the inventory of facts, the concept may be changed and made more accurate. Teachers have an important role in providing opportunities for students to have experiences that will add to their inventory of facts and opportunities to discuss the facts they have acquired and the concepts they have formed.

INTERRELATIONSHIPS BETWEEN CONCEPTS

Concepts are interrelated, with two concepts often sharing some of the same facts. A "garage," for example, can house a car but it can also be a "workshop" or a

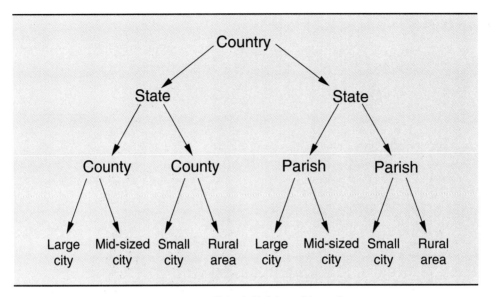

Figure 4–2 Political divisions hierarchy.

"storage area." People are flexible in the concepts they form. This flexibility allows us to account for the range of diversity in our social world.

Many concepts include other concepts as *subconcepts.* For example, the concept of "country" includes the subconcept of "state" and also other subconcepts. "State" in turn includes "county" or "parish" in addition to other subconcepts. Related concepts such as these form a hierarchy (Figure 4–2). In a hierarchy a concept can incorporate subconcepts. In turn, the same concept can be subordinate to another concept, the *superordinate concept.* In the hierarchy described in Figure 4–2, "country" includes the subconcept of "state"; it is superordinate. "State" in turn includes the subconcept of "county." "County" includes the subconcept of "small city." As another example, "interdependence" is a concept that requires the learner to first understand the subconcepts of "dependence" and "independence."

Some concepts are related to other concepts in a different way. In this instance, each of the two concepts is equivalent in some way; neither is a subconcept of the other. They may be related in terms of just one characteristic. These are called *coordinate concepts.* For example, consider the concept "county." What is a coordinate concept for "county" in the United States? There are many characteristics of the concept that could be considered. Here are three characteristics.

First, a county is a governmental unit. Other such units are borough, city, state, and nation. None of these is equivalent to the concept of county. Borough and city are both subconcepts of it. County, in turn, is a subconcept of state and nation.

Second, a county is an identifiable region. What are other identifiable regions? Some of them are backyard, home, neighborhood, world, and solar system. None of these is a region similar to the county. Backyard, home, and neighborhood are all subconcepts of it. Country is a subconcept of world and solar system.

Third, a county is a provider of services to its people. It provides a variety of services, which can include road upkeep, education, and police patrols. Who else provides the same types of services to its people to the same extent? Here, only one instance is found: the Louisiana parish. Only the parish is the coordinate of the county in the United States. It has a similar function; it is a governmental unit. It has a similar region. It also provides similar services to people. The Louisiana parish is unique in the United States. Its name can be traced back to early French settlers. Although its name is unusual its function and structure is similar to that of the counties found in other states.

Many concepts, such as interdependence or socialism, include several subconcepts. To accurately construct the concept being taught, students first need to understand its subconcepts. A teacher's lesson may not be successful because students do not understand a critical subconcept. Some concepts also have important coordinate concepts that need to be understood. For example, a coordinate concept of socialism is capitalism. Students may become confused when trying to sort out the differences and understand the similarities between these two coordinate concepts unless the teacher has built into the lesson many opportunities to compare and contrast the sets of characteristics that describe each of these concepts. Teachers must understand the relationships between concepts if they are to successfully teach concepts and diagnose difficulties students are having in constructing these concepts. A concept analysis (see Table 4–1) can help a teacher understand both the characteristics of a concept and its relationship to other concepts. An analysis of key concepts to be taught in a lesson or unit will help a teacher identify both examples and nonexamples to use during instruction.

Table 4–1

A Concept Analysis

To carry out a concept analysis the following information is gathered:
1. concept
2. definition
3. characteristics
4. examples
5. superordinate concepts
6. subconcepts
7. coordinate concepts (Eggen & Kauchak, 1988)

A concept analysis of "county" follows:
1. Concept: county
2. Definition: the largest territorial division for local government within a state of the United States of America
3. Characteristics: an identifiable region within a state, a governmental unit, a provider of local services such as law enforcement and education
4. Examples: Wayne County, Michigan (large city), Fayette County, West Virginia (rural and small town), and Tuscaloosa County, Alabama (small city and rural area)
5. Superordinate concept: state
6. Subconcepts: large city, mid-sized city, small city, rural area
7. Coordinate concept: parish

Can you identify a concept that might include "socialism" as a subconcept? Possible concepts that include socialism as a subconcept are "political system" and "economic theory." Each of these includes socialism as one system or theory along with others. Can you identify a subconcept of "socialism"? Possible subconcepts of socialism include "governmental ownership" and "state control of production." Can you identify a coordinate concept for "socialism"? Did you suggest a political system or an economic system as a coordinate concept? Two concepts among those that could be suggested are capitalism and communism.

Concepts are a major portion of the content of the social studies. They take a large number of facts and process them into manageable pieces. Individuals must learn each concept and process the information it represents on their own. As a result, each of us has a somewhat different understanding of a concept. The strength of a well-defined concept is such that even though we each form our own mental construction of that concept, its essential characteristics are recognized by all of us.

RECOGNIZING AND WORKING WITH CONCEPTS STUDENTS HAVE FORMED PRIOR TO TEACHING

Students come to school with many concepts already formed (Harlen, 1985, p. 76). These concepts often differ from those of professionals in a field, who may view students' concepts as inaccurate. To students, however, they are sensible and useful concepts. Teachers can influence students' thinking and concepts in ways that are intended, or they can influence them in unanticipated ways, or they may not influence them at all (Duit, 1987).

WHEN MIGHT TEACHING HAVE LITTLE EFFECT ON STUDENTS' CONCEPTS?

First, students have already formed concepts on their own, sometimes through giving an idea a lot of thought (Feldsine, 1987). Many concepts develop as students try to make sense of their social environment. These concepts are likely to be firmly held (Harlen, 1985). In school, students are sometimes involved in situations using concepts that the teacher defines differently than do the students. One or two experiences in school may not be enough to convince students that they need to reconstruct their concepts.

Second, teachers are often unaware of students' inaccurate or incomplete concepts. Through setting up an open-ended exploration activity teachers can observe, listen to, and work with students while noting and gauging their current understanding of a concept.

Third, teachers often make unfounded assumptions about the teaching and learning process. Sometimes teachers assume students have formed no prior concepts. At other times teachers assume that if students have concepts prior to teaching, these will be easily replaced by concepts taught. Both assumptions are often false. Much of the time students have prior concepts that they do not reconstruct easily.

Fourth, teacher and students often do not really communicate with each other. Teachers try to convey meaning using words, diagrams or symbols. When the student focuses on these he or she has to find meaning in them. The meaning constructed may not be the meaning intended by the teacher. This is particularly likely if the language used by the teacher, or textbook or worksheet, is not familiar to the student. Then:

- The student may ignore what the teacher is saying.
- The teacher may ignore what the student is saying.
- The teacher may insist that students use the "correct" words. (Students sound like they understand the concept and its attributes the teacher is trying to teach, but actually they are just making noises that *sound* like the understanding is there.) (Harlen, 1985)

HOW CAN TEACHERS INFLUENCE STUDENTS' CONCEPTS?

First, to successfully influence students' concepts, teachers need to be aware of the ideas students are bringing to the lesson. What do they think this is? Why? What words do they use to describe or explain it?

Second, teachers need to provide students with an opportunity to become familiar with the context in which the concept to be discussed belongs. Whenever possible this should involve students in firsthand experience. This encourages students to try out their ideas by investigating a situation or objects for themselves. The exploration phase of a learning cycle is an appropriate time to accomplish these activities.

Third, communication is important, particularly during the invention phase of a learning cycle, when students are guided to construct a new concept or reconstruct an existing one. Students should present their ideas to others and learn to appreciate the ideas of other students and of the teacher. Often small group discussion will challenge students to find evidence for their ideas. Large group discussions will bring a number of ideas together for consideration.

Fourth, during the investigative and discussion process characterizing the invention phase of the learning cycle, students should be offered the concept as constructed by the teacher and should be encouraged to explore it for themselves without the teacher's insistence that this is the only correct view of the concept.

Fifth, the value of the concept presented by the teacher should be made evident through expansion, using it to solve new problems and applying it to make sense of the new experiences. Through reasoning, the consideration of observations and experiences, and communication, students may realize that different ideas exist and they may decide that another idea is more usable and appropriate.

PLANNING A LESSON THAT HELPS STUDENTS CONSTRUCT A NEW CONCEPT OR RECONSTRUCT AN EXISTING ONE

How does a teacher plan, implement, and evaluate a lesson designed to help students restructure their existing concepts or construct a new concept? Planning involves: identifying the concept to be taught, selecting the attributes that will be used in defining the concept, and deciding which information will be used to illustrate the concept. A lesson that focuses on the construction or reconstruction of a concept involves students in direct experiences where they work with information and analyze its attributes. Process skills are used to help students structure information to develop the concept. A lesson focusing on a concept differs only in emphasis from one focusing on process skill development. Learning a concept involves using process skills to invent concepts. Learning a skill involves using process skills to invent an understanding of the process skill itself. A teacher may use the same set of materials to help students construct a process skill or a concept. This difference is most clearly seen in the guiding questions a teacher asks during the lesson. These questions will differ depending on whether the focus of the lesson is a skill or a concept.

A Practice Activity

Which of the following would be an appropriate objective in a lesson focusing on a concept?

1. State the difference between something we need and something we want but do not need.
2. Identify the ethnic group associated with a specific mode of traditional dress.
3. Categorize various modes of dress associated with different ethnic groups.
4. After collecting climatic data, make inferences regarding the relationship between climate and the fabrics used in traditional dress in various cultures.
5. After visiting the state legislature building and observing legislators at work, describe the role of a state legislator.

☞ *Objectives 1, 2, and 5 represent lessons that focus on concepts. In order to accomplish objective 1 the concepts of "wants" and "needs" must be developed. In objective 2 students need to construct concepts describing the attributes, including dress, of different cultural groups. Objective 5 involves developing a concept of "state legislator." Objectives 3 and 4 are focused on process skills. Objective 3 works with classifying while objective 4 works with inferring.*

SELECTING CONTENT

Concepts selected for teaching should be developmentally appropriate and consistent with the goals of the social studies. Various sources can be used to select concepts to be taught, including state department of education social studies objectives, school textbooks, texts used in introductory college courses in the social sciences, and social studies methods textbooks (Schug & Beery, 1987).

After a concept is selected, the teacher must identify the attributes important to an understanding of the concept. This is not always easy to do. It can be difficult to decide what the attributes of a concept are and which ones separate it from related concepts. Sometimes it is helpful to look up the definition or description of a concept given in specialized dictionaries or college textbooks. Definitions found in all-purpose dictionaries are often not specific enough to be helpful to a teacher in planning a lesson.

PREPARING INFORMATION USED IN THE ACTIVITY

After the social studies concept is identified for a lesson and its attributes are described, the teacher needs to select and prepare information for the lesson. Examples illustrating the concept being taught are selected. A teacher who will teach the concept of "rituals" might bring in birthday cake candles, party hats, horns, ribbon, and wrapping paper or a wedding ring, wedding announcement, rice, bridal veil, and a picture of a wedding cake. These are items that students can touch, see, smell, and hear. Nonexamples are also selected.

Real items, such as birthday cake candles, ribbon, and wrapping paper, or a wedding ring, bridal veil, and rice help students understand: (1) social studies activities in the classroom relate to the real social world outside the classroom; (2) ideas and skills gained in the classroom are applicable in the social world outside the classroom.

Information used in a lesson focusing on a concept is a part of the social world. The more concrete the information, the more accurately reality is represented. When students can make their own observations of something they are more likely to focus their attention on the lesson, enjoy it, and reconstruct their ideas to develop a more appropriate understanding of the concept.

Students should have the opportunity to interact with and explore information in an activity as much as possible. If birthday candles and paper hats or a bridal veil and rice are the source of information for the lesson, these items can be passed around or placed on a table so students can feel, smell, and look at them closely, thereby familiarizing themselves with the information central to the activity. To internalize ideas about the world, students of all ages, but especially younger students, need to be actively involved in manipulating and interacting with concrete examples. At all ages, the more realistic the information, the more complete students' observations will be. More complete observations, in turn, are more likely to result in more accurate understanding. However, a Titan rocket or a weather satellite can't be brought into the classroom, and a field trip to visit it is not always possible. In such cases, pictures, computer software, or other media are helpful substitutes for the real items. What is important is to avoid teaching concepts solely with words. When words alone are used, students tend to memorize the words instead of examining the mental images the words represent. Their understanding is limited to what they can recall from only the verbal memory. Concepts are treated as facts, and as facts, they are no longer able to summarize information and organize the social world for students (Eggen, Kauchak, & Harder, 1979).

When the amount of information is limited, it might be better used in demonstrations, on examination tables, or in a learning center around which groups of students interact prior to a class discussion. Activities with expensive, rare, or delicate items might involve students in watching rather than in manipulation or doing. Such activities should be held to a minimum because they place limits on active involvement.

In organizing information selected for an activity, the teacher must weigh several factors:

- the amount of time available
- students' activity level
- the relative importance of the individual concepts and process skills

The amount of structure imposed by the teacher will vary depending on the priority each factor is given. Overorganized information does not allow students to grapple with the information and construct an understanding of it in their mind. They are likely to simply memorize it and are deprived of the opportunity to practice their skills through working with the information until it has meaning to them.

IMPLEMENTING THE LESSON

When the lesson is implemented, students are initially given information to explore. The information they work with can be in the form of objects, videotapes, books, computer software, interviews, role plays, or almost anything else.

During the teacher-guided invention phase, students share observations of the information provided. Questions such as "What did you see, notice, hear about . . . ?" can be asked. When social scientists investigate an area, they are not sure which observations are important. As many observations as possible should be made and recorded. Students often make more accurate observations when provided with an opportunity to interact personally with materials. They are also helped by simple illustrations and tables and charts drawn on the board or overhead projector. The whole class can see clearly what is happening. Points are clarified and essential aspects of the information emphasized.

After students make observations, many different things can occur. Frequently, the teacher chooses one of two options to develop the lesson. Option 1 is more teacher directed. Teachers present a best example to use as a standard in judging other examples. For example, a best example to teach the concept of ritual to a second grader might be blowing out the candles on a birthday cake or watching fireworks on the Fourth of July. For a seventh grader, two best examples of rituals might be spending time each September reading all the posters candidates develop for election to student government at school or scouting out where one's classrooms are located before the beginning of the school year to form a mental map of the routes needed to get from class to class. These best examples help students form a mental image that they may recall at a later time to help them decide if something is a ritual even if they cannot state a verbal definition. One caution in choosing the best example of a concept: Try not to select a stereotype; it will unnecessarily promote stereotyping.

Option 2 is less teacher directed. Students form inferences on their own or with help from prompting and probing questions that focus on identifying the attributes being used to define the concept. Sometimes students need additional information and need to make more observations in order to form inferences. After making and sharing observations, students are asked to identify patterns in their observations. Examples of questions to use include: What common characteristics do we see in each example? What belongs under what? What would you call this group? (Taba, 1967)

During this process, students are making generalizing inferences. If they have difficulty, the teacher may provide additional information or refocus students' attention on earlier information.

In the less teacher-directed approach, the teacher should be supportive but questioning and noncommittal rather than providing explanations. Such questioning focuses students on their own interactions with the information. Teachers remain supportive, but they respond to suggestions with questions such as: "Does all of the information agree with what you say?" This reminds students that they are working toward developing descriptions of the social world that accurately describe reality.

After students arrive at the concept, the invention phase of the activity moves to closure through verbalization of the concept. Students can define the concept in words that include the information at hand. The statement defining the concept is written out for students to see. When the concept is written out, students examine it critically to ensure that it is complete and accurate. The teacher checks to see whether individual students understand the concept. Various students develop an understanding at different rates. A concept is written out to focus students' attention on its attributes and to help them evaluate their discussion of it and reach a closure.

Students may also examine the adequacy of a concept definition developed in class by checking the attributes in the definition against the examples provided. Their definition of "rituals," for example, might include the attribute of "using items that are not used in ordinary daily activities." Students would need to check items associated with rituals that have been brought into class to determine whether this attribute is evident in these items. As students practice applying attributes in the definition of a concept to available examples, they further refine the definition and are more likely to develop a more complete and accurate concept.

EVALUATION

Measurement items used to evaluate students' construction or reconstruction of a concept should help the teacher determine whether students can use the concept in other situations with examples not previously encountered.

LEVELS OF LEARNING

Measurement items may evaluate any of the levels of learning described by Bloom (1956). (See Table 4–2.) Knowledge-level learning usually consists of students reciting information and teachers reinforcing appropriate responses. Examples of such learning are memorizing the articles of the United States Constitution or a list of

Table 4-2
Levels of Learning (Benjamin Bloom)

LEVEL	LEARNING CLASSIFICATION
1	**Knowledge** Recall specific information, concepts, generalizations.
2	**Comprehension** Translate, interpret, explain, summarize, extend information.
3	**Application** Use concepts, generalizations, processes in a new situation.
4	**Analysis** Identify parts, elements, and their relationships.
5	**Synthesis** Put parts together, develop a plan, and communicate in a new way.
6	**Evaluation** Make a judgment using a specific set of criteria.

Source: Adapted from Taxonomy of Educational Objectives Handbook 1: Cognitive Domain, *by Benjamin Bloom (ed.), 1956, New York: David McKay.*

famous women. Students are often asked to reproduce the original content in basically the same form in which it was taught. With a concept, this could involve recalling the definition for that concept as it was defined in class or in the text.

Higher-level learning involves the assimilation and interpretation of knowledge. Going beyond simply being able to recite an idea, the student learns an idea so that it has meaning. Higher-level learning is evaluated in terms of whether the student can apply the concept in a new situation.

ESTABLISHING WHETHER THE STUDENT IS SUCCESSFUL

A major criterion used in judging the success of a lesson focusing on a concept is whether the student is able to use the concept to understand aspects of the social world not previously explored in the lesson. Can students apply the concept in new and original situations? For example, if students have developed the concept of "rituals" through considering some items associated with them, can they determine whether something is a ritual by being given information about the items associated with it?

MEASUREMENT ITEMS

Two types of measurement items can be used—production and recognition. Production items ask students to:
• produce their own examples of a concept
• describe or give a definition of the concept in their own words
• provide an example of the concept (Sunal, 1990)

For example, a production item used to measure students' understanding of the concept of "rituals" might ask: "List three examples of things you do that let everyone know it is the last day of school."

Recognition items provide students with a number of choices from which they recognize correct alternatives. The choices provided include options that were not previously discussed in class. A recognition item designed to measure the concept "rituals" would be: Which of the following are used in celebrating Halloween?

costumes	bunnies
jack-o-lanterns	fireworks
shamrocks	candy

Production and recognition items each have advantages and disadvantages. Recognition items are often harder to prepare than production items, but they check each student on the same information. As a result, comparisons can be made between students and across groups. Production items are easier to construct but often harder for students to complete and may make some students anxious. They allow the teacher to see more clearly what is going on in each student's mind.

KNOWLEDGE LEVEL

Items that evaluate a concept at the knowledge level will measure the ability to remember information previously presented in class about the concept. This includes:

- its definition
- its attributes
- examples used in class

Students are evaluated on whether they remember the information in basically the form in which it was presented. They are not evaluated on whether they can generalize the concept to new situations.

HIGHER LEVELS

Measuring a concept at higher levels involves students in working with examples not previously discussed. Both production and recognition items will measure higher levels of concept understanding. Teachers using recognition items should be sure to select examples measuring the concept being taught, rather than some other type of content. It is necessary to avoid exotic or unfamiliar examples, as these measure student knowledge of the examples rather than understanding of the concept. For example, if a teacher trying to measure student understanding of the concept "rituals" provides water (an item used in rituals celebrating the Loy Kratong festival in Thailand where people throw water on each other) as one alternative, the validity of the item would be questionable unless it is likely that the students would have explored the appropriate Thai festival. If students did not know that throwing water on people might be part of a festival, then the item would be measuring this fact rather than their understanding of the concept. This can be avoided by providing enough description in the examples to overcome any lack of prior knowledge.

MEASURING NONREADERS' CONCEPT DEVELOPMENT

Measuring the construction of concepts by young students can be difficult because so many are nonreaders. Drawings and pictures can be used instead. For example, a lesson on the concept "rituals" could be expanded using an art activity where students draw an example of items associated with celebrating a holiday that wasn't discussed in class. Another option is showing students pictures and then asking them to color or mark all the pictures that are examples of items associated with rituals. More information on evaluating nonreaders is presented in the chapter on evaluation.

THE EXPANSION PHASE

This last part of the lesson involves applying the concept in new situations. This helps students resolve any uncertainties that might exist. The expansion part of the activity gives teacher and students an opportunity to evaluate how well the concept has been understood.

GUIDING YOUR PRACTICE

The following activity is designed to guide your practice with the idea this chapter has helped you reconstruct: how to teach concepts.

A Practice Activity

Where possible, discuss your responses to this practice activity with a classmate.

Examine the following objective: "After examining a situation involving two children and one gift, students will define 'jealousy'." What is the major concept used in this objective? If this objective is to be accomplished, students must be able to use which process skill?

☞ *The concept of "jealousy" is emphasized in this objective. In order to accomplish this objective, students must have skill in making predictions.*

Rephrase the objective so that it focuses on a process skill rather than on the concept of jealousy.

☞ *There are a number of ways in which this objective could have been restated. One example is, "Students will predict whether an individual would be jealous when involved in a situation where there are two children and one gift."*

As part of the lesson's activities, students could role-play various situations in which a person displays jealousy. If this were part of the invention, why would the teacher be involving students in the role plays?

☛ *A teacher might involve students in role-playing situations in order to provide them with examples of the variety of events that might ignite jealousy.*

Think of an example of a role-playing situation that a teacher might involve students in.

What do you think are the most important attribute(s) of the definition of jealousy?

Formulate the definition of jealousy as a second grader might explain it.

What is the definition of jealousy as a fifth grader might explain it?

☛ *Expansion in this lesson might involve students in developing and performing a scenario where jealousy is displayed.*

FINAL PRACTICE

As a final practice, describe a role play that might be used with fourth graders to teach the concept of "sharing."

What are the important attributes of sharing in this role play?

INDEPENDENT ACTIVITY

Examine the lesson plan on the concept of "interdependence" in economic education in chapter 13. Then review the exploration activity. Would this activity enable the teacher to diagnose students' prior knowledge?

Examine the invention activity. Are students developing their definition of the concept or is the teacher giving them one? Is there an example in the activity that might help students develop a mental image they could use in the future when they try to recall the concept this lesson teaches? Is there a closure that the teacher could use to determine whether to go on to the expansion activities?

The expansion activities involve students in applying the concept in a situation different from that in which they learned it. How do the expansion activities do this?

Now that you have had an opportunity to examine a lesson focusing on a concept, describe a set of activities to teach another concept. Suggest activities to help students construct the concept of "island." Begin with an activity for the exploration. Remember that it should focus students' attention, diagnose their current conception, and relate prior to new learning.

Suggest an invention activity. Can you suggest one that would present students with a best example of the concept? Remember that teachers are a little more directive during the invention phase of a learning cycle.

Suggest an expansion activity. If possible, include more than one of the following: guiding students' practice, final practice, independent activity.

SUMMARY

Concepts are an important part of social studies content. The teacher helps students identify and define concepts. This is accomplished through developing lessons that provide students with activities in which they can examine both examples and nonexamples of the concept being constructed. Once students have constructed a definition of the concept, teachers provide them with opportunities to practice applying it in a variety of situations, thereby stabilizing their understanding of it. Students need exploration activities that challenge them and cause them to recognize a need to reconstruct existing concepts or to construct new concepts. Invention activities involve students in working with information provided by the teacher. Questions are used to focus their attention on the attributes the teacher is using to define the concept being taught. A closure is achieved during the invention phase as students define or describe the concept. During the expansion phase, students apply the concept to situations different from those in which it has already been used. When students have had several opportunities to apply the concept in new situations they will be able to stabilize it in their long-term memory.

REFERENCES

Bell, B. & Barker, M. (1982). Toward a scientific concept of animal. *Journal of Biological Education, 16*(13), 197–200.

Beyer, B. & Penna, A. (eds.). (1971). *Concepts in the social studies.* (Bulletin 45). Washington, D.C.: National Council for the Social Studies.

Bloom, B. (ed.). (1956). *Taxonomy of Educational Objectives Handbook 1: Cognitive Domain.* New York: David McKay.

Duit, R. (1987). Research on students' alternative frameworks in science—topics, theoretical frameworks, consequences for science teaching. *Proceedings of the Second International Seminar Misconceptions and Educational Strategies in Science and Mathematics,* Vol. 1, Ithaca, NY: Cornell University, 151–162.

Eggen, P. & Kauchak, D. (1988). *Strategies for teachers: Teaching content and thinking skills.* (2nd ed.) Englewood Cliffs, NJ: Prentice-Hall.

Eggen, P., Kauchak, D., & Harder, R. (1979). *Strategies for teachers.* Englewood Cliffs, NJ: Prentice-Hall.

Feldsine, Jr., J. (1987). Distinguishing student misconceptions from alternate conceptual frameworks through the construction of concept mapping. *Proceedings of the Second International Seminar on Misconceptions and Educational Strategies in Science and Mathematics,* Vol. 1, Ithaca, NY: Cornell University, 177–181.

Harlen, W. (ed.). (1985). *Primary science: Taking the plunge.* London: Heinemann.

Klausmeier, H., Ghatala, E., & Frayer, D. (1974). *Conceptual learning and development: A cognitive view.* Orlando, FL: Academic Press.

Schug, M. & Beery, R. (1987). *Teaching social studies in the elementary school: Issues and practices.* Glenview, IL: Scott, Foresman.

Seiger-Ehrenberg, S. (1991). Concept development. In A. Costa (ed.), *Developing minds: A resource book for teaching thinking,* Revised edition, Vol. 1, Alexandria, VA: Association for Supervision and Curriculum Development, 290–294.

Stanley, W. & Mathews, R. (1985). Recent research on concept learning: Implications for social education. *Theory and Research in Social Education, 12,* 57–74.

Taba, H. (1967). *Teacher's handbook for elementary social studies.* Palo Alto, CA: Addison-Wesley.

Tennyson, R. & Cocchiarella, M. (1986). An empirically based instructional design theory for teaching concepts. *Review of Educational Research, 56,* 40–71.

CHAPTER 5

OVERVIEW

Generalizations describe the relationship between two or more concepts. Students often have constructed generalizations from their limited experience with the social world. Such generalizations are reconstructed as they gain more experience (Eggen & Kauchak, 1988). The social studies curriculum, in providing students with opportunities to increase their knowledge of the social world, can help students acquire and develop the content and skills needed in constructing or reconstructing generalizations. The form of instruction typically called "inquiry" uses skills designed to help students learn generalizations. It should be an important part of the social studies program with older students since they will have acquired the skills and concepts necessary to work with generalizations.

This chapter illustrates how the learning cycle is used in an inquiry or generalization-constructing lesson. The reader is involved in activities that enhance involvement with the chapter's material. In order to accomplish its goal, this chapter is organized as a learning cycle. You will be working through the learning cycle as you read the chapter and do the activities integrated into it.

Constructing Generalizations in Social Studies

OBJECTIVES

1. *Suggest appropriate activities to include in an inquiry lesson teaching a generalization.*

2. *Describe the teacher's role in an inquiry lesson that develops a generalization.*

3. *Describe how the process of developing and revising generalizations is continuous.*

4. *Describe the role of generalizations in social studies content.*

5. *Describe how the ability to construct generalizations is important in the decisions citizens must make in society.*

EXPLORATION IN CONSTRUCTING GENERALIZATIONS

Let's begin our consideration of how to help students construct generalizations by completing the exploration activity presented below.

Time for Reflection: What Do <u>YOU</u> Think?

PATTERNS IN ECONOMICS

Look at products in your kitchen such as baking soda, or at your personal-care items such as shampoo, aspirin, shaving cream, or lipstick. How many are brand-name items? How many are generic or store-brand items?

Collect some additional information. What totals do you find among an acquaintance's kitchen or personal-care items? How many are brand-name items? How many are generic or store-brand items?

Which is more common among your items, generic or brand-name products?

Which is more common among your acquaintance's items, generic or brand-name products?

Which is more common when the items you both have are put together, generic or brand-name products?

Think about the products you both use and those that other people you know use. Do you think generic or brand-name products are more widely used in your community? Why do you think this type of product is more frequently used in your community?

In the activity above, you looked at kitchen or personal-care items you use and surveyed what someone else uses. Then you tried to identify whether generic or brand-name products are used more frequently by each of you. Next, you were asked to combine the items both of you have and to determine whether brand-name or generic items are used more frequently among the combined group. Then you were asked to suggest which type of product would be most frequently used in your community. To do this you probably used some of the information you collected from people with whom you are familiar. Finally, a problem was presented: "Explain why brand-name or generic products are more popular."

In a lesson in which a generalization is constructed, a problem or question is presented. By having students deal with data related to the topic during the exploration phase, the question is raised in the learner's mind. The teacher helps identify the question in students' minds by using several strategies. First, the teacher puts students in a situation where the information they acquire sets up some conflict or raises a question in their minds. In addition, the teacher involves students in making firsthand observations that give them information that leads to a sense of conflict and raises questions. The activity students are involved in also requires them to recall information they already have. They often find that the information they have is not sufficient to resolve the conflict they are experiencing or to answer their questions. The activity also encourages students to organize the information they have to determine whether it is sufficient.

In this exploration, you collected the data by surveying products you and another person use. At the end of the exploration a problem was presented. This problem was phrased as a question: "Why have you decided this is more frequently used?" It is a problem that naturally arose from the activity with which you were involved.

INVENTION IN CONSTRUCTING GENERALIZATIONS

GENERALIZATIONS

Generalizations relate concepts to each other, further summarizing our experiences (Eggen & Kauchak, 1988). Generalizations are even more useful than concepts because they can summarize more information than concepts do. They can also describe our social world more accurately. Generalizations:
- state relationships between two or more concepts
- often identify cause and effect
- can be used to predict a future occurrence of the relationship stated in the generalization (Eggen & Kauchak, 1988, p. 58)

In the following discussion, a third grade student named Spencer uses both concepts and a generalization:

> "The President makes speeches. The President meets important people. He signs laws. The President gives big dinners. He talks to television reporters and answers their questions. You have to be good at doing a lot of different things to be President."

Spencer uses several concepts including "the President," "speeches," "laws," "dinners," and "reporters." These concepts summarize Spencer's experiences with each of these events and items. Spencer makes a generalization that goes further than the concepts he was working with. He relates being president to having skills in many areas.

SEPARATING FACTS FROM GENERALIZATIONS

Sometimes people mistake generalizations for facts. For example, "Riding in a limousine means you have a lot of money" is a generalization, not a fact. It is a generalization for two reasons. First, the statement wasn't formed from observation alone. We may have seen the limousines and the passengers riding in them. We may have noted the quality of the clothes the passengers are wearing. But we have not seen their bank records or credit card bills. We are making assumptions based on what we have observed and we have gone beyond those observations.

Second, the information in the statement is a summarization, not a report of a single event. Generalizations summarize relevant characteristics of observations that have been made. Because we have not seen all possible cases, we generalized from what we did see to make a statement. For that reason it is a generalization from what was observed. We agree with the statement because no contradictory case has been observed. If a contradictory case is eventually observed, the generalization can be changed.

Generalizations such as the limousine example occur when we make inferences from experiences we have had and generalize them to include all possible examples. They can be used to form a hypothesis or suggested explanation for which data can be collected. With the limousine generalization we may talk to various limousine riders and find out that they are not wealthy. For example, they may have hired the limousine to celebrate a personal event like prom night or an anniversary. The results of our data collection may lead us to change our original hypothesis. Generalizations may be an inference from which a hypothesis is formed or they may be a conclusion formed as a result of checking a hypothesis. Which of the following do you think is a generalization? *Margaret Thatcher was Prime Minister in the United Kingdom* **or** *Americans are not sure that a woman can capably carry out the job of President?* The first statement is a fact; the second is a generalization since it is not formed from observation alone. It involves us in generalizing an inference we have made from our observations. The statement tries to summarize what people are thinking. Because of these factors it is a generalization.

GENERALIZATIONS CAN BE USED TO PREDICT

Generalizations can be used to predict actions and events. Using the generalization about limousine passengers, we can predict that a person who rides only in limousines would be considered wealthy by others in the community. Using the generalization, "Americans are not sure that a woman can capably carry out the job of President," what prediction might you make about the chances of a woman's being elected President of the United States during the next presidential election? Using this generalization, you would predict that the chances of a woman's being elected President during the next election are poor.

The predictive capability of generalizations is important because being able to predict events and actions gives us some control over our lives. Social studies education is concerned with helping students learn to predict and control events in their own lives and as citizens of their society. Teachers help students form generalizations and use them to make predictions. They also help students discover inaccuracies in the generalizations they have formed and reconstruct them so that they have better predictive value.

PRINCIPLES OR LAWS

Generalizations have different levels of acceptance by people. Some are accepted as true, with no common exceptions. These are principles or laws. For example, "All people must eat to survive" is a generalization that can be accepted as true and without exception. Other examples of principles or laws are: "Change is inevitable;" "All individuals exhibit behavior;" "The earth's surface features vary as a function of geologic events, weather, and human culture."

On the other hand, "Riding in a limousine means you have a lot of money" is a generalization for which we can find exceptions. This generalization is not accepted as true without any common exceptions. So, it is not a principle or law. As a generalization, its level of acceptance is lower than that of the generalization, "All people must eat to survive." Because both examples describe patterns identified from numerous individual instances, these are generalizations, not facts (Seiger-Ehrenberg, 1991; Eggen & Kauchak, 1988). Can you identify a social studies generalization that you think is an example of a principle or law? If possible, discuss it with a peer to find out whether he or she also thinks it is a principle or law.

ACADEMIC RULES

Academic rules are another form of generalization (Eggen & Kauchak, 1988). Often students memorize and use an academic rule without understanding the rule and its use. Once students are to be able to apply an academic rule at appropriate times teachers must help them understand the concepts found in the rule. Memorization of a rule when there is little understanding of the concepts it includes is limited learning because students will not be able to judge when to apply it. An example of a rule is: "Latitude is the distance in degrees measured from the equator toward one of the poles."

A Practice Activity

In teaching the example, "Latitude is the distance in degrees measured from the equator toward one of the poles," what concepts do you think students would have to know to understand it? What skill(s) might they have to understand?

☛ *Concepts that you might have identified include: distance, degrees, measurement, equator, and poles. A student would also need skill in measuring to understand this rule. Certainly students should have been introduced to the idea that there are 360 degrees in a circle and should have practiced measuring various degrees.*

Generalizations are the most abstract form of content and the most difficult to learn because of their abstractness. They can describe a simple relationship between a few concepts or a highly complex one between many concepts. They may have only limited explanatory power or they may have the greater degree of certainty that is associated with principles or laws. Generalizations are used to organize facts and concepts as they summarize them and describe the relationships between them. Once the organization occurs, and a generalization is formed, it is used to make predictions. Generalizations are the form of social studies content that best explains our social world.

GUIDING STUDENTS' LEARNING OF GENERALIZATIONS

A lesson focusing on a generalization begins with an exploration activity in which a problem or question is identified. This is the first phase of the lesson. To review, the complete learning cycle used in teaching a generalization consists of the following phases:
- *Exploration:* Identification of a problem or question.
- *Invention:* Formation of a hypothesis responding to the problem/question; gathering of data (information) to check the hypothesis; evaluation of the data to decide whether or not it supports the hypothesis.
- *Expansion:* Application of the generalization constructed if the hypothesis is supported or a reconstruction and checking.

PROBLEM/QUESTION

The problem or question developed in the exploration phase is the basis of the lesson. It must be one where a cause and its result can be identified if hypothesizing is going to occur in the process of seeking a solution (Beyer & Penna, 1971). For example, in a discussion on consumer demand the question may arise, "What is the favorite dessert at this school?" This can be a problem that leads to the construction of a generalization, particularly if it is developed further into a question such as "What is the favorite dessert at school, and why is it the favorite dessert?" There are two important parts to this question: 1) what the favorite school dessert is and 2) the reason for its popularity. The reason for its popularity results in a particular dessert being identified as the favorite dessert. It is the cause of the popularity of a particular school dessert. The favorite school dessert, in turn, depends on the reason. It is a *result* of the reason for popularity. If it happens to be popular because it is the *sweetest* school dessert, its popularity could disappear if the cook comes up with a sweeter dessert. (Note that a hypothesis that is a generalization has been developed in relation to this school dessert question: "The favorite school dessert is the sweetest dessert served.") In order to carry out an inquiry that results in a generalization it is important to consider which part is the *cause* and which is the *result*. Teachers need to help students explore this relationship. In this instance, the cause is "sweetness" and the result is _____. (What do you think the favorite sweet school dessert would be?)

What generalization might these boys be forming by tasting snails at a European food fair?

A generalization relates concepts (such as sweetness and the favorite dessert) in some way. In order to understand the relationship, both teacher and student need to be able to separate out the concepts in the generalization and then decide how they are related (cause and result). If the inquirer cannot clearly identify the concepts in a generalization and figure out which is the cause and which is the result, it is not likely that the inquirer will be able to decide whether the information gained in the inquiry does or does not support the generalization (Eggen, Kauchak, & Harder, 1979). Elementary students, in particular, may need help in sorting out cause and result. They have less experience, fewer skills, and are familiar with fewer concepts than are the older middle school students. Even with these limitations, they can begin working with generalizations. The teacher, however, must be aware of their limitations and must be prepared to provide materials and experiences that strengthen students' abilities to work through an inquiry and construct a generalization.

Before beginning the lesson, teachers need to think about: the concepts involved in the problem or question, possible hypotheses (generalizations) that could resolve the problem, and what kind of information students will need to collect to determine if their hypotheses are supported.

Let's analyze another problem/question. "Why are brand-name or generic products the most commonly used in your community?" In this question, the *cause* being explored is the reason(s) that people choose to use either brand-name or generic products more frequently. Some of these reasons could be lower cost, familiarity through advertising, or status appeal. The *result* is the type of product (brand-name or generic) purchased most often by people. The type of product purchased depends on the buyer's reason(s) for purchasing that type of product. It is a *result* of the reason(s).

Younger students can carry out inquiries when they are working with familiar items or situations. They may also be able to carry out a less complex inquiry in which they are gathering information that is easily acquired. For example, students might study pictures of Fort Duquesne (now Pittsburgh) in Pennsylvania and wonder why it was built in that location. After examining maps, they might decide that "It was built there because three rivers come together at this point: The Monongahela and the Allegheny join to form the Ohio." They can check this hypothesis by examining reference books that describe why the fort was built at this location. With this inquiry students should have to be able to explain that the location resulted in the fort's being built on the intersection of the three rivers. This is a workable relationship for younger students.

HYPOTHESIS FORMATION

The hypothesis developed as a solution or answer to the question is phrased as a generalization. Once students know what the problem or question is and want to pursue it, they must be led systematically and creatively to think about a solution (Maxim, 1987). This occurs in the invention phase of the learning cycle. Students usually need to be asked some questions to get them thinking about what information is needed to decide whether their hypothesis can be supported. Some questions the teacher might ask are:

> What do you know about this?
> How could this information help us come up with an answer to our problem?"
> Based on what we have discussed, what are some answers you can suggest?

Small groups offer an opportunity for the give-and-take of ideas and are effective when trying to develop a hypothesis. Developing a useful hypothesis is likely to be an activity that students find challenging. Small-group formation of a hypothesis is usually less stressful, more fun, and more productive than attempting to develop one individually (Eggen & Kauchak, 1988). When a hypothesis is developed by the whole group it is less likely that each student will be involved and that a variety of ideas will be fully represented as the hypothesis is developed.

Think back to the exploration activity above. You were asked: "Why do you think this type of product (brand-name or generic) is more frequently used in your community?" In answering this question you were forming a hypothesis that was phrased as a generalization. If you were able to do a broad-based survey of the buying habits of members of your community you would be able to determine whether your hypothesis is supported. Whether or not your hypothesis is supported you would be able to construct a generalization. You might, for example, construct one of the following generalizations:

> People buy generic products because they are cheaper.
> People buy generic products because they think they are the same quality as brand-name products as well as being cheaper.

DATA GATHERING

The invention phase continues as students gather data or information to check their hypothesis. Teachers need to provide guidance by asking questions such as:

What are some possible sources of information?
What methods would help us gather information? (for example, direct observation, surveys, library research)?
Which one(s) will we use with our problem?
Will this provide us with enough data (information) to check our hypothesis or will we need to combine it with another method to gather some different data?

Once students have decided how they will gather data or information to check their hypothesis, they are given time to do this. Some data gathering may be done out of school. Some in-school time is also necessary, however, because students often need to discuss a next step in data gathering with their teacher or need advice on how to find and use a data source not considered earlier. Teachers frequently may have appropriate data sources available in class so they can provide guidance in their proper use to save time.

As students gather data, they need to decide how to organize, classify, and categorize it. Data should be presented in a way that allows it to be easily and clearly shared with others. Students might use maps, charts, graphs, bulletin boards, drawings, oral reports, written reports, dramatic skits, panel discussion, models, or demonstrations. Well-organized data enables students to use it more successfully to decide whether their hypothesis is supported. Poorly organized data is likely to be of little use since it may not display identifiable patterns and may encourage false conclusions about whether or not a hypothesis is supported. For example, students may survey family members regarding why they buy brand-name or generic products. Their survey could include questions about paper products such as paper towels and toilet paper. It could also include questions about food items such as canned vegetables. When the data is organized, students might lump the responses about paper products and food items together. In doing so, they may decide that "people buy generic items instead of brand-name items because cost is more important than quality."

If they separate out the responses, they may find that people are more likely to buy generic paper products and brand-name food items. The reason for this difference is that the people they surveyed thought there was only a small difference in quality between generic and brand-name paper products and so were unwilling to pay more for brand-name products. People perceived the food items as quite different in quality, finding generic vegetables, for example, much tougher and stringier than brand-name vegetables. In this case they were willing to pay more for what they perceived as much higher quality. The generalization that would result from organizing the data by type of item purchased would be that "quality is more important than cost when people decide whether to buy a brand-name or a generic item." If the students' hypothesis had been "cost is more important than quality when people decide whether to buy a brand-name or a generic item," the first way of organizing data would have falsely supported this hypothesis. The second way of organizing data would not have given support to this hypothesis and students would need to develop a different hypothesis that focuses on quality and not on cost.

Teachers should encourage students to share their information with the class. Data collected by one group of students may lend support or reduce support for one or more of several competing hypotheses. Sharing of information is also likely to broaden students' understanding of a problem as they come into contact with a wider range of data. Student understanding can also be broadened when data is presented in varying formats by different groups.

EVALUATING THE HYPOTHESIS

After data is presented, students decide whether or not their hypothesis is supported. Three results are possible:

1. If the data is inadequate to make a decision, students decide they need additional data.
2. If the hypothesis is supported, students invent a generalization.
3. If the hypothesis is not supported by the data, students need to reconstruct their hypothesis.

EXPANSION IN DEVELOPING GENERALIZATIONS

Figure 5–1 describes the process of developing and reconstructing generalizations. To some extent, this is a never-ending process because generalizations never address all possibilities. They are statements informing us that "in general, this is the case"—not "this is always the case." Teachers help students construct usable generalizations. They also help students understand that once they have a usable generalization, they need to proceed with using it. It can be reconstructed later if they find it no longer addresses data they have.

During the last phase of the inquiry, the expansion, students take different paths, depending on whether the data they have collected related to their hypothesis is inadequate, supports the hypothesis, or does not support it. If the data collected is inadequate and no decision can be made regarding whether or not a hypothesis is supported, students need to decide whether there is a way to collect more data and/or more appropriate data. If this can be done, they should plan how to do it and then collect the additional data. In considering whether they can obtain adequate data, students may find that it is not possible; the information may not exist. For example, they may be interested in how many children learned to read in their community during the first half of the 1800s. There may be no records in existence that would give

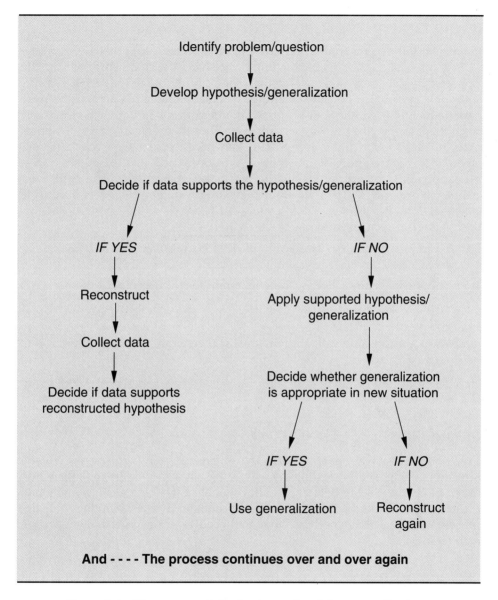

Figure 5–1   The process of developing and revising generalizations.

them the information they need. They may, however, be able to make inferences based on information available in similar communities. Under such circumstances, the students would be asked to tell how satisfying or reliable they
believe this generalization to be or they may wish to pursue a different but related problem for which more information is available.

APPLICATION OF THE HYPOTHESIS

If students find that the information they have collected supports their hypothesis, they can expand their understanding by applying the generalization from the supported hypothesis in another situation. For example, if the students used a survey of products in their home to determine whether brand names or generics were more frequently used, they could survey another group, perhaps senior citizens. When they do this, they will be deciding whether their generalization is appropriate in that situation. If it is appropriate, they need to use it again in another situation. If it is not appropriate, they need to reconstruct it and begin the process of collecting data to find out whether the reconstructed generalization, or new hypothesis, is supported. The data from the surveys might yield several possible generalizations. For example, after a survey of products in their homes, students might form this generalization:

> People with children buy brand-name products because they want to be guaranteed a level of minimum quality.

After a survey of senior citizens, students might form the generalization:

> Senior citizens buy generic products because they are on a fixed income and need to buy cheaper items.

Students might conclude their study with a final generalization that reflects all of their research:

> People buy different types of products—brand names or generics—at different stages in their lives.

RECONSTRUCTION OF THE HYPOTHESIS

If their hypothesis was not supported, the students repeat the processes of gathering, organizing, and presenting data, deciding whether their hypothesis is supported by this new set of data. If it is, they will have invented a generalization as a result of their second attempt to solve the problem. If their data does not support the reconstructed hypothesis, they will need to reconstruct it again and repeat the process.

DECIDING HOW WIDELY A GENERALIZATION CAN BE APPLIED

"Is our generalization always true?" When their hypothesis is supported by the data they gathered, students need to decide how widely the generalization can be applied. For example, do people in larger (or smaller or more ethnically diverse or more industrial) communities make the same choices when deciding to buy either the brand-name or the generic product? Students may decide that they can confidently say that people in their community buy either brand-name or generic products more frequently because of a particular reason. They may also decide that although there is some evidence encouraging them to apply their generalization to other situations, they will need to collect more data before they can generalize beyond the people they are able to talk to. When students begin to apply a generalization, it is always necessary to encourage them to think about any limits present, to ask the question "Is this always true?"

EVALUATING THE INQUIRY PROCESS

Students should be assisted in reviewing their activities to determine which were productive and which could have been done differently. For example, some data sources may be very helpful while others are limited. Some ways of organizing data may be more effective than others. Evaluating their activities enables students to make decisions, better direct their own learning, and become more dependent on internal rather than external reinforcement. This is important in social studies teaching, as the goal is to create citizens who are independent judges and decision makers.

Time for Reflection: What Do <u>YOU</u> Think?

Your expansion activity is to describe briefly an inquiry lesson that would involve students in using survey methodology to investigate a problem in their community.

- Objective

- Exploration Activity

- Problem or Question That Might Be Generated by the Exploration Activity

- Two Possible Hypotheses for Which Data Might Be Gathered

- Invention Activity

- Expansion Activity

SUMMARY

The development of generalizations is a process that never ends. A generalization is constructed and then is applied in a new situation. It may then be reconstructed or accepted as usable in the new situation. It is checked each time it is used. The three phases of the learning cycle help students identify a problem, hypothesize a solution, collect data with which to check the solution, determine whether the solution is supported, and either reconstruct the hypothesis or apply a supported hypothesis (generalization) in another situation. One important advantage of planning a generalization learning cycle is the inclusion of the significant step of checking the generalization in a new situation during the expansion phase. Students need to use the generalizations they learn in a variety of situations if they are to stabilize them in their minds. They also need to discover that the generalization they construct might not satisfactorily explain a different situation. They must be able to recognize cases in which their investigation did not use appropriate procedures or resources and situations requiring additional or different information. Since the modern world involves students in complex, changing societies it is important that they use generalizations in a variety of situations and learn when they are appropriate and when they need to be reconstructed. If students are not able to do this, they will be less able to participate fully as responsible citizens in society.

REFERENCES

Beyer, B. & Penna, A. (eds.). 1971. *Concepts in the social studies.* (Bulletin 45). Washington, DC: National Council for the Social Studies.

Eggen, P. & Kauchak, D. (1988). *Strategies for teachers: Teaching content and thinking skills.* Englewood Cliffs, NJ: Prentice-Hall.

Eggen, P., Kauchak, D., & Harder, B. (1979). *Strategies for teachers.* Englewood Cliffs, NJ: Prentice-Hall.

Maxim, G. (1987). *Social studies and the elementary school.* Columbus, OH: Merrill.

Seiger-Ehrenberg, S. (1991). Concept development. In A. Costa (ed.), *Developing minds: A resource book for teaching thinking,* Revised edition, Vol. 1, Alexandria, VA: Association for Supervision and Curriculum Development, 290–294.

CHAPTER 6

OVERVIEW

Planning for teaching is a complex process. As they plan, teachers make decisions in three areas. First, they must decide what their students are developmentally and culturally ready to learn (see chapters 2, 9, and 14). Second, they must decide what is appropriate to teach. Third, they must decide how they will teach. This chapter focuses on steps two and three, deciding what to teach and how to teach it.

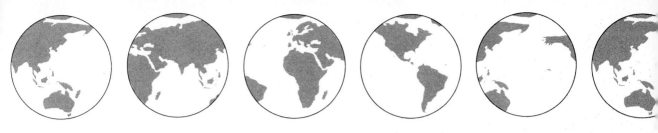

Planning for Teaching

OBJECTIVES

1. List the three major sources of the social studies curriculum.
2. Explain the influences of state and local courses of study, state testing programs, and textbooks on the social studies curriculum.
3. Identify steps in planning for teaching.
4. Describe how units of study can be identified.
5. Describe factors to consider in choosing appropriate topics for lessons within a unit.
6. Explain the importance of objectives in planning and teaching lessons.
7. Differentiate between knowledge, skill, and attitudinal objectives.
8. Practice writing and rewriting objectives.
9. Explain how and why the discussion of what objectives should be written is different from how to write objectives.
10. Identify at least three considerations that a teacher needs to keep in mind when planning a lesson.
11. Describe how the actions of a teacher during a lesson are different from those of the learner.
12. Identify the different parts to include in a unit and explain how the three kinds of lessons are different from one another.
13. Identify differences between an interdisciplinary and a multidisciplinary unit.

DECIDING WHAT TO TEACH

SOURCES OF CURRICULUM

Curriculum can be defined as what is taught. Social studies curriculum includes facts, skills, concepts, generalizations, attitudes, and values. Where does curriculum come from? Three primary sources of the curriculum are the society, learners, and knowledge (Tyler, 1949).

SOCIETY

Each society has unique perspectives regarding what is important. Curriculum must respond to widely recognized social needs. Therefore, each society and to some extent human society as a whole are sources of the social studies curriculum (see also chapters 12 and 14). For example, if the development of citizens who participate in government through voting and paying their taxes is widely recognized as a social need, the social studies curriculum will be expected to work to satisfy this need.

Within many societies are different subcultures. In such societies, these subcultures also contribute to the social studies curriculum. The contributions of each subculture are recognized in the curriculum and the needs of students from that group are recognized and addressed. For example, Korean-American students bring to the classroom an ancient culture with a strong respect for family and education. These students may have a great need to find a way to accommodate their views of family to those of mainstream United States society.

The local community may also have special needs or characteristics that influence the curriculum. For example, a community where the residents are very mobile might select a curriculum with a content that reflects national questions, whereas a stable community might place a larger emphasis on local issues and history. A racially and ethnically diverse community has special needs and offers unique possibilities for study that a homogeneous community does not have.

LEARNERS

Information about learners and their needs (see chapter 1) results in the identification of physiological, emotional, social, and cognitive needs that are addressed by the social studies curriculum. The need to develop self-esteem and to recognize areas in which a student can provide leadership to others, for example, can be incorporated into the social studies curriculum.

KNOWLEDGE

Social studies process skills, facts, concepts, generalizations, attitudes, and values represent the knowledge sources for the social studies curriculum. These are complex in social studies since the subject matter knowledge is drawn from all the social sciences, from the humanities and sciences to some extent, and from the integration of various aspects of these areas (see chapter 1).

Time for Reflection: What Do <u>YOU</u> Think?

- Suggest at least one other need, in addition to the one cited in the text above, that the society in your country would widely recognize and that the social studies curriculum would be expected to incorporate.

- Suggest two additional personal needs that the social studies curriculum should address.

- Transportation is a topic found in many social studies curricula. Which social sciences might it draw its subject matter from?

- Which humanities and/or sciences might contribute to the subject matter of this topic?

- Is this a topic that draws its subject matter from an integration of several areas, or does it draw mostly from one area?

CONTROVERSY OVER THE SCOPE AND SEQUENCE OF THE SOCIAL STUDIES

The three major sources for the social studies curriculum produce a huge volume of material that conceivably could be part of the curriculum. This has led to a long debate over what the scope of the curriculum should be and then over the sequencing of what is included. In recent years documents such as *Charting A Course: Social Studies for the 21st Century* (1989), *Historical Literacy: The Case for History in American Education* (1988), *America in Transition: The International Frontier* (1989), and *Guidelines for Geographic Education* (1984) have all addressed the issue of what the scope and sequence of the social studies curriculum should be. These reports, and others, are representative of major trends and issues in social studies education during the 1980s and into the 1990s. These reports tend to emphasize history and geography as the major sources of knowledge in the social studies curriculum. They also stress an international perspective in teaching geography, history, and current events. Others have argued against an identification of history and geography as the major sources of social studies curriculum. Walsted and Soper (1988) argue for greater study of economics while Evans (1989) argues for an emphasis on consideration of current events and social issues in the curriculum.

Recognizing the different needs of states and communities, the National Council for the Social Studies (NCSS) has published many articles in its journal, *Social Education,* explaining various proposals for a social studies curriculum. NCSS does not endorse any one specific curriculum, although it has sponsored and taken part in several examinations of the curriculum in recent years. Instead, they recommend that school systems and states examine such curricula and select what they believe is best for their students. Three scope and sequence alternatives are featured in the October, 1989 issue of *Social Education:*

> "Social studies within a global education" proposed by Kniep, stresses the role of social studies in education for an understanding of global issues and interrelationships.
>
> "Designing a social studies scope and sequence for the 21st century" by Hartoonian and Laughlin identifies ten themes to be included at each grade level.
>
> "In search of a scope and sequence for social studies: Report of the National Council for the Social Studies Task Force on Scope and Sequence" suggests some changes in the expanding environments approach.

There has been controversy over the expanding environments approach in social studies (see Chapter 1). Many social studies educators agree that the expanding environments approach is limiting (Akenson, 1987; Larkins, Hawkins, & Gilmore, 1987; LeRiche, 1987; Haas, 1991). They argue that students can study various cultures and historical periods beginning in the primary grades (Crabtree, 1989). Others advise against a set of recommended content for each grade level. They prefer a curriculum based upon issues or interests of students. These might reflect current local and national concerns or longstanding issues from history and the social sciences (Engle & Ochoa, 1988).

The future content of the social studies curriculum in terms of its knowledge sources is undecided. Decisions are usually made on a state level, and occasionally at the local level. California adopted a curriculum focused on history and geography that does not use an expanding environments approach. New York has a very different curriculum that stresses social science concepts with a periodic application and integration of these concepts. Teachers need to be aware of controversy over the social studies curriculum and to participate as much as possible in decisions that are being made in regard to it (Larkins, Hawkins, & Gilmore, 1987; Haas, 1991).

INFLUENCES ON SOCIAL STUDIES CURRICULUM

While there are three major sources of curriculum in the social studies, there are narrower influences that affect the specific content of the curriculum taught. These include state and local courses of study, state testing programs, and textbooks.

STATE AND LOCAL COURSES OF STUDY

A state or school system course of study may be mandated or may serve as a guide. Where it is mandated, teachers must use it as their basic curriculum. Mandated courses of study are usually considered to represent the minimum curriculum. Teachers are encouraged to add to it in both breadth and depth. To help you make decisions you will need to know the answers to several questions. Does your state have a course of study in social studies? Does your local school system have a social studies course of study? Is any of these a mandated course of study? Local courses of study may exist where no state curriculum is mandated. Or they may exist to add breadth and depth to the state course of study. These may also be mandated or may serve as a guide. State and local courses of study intended to serve as a guide should be considered just that—a guide. The teacher is expected to use the guide to focus and structure the curriculum but is usually encouraged to go well beyond it.

Mandated courses of study sometimes result from a belief that teachers are not presenting a full social studies curriculum and/or are not devoting an adequate amount of time within the classroom day to social studies. Mandated courses of study often also result from a belief that it is important to outline a course of study since teachers and/or local school systems may be unable to determine an appropriate and relevant social studies curriculum for their students. Of course many educators would disagree, believing that teachers and local school systems know their students' needs best. Today, many states have official courses of study and, of these, many are mandated.

STATEWIDE TESTING PROGRAMS

Statewide testing programs are common. Standardized tests are often used because they allow comparison of student achievement between school systems within the state and with students in other states (see chapter 9). They are also often used because developing a test to fit a particular state course of study is expensive and time consuming. Since standardized tests are not developed to reflect a particular course of study, they test material that is not necessarily in a state or local course of study. Does your state use standardized tests in testing its students? If so, what tests are used and what grades are they used in? Teachers find that they must teach tested material if their students are to do as well as possible on all parts of the test. As a result, the material tested is added into, or sometimes replaces, the social studies curriculum outlined in the state or local course of study.

SOCIAL STUDIES TEXTBOOKS

Textbooks are another influence on the curriculum. Many teachers depend heavily on the textbook (see chapter 1). As a result, it may dictate the curriculum. Because of mergers in the textbook industry, there are fewer than ten elementary and middle school textbook series in social studies today. Textbook publishers try to satisfy as many users as possible. As a result, no textbook is likely to provide a curriculum that perfectly fits a state or local course of study, or the needs of a particular group of students. Some textbook series are written to sell to states with large populations. These states, such as California and Texas, have textbook selection committees who choose series to be purchased in the state. A series that is selected in such a state will have a large number of buyers. Therefore, publishers are likely to produce textbooks that will fit the courses of study in these few states. This means that the series may not fit well with courses of study in other states. With few textbook series available, the possible choices are also few. An additional problem is that a textbook is also unlikely to present all the material found in a particular standardized test. A curriculum dictated by a single textbook will have many limitations.

PUTTING IT ALL TOGETHER

Teachers are faced with many decisions and sometimes with conflicting goals. Determining what the social studies curriculum will be when there are so many sources for that curriculum and several conflicting influences is one of the factors that makes teaching such a challenging job. Nevertheless, many teachers take time to reflect on what needs their students have, what abilities they have, and which curriculum will best help them develop into caring, participating individuals and citizens. What is taught in social studies is typically influenced by state and local courses of study and by textbooks and by state mandated tests. In these cases, teachers have guidelines and limitations for choosing units.

Teachers often work with other teachers as they make decisions regarding the social studies curriculum. Sometimes these are impromptu occasions when, for example, teachers at the same grade level start talking about their curriculum while eating lunch together. At other times teachers set up curriculum development teams at their grade level, in their school, or in their school system, which work on the social studies program. Both impromptu and planned efforts can have positive effects. Duplication of effort can be reduced as teachers share ideas and materials. Greater reflection can also occur as teachers listen to others' thoughts and weigh different ideas. Units developed by teachers working together are discussed later in this chapter in the section on multidisciplinary and interdisciplinary units.

THE UNIT

IDENTIFYING UNITS OF STUDY

After identifying the curriculum content for each grade level, the year's work should be divided into units of study. Units are carefully organized sets of lessons on a topic that help students understand the interrelationships between the selected skills, facts, concepts, generalizations, attitudes, and values. Units are particularly important in social studies because they enable teachers to help students work with the content in a variety of ways. Single, isolated lessons cannot accomplish these goals. Units are developed to answer questions such as:

> What are the characteristics of friends?
> How does the law affect me?
> Why is the United States of America an important and powerful nation?
> How can we learn about the quality of the environment in our state?
> How do people get money?
> Why are families important?
> What is it like to live in Japan? Alaska? India? Mexico? Nigeria?

How can we improve our community?
Who are America's heroes and heroines?
How can we improve our environment?
How do laws change?
What is the job of the president of the United States of America?
Who are some famous American immigrants?
How have equal rights been attained in the United States of America?
Why do we need to take a census?
What is "in America's best interests?"
How does advertising try to influence consumers?
How do Americans go about voting?

The length of units varies from a few days to an entire semester or year. The unit is completed when the students can give a satisfactory answer to the title's question. Older students or those with more mature thinking skills give answers of greater complexity. Two important reasons for unit teaching are to allow for individual differences and to allow students to help determine the length and depth of the study by asking questions related to the topic. Longer units may be divided into subquestions whose answers help answer the larger question.

A Practice Activity

Look at the first four unit questions listed. Explore some subquestions for each of these unit topics.

☞ *Phrasing your unit topic as a question is helpful in planning the unit. As subquestions are generated, individual lessons or sets of lessons can be developed to help students construct answers to those questions. Possible subquestions are: Why do we need friends? What happens when people do not obey the law? How are laws created? What important natural resources are found in the United States? How are United States citizens different from those in other nations? Which state laws are designed to protect our environment?*

Units include three specific kinds of lessons: *initiatory, developmental,* and *culminating.* The goals of the initiatory lesson are similar to those of the exploration phase of a learning cycle. Both:
- introduce the study by motivating students to become involved in aspects of the topic by presenting them with information that challenges their current ideas
- use students' previous knowledge and experience
- ask questions about the topic

The initiatory lessons serve as the exploration of a unit's topic.

The developmental lessons include learning the concepts, generalizations, and skills needed to answer the question of the unit. The developmental lessons do what the invention phase of a learning cycle does. If the unit is short in length, such as a unit on "How do citizens vote for the president?", the unit may be one learning cycle. If the unit is long, such as one dealing with "How do people in our community earn money to satisfy their needs and wants?" then the developmental lessons may include a series of learning cycles each teaching a different concept, generalization, or skill. A longer unit, for example on economics, might include several learning cycles that answer subquestions like: Why do we have scarcities? How do producers try to reduce the impact of scarcity? How can informed consumers help reduce the negative impacts of the energy crisis? and How does the need to combat a scarcity of food and energy affect the people of today's world?

The unit's culminating lesson reviews what has been learned and may also include the application of the information to new areas. Thus, although sometimes just a review of the knowledge imparted, the culminating activities are often an expansion of what has been learned.

There are some similarities between a unit and a learning cycle. However, in addition to the three types of lessons, units include a clear statement of the knowledge, skill, and attitudinal objectives and descriptions of the methods of evaluation appropriate for the unit (see chapter 9). Other helpful inclusions are bibliographies for both students and teacher and a clearly stated rationale or reason for teaching the unit.

The teacher decides which process skills, concepts, generalizations, attitudes, and values are central to a social studies unit. Lesson plans are then designed to provide students experience with this material. A unit must relate important material to the student. This relationship is built to foster the student's development as an individual and also as a citizen. In deciding which material is central to a unit, the teacher should consider student interest and experiences, the teacher's own interests, the cultural composition of the class, and contemporary events.

In the rationale statement teachers explain why the topic is studied. Appropriate reasons might include:

- The topic is of particular interest to the students.
- The topic helps students solve interpersonal problems in the classroom.
- The topic is timely and deals with a current problem or issue of concern locally, in the state, or nationally.
- The topic is mandated by the state curriculum.
- The topic expands students' knowledge to include an important area or issue needing formal instruction if it is to be understood.

The rationale also tells how this topic is related to other topics that have or will be studied by the students. For example, the students may study the Constitution and Bill of Rights because it was the next major statement concerning liberty and political rights after the colonies issued the Declaration of Independence and fought the Revolutionary War. The rationale also discusses briefly which skills will be introduced or reviewed during the unit. In a unit about the Bill of Rights, students might interview workers in the community and find out if and how the

Bill of Rights affects their work. Or, in a community where unemployment has recently increased, a teacher might develop a unit that examines the emotional and economic needs of families and helps students identify ways they can constructively and creatively spend time with family members without spending money.

Beginning teachers often focus on units mandated by state or local courses of study. As they gain experience and satisfy basic requirements, they move onward to units that respond more closely to the individual interests and needs of their students. Beginning teachers should write a unit rationale that goes beyond the statement, "Topic is mandated by the state curriculum." It is appropriate to recognize that the decision to plan and teach the unit did begin as an attempt to satisfy a mandate. However, the rationale should also explain how the unit will result in meaningful learning by students.

■ DECIDING HOW TO TEACH

PLANNING AND DECIDING HOW TO TEACH

Once units and topics within units have been outlined, it is time to begin planning for the teaching of the unit. All teaching begins with planning. Teachers may begin by preparing a resource unit that contains a rationale, set of objectives, list of potential resources, and short descriptions of activities that might be used to accomplish the objectives. Eventually, the teacher prepares a teaching unit detailing all instructional resources, including the lesson plans, evaluations, and resource materials.

Identifying objectives—what students are to learn—is the first step in planning. Later in this chapter, objectives are defined and their construction is described. After objectives are identified, the teacher considers possible instructional strategies such as simulations, biographies, and surveying that can be used to accomplish the objectives. The next chapter discusses many of the teaching strategies teachers can choose from. Teachers familiar with how to use a number of alternative instructional strategies have a better chance of matching an appropriate procedure to the objective than do those whose repertoire is limited. When the strategies for teaching have been selected and instructional materials identified and selected, the actual lesson plans can be prepared, implemented, and evaluated.

WRITING OBJECTIVES

Once the topic of a study is selected the teacher must decide just what about the topic the students should learn. The emphasis of every objective must be on the accomplishment of the student. During a lesson the students go through a series of activities that result in their learning content and perfecting skills and attitudes. The teacher does something very different. The teacher facilitates student learning and development and assesses student progress toward learning. Objectives must always be worded so that it is clear what the student will accomplish during the lesson or unit. Objectives should not focus on what the teacher will do. Objectives help a teacher perform two important tasks:

1. keep clearly in mind what students are to learn during the lesson
2. identify what information and behaviors will measure student accomplishment

In assessing teacher performance, evaluators often ask, "Did the teacher teach to the objective?" However, in a complete evaluation of a social studies professional, the question becomes, "Did the teacher teach the students valuable and important things that will help them become good citizens?"

TYPES OF OBJECTIVES

Content knowledge, skills, and attitudes are all essentials in the social studies curriculum. Therefore, objectives of each type must be written, taught, and evaluated. The process of writing objectives helps the teacher consider what the important things are that the students should be doing and learning in their social studies activities. Every objective must be weighed carefully to determine if it must be included to help students learn content knowledge, skills, or attitudes that will be important to their functioning as responsible citizens in a democratic society.

When first writing objectives, students often worry most about how to properly word objectives. The wording of objectives is important and must communicate clearly to the reader. Some educators say that objectives should clearly state what a student will be able to do after instruction that he or she could not do before being involved in instruction. This view of an objective sees the student's mind as an "empty vessel" that is "filled up" during instruction. Clearly, during social studies instruction students do acquire new content knowledge. They may learn that the president of the United States is the commander-in-chief of the military forces. At other times students may learn to perform specific skills such as reading a population graph. However, meaningful learning often requires the learners to use skills they already have to reorganize their knowledge. This means that there are times when what the learners are doing during the instructional process is more important than new knowledge. This view places a greater emphasis on the development of skills.

Perhaps you have already learned to write behavioral objectives that include three parts:

1. under what conditions (specific sources of information)
2. the action of the student (action verb)
3. the degree of acceptable accomplishment (minimum performance level) (Mager, 1962)

An example of such an objective is:

> Given a map of the world and the latitude and longitude coordinates of ten national capitals, the student will correctly locate the capitals with 90% accuracy.

Such wording of an objective illustrates all three parts. It is most appropriate for a lesson objective because it identifies the materials that are used. This form of objective is helpful when the student is practicing a skill that has several rules to apply when performing each task. However, many social studies lessons do not include tasks that follow a systematic series of steps. Jarolimek (1991) says that there is a middle ground in the wording of objectives. Social studies specialists tend to view behavioral objectives as statements of what students will learn or do during the instructional process. The key to writing such objectives is to use a verb that describes what is done by the learner during the lesson. Among the verbs that accomplish this are:

| name | list | identify | role play | choose | listen |
| compare | analyze | describe | graph | explain | tell why |

Examples of all three types of objectives that represent the "middle ground" suggested by Jarolimek are given below. Take note of how the descriptive verb hints at what will be done during the lesson and how to approach the evaluation of each objective.

Knowledge Objectives.   Knowledge objectives always mention the topics under study. Some examples are as follows:

1. Students will compare the lives of colonial children with their own lives.
2. Students will correctly locate the four large islands of Japan.
3. Students will give reasons why one brand of cereal costs more than another.
4. Students will state the meaning of Thanksgiving in their own words.

Skill Objectives.   Skill objectives describe the skills that will be learned or practiced during the study. Some examples are:

1. Students will gather data by interviewing.
2. Students will write reports in the form of a newscast.
3. Students will organize data on maps.
4. Students will classify the items on their list into those that are needs and those that are wants.

Attitudinal Objectives.   Attitudinal objectives express the things that we hope students will feel and believe in the future as a result of their study. Such behaviors come about as a result of the students' having formed conclusions and generalizations about the topic under study.

1. Students will be respectful toward older people.
2. Students will want to seek out opportunities to learn more about the president's activities.
3. Students will conserve energy in their daily activities.
4. Students will voluntarily tell others about the original Thanksgiving celebration in the United States.

This learning center could address knowledge, skill, or attitudinal objectives.

A Practice Activity

Review the objectives listed above and answer the following questions.

- What are the four different topics that the knowledge objectives deal with?
- What are the four activities that students will be doing in the lessons guided by the skill objectives?
- If the skill objectives all come from the same unit, what do you think the topic of that unit might be?
- Look at each of the four attitudinal objectives. What is the conclusion or generalization that you think the students would have had to make and believe in order to motivate them to perform the actions described in each of the attitudinal objectives?

☞ *Your answers to the topics under study should be similar to the following: (1) colonial life; (2) Japan; (3) economics or consumer behavior (4) Thanksgiving. The student activities are: (1) interviewing someone; (2) writing reports; (3) making maps; (4) classifying things.*

In the skill objective you will not be able to identify the topic. Some teachers do like to write longer skill objectives and include the topic. However, that is a matter of personal preference and not a requirement for a skill objective.

The conclusions or generalizations should be similar to: (1) Older people know a lot from their experiences that can help others. (2) Being president of the United States of America is a demanding job and requires a person to work hard and make lots of important decisions. (3) By using less energy we conserve our natural resources and environment. (4) When we celebrate holidays we are keeping those traditions of the past that people think are important to remember and practice.

Read each of the following objectives and decide if each is expressing a clear behavior or not. Then reword each objective, even those you believe are clearly worded, as there is always more than one way to word an objective clearly.

1. Students will identify the human influences they see on the environment.
2. Students will understand that people change the environment.
3. Students will describe how the business district of the city is different from a residential area.
4. Students will recognize the importance of the president.
5. Students will identify ways the Pilgrims survived in America.

☞ *You may have identified numbers 2 and 4 as not clearly worded. Some might also say that 5 is not as clear as it could possibly be. One way to help decide if the expected student behavior is clear in an objective is to try to write a test question or exercise for that objective. A clear objective gives precise direction to the content of a test question. However, if you think several rather different questions could measure the objective, then that objective could probably be more clearly written. In objectives 2 and 4 the verbs "understand" and "recognize" are open to a wide variety of interpretations. In deciding whether students "understand" at the end of a lesson, would the teacher be satisfied if the student made the statement, "People can change their environment"? Or would the teacher want the student to give examples of ways people have changed the environment? Or would the teacher expect a scientific explanation of what will or might happen in nature after people act in a particular way? Since it is not clear what the teacher expects the student to do as a result of accomplishing the objective, the objective is vague and needs to be rewritten.*

Objectives 2 and 4 can be made clearer by using different verbs that de-scribe how to recognize someone as important or understand the cause of a change. You might also have changed the phrase "identify ways" used in objective 5 to "explain how" or "name three actions" Pilgrims took to help them survive in America. Some people might consider the term "identify ways" a little too general. For objectives 1 and 3 you may have changed the verb to another rather similar action or you may have added a conditional phrase such as "Given a set of pictures" or specified a minimum number of exam-ples students need to give.

Now try your hand at writing a knowledge, skill, and attitudinal objec-tive. Use one of the following unit topics:

1. *"What was it like to live in Europe during the Middle Ages?"*
2. *"Why should Americans be concerned with protecting the tropical rain forests?"*

The more you write objectives and evaluate the objectives you read in the les-son plans of others, the easier it will become for you to master the mechanics of writing objectives. Near the beginning of each chapter of this book there is a list of objectives for the chapter and for each sample learning cycle or lesson. An ex-amination of these objectives will provide you with many more examples of prop-erly worded objectives. As you develop your skills in clearly wording objectives, you will find that you may even be able to rewrite this book's objectives more clearly! These lists of objectives play an important role in planning and evalua-tion. Not only will they help you in studying the chapters but they can also serve as a reference for style and as a guide in the selection of social studies objectives.

APPROPRIATENESS—GOING BEYOND THE MECHANICS OF WRITING OBJECTIVES

With effort, the mechanics of writing objectives will be mastered, but the ques-tion of *appropriate* objectives for social studies is one that has faced social studies educators for years. Moreover, it is one that will continue to be of concern given the dynamics of our society and the changes made even greater by today's tech-nology. For example, today a teacher might use an objective such as, "Students will identify ways in which technology threatens life on earth." In the 1950s the impact of technology was usually seen only as positive, so that an objective fo-cusing on negative impacts of technology would probably not have been used.

Social studies professionals have long been engaged in this task of finding ap-propriate objectives. Periodically, special interest groups and politicians become involved. The National Council for the Social Studies (NCSS) is the major profes-sional organization devoted to promoting social studies education. Their publications examine all of the issues related to social studies, including what should be taught and what methods are best to use in attaining specific goals. Membership in the NCSS or one of its state or local affiliate councils is one way in which teachers can receive ongoing and continuous help in examining the question of what should be taught to our future citizens and how this can best be accomplished.

DEVELOPING THE LESSON

Teaching a lesson begins with its planning phase. This is where the topic, objectives, and methods of presentation are identified. Writing the lesson plan helps the teacher:

1. organize its presentation
2. anticipate student responses and problems that may arise in students' understanding
3. plan management procedures such as passing out materials or moving into groups *(Clark & Yinger, 1979)*

The teacher should plan carefully so that most of the students' attention during instruction will be directed toward the behaviors needed to accomplish the objectives (Smith & Sendelbach, 1979). This is the meaning of the phrase "time on task." Interesting tasks and clearly given directions and procedures eliminate distractions and many discipline problems.

    Lesson planning involves applying theory about effectively helping students learn. This assures that students' attention is gained and directed and that thinking skills are practiced, used appropriately, and assessed for attainment. Table 6–1 is a lesson plan on productive resources that contains the parts described in this section.

Table 6–1

LEARNING CYCLE: Productive Resources

Theme: Productive Resources (For Primary and Intermediate Grades)

OBJECTIVES	PROCEDURES	EVALUATIONS
	Materials: *pictures of natural, human, and capital resources; pictures of livestock production.*	
	Introduction (Exploration)	
Students will review previous knowledge by identifying examples of natural, human, and capital resources.	Teacher asks, "Do you like brownies?" Teacher says, "Let's make some. What do we need to make the brownies?" List items on board. Affirm all these are necessary to make brownies.	Check to see students are paying attention and participating.

Students will define productive resources as the natural, human, and capital resources used to make a product or perform a service.

Teacher Presentation of Information (Invention)

Those things we use to help us make a product or perform a service are called "productive resources." Teacher writes: "productive resources" on board.

Teacher shows pictures of natural, human, and capital resources one at a time.

Teacher reviews term for first picture and writes it on board under "productive resources."

Teacher shows a second picture and asks, "What natural resources do you see in this picture?" Students respond. Repeat with additional pictures of human and capital resources. Other questions to ask include: "Are these people examples of human resources?" "Why?" "Why not?" Return to list for brownies. Ask students to classify each item on the list. Ask: "What can we say a productive resource is?" Write class definition on board. Have students write it in notebooks.

Correct classification of items on list is recorded on a checklist.

Class states a definition.

Student Practice (Expansion)

Given a set of pictures of livestock production, small groups of students will identify which of the items pictured are or are not productive resources in this business

In groups of 3, students will develop a list of items in the pictures that are productive resources used in livestock production and a second list of items that are not used. Then students will identify at least 2 examples of human, natural, and capital resources in their lists. Representative of each group writes on board.

Class and teacher compare checklists.

Teacher checks students' list for at least 80% accuracy.

Individual Practice (Expansion)

Homework: Talk with a parent or neighbor about his or her job and identify the productive resources required in it. Then put an (N) by those that are natural resources and a (C) by those that are capital resources. Be prepared to share this information tomorrow.

Students have information to share and participate in sharing it as indicated by a checklist.

Note: This lesson plan is a complete learning cycle. The introduction is the exploration phase. The teacher presentation of information is the invention phase. The student and individual practice are the expansion phase.

Lesson Plan Checklist

STUDENT'S NAME	PARTICIPATES IN CLASSIFYING ITEMS	PARTICIPATES IN SHARING INFORMATION ABOUT JOBS AND PRODUCTIVE RESOURCES

In the introduction the teacher focuses students' attention and creatively directs it toward the content of the lesson. This brings the students' prior knowledge and experiences into their working memory. In the lesson on productive resources this is done by asking the students to list what it takes to make brownies. Next, the teacher provides some information for the students to examine. This information may be in the form of an oral presentation by the teacher, or the teacher may select another form of stimulus such as a set of pictures, story, poem, recording, chart, map, or artifact to present knowledge. The information should challenge students' existing content knowledge, skills, or attitudes. In the lesson on productive resources the teacher displays pictures and identifies examples of natural, human, and capital resources in the pictures. After the information is examined by the students and teacher, the teacher has the class interact with the data. Often questions are asked to accomplish this. Sometimes the teacher directs the students to perform a task such as ordering the data from largest to smallest, after which they are asked to make an interpretation or to form a conclusion. During the class' interaction the teacher observes to see if most of the students have constructed the knowledge or skills presented. In the productive resources lesson the ability to classify the list of ingredients as human, capital, and natural resources provides this information. Once the teacher believes the students have classified appropriately, the lesson can proceed. If not, the teacher corrects the students' work and reteaches the portion where errors occurred. The teacher then provides another task in which groups or individuals again practice with the data. At this time the teacher observes more closely and may collect students' work to evaluate attainment of the lesson objectives. If all or some of the students do not attain the objectives, the teacher must review, reteach, and reevaluate those portions of the lesson where problems have been found before preceding on to the next lesson.

As the lesson is taught, the teacher observes and interacts with the students. The teacher also interacts with the materials and equipment used. This combination is no easy task. Many teachers have expressed the wish to be more than one person. Planning the lesson and the management of students and materials in advance are important to successful teaching. Multimedia materials help the teacher motivate and direct students' attention. These are a great help for the teacher as long as they work! Even the most experienced teachers can have major problems with media, such as burned-out bulbs in an overhead projector. Occasional media problems should not be a surprise nor should they be used as an excuse to avoid using media.

Researchers tell us that most teachers usually stick close to their lesson plans (McCutcheon, 1981). That is why the lesson plan should be thoroughly prepared. Teachers seem to plan more thoroughly when they are teaching new material because of their lack of experience in this particular situation. Beginning teachers need more detailed lesson plans because they have very limited experience in teaching students various content areas.

INTERDISCIPLINARY AND MULTIDISCIPLINARY UNITS

Social studies as a content area within the elementary and middle school has characteristics that make it different from other content areas. However, the social world we live in is not really separate from the physical world. Social studies incorporates reading/language arts, mathematics, art, industrial arts, music, and physical education as tools used in studying and understanding its content. It incorporates science and technology directly in areas such as geography and less directly in areas such as economics, sociology, history, and political science. No area of social studies can be totally separated from other content areas. All interact in our world today and always have affected each other. It is important to help students build relationships between content areas. By so doing we bring schooling closer to life outside the school, where the world is one integrated experience and is not compartmentalized into content areas. We also broaden and strengthen the social studies content we teach.

INTERDISCIPLINARY UNITS

Integration of content can take place in interdisciplinary or multidisciplinary units. Interdisciplinary units involve looking at a topic from the perspective of a variety of disciplines within social studies. If the topic is native Hawaiian culture, for example, students might be involved in activities that originate in history, anthropology, geography, economics, sociology, and political science. Such a unit would try to integrate the disciplines within the topic (see Table 6–2).

While most social studies teachers in the elementary and middle school do take an interdisciplinary approach on social studies, it is often helpful to consider the range of disciplines that can be integrated into a unit. When such consideration occurs, areas that may have been viewed as less likely to contribute to the unit are often found to be more relevant than anticipated.

Table 6–2

Possible Topics in an Interdisciplinary Social Studies Unit on Ancient Hawaiian Cultures

Anthropology: *Early customs and dress*
Economics: *Trade between local islands and across the Pacific*
Geography: *Routes of travel to Hawaii, major volcanoes, locations of towns*
History: *Early settlement, contacts with other Pacific societies*
Psychology: *Role of the individual, values*
Political Science: *Rulers and the ruled*
Sociology: *Types of workers, social structure*

MULTIDISCIPLINARY UNITS

Another type of unit is multidisciplinary. It may be used by teachers in self-contained classrooms in cooperation with special teachers from art, music, and physical education or in departmentalized schools between groups of teachers or cooperatively by the entire staff. Multidisciplinary units integrate content from a variety of subject areas. A multidisciplinary unit on native Hawaiian culture, for example, might involve aspects of knowledge, and skill and attitudinal objectives in a large number of different subjects. Examples of topics from many subject areas that could be incorporated into a multidisciplinary unit on ancient Hawaiian culture are given in Table 6–3.

A Practice Activity

After examining the examples given in Table 6–3, suggest one more topic that might be included under social studies.

Select another content area from Table 6–3 and suggest an additional topic for it.

Table 6–3

Possible Topics in a Multidisciplinary Unit on Ancient Hawaiian Life

Social Studies

governmental structures, economic system, location of population centers, archeological sites, land use, family groups, personal rights, occupations, and religious practices

Science

volcanic eruptions, igneous rocks, plate tectonics, soils, topographic maps, rain forests, weather, plant life, and animal life

Mathematics

graphing elevations, calculating volume of material erupted in volcanic eruptions, calculating population figures, and information on Hawaiian mathematics

Art

landscapes, bark cloth designs, volcanic sunsets, use of pumice in landscaping, sculpturing of volcanic rocks, and scale drawings

Music

traditional Hawaiian music, creating original vocal and instrumental songs that convey surf and volcanic sounds

Foreign Language

Hawaiian words, modern place names and their origins

Typing/Computers

typing stories, developing or using a database on Hawaii and volcanoes, using a modem to contact people in Hawaii, word processing articles, fliers or pamphlets, and graphic illustrations

Industrial Arts

using pumice as a grit, using obsidian for knives, and using granite in buildings and carving

Physical Education

rope climbing, mountain climbing, surfing, fishing, traditional games, and dancing

Home Economics

traditional foods, traditional food preparation and cooking, Hawaiian pie, and flambé desserts

Agriculture

traditional agricultural methods and crops

Health

native medicines, tropical diseases, and epidemics brought to islands by Europeans

Language Arts

folklore, reading European reports of early contacts with Hawaiians, writing descriptions of native Hawaiian life before first contact with Europeans, writing after looking at pictures or videos of Hawaii, writing poetry describing tropical plants, making a video acting out scenes from traditional life, and writing a comparison of traditional life on two different islands

REASONS FOR USING INTERDISCIPLINARY AND MULTIDISCIPLINARY UNITS

Interdisciplinary and multidisciplinary units involve students, teachers, and families within a small group of classes, a whole grade, or across grades in a school. These units reach the "whole" student, involving him or her in a range of creative, logical, analytical, and communicative activities. They also provide opportunities for social and tutorial interactions among students in different classes and grades and with a variety of adults.

Interdisciplinary and multidisciplinary units help students see connections between content areas on one topic and disciplines within a content area. Students' interest and achievement is heightened and reinforced throughout the day. Different learning and teaching styles can be incorporated to meet the needs of all students in both heterogeneous and homogeneous grouping. Teachers as well as students share, learn, and grow (Steinheimer, 1990a).

PLANNING INTERDISCIPLINARY AND MULTIDISCIPLINARY UNITS

How is an interdisciplinary or multidisciplinary unit planned? One method that often works well is brainstorming to create a web (Steinheimer, 1990b). Creating a web (see Figures 6–1 and 6–2) and planning the timetable for teaching the topics selected for the unit can involve the following steps:

- Ideas for activities in the unit are brainstormed. This can work well when a group of people sit around a large sheet of butcher paper. As ideas for activities in the unit are generated, one person writes them with a marker on the paper. Any number of teachers representing a variety of content areas within a discipline or in several disciplines can participate. Special education teachers and other staff not identified with a particular content area can also be involved. As topics are generated, participants can combine and build upon the ideas of others.
- No evaluation of any activity occurs during the brainstorming. Table 6–2 and Table 6–3 are examples of webs developed in this way. Additional categories can be added to both interdisciplinary and multidisciplinary webs.
- When the initial brainstorming is completed, the suggestions are organized into a working web such as the one shown in Figure 6–1.
- The most appropriate of the activities brainstormed are selected.
- A culminating event or activity involving the range of areas represented in the unit is developed. This should serve as a final integration of the unit.
- A timetable is developed that indicates when various topics will be taught. Table 6–4 illustrates a timetable for a multidisciplinary unit.

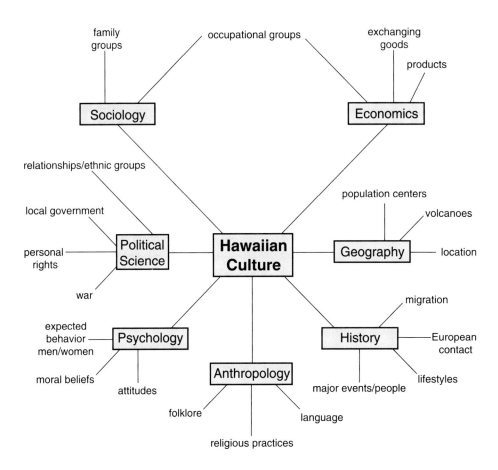

Figure 6–1 An interdisciplinary unit web.

Multidisciplinary units can be developed around a social studies topic or they can be developed around a topic from another content area. In either case, social studies plays an important role in such units. As a web is developed, connections between activities listed for different content areas are often made. Figure 6–2, for example, lists soils as a subtopic under science. In agriculture, crops and farming methods are discussed. In social studies, occupations are discussed. Neither of these subtopics can really be separated from the other. Teachers involved in the unit need to help students make these connections. They also need to work with each other in teaching these related topics. Knowl-

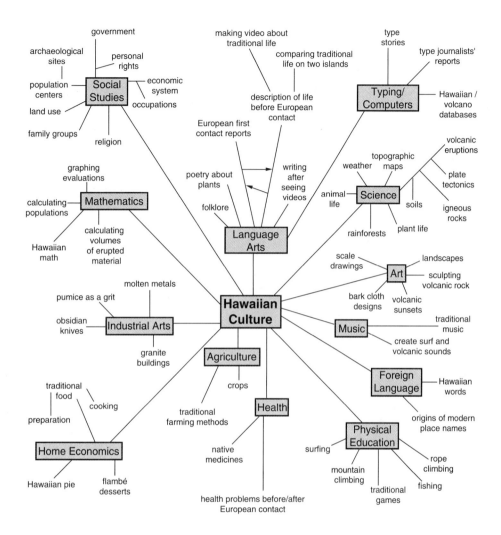

Figure 6–2   Brainstormed multidisciplinary unit web.

edge of both what and when something is being taught in another subject helps teachers plan for and encourage students to make connections and see relationships.

Often, the teacher from whose content area the topic originates takes the lead role in organizing the unit. Since such leadership requires a lot of energy and time, teachers often switch leadership and support roles with various units.

Table 6–4

Multidisciplinary Unit Timetable

CONTENT AREA	WEEK 1	WEEK 2	WEEK 3	WEEK 4	CULMINATING ACTIVITY
Social Studies	land use	government	family groups	economic system	H A
Language Arts	folklore	plant poetry	European contact reports	writing about videos	W A
Science	rain forests	plants/ animals	volcanoes	weather	I
Mathematics	calculating populations	graphing elevations	calculating erupted material	Hawaiian math	I A
Computer Studies/ Typing	type stories	databases	volcano data bases	type journal- ists' reports	A N
Music	traditional music	surf sounds	volcano sounds	vocal music	F
Art	landscapes	bark cloth	volcanic sunsets	scale drawings	A
Industrial Arts	pumice as grit	obsidian knives	molten metals	granite buildings	I R
Home Economics	traditional food	Hawaiian pie	flambé desserts		(ALL
Agriculture	crops		traditional farming		AREAS)
Health		native medicines			
Foreign Language	Hawaiian words			place names	

A Practice Activity

As a practice activity, build a small interdisciplinary web for the topic *transportation*. Try to think of one activity for each of the social science disciplines underlined that would be appropriate for important or useful objectives concerning transportation. Brainstorm ideas with a peer, if possible.

Economics   *History*   *Geography*   *Anthropology*

TRANSPORTATION

Political Science   *Sociology*   *Psychology*

As another practice activity, build a small multidisciplinary web for the topic *transportation*. Try to think of one activity for each area listed. Brainstorm ideas with a peer, if possible.

Social Studies   *Language Arts*   *Science*   *Mathematics*

TRANSPORTATION

Art   *Music*   *Industrial Arts*   *Health*

SUMMARY

This chapter has discussed deciding what to teach and how to teach it. There are several major influences on the social studies curriculum. These result in a huge number of possible topics and issues that can be studied in units. There are several forces that push and pull at teachers when they decide what to teach. These include official courses of study, standardized tests, and textbooks.

Once a decision is made regarding what is to be taught, planning for teaching follows. Thorough planning is important to effective teaching. Teachers begin by developing clearly stated objectives that reflect what students will learn and do during lessons and how learning can be assessed. Planning for teaching involves determining what needs students have and what their abilities and interests are. It involves utilizing the cultural background each student brings to the classroom.

Units are developed that integrate process skills, facts, concepts, generalizations, attitudes, and values. Through units, students construct a wide range of social studies knowledge. They also are assisted in understanding that knowledge does not consist of isolated pieces of information but is an integrated whole. Many social studies units are interdisciplinary, integrating many areas within social studies. Units can also be multidisciplinary, integrating social studies with other disciplines as varied as mathematics and industrial arts.

REFERENCES

Akenson, J. (1987). Historical factors in the development of elementary social studies: Focus on the expanding horizon. *Theory and Research in Social Education, 15*(3), 157–171.

Bradley Commission on History in Schools (1988). *Building a history curriculum: Guidelines for teaching history in schools.* Washington, DC: Educational Excellence Network, ERIC ED 310 008.

Clark, C. & Yinger, R. (1979). Three studies of teacher planning (Research Series No. 55). East Lansing, MI: Institute for Research on Teaching, Michigan State University.

Crabtree, C. (1989). Returning history to the elementary school. *Historical literacy: The case for history in American education* (P. Gagnon and the Bradley Commission on History in Schools). New York: Macmillan.

Curriculum Task Force of the National Commission on Social Studies in the Schools (1989). *Charting a course: Social studies for the 21st century.* Washington, DC: National Commission on Social Studies in the Schools, ERIC SO 020 553.

Eggen, P. & Kauchak, D. (1988). *Strategies for teachers: Teaching content and thinking skills* (2nd ed.). Englewood Cliffs, NJ: Prentice-Hall.

Engle, S. H. & Ochoa, A. S. (1988). *Education for democratic citizenship: Decision making in the social studies.* New York: Teachers College Press.

Evans, R. (1989). Diane Ravitch and the revival of history: A critique. *The Social Studies, 80*(6), 85–88.

Haas, M. E. (1991). An analysis of the social science and history concepts in elementary social studies textbooks, grades 1–4. *Theory and Research in Social Education, 19*(2), 211–220.

Hartoonian, M. & Laughlin, M. (Oct. 1989). Designing a social studies scope and sequence for the 21st century. *Social Education, 53*(6), 385, 388–398.

Jarolimek, J. (1991). *Social studies in the elementary school.* (8th ed.), New York: Macmillan.

Joint Committee on Geographic Education of the National Council for Geographic Education and the Association of American Geographers (1984). *Guidelines for Geographic Education.* Washington, DC: Association of American Geographers.

Kniep, W. (Oct. 1989). *Social studies within a global education, 53*(6), 385, 399–403.

Larkins, G., Hawkins, M., & Gilmore, A. (1987). Trivial and noninformative content of elementary social studies: A review of primary text in four social series. *Theory and Research in Social Education, 14*(4), 299–311.

LeRiche, L. (1987). The expanding environments sequence in elementary social studies. *Theory and Research in Social Education, 15*(3), 37–154.

Mager, R. F. (1962). *Preparing instructional objectives.* Belmont, CA: Fearon Publishers.

McCutcheon, G. (1981). Elementary school teachers' planning for social studies and other subjects. *Theory and Research in Social Education, 9*(1), 45–66.

Smith, E. & Sendelbach, N. (1979). Teacher intentions for science interaction and their antecedents to program materials. Paper presented at the annual meeting of the American Educational Research Association, San Francisco.

Steinheimer, M. (1990a). What's in a term? *Science Scope.* (May), 41.

Steinheimer, M. (1990b). *Making connections: A workshop on developing and implementing multidisciplinary and interdisciplinary units.* Maryland Heights, MO: Pattonville Heights Middle School.

Task Force on International Education (1989). *America in transition: The international frontier.* Washington, DC: National Governors' Association, ERIC SO 020 208.

Task Force on Scope and Sequence, National Council for the Social Studies (Oct., 1989). In search of a scope and sequence for social studies: Report of the National Council for the Social Studies task force on scope and sequence. *Social Education, 53*(6), 376–385.

Tyler, R. (1949). *Basic principles of curriculum and instruction.* Chicago: University of Chicago Press.

Walsted, W. & Soper, J. (1988). *A report card on the economic literacy of U.S. high school students.* New York: Joint Council on Economic Education, ERIC ED 310 005.

CHAPTER 7

OVERVIEW

Teaching materials and the strategies used in teaching are of critical importance in social studies lessons. Materials are important in helping students form abstract social studies concepts. But they must be carefully selected. Teaching strategies can effectively assist students in forming concepts and generalizations, or they can limit learning. Teachers need to be familiar with a wide range of teaching strategies.

This chapter continues the discussion begun in the last chapter regarding how to teach. It is designed to serve as a resource describing a variety of instructional strategies. Teachers may teach the same skill, concept, or value in the social studies curriculum using a variety of strategies. No single strategy is always best. Therefore, this chapter describes many strategies and invites teachers to begin by using a few strategies until they feel they have mastered their use. Then, this chapter can serve as a resource describing additional strategies that teachers can gradually add to their repertoire.

In describing strategies and materials, the chapter organizes them in relation to the part of the learning cycle in which they most frequently are used. Strategies that lend themselves to the first part of a lesson, the exploration, and to the last part of a lesson, the expansion, are described first. Often these will be appropriate for use in either of these less teacher-guided parts of a lesson. These include role playing, simulations, guest speakers, and field trips. Then, strategies frequently used in the more teacher-guided part of a lesson, the invention, are described. These include direct instruction, textbooks, questioning, discussion, learning centers, and games. Finally, strategies and materials that are used in all parts of a lesson are discussed. These include cooperative learning and commercial units and materials as well as those sponsored by agencies such as the American Bar Association or a state electric power company.

Instructional Strategies and Materials for Teaching Social Studies

OBJECTIVES

1. Identify the advantages and disadvantages of the role playing and simulation methods.
2. Explain why teachers must be aware of student feelings and talents when using role playing or simulations.
3. Describe strategies for effectively incorporating a guest speaker and a field trip into the curriculum.
4. Describe the types of content that may be appropriately taught by direct instruction.
5. Identify the major functions of a teacher during direct instruction.
6. Describe how a discussion varies from a question-and-answer teaching method.
7. Describe how a textbook may be appropriately used.
8. State the goal of questioning strategies.
9. Describe at least five characteristics of learning centers.
10. Identify uses of games in social studies.
11. Identify the characteristics of cooperative learning.
12. List three reasons social studies teachers might give for using cooperative learning experiences.
13. Explain the difference between commercial units prepared by publishers and those prepared by sponsors.

STRATEGIES AND MATERIALS USED IN THE EXPLORATION AND EXPANSION PHASES OF A LESSON

Both the exploration at the beginning of a lesson and the expansion at its end are less teacher guided than is the invention, where a skill, concept, or other idea is constructed. As a result, strategies appropriate for one of these phases are typically also appropriate in the other phase. Those strategies identified in this section of this chapter may also be used in the invention phase, but lend themselves better to the exploration or expansion. Likewise, the strategies described below as appropriate for the invention phase might also be used in other phases but tend to be best suited for the invention.

USING ROLE PLAYING AND SIMULATION

Role playing and working through simulations are especially good activities in the exploration or expansion phases of the learning cycle and in the initiatory or culminating portions of a unit. Both provide opportunities to:
- learn content
- use critical thinking
- make decisions
- practice social and communication skills

They also provide students with opportunities to:
- hypothesize
- test
- revise
- retest their ideas

In role playing and simulations, students prepare for future experiences in a non-threatening environment and receive help in developing sensitivity and tolerance for others.

Done individually, role plays tend more to examine value and social issues while simulations tend to stress content and cognitive skills. Many simulations also incorporate role playing, adding to their interest and complexity.

ROLE PLAYING

Role playing examines interpersonal relationships and social behavior. Required to articulate and criticize the views and behaviors of the characters in the role play, students become conscious of their values. Such student behaviors make role-playing an important method to use in developing empathy, values, and morals. Young students role play situations with which they are familiar, such as selecting team members or telling the truth (see also chapter 10). Older students may also confront familiar problems, or they may explore real problems faced by historical figures, before learning how the problem was solved by the individual. This will be discussed in more depth in chapter 12.

To be effective, role-playing must be carefully taught. The teacher must maintain a supportive class environment and be sensitive to the various personalities of the students. The class must remain orderly, as laughter will interrupt the thinking and willingness of some students to participate. All students must be actively involved in the role-playing lesson, including the listeners. The teacher draws out all students and keeps a few from dominating the lesson.

Role-playing carries the risk of displays of emotions that might cause embarrassment or lead to possible criticism or ridicule. If the teacher takes the time to develop a class atmosphere in which students respect individual differences and feelings, such problems can be avoided.

A well-designed role-playing lesson typically has eight parts:

1. A **warm-up** makes the students aware of the general type of problem and then introduces the specific role play to be considered. Student understanding is checked with specific questions about the various characters and their views. Predictions of possible actions help identify alternatives.
2. **Selection of participants** is done with consideration of the personalities of the students and the goal of the content of the role play. Different groups of students may replay the scene or subsequent scenes for the problem. Shaftel and Shaftel (1982) suggest that the more mature students should not be the first to act out a scene as their choices might eliminate the consideration of alternatives and their consequences.
3. **Setting of the stage** occurs next. It is a general agreement by the players on the content of the scene to be portrayed, but not its outcome. No set speeches are prepared. An example of setting the stage is:

   The scene is a conversation between a student and parent just after the parent has been called by the principal. The principal has said that the student cheated on a test.

4. The **listeners** in the audience are prepared for their role. They receive suggestions of what to listen for. The goal is to keep them intellectually involved in the role play and to prepare them to take part in the discussion that will follow. Different members of the audience may be assigned specific tasks, such as observing a character's responses or predicting a character's next behavior.
5. The actual **role play is introduced** by establishing who the participants are and when and where the action takes place. An example of an introduction of the role play is:

   Mary is the mother who has just heard from the principal, about her son cheating on a test at school. Tom is the son who enters the house through a door over there and sees his mother.

6. Following the enactment, the teacher leads a **discussion** that investigates the realism of the ways the roles were portrayed. The words and actions of the characters are evaluated. A discussion of alternative responses that could have been made by the characters and their consequences dominates this section.

7. A **reenactment** of the role play follows the discussion. Students portray different interpretations by the characters, so a new set of alternatives and consequences are examined. Additional scenes in the drama may also need to be portrayed. Different groups of students may act out these scenes to increase participation.

8. To bring **closure,** the teacher and students examine how representative the problem they enacted is. They may also draw some generalizations about the ways people respond or should respond when facing a problem. During this time students may share similar problems with which they are familiar. However, a teacher should never prod students into revealing personal problems that might cause embarrassment. Teachers should remember that they may be concerned, but they are not trained counselors. Therefore, some appropriate questions to ask are: "Have you ever heard of someone having a similar problem?" "Was the outcome realistic?" "What were important comments or actions that led to this outcome?" "What might have been said or done to change the outcome?" or "Can you imagine a situation in which a similar problem might take place?" But the question, "Have you ever personally experienced this type of problem?" is not appropriate. (Shaftel & Shaftel, 1982)

SIMULATIONS

Simulations are activities that are similar to a real world situation or problem, which have been simplified for use by students in a short time period. In the simulation, the students perform tasks or assume roles and seek to act out a problem situation. Participants are provided with descriptions of their tasks, roles, and the problem situation.

Simulations are appropriate for all ages, but most commercially available ones are written for students in grade 4 or older. Simulations have been written concerning a wide variety of political, family, economic, and social problems in various historical and geographic settings. Very young students might take part in assembling paper masks on a simulated assembly line or in a simulated early-American school day. Older students might take part in a simulated African market, court of law, or stock market investment. Teachers can construct simulations, locate them in the ERIC file, or purchase them from special publishers. Many computer programs are examples of simulations. Computer simulations usually provide interesting graphics and keep score of student progress. (For more details see chapter 8.)

Students apply their knowledge and skills as they solve the simulation's problem. Sophisticated simulations may last for several days or weeks and present additional problems for the players to solve as the simulation progresses. The students' solutions vary depending on the players involved.

As with role-playing, the teacher has important tasks to complete. These include:

- preparation of materials
- introducing the simulation
- conducting the final debriefing discussion

When they begin the activity, the students must have all materials ready to use and must clearly understand the problem and issues of the simulation. Roles need to be handed out with care. Ideally, all roles are equal in the amount of time and work needed for preparation. Simulation materials should provide each student with a detailed written description of his or her role, including talents, concerns, and viewpoints about the topic. Teachers and students should be aware that the best-sounding role titles may not indicate the most crucial roles. The success of simulations depends on the willingness of the students to be active and to use their talents to influence the decisions.

When the teacher is certain that the problem and roles are clearly understood, the simulation begins. When the problem is solved, the simulation is completed. The debriefing of the simulation is crucial. Questions to be examined in the debriefing should require the students not only to recall events but to reflect on their consequences and importance to the solution. Debriefing questions include:

- How realistic was the simulation?
- Did the participants perform their roles realistically?
- Are the participants happy with the outcome? What do they think could have been done differently to increase their satisfaction?
- What additional knowledge might help them better perform the simulation?
- Do the students want to perform the simulation again? Do they think that their increased learning would be worth the additional time to prepare and rework the simulation?
- What are some other possible outcomes for the simulation had different views prevailed?
- What did we learn from this simulated activity that might help us to understand other similar problems?

With use of a simulation there will be some element of competition among the participants. However, the teacher should not stress the goal of winning but rather of solving the problem in a realistic manner. Solutions to problems often require compromise and cooperation. The objective of a simulation is that the students learn through the process (which includes the debriefing), not that they get the "right" or "best" solution to the simulation's problem. Too much emphasis on competition or high grades may reduce the impact of simulations. If grades are given in connection with a simulation, they should come from a test or essay, written after the completion of the simulation and the debriefing discussion.

THE GUEST SPEAKER

A guest speaker is usually welcomed with great interest by students. The speaker can do more than just talk. He or she might bring collections and artifacts and spend most of the time answering questions. Another speaker might demonstrate crafts such as spinning. Collectors and demonstrators are more appropriate for younger students. Whatever the focus of the speaker, the teacher needs to carefully prepare both the speaker and the students for the visit to attain maximum learning. Students should spend some time working with the speaker's topic prior to the visit. For this reason, guest speakers are most frequently found during an expansion. However, sometimes they can involve students in an exploration of a topic. They might also be occasionally used to help students construct learning during an invention. As part of the preparation for a visit from a guest speaker, teachers should provide the speaker with:

- an overview of the unit's goals
- key questions and points for the speaker to address; student-generated questions are also helpful
- a brief description of the class and their interests and maturity level
- an opportunity to describe specific equipment or assistance needed so the room can be prepared in advance.

The students should be prepared for the visit of the speaker by:

- hearing a description of who the speaker is and why he or she is coming
- generating a list of questions to give the speaker in advance
- discussing procedures for the speaker's presentation, including appropriate courtesy toward the speaker
- deciding how to record the information the speaker will present, for later use
- deciding who will assist the speaker in and out of the room with his or her materials

After the speaker's presentation, the class should:

- discuss and recall what was learned and relate it to the unit under study
- express their thanks to the speaker in writing or through drawings

A lesson plan should be developed that indicates the objectives the speaker's visit will meet. It should also describe how the students will be prepared for the visit, what will occur during it, how it will be expanded upon, and how it will be evaluated. Without a plan the visit is likely to be interesting, but it may not relate well to the social studies content with which students are working.

A Practice Activity

Think about the community in which you now live. Suggest one commercial enterprise that might provide a guest speaker for a unit on the life in your city during the period 1890 to 1914.

☞ *There are many possible responses. Among them are an antique dealer or the owner of a family-operated business.*

Suggest one government agency that might provide a guest speaker for the same unit.

☞ *Again, there are many possible responses. Two are a representative of the city planning office and of the fire department.*

Suggest a topic that a student's family member might talk about in class relating to this unit.

> ☞ *There is a huge variety of topics that could be discussed. Two possible topics are descriptions of "what school was like" or "what we did for fun after school and on weekends."*

THE FIELD TRIP

Field trips can focus on an opportunity to meet with people, or they can focus on an opportunity to explore a site. Field trips are usually a highly rewarding activity that typically produces meaningful learning. Preparation for a field trip involves planning for what will happen before, during, and after the trip. As a result, field trips, like guest speakers, are most often included in the expansion phase. Planning for a field trip involves:

- checking with the principal about your school's procedures for field trips
- deciding what objectives will be met by the field trip
- visiting the site beforehand to decide what should be seen and done:
  - talking with the education coordinator or site representative if one is available
  - actually walking and/or driving through the field trip in a trial run
  - taking notes on which aspects of the trip will address the objectives you have developed
  - identifying technical language and content knowledge students will need to learn in preparation for the trip
  - determining approximately how much time the trip will require
  - identifying any special safety precautions that will need to be taken
  - making arrangements for students with handicaps
- making arrangements in writing for the trip well in advance, including:
  - reservations at the site, giving information about:
    - the date and times of arrival and departure
    - the number of students and adults involved
    - approximate ages and grade level(s) of the students
    - your name, address, and phone number
  - arranging for guides and/or speakers
  - planning transportation, meals or snacks, and accommodations (as needed)
  - planning supervision of students
- sending permission forms home well in advance:
  - using standard school system forms or including the following information if you must make up your own form:
    - a brief description of the trip and its purpose
    - individual student needs (How much money should students take? Is a sweater or jacket needed?)
    - the date by which permission forms must be returned
    - a place where a parent or guardian signs, giving permission

- notifying students and their families of any costs associated with the trip well in advance and making plans for how to accommodate students whose families cannot afford the costs involved
- discussing the field trip with students:
    - identifying the focus of the trip for students
    - identifying specific items/events to watch for, look at, or be involved in
    - helping the students plan questions to ask and when to ask them (as appropriate)
    - helping students plan a system for recording their observations
    - discussing appropriate behavior throughout the trip
    - identifying seatmates and partners
    - having students make nametags giving their name, school, and the school's phone number (or make the nametags for very young students)
- obtaining permission, as necessary, for record keeping that involves taking photographs, making rubbings, audiotaping, or videotaping
- planning and carrying out follow-up activities related to the focus of the field trip with students, including thank-you notes where appropriate.

A lesson plan should be prepared for the field trip including clear objectives, a procedure, and a plan for evaluation of learning.

A field trip offers this student a unique opportunity to operate a bellows once used by a nineteenth-century blacksmith.

STRATEGIES USED DURING THE INVENTION PHASE OF A LESSON

DIRECT INSTRUCTION

Direct instruction involves teaching students content knowledge in the form of facts, rules, and action sequences. This will occur during the second, more teacher-guided phase of a lesson, the invention. The teacher usually accomplishes this through lecture mixed with teacher–student interactions involving questions and answers, review and practice, and the correction of student errors. This is a fast-paced lecture that is highly organized and focuses on a limited amount of clearly identified facts, rules, or action sequences (Borich, 1988, p. 143).

Some of what we learn, we need to learn through memorization and a teacher-directed presentation. For example, the names of the countries that border our nation are memorized, as are the number of feet in a mile and centimeters in a meter. Information about government, cities, political events, religions, and ethnic groups is often taught by direct instruction in social studies. Can you suggest one other category of information that might be appropriately taught through direct instruction?

Because each of us deals with so much information in the modern world, some of that information must be learned by direct instruction. This would include skills such as how to lay out a bar graph, what various symbols might mean on a map, or how to use a camera to take pictures for a social studies project. Can you suggest one other skill used in social studies that might be appropriately taught through direct instruction?

OBJECTIVES

Objectives for a direct instruction lesson can focus on verbs such as the following.

For cognitive objectives:

to recall	to use	to organize
to demonstrate	to list	to paraphrase

For affective objectives:

to listen	to comply	to obey
to display	to express	to prefer

For action sequence objectives:

to follow	to repeat	to place
to perform accurately	to perform independently	to perform proficiently

This type of instruction involves students in applying facts, rules, and actions. Usually, in direct instruction, a single lesson is planned for a specific outcome rather than a series of lessons leading to an outcome.

PROCEDURES

Direct instruction typically involves the whole group. Most often, the teacher gives instruction, and the students receive it. It should involve students in asking questions, making comments, taking notes, and other activities that make them active rather than passive learners. It should be well-organized, change pace, and be of appropriate length.

Direct instruction often takes place in three formats in social studies teaching. These are lecture or teacher presentation, class discussion, and demonstration.

LECTURE OR TEACHER PRESENTATION

The lecture or teacher presentation is the format most associated with direct instruction. Some lecture is possible with students of almost any age. However, the amount of time devoted to it increases proportionately with the age of the child. First grade students should be exposed to a presentation of no more than ten minutes if it is relevant to something they are involved in and generates enthusiasm.

For example, if students are going to operate a classroom store as part of a study of concepts such as "buyers" and "sellers," the teacher may show them how to set up a list of the store's inventory. Then the students can be shown how to use columns in which they enter the quantity of an item available at the end of the day, the number sold that day, and the number added to the inventory that day. The teacher is modeling a simple accounting procedure. Students probably could have devised their own system. The teacher, however, may wish to involve them more heavily in buying and selling activities and is creating more time for these activities by modeling the use of an accounting system.

With older students, a teacher's presentation may be longer. For example, with sixth graders, a teacher may use a presentation to prepare them to take oral histories from local residents (see also chapter 12). The teacher may enumerate materials needed, such as a tape recorder and tapes, discussing how to place the tape recorder so that it records clearly but is not too obvious. The teacher might describe strategies to put the person being interviewed at ease and list questions the students should ask to begin the interview. Finally, the teacher might describe ways of showing appreciation to the person interviewed, such as thank you letters or home-grown flowers.

Direct instruction involves preparation by the teacher, as do all forms of instruction if they are to be effective. Teachers should:

- begin with a daily review, check the previous day's work (as needed), and reteach (as needed)
- present new content in an organized manner
    - begin with an overview
    - follow with a question, problem, or controversy in the introduction or use one soon after to generate interest
    - move quickly in small steps (as needed)
    - evaluate previous learning while introducing new content

- present content organized in an outline or a set of notes
- use examples such as pictures to help students remember important points
- emphasize main points
- change pace often, for example, moving from lecture to a visual aid to questions and back to lecture
- have students take notes to help them remember what is being presented
- pause at appropriate times to give students time to take notes and to think about what is being said
- guide student practice
  - use a lot of questions
  - prompt students when they are first practicing the content taught
  - check each student's learning
  - guide student practice until all are performing at an 80% or better accuracy level
- provide feedback and assistance and reteach as needed
  - assist by simplifying questions, giving clues, explaining or reviewing steps, or reteaching last steps
  - reteach, using smaller steps, if necessary
- provide independent practice to create automatic responses
  - use seatwork
  - practice until content is overlearned
  - monitor practice to make sure students are fully involved
  - practice until an accuracy level of 95% or higher is achieved
- review content learned every week and every month and reteach when necessary (Rosenshine, 1983, p. 338)

CLASS DISCUSSION

A well-organized class discussion can also be a form of direct instruction. Not all class discussions are direct instruction, however. Class discussions, their characteristics, and appropriate topics for discussions are described further below. Direct instruction is frequently used to teach skills, especially those tasks that require carefully following a specific set of steps in a set order.

DEMONSTRATION

Demonstrations are another form of direct instruction. They are used to model a behavior. After the students have observed the behavior, they practice it. Demonstration is most effective if the practice activities have been carefully planned. A teacher may use demonstration to teach students a wide variety of behaviors, for example, how to find directions with a compass, how to turn on and load a computer, and how to introduce oneself to a person about to be interviewed. These are all behaviors the students are expected to model closely in their follow-up activities. Other demonstrations may provide students information they use in a follow-up activity where they do not model the teacher's behavior. For example:

> The teacher may demonstrate a rainfall gauge by setting it up, reading it every day at the same time, emptying it, and then reading it again the next day. The students learn to read the gauge. After taking rainfall readings for a month, they construct rainfall charts. Then they look up rainfall figures for other communities during the same month and compare them to those in their community. The demonstration with the rain gauge has enabled them to understand how rainfall figures are obtained, to apply this knowledge when they read rainfall figures, and to explain what they mean.

Direct instruction has a role in social studies education. As with all other forms of instruction, it can be used appropriately but only if well planned and well organized. Most of all, it must fit meaningfully into student activities if it is to be effective.

ASSESSMENT

Assessment can take several forms (see also chapter 9). One form is through multiple choice, fill in, or matching items. These items might ask students to list dates of events. Another form of assessment involves summarizing or paraphrasing the facts or rules learned. Here the student states what important ideas were learned or conclusions reached. A third form of assessment involves applying facts and rules in a situation that is slightly different from the one in which the content was learned. An example is reading data from a new map or chart.

Time for Reflection: What Do <u>YOU</u> Think?

Your students have conducted a survey in which they each asked ten different people what they believe to be the best use for an empty piece of land in your community. The data now needs to be organized into a bar graph. The students have not done this type of a task before. You must instruct them in how to make the bar graph. Since there is so much data, you have decided that the students should cooperate in groups of four to make graphs. You are going to demonstrate how the groups should go about making the bar graphs. What are the steps you will demonstrate and expect each group to follow in preparing a bar graph?

DISCUSSION STRATEGIES

Discussion is verbally sharing ideas with the goal of improving thinking on a topic. A discussion requires sharing and is not dominated by one person, especially the teacher. It is a form of direct instruction. Students share ideas, reasons, facts, and questions. Students who take part in successful discussions come to the situation with:

- a set of skills they have learned and are willing to use
- some knowledge about the topic to be discussed

The knowledge may come from real life experiences or may be acquired indirectly through printed media. The teacher can do much to create the willingness to participate through personal modeling of the skills and by recognition of the students' efforts in the discussion. Arranging seats so that students have eye contact and can easily hear each other also promotes the interchange of ideas. However, a discussion will not be successful if the students do not possess and use such skills as:

- listening to others
- asking questions to draw out or clarify the ideas of others
- paraphrasing the views of others
- identifying areas of agreement and disagreement

Students must be taught such skills and be involved in practicing them. When a discussion involves the whole class, the teacher can review proper procedures and monitor the progress of the group. When dividing the class into smaller groups, the teacher may want to provide students with a group discussion guide that presents topics and asks students to perform certain tasks in keeping with the skills required for discussion of the topic. Table 7–1 illustrates a small-group discussion guide.

Learning through discussions will be more successful if the teacher brings the discussion to a closure. Individual written responses are one way to accomplish this task. Other ways are to have students summarize the various viewpoints and have students who support a view indicate their agreement by a show of hands. Since discussions do not always lead to similar conclusions, teachers should also address this point at the end of the lesson. This may be done by asking the students if they can still be friends even though they disagree on this topic or by reminding them of the role of dissent in a democracy.

Table 7–1

Discussion Guide: What Is This Artifact?

Each member of your group should examine your group's artifact carefully. When everyone has had a chance to examine the artifact, discuss and answer the questions below. As you discuss the questions, think about the following:

- Do you know what every other person in your group thinks?
- Did everyone have a fair chance to give their ideas?
- What should the group do if you don't have the same idea at first?
- What should the group do if you can't all agree on an idea after talking about everybody's ideas for a while?

Give the artifact a name.
What do you think the artifact is used for?
What is it made of?
How would you make it?

Discussions can involve a whole group of students or can take place in small groups. When the whole class is involved in a discussion, they are usually working toward the construction of a concept, generalization, value, or other portion of social studies content. This occurs during the invention phase of a lesson. Small-group discussions are often used during the exploration and expansion phases of a lesson. At this time, students take the knowledge or skill they have constructed and consider their application in another situation. They may try them out in a new situation and then discuss how well it worked. Or they may plan their effort and then try out their plan. In either case, students are trying to expand the use of the knowledge or skill in hypothetical or new situations. This is difficult to accomplish as a large group. Small-group discussion is more likely to involve each student than is large-group discussion. In this respect, small-group discussion provides a greater opportunity for each student to contribute to or expand upon the lesson.

TEXTBOOKS

TWO DIFFICULTIES IN READING TEXTBOOKS

Textbooks often define the social studies curriculum and the units within it. Today's social studies textbooks contain many pictures, illustrations, maps, and graphs. The teacher's guides also suggest activities to help introduce and expand upon the text's presentation. Still, many students have difficulty with reading social studies textbooks (Anderson & Armbruster, 1984). The two difficulties students have stem from a lack of experiential background and the complex social studies content (Hoge, 1986). Students who have little experience outside their neighborhood or local community may also find it hard to be interested in learning about faraway places. Students who have little sense of personal or family history may find it difficult to relate to historical settings (Hoge, 1986).

Social studies textbooks tend to have a heavy technical load of concepts and generalizations. Technical concepts are specialized ideas in social studies such as "delta," "interdependence," "economy," and "constitution." Technical concepts are related in some way to form generalizations. For example, "The *economies* of countries in today's world are *interdependent* upon each other." Most students have an incomplete and inaccurate understanding of these concepts, if they know them. Many social studies textbooks pile too many concepts and generalizations into a few paragraphs without enough supporting examples and with little discussion. Textbooks are made more complex because they include hard-to-pronounce names of cities, faraway countries, and foreign-language names. There are frequent references to long periods of time and huge distances. What does a ten-year-old student think when a textbook says: "Our country was founded over two hundred years ago," or "long, long ago?" What do expressions such as "far to the north" or "over a thousand miles to the east" mean to students who are not sure which direction is which and have never traveled further than across the state? (Hoge, 1986, p. 1)

DOING A CONTENT ANALYSIS OF A TEXTBOOK

Teachers should carry out a content analysis of their school's curriculum guide and think about what they intend to teach. When they have identified a unit they plan to teach, they should examine a copy of the textbook to see whether it contains relevant material. Next, teachers should analyze the unit in a student edition of the text before reading the teacher's guide. Many teachers use textbooks as resources for students. Often, textbooks from different publishers are used. When textbooks are used as a resource, they support a unit but do not directly determine its context.

A Practice Activity

Try a textbook unit content analysis now. Pick up a student copy of a social studies textbook, choose one unit, and ask yourself the following:

- What should be learned from reading this unit?
- What is most important here?
- What are the most important facts presented?
- What are the most important concepts presented?
- For which of these concepts can students now give an example?
- Which concepts are likely to be completely new to students?
- What are the most important generalizations presented?
- What process skills are presented or required?
- What attitudes are evident?
- What values are incorporated?
- Which words will students have difficulty pronouncing?
- Do the objectives match those in the state or local curriculum guide?

☞ *The procedure above is also useful in carrying out a content analysis of a curriculum guide, a prepared unit, or other teaching material. A content analysis can help teachers identify the most important skills, facts, concepts, generalizations, attitudes, and values in the textbook's unit. If these match what the teacher intends to teach, the textbook will provide good support. If they do not match, or only partially cover important material, the teacher will have to make sure other resources are available to accomplish all of the objectives. The teacher may also choose to develop a teaching plan for a unit based on the textbook.*

DEVELOPING A TEACHING PLAN FOR A TEXTBOOK-BASED UNIT

Once the content of a textbook unit has been analyzed and the most important process skills, facts, concepts, generalizations, attitudes, and values identified, the teacher can develop a teaching plan. The teaching plan should set up learning cycles for the important material identified. Material identified as less important can be read from the textbook. If students can learn important material, other material can be given a more cursory treatment. Generally there is such a heavy technical load of concepts and generalizations that it will not be possible to develop a learning cycle to teach each of them. Therefore, it is critical to identify what is most important and to implement learning cycles to teach it. The textbook can be used in any portion of the learning cycle, but it is best used during the invention phase. A new teacher may have difficulty accomplishing such effective teaching because of the demands of many subject areas. It usually is not possible for new teachers to develop more than two or three complete, well-elaborated units in each subject area during the first year of teaching. Therefore, a new teacher should identify the two or three most important social studies units in the textbook and develop a teaching plan using learning cycles for those units. During the following year, the teacher can add two or three more units. Within just a few years, the teacher will have developed appropriate teaching plans for all the units to be taught.

As learning cycles are developed, the teacher must accomplish several things:

1. develop for students (often vicariously) the required background of experience
2. accommodate the varying reading skills of the students
3. provide direct instructional help with locating places, comprehending long periods of time, understanding technical concepts, and pronouncing foreign-language names
4. select appropriate learning activities for learning cycles

Experiential background can be built by field trips, films, video, computer software, slide shows, guest speakers, travel brochures, study prints, cultural artifacts, hobby collections, native foods, and trade books.

When reading the textbook, students can use a variety of strategies that will help them with text material. Study guides can help students identify important facts, concepts, and generalizations. In cooperative study groups, students can each read passages and share their study-guide responses. Poorer readers can be grouped with stronger readers so that difficulties in reading passages can be quickly overcome by asking another group member how to pronounce a word or for help with a sentence. Passages can be tape recorded by the teacher, an aide, an adult volunteer, or an older student. Such tape recordings are helpful to some students who are having difficulty reading passages. More able students can translate passages into their own words and share them with classmates (Hoge, 1986). Such translation is often easily done using word-processing programs such as *Bank Street Writer.*

Globes and wall maps should supplement textbook maps. As students read in the textbook, they should be encouraged to find places mentioned and to consider their relative location:

- how far away they are from important places your students know
- what they are close to
- how long it will take to get to these places

Hoge (1986) also suggests that students will need help with time concepts. They can use time lines (computer software programs such as *Time Liner* by Tom

Snyder Productions can be helpful) and strategies such as calculating the number of generations, at twenty years per generation, back to a time being described and then making a chart with a cut-out or stick figure representing each generation.

In all their work with the social studies textbook, students should be told why they are reading a textbook. They should know what facts, concepts, and generalizations are important. They should be assisted in identifying important passages and in interpreting in their own words what the textbook says.

QUESTIONING STRATEGIES

"Teachers should ask more questions that require students to think and discover answers." "Teachers should ask questions that help students learn how to develop a good moral character." "Teachers should ask questions that require students to locate places on a map. Americans are geographically illiterate."

These are statements that have been made by adults concerned with the quality of education their children are receiving. Each statement suggests method— how students should be learning the content—as well as the content to be learned.

Learning begins by asking questions. Elementary and middle school students usually find it easy to come up with questions to ask about a situation or an event. When they can't, they probably think they shouldn't. Asking questions should be encouraged. Raising a variety of questions, including poorly expressed and vague ones, is important to learning. Questioning is how a person fills in links between one experience and another and makes personal sense of the world. Teachers assist this process with the questions they ask students to consider.

Learning is helped if teachers, and eventually students, recognize the distinction between social science questions and philosophical questions. Social sciences address questions about the social world and how it behaves. The answers can be tested by investigation or by consulting an expert.

A philosophical question such as "What is the purpose of my life?" cannot be answered by investigation or by consulting an expert. Such questions have answers people have agreed on. These answers are not based on proof. Within the range of questions that social studies attempts to answer at the elementary and middle school levels, the best questions are those for which students can find answers through their own activity. When students ask a question such as "Why do people always seem to want what they don't have?" they are not aware that they are asking a very different kind of question—a philosophical question—and that social studies might not be able to answer it. To develop this awareness is a significant part of their education, but it will come only very slowly (Paul, 1991; Harlan, 1985).

Questions are a part of all sections of a lesson. However, they are most heavily used during the teacher-guided invention section of a lesson. Each section of a lesson has different objectives. Before writing a series of questions to ask students on a lesson plan, teachers must consider, "What objectives am I trying to accomplish with these questions?" Some questions ask for simple direct answers while others require many facts and the understanding of complex relationships before an answer can be arrived at. Some questions have correct answers while others have only best guesses or hopes.

There are many types of questions and many questioning strategies. Questioning is both a specific type of strategy for teaching and also an integral part of the other strategies discussed in this chapter. A questioning strategy refers to the types of questions asked, including the complexity of the questions, their goals, and the order in which such questions are asked.

Two types of questions, narrow and broad, have been described by Schug and Beery (1987). When checking for the understanding of specific information, either from memory and observation or for the purpose of focusing ideas on a simple problem, the teacher asks narrow questions or those with a few, specific answers, such as: Who made it possible for Columbus to sail to the New World? Where did the Pilgrims live? How does a coffee grinder work? Why did the French send traders to America?

Broader questions are more challenging and interesting because they require the student to draw conclusions, make generalizations, or decide on best strategies and behaviors. They also ask students to speculate. Potentially, broad questions have many correct answers. Such questions can be asked about both content and values. Some examples are: What do you have to do to be elected president? What accounts for the increase in the pollution of our state's air and water? Why didn't many people settle in Florida until the middle of the twentieth century?

USING QUESTIONS TO CAUSE THINKING

Very young children learn to listen to the language used by the teacher and to respond to cues in it (Davis & Tinsley, 1967). Students cue in on the level of thinking indicated by the teacher's questions. They respond with a matching level (Cole & Williams, 1973). Teachers who ask broad questions have students who use more divergent thinking (Gallagher & Asher, 1963). Research indicates that when teachers use broad questions, their students score higher on standardized achievement tests and on tests of critical thinking (Redfield & Rousseau, 1981). The implication of these research studies is that teachers can cause students to think by carefully designing their questions.

Earlier chapters have described learning as a process in which several steps occur. These have been outlined by Costa (1991, p. 195) as a model of intellectual functioning. During the *exploration* part of a learning cycle, we get information through the senses or from our memory. During the *invention* phase, we compare that information with what we already know and we draw meaningful relationships. During the *expansion* phase, we apply and transfer those relationships to hypothetical or new situations and evaluate what we have done. Teachers and students must ask questions appropriate to the objective(s) of each phase of the learning cycle if students are to successfully work through it.

Exploration Questions. Teachers help students draw information from their memory and gather information from their senses. Objectives that teachers use at this time utilize verbs such as: complete, count, match, name, define, observe, recite, select, describe, list, identify, and recall (Costa, 1991). Narrow questions are used to help recall or gather specific information related to the topic under study. Broad questions are used to encourage students to make conclusions and predictions. Examples of questions used during an exploration are:

Name	What are the states that share boundaries with Kansas?
Count	How many cities in Pennsylvania have populations of over 1,000,000 people?
Match	What country goes with this national dress?
Describe	How does this poem make you feel?
Select	Which words on this list refer to landforms?
Complete	Lewis and Clark explored what territory?
Recall	How did you feel about not being picked to be in the role play?
List	Who were the first four presidents of the United States?

Invention Questions. During the invention phase, teachers help students process information they have gathered in the exploration. Questions prompt students to draw relationships among the information they have gathered to try to establish cause and effect. Verbs used in objectives for this phase of the lesson include: synthesize, analyze, categorize, explain, classify, compare, contrast, state causality, infer, experiment, organize, distinguish, sequence, summarize, group, and make analogies (Costa, 1991). Narrow questions in this phase tend to have several possible answers as opposed to just one answer. Broad questions tend to be limited to small problems. Examples of questions related to objectives used during the invention:

Explain	Why did Henry Ford use the assembly line to produce cars?
Make Analogies	What other laws are similar to this one?
Organize	How can you show this data so that it is easy to see the population increase every year?
Contrast	How are lakes different from ponds?
Compare	How does the average monthly temperature of New Orleans compare with the average monthly temperature of Singapore?
Sequence	Can you put these events in chronological order?
Infer	After reading these newspaper accounts, what can you infer about people's support of the women's suffrage movement in 1900?

Expansion Questions. During the expansion, the teacher asks questions that require students to use the concepts or generalizations they have developed in hypothetical or new situations. Students are encouraged to think creatively, use their imagination, consider or apply values, and make judgments. Verbs used in objectives during this phase include: apply, imagine, plan, evaluate, judge, predict, extrapolate, create, forecast, invent, hypothesize, speculate, generalize, build (a model of), and design (Costa, 1991). Few, if any, narrow questions are asked. Instead, almost all of the questions are broad questions in which students recall and apply recently learned skills and ideas. Students combine and sequence ideas, make value judgments, and develop plans, strategies, hypotheses, and their own simple theories. Examples of questions used in the expansion are:

Speculate	If our population continues to grow as it has been, what will life be like here in our community in the year 2050?
Generalize	If global warming continues and the polar ice caps melt somewhat, what will happen to coastal cities that are located in low-lying areas such as New Orleans and Lagos, Nigeria?
Evaluate	Which of these plans is the fairest way of ensuring that everybody has an opportunity to find out about job openings in this company?
Judge	Which of these is the best example of Middle Eastern palace architecture?
Hypothesize	What type of voter (age, sex, race, income level) will this political candidate most likely appeal to?

TIME TO THINK

An important consideration in asking questions is called wait-time. *Wait-time* is the amount of time that a teacher waits after asking a question for the student to answer before rephrasing or rewording the question. Rowe (1968) found that most teachers did not allow a student time to think before answering a question. She recommended that teachers allow at least five seconds of wait-time. Broader questions with more complex answers require time to think before answering. The very broad questions, especially those associated with the expansion phase, benefit from more time to identify an answer. Additional time is also important if students are to judge their ideas for themselves and revise their answers. Using small-group discussion followed by whole-class discussion is a procedure that allows students more time to think and reduces pressure on individual students.

THE LEARNING CENTER

Learning centers involve students in making choices among the activities they do at the center and in evaluating their own progress. This opportunity to choose is given to students because of the belief that students can best select the way to learn (Blake, 1977). Some teachers devote most of the day to individualized learning through learning centers while others combine learning centers with a variety of teaching strategies.

Just as the use of learning centers is flexible so also is the appearance of learning centers. The availability of space plays an important role in the physical appearance of a learning center. In a cramped area the learning center may be confined to a single box with students returning to their desks to work on each activity. In other settings learning centers may be on large bulletin boards or in sections of the room that are divided into cubicles for different types of activities. Books, games, short stories and descriptions, filmstrips, pictures, artifacts, practice drills, creative writing exercises, and arts and crafts activities all have appropriate places in learning centers. The objectives of social studies learning centers vary widely. They may be either gaining knowledge, developing skills, or examining attitudes and values, or two or more types of objectives may be combined.

Common characteristics of social studies learning centers include:
- clearly established learning objectives
- self-checking and self-evaluation procedures for individual activities
- progress charts or records for each student
- multiple activities to accommodate various learning styles
- student choice among the methods of attaining specific objectives
- enrichment materials for both remedial and advanced study needs

Learning centers are appropriate for all grades. They are easiest to use in self-contained classrooms where time is more flexible. Because learning centers have the ability to provide enrichment, remedial, and advanced activities without overtly labeling or removing students from the classroom, learning centers have a place in all classrooms. Carefully planned learning centers allow students the opportunity to make decisions concerning their learning. By involving students in such decision making, learning centers provide a meaningful learning experience that also builds self-esteem.

GAMES

Using games in social studies is a stimulating way to drill and practice skills and content. Sometimes games may be used to teach content. Many students have played small-group games since kindergarten. They usually view games as a challenge that is fun to meet.

Games can have several educational values in social studies. These include:
- following directions
- practicing social skills
- reviewing information
- using cognitive skills
- making decisions
- living with the consequences of decisions
- becoming aware of or learning new information (Haas, 1990)

Few commercially prepared games focus on social studies content. Those that do often involve money, investment, place locations, or careers and may be useful. Games designed for adults such as *Life, Monopoly, Trivial Pursuit,* or *Strategy* sometimes ask questions from categories of knowledge such as history and can be used with middle school students.

Teachers can make small-group games by adapting commercial games or by changing the content to reflect their social studies lessons. The format, game board, cards, and/or rules of a commercial game can all serve as idea starters for games teachers make. Because teachers are busy people, it is important to make games that are simple and do not require a lot of artwork or other time-consuming activity. Teachers should consider using computer software to make titles for games and game cards. These can be laminated to increase sturdiness. Brightly colored markers and commercially prepared stickers and letters can also make a game attractive to students while reducing the time needed to construct the game. Older students, and often younger students, can color game items, draw lines, and do much of the work in game construction with guidance from their teacher. Students often like finishing a game the teacher has begun making. Guidelines for making small-group board games have been suggested by Mary Haas:

- Select one or more concepts to emphasize. Some examples are:

symbols	legends	grid
directions	locations	landforms
famous people	landmarks	bodies of water

- Decide what the student must do with each concept. Some examples are:

name it	define it	collect it
move to it	match it	count it

- Determine how to win the game.
- Designate the order of play.
- Write the rules for the game as numbered commands. (Modeling the rules after commercial games with which the students are familiar helps all students, but especially the very young, to play.)
- Create place markers, or borrow them from a commercial game, and clearly identify pathways to be followed in advancing along the board. (Haas, 1990)

Board games provide a great variety of opportunities for challenging students because of the many ways they can be played. Maps and diagrams may be used on a game board to provide a source of data for answering questions as well as for decoration. Card games are appropriate for matching tasks. Students can match symbols, words with symbols, the drawing of a state or nation with its name, capital, or continent. Dominoes are another game in which concepts and definitions or words and graphic symbols can be matched.

Games are educational and they are fun. They also provide an opportunity for students to practice social skills. Small-group games provide many opportunities for individual players to interact directly with the educational content. In a small-group game, only a short amount of time elapses between each student's turn. Teachers in the intermediate grades and middle school often prefer to use whole-class games and to model them on television game shows. In such games students answer questions that review the content of social studies lessons. Stu-

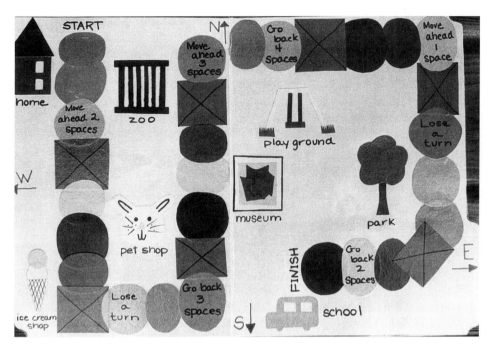

Games can be made that refer to features with which students are familiar, such as a pet shop and a playground.

dents may also help prepare the game by writing questions to be asked. Students are motivated by the opportunity to perform the leadership roles in such games and by the competition between teams during play. Whole-class games provide the student with only a few opportunities to answer questions personally. One way to increase the number of questions a student must answer is to form teams and require all students on the team to agree to an answer. Another procedure is to have each student on the team write the answer on a piece of paper and to collect the papers. One or two of the slips of paper can then be randomly drawn and a point awarded for each correct written answer. Whole-class games are best when used for a short period of time; they provide an excellent way to review the day's lesson.

COOPERATIVE LEARNING

Cooperative learning is an approach or a set of strategies especially designed to encourage student cooperation while learning. It can be used in all phases of a learning cycle. In a review of research on the use of cooperative learning in virtually all academic disciplines and in a variety of settings in the United States and in other nations, Slavin (1987) reports that all students learn as well or better when using cooperative learning than with competitive and individual learning. Johnson, Johnson, Holubec, and Roy (1984) point out that students receive a wide range of positive mental health benefits including a positive self-image and an improved attitude toward, and acceptance of, classmates. Small cooperative groups increase the opportunity for positive reinforcement and reduce the risks of negative reactions and ridicule in giving a wrong answer. To be successful, cooperative learning strategies must be carefully taught, designed, and reinforced by the teacher. Cooperative learning experiences contain four basic elements:

1. Positive interdependence is promoted through the division of work load and responsibility and through joint rewards.
2. Students are individually held accountable for their own learning and also for the learning of all others in the group.
3. Assignments are frequently divided into parts with each student mastering parts and then instructing the other students.
4. Students have a face-to-face encounter with each other on the topic being studied.

Discussions, explanations, questioning, and other verbal exchanges play an important role in sharing, reviewing, and rehearsing the content. Traditional group work often fails because one student takes over the leadership and makes decisions that affect only his or her own learning (Slavin, 1987).

Cooperative groups are heterogeneous. Leadership responsibilities for both the content of the lesson and the success of the group are given to all. For example, one student may be the group's recorder, writing down what decisions have been made and keeping notes; another might be in charge of materials, collecting those that are needed and organizing them; another may be the group's spokesperson, while another may be the group's organizer—making sure everyone has a chance to contribute to the discussion and that each person has a clear task to do. These roles are usually alternated between members of the group if it works together over a period of time on different topics. The functioning of the group is monitored by both the students and the teacher. The teacher instructs students in effective group processes (which creates a nonthreatening working environment), intervening when members encounter difficulty with group processes.

Recognition, including grading, is done with an eye to the success of the group as well as of the individual. Grades can be assigned by combining individual scores and the group's mean. This practice has been found to result in higher group mean scores and in a feeling among students that their classmates wanted them to learn (Madden & Slavin, 1983). Teachers and students also evaluate and grade the working process of the group as well as the final product or presentation. In cooperative learning classrooms, students who try hard, attend class regularly, and help others learn are praised and encouraged by others in the group. (Slavin, 1978).

Instruction in cooperative learning begins with short lessons with carefully structured materials presented by the teacher. For example, the teacher may show students how to classify a set of pictures. As students become more familiar with the processes, lessons may be longer and involve the students in selecting topics and subtopics and assigning membership responsibilities.

When students are ready to work cooperatively with larger amounts of material, they can be involved in an approach where students divide up a topic that has a large amount of material related to it, for example, the Depression in the United States in the 1930s.

- One group member may focus on "What were the major causes of the Depression?"
- Another may focus on "What were the effects of the Depression in our community?"
- A third may focus on "What major solutions were experimented with to try to ease the Depression?"
- A fourth may focus on "What was the role of the president, Franklin D. Roosevelt?"

Each member may work with students in other groups who have the same question to develop an answer to. The answer is then shared with the student's original group. This procedure is called a jigsaw and is best when there is a lot of material available on a topic so it has to be broken down into subtopics. Another approach is to have each group member develop a response individually and then share it with his or her group.

Cooperative learning can enable students to work with both large and small amounts of material. In this setting each student's strengths are used as each makes a recognizable contribution.

COMMERCIAL AND SPONSORED UNITS AND KITS

Meaningful learning requires learners to process a variety of data sources. Traditionally as students progressed through school their direct contact with data tended to disappear, and the abstract written or spoken word dominated their studies. Today this is no longer the case. Textbooks are filled with colorful illustrations while the teacher's guide contains suggested activities that frequently involve students in gathering and processing their own data related to the topic of the text. Teacher's guides are no longer single books but contain transparencies, transparency masters, and assignment sheets in large looseleaf binders. A few texts have related computer software, filmstrips, and videotapes. The entire product lines of some companies specialize in single media sources such as computer software, filmstrips, videos, or primary document facsimiles. Carefully prepared teacher's guides and student worksheets usually accompany such products to assist in learning the content. A few companies prepare multimedia learning kits or units. Teacher's guides and student project sheets, large pictures, posters, filmstrips, models, artifacts, and both factual and fiction books related to a specific topic or problem may be included in kits and units. The production of educational units and kits is not limited to professional educational publishing houses.

Museums, government agencies, industries, and special interest groups all produce learning materials for classroom use. Often they hire specialists in education to work with them and produce professional-looking learning materials. Such materials have often been called "free and inexpensive teaching materials." "Sponsored materials" is a more appropriate term (Haas, 1985). Many sponsored materials are appropriate for classroom use. Teachers should make use of them where possible, in any stage of a learning cycle.

However, such materials express the viewpoint of the producer or sponsor. Sponsored materials are not subjected to the reviews and pressures that commercial educational publishers face. Rarely are sponsored materials reviewed by state or local adoption committees. When teachers wish to use materials that have not been screened by official adoption committees for overall appropriateness, they have the additional evaluation responsibilities of examining the methods used to present the sponsor's message and of judging the potential impact of that message on the students.

Commercially prepared kits and units can be a great timesaver for teachers. However, learning kits vary greatly and each must be examined for its own merit. They must be judged on whether they match the curriculum and abilities of the students. Without such a match, even a high quality kit will make a limited contribution to meaningful learning. Important additional criteria for judging social studies kits and units are:

- How accurate is the information presented?
- Is the material in the kit illustrative of the multicultural nature of the society?
- Do the materials present multiple viewpoints in an unbiased manner?

Time for Reflection: What Do <u>YOU</u> Think?

The practice activity below will involve you in deciding which type of material or strategy you would use in teaching each part of one lesson. Would you focus on using questioning? on using a learning center? on using direct instruction?

☞ *You are teaching a unit on Norway. Children's literature, particularly stories about trolls, is used as a resource in much of the unit. Students talk about the trolls and how they might reflect the Norwegian culture they came from. They also talk about references in the stories to geography, weather, occupations, music, and religion. Briefly describe a lesson in this unit, fo-*

cusing on the strategies and or materials you would use in each part of the lesson.

What is the lesson objective?

What are some materials and/or strategies to be used in the exploration part of the lesson?

What are some materials and/or strategies to be used in the invention part of the lesson?

What are some materials and/or strategies to be used in the expansion part of the lesson?

SUMMARY

There are many things to consider in preparing a curriculum and the units and lessons that carry it through to student learning. While many people's ideas go into the process, the teacher still has a major role. The final selection and interpretation of the objectives and the ways the objectives are carried out in the classroom are the individual teacher's decisions. Specific instructional strategies tend to be more widely used in the exploration and expansion phases of a lesson while other instructional strategies are more widely used in the invention phase. Most strategies can be used with a wide variety of content and students. There are many sources of information and a variety of ways to present the information. The teacher needs to be familiar with the various procedures needed to successfully implement the instructional methods selected. Thorough planning is necessary to implement the strategies and use materials appropriately.

Some Sources of Materials for Social Studies Teaching

Interact
P.O. Box 997–Y91
Lakeside, California
92040

Ethnic Arts and Facts (Kits)
P. O. Box 20550
Oakland, California
94620

*SPICE (International
and Cross-Cultural Materials)
Room 14
Littlefield Center,
300 Lasven Street
Stanford University
Stanford, California
94305–5013*

*National Women's History Project
7738 Bell Road
Windsor, California
95492-8515*

*Social Studies School Service
10200 Jefferson Boulevard
Room 48
P.O. Box 802
Culver City, California
90232-0802*

REFERENCES

Anderson, T. & Armbruster, B. (1984). Content area textbooks. In R. Anderson (ed.), *Learning to read in American schools.* Hillsdale, NJ: Lawrence Erlbaum Associate Publishers.

Armstrong, D. (1989). *Developing and implementing the curriculum.* Boston: Allyn and Bacon.

Blake, H. (1977). *Creating a learning-centered classroom.* New York: AMD Visual Library.

Borich, G. (1988). *Effective teaching methods.* Columbus, OH: Merrill.

Cole, R. & Williams, D. (1973). Pupil responses to teacher questions: Cognitive level, length, and syntax. *Educational Leadership. 31*(November), 142–145.

Costa, A. (1991). Teacher behaviors that enable student thinking. In A. Costa (ed.), *Developing minds: A resource book for teaching thinking,* Vol. 1, Alexandria, VA: Association for Supervision and Curriculum Development, 194–206.

Davis, O. & Tinsley (1967). Cognitive objectives revealed by classroom questions asked by social studies student teachers. *Peabody Journal of Education, 45*(February), 21–26.

Gallagher, J. & Ashner, M. (1963). A preliminary report: Analysis of classroom interaction. *Merrill Palmer Quarterly, 9,* 183–194.

Haas, M. (1985). Evaluating sponsored materials. *How To Do It Series 4 Number 3.* Washington DC: National Council for the Social Studies.

Haas, M. (1990). The role of games in the elementary school. *Social Studies and the Young Learner. 3* (Nov./Dec.), 9–11.

Harlan, W. (1985). *Teaching and learning primary science.* New York: Teachers College Press.

Hoge, J. (1986). *Improving the use of elementary social studies textbooks.* ERIC Digest No. 33. Bloomington, IN: Clearinghouse for Social Studies/Social Science Education.

Johnson, D. W., Johnson, R. T., Holubec, E. J., & Roy, P. (1984). *Circles of Learning.* Alexandria, VA: Association for Supervision and Curriculum Development.

Madden, N. & Slavin, R. (1983). Effects of cooperative learning on the social acceptance of mainstreamed academically handicapped students. *The Journal of Special Education, 17,* 171–182.

Paul, R. (1991). Dialogical and dialectical thinking. In Costa, A. (Ed.), *Developing minds: A resource book for teaching thinking,* Revised edition, Vol. 1, Alexandria, VA: Association for Supervision and Curriculum Development, 280–289.

Redfield, D. & Rousseau, E. (1981). A meta-analysis on teacher questioning behavior. *Review of Educational Research, 51*(Summer), 234–245.

Rosenshine, B. (1983). Teaching functions in instructional programs. The *Elementary School Journal, 4,* 335–351.

Rowe, M. B. (1968). Science, silence, and sanctions. *Science and Children, 6*(March), 11–13.

Schug, M. & Beery, R. (1987). *Teaching social studies in the elementary school: Issues and practices.* Glenview, IL: Scott Foresman.

Shaftel, F. R. & Shaftel, G. (1982). *Role Playing for Social Value* (2nd ed.). Englewood Cliffs, NJ: Prentice-Hall.

Slavin, R. E. (1978). Student teams and comparison among equals: Effects on academic performance and student attitudes. *The Journal of Educational Psychology, 70,* 532–538.

Slavin, R. E. (1987). Cooperative learning and the cooperative school. *Educational Leadership, 45*(3), 7–13.

CHAPTER 8

OVERVIEW

Audio-visual and electronic media have become a pervasive part of our social world. These media are diverse, offering teachers a wide range of tools with which to assist students in social studies. This chapter gives an overview of the range of audio-visual and electronic media available and discusses the implications for their use by teachers.

Using Audio-Visual and Electronic Media in Social Studies

OBJECTIVES

1. Indicate how videodiscs, recordings, films, filmstrips, videos, and television can be used to make social studies concepts and generalizations less abstract for students.

2. Describe how each of the following might be used in the social studies program: simulation software, databases, CD ROM, computer-based microworlds, local area networks, and hypertext/hypermedia.

RECORDINGS, FILMS, FILMSTRIPS, VIDEOS, TELEVISION, AND VIDEODISCS

RECORDINGS, FILMS, AND FILMSTRIPS

A recording engages students' sense of hearing while a picture engages their sense of sight. Students can make different observations from a recording than from a picture. When the two are combined, an opportunity to process many more observations is created. A filmstrip with an accompanying tape recording is often a better alternative than a picture because it adds an auditory dimension to students' observations in addition to presenting a number of pictures relating to a topic. A film is an even better alternative than a filmstrip because it adds movement and many more scenes. The more senses involved, the greater the range of observations a student can make and the more information that can be gathered.

Each of these resources must be previewed by the teacher before it is used with the students. Some films, filmstrips, and tapes may not be worth the time used to view or listen to them because they are outdated and biased, have little useful information, or are of poor quality. Teachers need to develop lists of topics for which these resources are appropriate. Before using one of these resources, teachers need to decide on its purpose. Will it be used to stimulate students' exploration of an area? Will it be used to help them invent a skill, concept, or generalization? Will it be used to expand a skill, concept, or generalization students have invented? When using one of these resources, teachers need to introduce students to the focus of the resource before it is used. Students should know whether they will see a new skill demonstrated, whether they will be presented with information that cannot be personally experienced except by audio-visual means, or whether they will be acquainted with a new or different viewpoint on a topic or issue. Teachers should next outline what key observations students should try to make and discuss how these observations will be recorded. After viewing or listening, students should share and discuss their observations. After students share their observations, teachers should ask questions they have prepared to extend the observations. Students might also have to view or listen to the resource over again to note points they missed the first time. Expansion activities should build on the experience with the resource.

A Practice Activity

- Think about commercial films you are familiar with. Identify at least one that might be used to support a social studies unit.

- What social studies unit could this film support?

- Identify a recording that might be used in a social studies unit.

- What social studies unit could this recording support?

VIDEOS

Videos should be selected and used much as any film is. An advantage of video is that it can be made by students and their teacher. It can be a record of a field trip, a guest speaker's visit, student presentations, local sites of interest in the social studies program, or of any number of other events and activities.

When a video is created it should be planned in detail first. A script for the video must be prepared by the students, teacher, or students and teacher working together. The script may lay out the exact words to be spoken, as in the case of a class play. More often, a script may only indicate a sequence of activities and who will be involved in each. The activities and words spoken are often planned in general with specific details ad libbed. Students can also use computer programs such as *Dazzle Draw* to make a title, division screens, and credit listings.

Videos have the advantage of allowing for retakes should a major blunder occur during videotaping. Teachers should develop a lesson plan when making a video that includes:

- objectives
- a workable plan for the content of the video
- clear instructions for its production
- an evaluation of its ability to meet the objectives
- ideas for how it can be expanded upon and used after it is made

Interviews and city council sessions are examples of the events that can be videotaped for later use in the classroom. Videotaping can be combined with a field trip. Students can view the video later to review the event, to gather additional information, and to support points made in discussion. When videotaping occurs on a field trip the teacher should ask another adult to do the taping since working with the equipment is likely to distract the teacher from his or her responsibilities to the students.

A Practice Activity

Assume you are taking your students on a field trip to the regularly scheduled meeting of town officials, such as the mayor and city council. You have decided to have a parent videotape the experience and have obtained permission to do so.

- Suggest one objective for this activity.
- Suggest a follow-up activity during which the videotape would be used.

☞ *There are many possible objectives. For example: "Students will identify the roles the mayor and city council members play during a meeting" or "Students will describe opposing views of the mayor and city council members on the issue of recycling." There are also a number of ways in which the videotape of the meeting can be used in class. It might support statements students make during discussion of the meeting they attended, or it might be used by students to carry out an analysis of specific portions of the meeting.*

TELEVISION

Television can be a resource for social studies in the classroom and at home. Many television programs are excellent resources for teaching. These include programs exploring various cultures, holidays, geography, and animals in different nations and in different regions of North America. Another teaching resource is programs dealing with issues or policies. Some of these are produced locally and of immediate interest in the local area. Nationally produced programs are sometimes of interest in a particular community. Locally produced programs often introduce students to:

- local sites of historical or geographical interest
- local and state government officials
- members of interest groups such as environmental support groups or the League of Women Voters
- citizens not affiliated with any group who are concerned about an issue or have a hobby or skill that is of interest

Programs produced for national distribution sometimes are accompanied by guides that help teachers incorporate them into their curriculum.

In selecting programs, teachers generally do not have an opportunity to preview the show. They must depend on descriptions found in the teaching guide accompanying it, or more likely on the description of it in a newspaper or commercial television guide. For this reason many teachers may prefer to tape a program and show it in class. This is considered fair use and is permitted if the tape is shown once in class within ten days and cleared within 45 days after it is used. Showing such videotapes in class ensures that all students have the opportunity to view the event to be discussed. Since most students watch television at home for entertainment they are not likely to have developed critical viewing skills (De Costa, 1990). It may be preferable to have them view videotaped programs in class where the teacher can guide their viewing and help them view a program critically.

In many states the Public Broadcasting Service (PBS) provides educational services directly to schools. Two kinds of rights to programs are purchased by PBS. Some programs are broadcast for immediate use in the school. These are often accompanied by viewing guides and other materials for use by teachers and students. Others can be copied and kept by schools to be used as teachers need them. Programs helpful in teaching social studies include those that describe nations and regions of the world, dramatizations of historical events, and dramatic illustrations of problems dealing with economics and government. These programs are different from many commercial television programs because they directly teach concepts using animation and examples closely related to the experiences of students. Teachers need to check every year with their local public broadcasting station to find out what new resources will be available.

It is always important to talk with students both before and after the program is viewed. Misconceptions can be analyzed as can bias, incomplete reporting, and other problems. Areas where the program's quality was high should also be discussed. Such areas might include the presentation of multiple viewpoints about an issue, an attention to details, an in-depth coverage of a topic, citation of sources, and the use of language that is clear and free from bias, leading, or prejudicial terms. Students will be more likely to recognize areas of quality in other programs they watch if their attention has been drawn to such concerns in class.

When a program is selected for students to view either in school or at home, a viewing guide should be prepared. The guide should include the following parts: An exploratory section containing
- a descriptive statement that previews the program
- a statement designed to motivate the student to watch the program, and explaining why the program is worth watching
- several questions that ask the student to think about the topic and recall what they know about it.

A section that guides students to invent important concepts or generalizations presented in the program by providing them with
- a list of questions and issues to watch for during the program
- a list of specific data to record while watching.

A section that expands on the information presented in the program by asking students to apply the information in the program. Possible expansion activities include
- activities to complete by themselves, such as building a model
- readings that discuss the topic of the program
- consideration of a list of related issues that will be discussed in class.

If the program is to be watched at home, the viewing guide should be sent home with a note requesting that parents watch the program with their children, discuss questions and concerns raised, and be involved in expansion activities.

When students make their own videotapes, they will have many decisions to make, encountering many of the problems a producer has. This will help them more critically appraise programs they see on television. Since many people get much of their information on current affairs and about the world in general from television, it is important to develop critical viewing skills.

A Practice Activity

- Look through a television guide or a local newspaper's television section, or think back on programs you have viewed during the past week. Identify one program that might be used in social studies.

- Suggest one objective for viewing this program.

- Describe how you might follow up on the viewing assignment in class the next day.

VIDEODISCS

Schools are beginning to acquire videodiscs that have as many as 54,000 frames on them. The images on these discs are shown on a computer screen. When used in this way they require a videodisc player and a monitor. The videodisc images can be projected on a screen using a liquid crystal display placed on an overhead projector.

The images on the disc can be rapidly accessed. This speed enables teachers to quickly add new information to a lesson. Teachers are also able to call up immediately new images to answer questions arising in class. Most often teachers use information directly from a disc as a means of presenting new information in a lesson. Most videodiscs can also be commanded by a remote control by punching in the number of the frame to be viewed or using a bar code reader to scan a series of coded lines to identify the correct frame. It is not difficult to use a computer to command the videodisc to show an image. This can be done in many ways. Authoring systems are available that help a teacher organize many images. A simple program can also be written in BASIC by the teacher by typing: PRINT D$; "VIDEO 1990,2457." This will command the disc player to play from frame 1990 to frame 2457, about 20 seconds of video.

With a videodisc, a teacher can:

- Arrange pictures to provide a clear demonstration of how to do something, such as making an arrowhead.
- Coordinate a series of pictures to illustrate an explanation or lecture.
- Save presentations for use in review and individual study. Students who were absent from class can make up work missed with a presentation that has been saved. Presentations can be saved by transferring them to video-tape or they can be saved as a computer program.
- Individualize lessons or create evaluation instruments using visuals on a videodisc. Some disc publishers give schools permission to use material from their discs. The material might come from several discs and be put together to address a topic.

As indicated above, images from videodiscs can be saved into a computer and stored on a diskette. This requires a device known as a digitizer or a video capture board. This device allows the user to take a single image and input it into a computer. Once it is inputted it can be displayed on the monitor and saved just as any other image on a monitor is saved. It can be printed, enlarged, reduced, captioned, etc., just as other screen images are treated.

These discs are a wonderful resource. Each one contains far more images than a teacher would possibly have in a picture file. A caution is necessary, however, because selecting and organizing images from a videodisc is time consuming. Transferring them into a computer program is also time consuming. But the time required in selecting, organizing, and transferring these images (and in learning these processes) is time well spent, as these activities have great potential. Many teachers develop two or three packages in a year, and save them for future use. Middle school students, with a little practice, can also use the videodisc and computer to illustrate their presentations and reports and share them with classmates.

COMPUTERS

Computers have entered elementary and middle school classrooms in large numbers. Many classrooms today have at least one computer. In some settings students use computers in laboratories set up within the school. Students often tend to be more comfortable with computers than do their teachers. Many teachers have not completely integrated computers into their classrooms, seeing them as machines that students use for drill and practice, rather than as tools having as integral a role as the chalk and chalkboard. It does appear that more and more teachers are gradually learning to integrate computers into their classrooms. Computers themselves are changing. Hypertext, integration with videodiscs, and

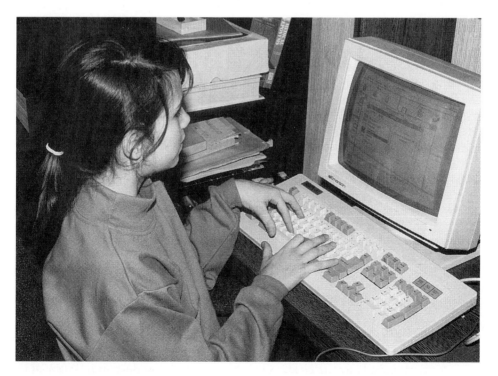

Computers have become an important tool for students.

other developments also make this a rapidly changing area, one that is a challenge for teachers to keep up with.

In such a situation it is best to begin at a modest level and gradually increase the use. Initially teachers should use computers and the software available to them. Gradually, teachers can investigate adding on recording, video, and other aspects. Computer use must be integrated into the curriculum to obtain the best results. If computer use is limited to a special time and/or to drill and practice activities, they have isolated limited effects on learning.

Less software is available for social studies than for some other content areas, such as mathematics. Teachers tend to use software tutorials and drills in social studies to deliver or reinforce factual knowledge. Much of the current software that is available stands alone and is not part of a larger curriculum package (S. White, 1988). The teacher's task is to find ways to bring the software into the curriculum at appropriate times.

SOFTWARE

SIMULATIONS AND DECISION-MAKING SOFTWARE

More computer simulations and decision-making software are becoming available. The ability of the computer to rapidly scan information makes a wide range of simulations possible. The computer can record students' decisions as they use a simulation and quickly provide them with an appropriate new set of information or a new problem. Because computers can branch, simulations can take different courses depending on decisions students make or the introduction of random variables. Students can play a simulation many times and get different outcomes each time. This allows them to experiment with different theories and viewpoints. Graphics add interest and supply data as a simulation is used. The thinking skills required to complete a simulation have increased as programming techniques have advanced.

A popular early simulation, *Oregon Trail* (MECC), is even more popular in its revised version. In it, upper elementary and middle grade students become pioneers traveling in a covered wagon to nineteenth-century Oregon. They must purchase their supplies and face hazards along the way and perhaps die just as did the original travelers of the Oregon Trail. *The Golden Spike* (National Geographic) involves students in building the United States' first transcontinental railroad in the 1860s.

These programs can easily be part of a larger curriculum where teachers involve students in outlining, time lines, and creative writing (Medeiros, 1990). For example, students might outline the events that happened to them while on the Oregon Trail and then use the outline to write a letter to their family back East. Or they might write about a day in the life of a worker building the transcontinental railroad. Simulations and decision-making programs for upper elementary and middle grade students that demonstrate high levels of sophistication are *Sim City* (Broderbund), *Where in Time Is Carmen San Diego?* (Broderbund), *Where in the World Is Carmen San Diego?* (Broderbund), and the *Decisions, Decisions* series (Tom

Snyder Productions). *On the Playground* (Tom Snyder Productions) is an example of such a program for primary grade students.

Simulations and decision-making programs let students step into a social, governmental, or historical setting, make decisions, and see their consequences. Different events occur depending on what decision is made. As a result, the program can be used many times with different events happening each time. The consequences also differ, depending on the choices one makes. These programs allow students to explore situations that cannot be personally explored in any other way. The consequences experienced in the simulation can be thought-provoking yet not scary, since students realize this is not really happening to them. Errors can be examined. Students can repeat the simulation and try out different choices. The opportunity to experiment helps them use critical thinking skills and gain a realistic sense of their personal intellectual and political power.

Many of the simulations mentioned can be played by one student. The dynamics of group interactions, however, are an important part of social situations. Tom Snyder Productions has adopted the philosophy that the computer assists teachers who love to teach. They advocate the use of a single computer in a classroom and have developed simulations and decision-making software in which the entire class or groups of students can work through the program simultaneously. These simulations stimulate discussion among students and encourage such social skills as cooperation, compromise, and consensus formation. Students discuss alternative solutions and have their thinking challenged before reaching a decision. They find that not only do individuals hold different positions but that groups make varying decisions. The research literature points to positive affective outcomes and gains in cooperative learning capabilities among students using computer simulations (Ehman & Glenn, 1987).

Some teachers take a different approach, assuming that students learn most when they build their own model and represent it (S. White, 1988). Roessler (1987) describes a simulation students built that helped them learn about and better understand the Depression. Such an activity is also an excellent opportunity for a multidisciplinary study using skills of a computer class and a social studies class.

PROBLEMS IN A GAME FORMAT

Drills and programs for the practice of cognitive skills were among the first types of software developed. Today's software has found ways to use the game format to motivate students to practice series of skills. Decisions are made on the basis of factual information gained through using resources such as an almanac, data sheets, and maps. Students are encouraged to plan strategies to accomplish their assigned tasks. Accurate records of all student moves are kept. Competitive rules can be programmed to apply when appropriate. Often the teacher can change the time allowed a group using the computer as students increase in their knowledge. The additional sophistication of such programs carries them beyond the level of memorization to the application of skills and the analysis of relationships among data. An example of such games is *The Ripple that Changed American History* (Tom

Snyder Productions), which helps students develop an awareness of significant events and dates in American history. Another example is *National Inspirer* (Tom Snyder Productions), which requires map reading and interpretation as students learn the locations of the physical features and natural resources of the United States.

EVALUATING SOCIAL STUDIES SOFTWARE

Computer software designed for use in social studies needs to be carefully selected. Most schools have limited software purchase budgets. There is always more software available than there is money to buy it. Each piece of software purchased should be appropriate to the goals and objectives of the social studies program. The Software Evaluation Form in Figure 8–1 is for general use with all types of software. It provides for checking for the presence or absence of program characteristics and for stating one's own position on the necessity of the characteristics in the program (Haas, 1986).

DATABASES

Databases are another computer-based tool that has entered social studies programs. With a database, information on a topic, such as the populations of state and provincial capital cities in North America, can be entered. Then students can call up those cities that have a certain characteristic, such as population over 100,000 or under 500,000. The information can be sorted in many ways depending upon what sort of information is needed. Once a database is set up it is always available to answer questions related to the information it contains.

Ready-made databases can be purchased. Four such databases are *Talking USA Map* (Orange Cherry Software), *World Geograph* (MECC), *NewsWorks* (Newsweek), and *The U.S. Constitution Then and Now* (Scholastic). *World Geograph* is typical of databases being developed. Students can compare data between any of 177 countries. They observe patterns in the data about different countries. They can also examine maps and print out data. Some textbook publishers have developed databases that correlate with their social studies series.

Students can make their own databases quite easily. Commonly available programs, such as *Appleworks* or *PFS-file,* have database components. Each student might carry out research and then enter the products of the research effort. For example, students could set up a database focused on early settlers in their community. After deciding what sort of information should be collected about each person (for example, name, birthdate, date of death, birthplace, whether married, number of children, occupation), each student searches out as much of the needed information as possible for a settler and enters the information into the database. Once the database is completed, students ask questions and sort the data to help answer their questions. They might, for example, use the database to find out how many of the male settlers were born overseas. Figure 8–2 depicts screens from a database developed by students.

Often when data is sorted to answer a question, new questions arise. As new questions arise students can carry out further research and add additional information

SOFTWARE EVALUATION FORM

Program Name _____

Author _____ Publisher _____

Type of Program _____ Age Level _____

At what point(s) in the curriculum does the program fit?

_____

List the content-specific concepts that the student must use in the program.

_____

List the relationships between concepts that students are required to know to use the program.

_____

Read each of the questions below and circle the correct response: YES, NO, or NA (not applicable). Then circle your feelings about the necessity of the characteristic: REQUIRED or PREFERRED. When you complete the questionnaire, examine the responses. Does the program have those characteristics that you believe are required? Are the NO responses for the most part in the preferred category or the required category? The final judgment will be somewhat subjective, but if you use the evaluation form, you will be forcing yourself to consider many aspects of software that you might otherwise neglect to consider.

Y/YES   N/NO   NA/NOT APPLICABLE   R/REQUIRED   P/PREFERRED

1. Are the objectives stated for the students?	Y N NA R P
2. Does the program attain its objectives?	Y N NA R P
3. Is the content free from negative stereotypes?	Y N NA R P
4. Does the program use correct grammar?	Y N NA R P

Teacher's Guide

If not available, circle this statement. If available, answer:

1. Are the objectives clearly stated?	Y N NA R P
2. Does the guide provide a complete written set of directions for the program?	Y N NA R P
3. Does the guide provide samples of what the student will see on the screen?	Y N NA R P
4. Are suggestions made for follow-up activity?	Y N NA R P
5. Is there a form of evaluation for students?	Y N NA R P

Technical Characteristics

1. Is the program free from programming errors?	Y N NA R P
2. Is the screen clear and easily readable?	Y N NA R P
3. Can the sound effects be turned off?	Y N NA R P
4. Are the graphics relevant and interesting?	Y N NA R P
5. Will the program be effective in either black and white or color?	Y N NA R P

Student Interaction

1. Are the instructions clearly stated?	Y N NA R P
2. Can the directions be skipped?	Y N NA R P
3. Does the program provide neutral or supportive feedback?	Y N NA R P
4. Is help provided to gain correct answers?	Y N NA R P
5. Is there more than one opportunity to answer the questions correctly?	Y N NA R P
6. Is the student required to input data?	Y N NA R P
7. Does the computer accept abbreviations?	Y N NA R P
8. Does the user control the speed at which the program progresses?	Y N NA R P
9. Are logical spelling errors accepted?	Y N NA R P

Administrative Details

1. Can the student stop and begin again where she/he left off?	Y N NA R P
2. Does the program test and record the student's progress?	Y N NA R P
3. Does the teacher have private access to the records of student work?	Y N NA R P
4. Can the teacher make individual assignments?	Y N NA R P
5. Can the teacher add to or change the questions?	Y N NA R P
6. How much class time must be allowed for proper use of the program?	Y N NA R P
7. How much individual and lab time will be needed?	Y N NA R P

Figure 8–1   Sample of a form used to evaluate computer software.

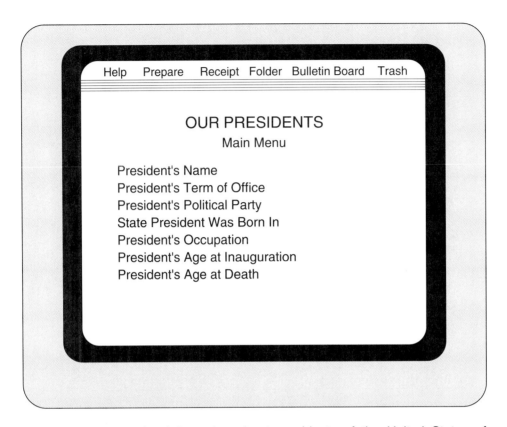

Help   Prepare   Receipt   Folder   Bulletin Board   Trash

OUR PRESIDENTS
Main Menu

President's Name
President's Term of Office
President's Political Party
State President Was Born In
President's Occupation
President's Age at Inauguration
President's Age at Death

This database contains information about presidents of the United States of America. Screen One lists the information items given about each president. The information is given in the database in the order listed on Screen One.

Figure 8–2   Three sample screens of a database developed by students.

to the database. Of course, sometimes the information just is not available. This teaches students that not every question can be readily answered. Making databases as a class effort demonstrates the power of information and also the power of cooperative effort. To construct a comprehensive database with a lot of information in it on one's own can be a daunting task, but it is one that is quite easily accomplished as a cooperative effort.

Spreadsheets can be used to extend data into the future. Data in a database can be put into a spreadsheet. Spreadsheets are able to add, subtract, multiply, and do many other operations with data. For example, a student might note that a certain amount of money is collected from a gasoline tax in a state each year. He may average this amount by dividing it by the number of people in the state. Then he can multiply it by an inflation factor after he notes that the population has been increasing one percent a year. He can predict that more people means more tax will be paid. The spreadsheet can predict what the amount collected will be in fifty years if the tax itself does not change. The spreadsheet will automatically increase

| Help | Prepare | Receipt | Folder | Bulletin Board | Trash |

Truman, Harry S.
1945 - 1953
Democratic
Missouri
Businessman
60
88

Screen Two gives specific information about a president, Harry S. Truman.

the population each year and calculate the tax. It can also calculate the total tax that will be paid over the fifty year period. Speadsheets allow students to play with changing one item in the data, such as the percentage of increase of the population annually, and then with changing another item, such as the amount of tax collected in the first year. As he plays with the data, the student can see how the larger picture is affected. This does allow students to begin to understand how long-range changes can be predicted and how long-range planning can occur.

To analyze the data that has been collected by hand or retrieved from a database, data analysis tools have been developed. *Polls and Politics* (MECC) is an example of a program that can be used with survey data. It helps students by visually summarizing the results of the survey in different ways, such as through a histogram. *Data Plot* (Muse) is an example of a program that does graphing. It can be used to summarize data onto charts and graphs. Both types of programs enable students to analyze and summarize larger amounts of data more quickly than can be done by hand. Research results (White, 1987; Underwood, 1985; Ennals, 1985) indicate that databases have positive effects on skills relating to information processing, data classification, and question asking.

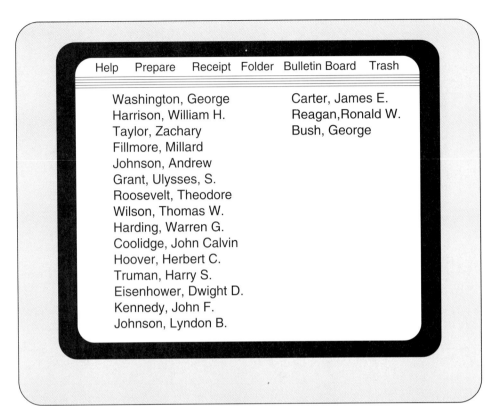

Help	Prepare	Receipt	Folder	Bulletin Board	Trash

Washington, George
Harrison, William H.
Taylor, Zachary
Fillmore, Millard
Johnson, Andrew
Grant, Ulysses, S.
Roosevelt, Theodore
Wilson, Thomas W.
Harding, Warren G.
Coolidge, John Calvin
Hoover, Herbert C.
Truman, Harry S.
Eisenhower, Dwight D.
Kennedy, John F.
Johnson, Lyndon B.

Carter, James E.
Reagan, Ronald W.
Bush, George

Screen Three is an answer to the question, "Which presidents were not lawyers?"

A Practice Activity

- After examining database Screen One in Figure 8–2, suggest two questions students might ask that could be answered by the information in this database.

- Suggest a question that could not be answered by the information in this database.

- What category(s) of information would have to be added to the database if it were to be able to answer this question?

CD-ROM

CD-ROM discs are available for both the MS-DOS and Macintosh families of computers. Grolier's American Electronic Encyclopedia (Grolier) and Microsoft Bookshelf (Microsoft) contain a huge amount of reference information. A computer and a CD-ROM device are necessary to use it. These discs give students access to information they need for conducting research. Usually such resources are located in a central area in a school where anyone who needs information has access to it. The user types in the topic of interest to get the information needed. The instructions for using the program usually tell users either what topics are available or how to type in the topic of interest and how to decide on possible alternative desired information.

COMPUTER-BASED MICROWORLDS

Microworlds are worlds programmed for the computer screen that encompass objects and processes that we can get to know and understand. The knowledge embodied in these experiences is made accessible because the microworld does not focus on problems to be done but on phenomena that are interesting to observe and interact with (Lawler, 1982, p. 140). These worlds are safe and manageable for the student (Papert, 1980).

LOGO is the computer language used most in constructing microworlds. This program has excellent graphics and drawing capabilities, making it useful in designing a microworld. The microworld should allow students to move objects within it and to restructure it as they see fit. In a microworld the user is given personal control over the creation and discovery process. Microworlds are a responsive environment that can be explored and extended by the learner (Tipps & Bull, 1985). The microworld is a place where a student does not have to wonder if adults are going to change the rules. It is a secure place where the student directs the analysis of new knowledge (Muller, 1985). The student can make up the rules the microworld operates by, set them into motion, and watch the effects. The student can also decide what objects will be part of a microworld and can change them at will and observe the effects of the change.

A useful microworld has the following characteristics:

- *Activity oriented.* The student manipulates concrete embodiments of the concepts to be learned. He or she experiences the concepts directly, not through language about them.
- *Simplifies the real world.* For clarity, microworlds often leave out aspects of the real world. Experience in the real world is juxtaposed with the computer world, so that each complements the other.
- *Clusters activities.* Any one concept is met in several different contexts and in different combinations.
- *Activities have a constructive component.*
- *Activities utilize the student's prior knowledge.* Such activities invite personal meanings and are motivational. They allow the involvement of the unique cultural heritage each student brings to the activities. Creativity is stimulated, fantasy is encouraged, and the student has fun.
- *Activities cut across content areas.*

- *Has several levels of description.* Students can move backward and forward from more experiential to more abstract activities.
- *Activities cater to a range of individual work styles.* (Weir, 1987, p. 105)

Perhaps the most work in social studies education has been done with microworlds involving geography. Figure 8–3 demonstrates a microworld a third grader drew when exploring geography. Students can begin with their own classroom, represented by a rectangle, and draw in desks, tables, and other furnishings. Radical rearrangement including moving doors and windows is possible. Students can set up the microworld so that when one item is moved, another moves also. For example, if the student really likes to sit next to the globe or the aquarium, every time this object is moved, the student's seat moves with it. In another type of microworld, students can set up a store and move goods in and out of it. Customers can enter and purchase goods. New goods can come in and be given prices depending on supply and demand or other criteria.

Microworlds allow students to build models of how a system works and extend changes into the future. This allows them to see how the system responds and to make more accurate predictions. Microworlds are an area that has seen less development than have other areas such as databases. This is an area with great potential and one that teachers should consider exploring with their students as opportunities present themselves.

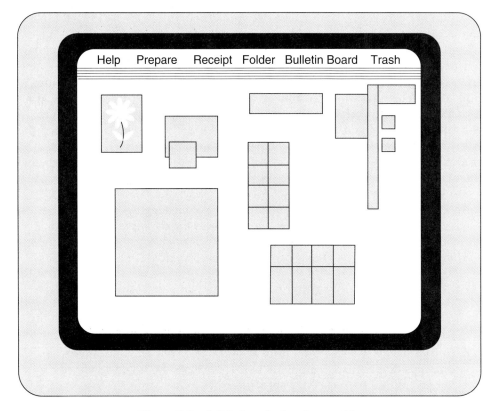

Figure 8–3   A third grader's microworld.

LOCAL AREA COMPUTER NETWORKS

Local area networks (LAN) use a computer to enable a group of people to communicate with each other and to work on a project together. Often these systems connect, or network, several computers through electronic mail (or E-mail). Figure 8–4 depicts three sample electronic mail computer screens. The network's computers can be located in one classroom, at various sites within a school, at various schools in a school system, in various school systems, etc. It is possible to network a school in New Jersey with one in Whitehorse, Yukon Territory, Canada with one in Brussels, Belgium. Networking outside of a single building is usually accomplished by sending messages over telephone lines using a modem. Within the local calling area the cost is no more than making a regular tele-

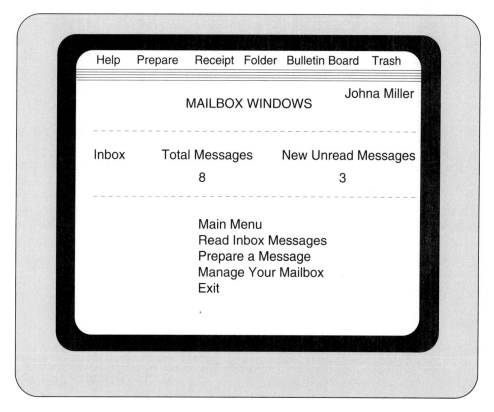

The reader has opened up her network screens. This screen shows the reader that she has eight messages in storage. Three of them are new messages she has not yet read. The main menu shows her the choices she can make. She can read her messages. She can choose to prepare a message to someone on a new topic or in response to an existing message. She can choose to organize her mailbox by adding names, removing names, grouping people in a different way, or by carrying out some other task. Or she can exit the network.

Figure 8–4   Three sample electronic mail computer screens.

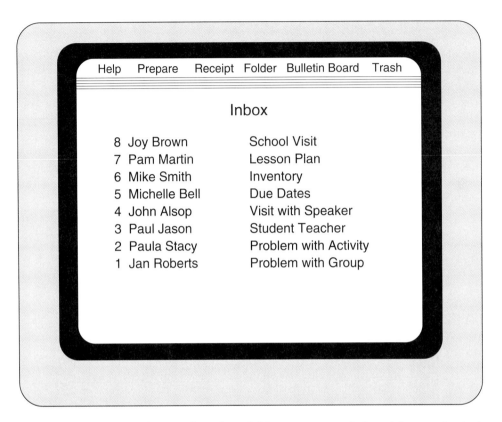

This screen shows the reader the eight messages in her inbox and what their topics are. The reader can begin with any one of the messages. She can read them all or choose to read one or more of them. She can prepare a message in response or choose not to respond.

phone call. Outside of the local calling area the cost is equal to that of making a long-distance call unless one has purchased an 800 number. Messages can be sent to one person on the network, to a set of people on the network, or to everybody. Messages are stored until the recipient of the message calls it up and responds to it or chooses to store it. Messages can be displayed on a computer screen and printed off or stored on a floppy disk. Some of the things networks can send are:

- word-processed messages
- spreadsheets and databases
- maps
- graphics
- forms
- tutorials

| Help | Prepare | Receipt | Folder | Bulletin Board | Trash |

MESSAGE CONTENTS

We are having a problem with the plan you gave us for interviewing the newspaper editor. We are asking about when the newspaper was founded and what its circulation was in the first three years.Then we are asking about its policy on publishing letters to the editor. Then we are asking about how much space is devoted to news, to sports, and so on. It seems like the topics are not really connected. With the first one, shouldn't we ask about its circulation now? With the second one, shouldn't we ask about whether a letter to the editor section improves circulation? Let us know what your thinking was. If you want, we will send you a list of the questions we think should be added in. We can send it to the other classes, too.

The reader has selected the message from Paula Stacy (#2). It is displayed on the screen. Now the reader must decide whether to respond immediately or to go back and consider the interview material sent earlier before responding.

Networks provide a new means of cooperation and knowledge sharing. Examples of ways networking can assist social studies teachers include:
- conducting surveys with a larger and more diverse set of respondents than would be available in a single class or school
- helping classes research their own questions, with students at several sites collecting data on the questions
- conducting larger studies on common topics in which individual classes investigate subquestions and share information
- sharing findings with others through graphics and writing

Broad questions that require much data to answer are especially appropriate for research via a LAN by elementary and middle school students. Examples of such questions are:
- Should separating garbage into recyclables and trash be mandatory?
- What are the important issues facing citizens in different parts of our state?
- How did a story affect different parts of the community?

- What are the favorite biographies students have read?
- Why should Americans be interested in saving tropical rain forests?
- What factors influenced the establishment and survival of neighborhoods and communities?

Commercially available programs utilizing E-mail and networking that operate in a way similar to that described above are KidsNet (National Geographic) and the AT & T Learning Network (American Telephone and Telegraph Company). Each of these involves a fee and provides software, the cost of telephone communication, and related curriculum materials. They involve students all over North America and, to some extent, overseas. It is possible, however, to set up a network within a local telephone calling zone with no costs beyond those of the computers, networking software, and a local telephone line—all of which might already exist in a school or school system.

A Practice Activity

· Suggest a research project related to political science which students could carry out using a local area network in their school system. If possible, discuss your ideas with a peer.

· Identify a grade level.

· Identify the topic of the research project.

· Identify the types of data to be gathered and analyzed.

HYPERTEXT/HYPERMEDIA

Few teachers have skills in programming computers, but they can have success in writing their own programs and assisting students to also prepare programs through the use of authoring systems. Hypertext/Hypermedia are examples of such programs that simplify programming. The advantages of hypermedia/hypertext are that it allows great flexibility, is interactive with the learner, and incorporates graphics and sound. Videodisc frames and voice sequences can also be integrated. Information is shared on nested screens called "stacks."

Each screen is actually like an index card. The developer writes and/or draws information on the card then puts it somewhere in a stack of cards. The stack can be shuffled in different ways. Buttons are put on the screen to give the user the option to go on to new information. With a simple stack the user progresses from card 1 to card 2 to card 3, and so on. By using buttons, the user can branch out and go from card 1 to card 40, back to card 1, etc. Another user might go from card 1 to card 2 to card 3 to card 4 and then to card 38 and back to card 4. Figure 8–5 shows a main pathway and one with branching.

The developer puts the cards in the deck and uses a button to take a reader to a card that branches out away from the main path being taken. No programming is required. The developer plans out each card, decides which ones are on the main path, sequences them, and then decides which cards will branch out and puts buttons on the main path cards from which branching occurs. The developer can return to the stack and add in another card at any point or take out an existing card at any time.

In hypertext, the first screen, for example, may show a map of Scotland. With a click of a mouse a new screen comes up identifying the map as Scotland. Clicking again, the user can return to the map or to any one of a number of other screens showing locations or features. The user might click on Glasgow. A new screen comes up that offers the user several choices:

- a map of Glasgow
- information on Glasgow's major industries
- information on Glasgow's form of government
- information on Glasgow's oldest building

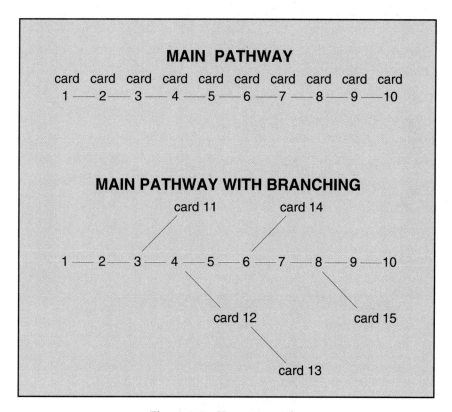

Figure 8–5   Hypertext paths.

The user clicks on one of these items and a new screen comes up giving the information selected. For example, if the user chooses the map of Glasgow, there will be some points (or buttons) that can be clicked on. These might correspond to famous sites or different regions of the city. When the user clicks on a region of the city, information is given about its history and current population. The user is also presented with questions requiring higher level thought processes than are used in investigating the map and the textual information presented. The user has the freedom to return to any previous screen or to select new information.

Students are able to move back and forth in these programs, review earlier information, and explore additional information in areas that they do not completely understand. Pieces can be added to the program to enrich it or to address areas of need identified among students. Hypertext allows a teacher or a student to develop software without knowing programming languages (Fiderio, 1988). Figure 8–6 shows screens that are part of a program developed by fourth graders.

Hypermedia is hypertext combined with motion videos, still pictures, and/or

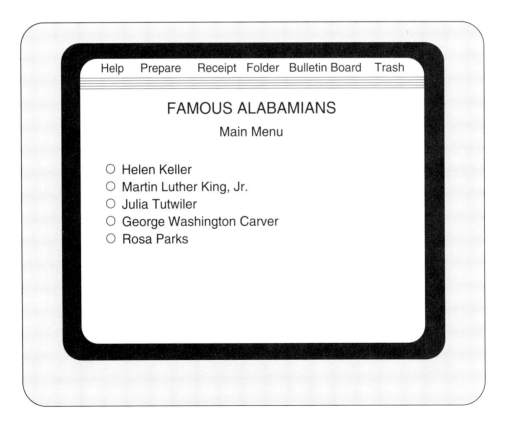

To use this screen, users move a mouse until it is pointing at the circle (button) that is beside the person they wish to know more about. They click on this circle.

Figure 8–6 Three sample hypertext program screens designed by fourth graders.

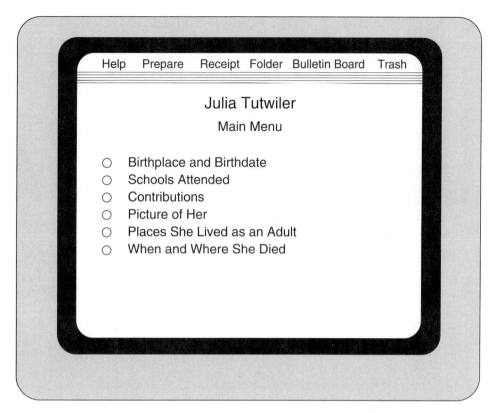

This screen gives users several options. Users select one and may later return to select another.

sound (Price, 1991). Motion video or still pictures are usually stored on videodisc or compact disc. Using hypertext, the developer can organize these stored images. They can be organized in sequence: image 1, image 2, etc. More often they are organized with branching by topics, so that images 1, 43, 690, and 758 may relate to George Washington while images 2, 3, and 101 relate to Thomas Jefferson. Branching is used from the main path. Since videodiscs and compact discs can contain up to 54,000 images (as does the National Gallery of Art videodisc, for example), they are most useful only when there is some easy way to access a specific image. So a *catalog of images* is created. Images can then be grouped and stored so that they can be called up as appropriate to a particular lesson or unit. Discs are also being developed that have sound accompanying images when appropriate.

It is possible to add an image into a computer program. When the program is used, the image comes up. Speech and music are another possibility in hypermedia. A guest speaker who comes into the classroom can be videotaped and the images fed into a computer and made a part of a new program. It is also possible to use a microphone to directly save what the speaker says and put it into a

| Help | Prepare | Receipt | Folder | Bulletin Board | Trash |

Contributions of Julia Tutwiler

Julia Tutwiler worked hard for two things. First, she worked hard for better education of women. She taught at schools for girls like the Tuscaloosa Female College. She was a principal of the Livingston Female Academy for twenty years. Now it is Livingston University so it is still around. Second, she worked hard for prison reform. She made sheriffs give prisoners safe drinking water and clean toilets. She got them to heat the prison in winter. She gave prisoners Bibles to read and made sure religious services were offered for them. Because of her work, a prison board was set up in 1886 in Alabama to make sure that prisoners had some minimum care. She was called "the angel of prisons."

○ If you want to know more about her work for women's education press this button.

○ If you want to know more about her work for prison reform press this button.

program. In addition, if he plays bagpipe music, this can be saved into the program. Some computers, such as the Macintosh LC, come with a microphone that allows direct saving into the computer. With others, speech and music are saved on a tape recorder. The tape recorder is attached to a computer and the music or speech can be saved from it into the computer. While not all tape recorders can be used, many are appropriate. CD-ROM is another link that can be made with hypermedia.

Using hypertext/hypermedia, students produce work that can become a permanent part of the classroom's materials and that will be of interest to other students (see Figure 8–7). They can produce reviews, summaries, book reports, research reports, and many of the other projects they do in the classroom. When introducing students to the use of hypertext/hypermedia, the teacher may find it helpful to train two students who each assist in training two additional students. Soon the new trainees will be able to train others. In a short time, every student will have been trained.

Commercial hypertext/hypermedia software packages that a developer can use are available. These include Guide (for IBM and Macintosh computers), HyperCard (for Macintosh computers), LinkWay (for IBM computers), SuperCard (for IBM computers), and Tutor-Tech (for Apple II computers).

Figure 8–7   This is a printout of a screen in a hypermedia program.

A Practice Activity

Identify a paper or presentation you have done for a college course that might have been put together using hypertext/hypermedia instead of preparing and typing it in a traditional paper or report format. Identify two ways you would change the traditional paper to use the unique opportunities that hypertext/hypermedia provide an author.

SUMMARY

Audio-visual and electronic media can serve as valuable learning tools in social studies. They can be used to enrich the content of the social studies program and to help students develop the processes used in exploring and learning that content. There is a nearly endless range of possible activities. Software programs are undergoing continual development as technology advances. Teachers may use commercially available software and packages that enable them and their students to develop their own programs. These media should be integrated gradually into the curriculum. Teachers might experiment with one or two media at first, adding media as they and their students gain expertise.

REFERENCES

De Costa, S. (1990). Using resources to teach the social studies. In C. Sunal (ed.), *Early childhood social studies,* (p. 223). Columbus, OH: Merrill.

Ehman, L. & Glenn, A. *Computer-based education in the social studies.* Bloomington, IN: Social Studies Development Center and ERIC Clearinghouse for Social Studies/Social Science Education.

Ennals, R. (1985). Micro-PROLOG and classroom historical research. In I. Reid & J. Rushton, (eds.). *Teachers, computers, and the classroom.* Manchester, England: Manchester University Press.

Fiderio, J. (1988). A grand vision. *Byte, 13*(10), 237–244.

Freman, E. & Levstik, L. (1988). Recreating the past: Historical fiction in the social studies curriculum, *The Elementary School Journal, 88,* 329–337.

Frye, N. (1964). *The educated imagination.* Bloomington: Indiana University Press.

Haas, M. (1986). Evaluating social studies software for the microcomputer. *The Arkansas Social Studies Teacher, II,* (Spring), 10–14.

Huch, C., Hepler, S., & Hickman, J. (1987). *Children's literature in the elementary school,* (4th. ed.). New York: Holt, Rinehart & Winston.

Lawler, R. (1985). Designing computer-based microworlds. *Byte, 7*(8), 13–16.

Medeiros, R. (1990). Social studies: Simulations, databases, and more for classroom teaching. *Electronic Learning,* (January), 10, 40–42.

Muller, J. (1985) The great Logo adventure. *Computers in the schools,* (Summer/Fall), 2, 60–63.

Papert, S. (1980). *Mindstorms.* New York: Basic Books.

Price, R. (1991). *Computer-aided instruction: A guide for authors.* Pacific Grove, CA: Brooks/Cole.

Roessler, M. (1987). Students design a depression simulation. *Social Education, 51,* 48–51.

Rose, S., Brandhorst, A., Glenn, A., Hodges, J., & White, C. (1984). Social studies microcomputer courseware evaluation guidelines. *Social Education, 48,* 573–578.

Tipps, S. & Bull, G. (1985). Teachers need time for turtles: Planning for teacher development with Logo. *Computers in the schools,* (Summer/Fall), 2, 39–44.

Underwood, J. (1985). Cognitive demand and CAL. In I. Reid & J. Rushton (eds.), *Teachers, computers, and the classroom.* Manchester, England: Manchester University Press.

Weir, S. (1987). *Cultivating minds: A Logo casebook.* New York: Harper & Row.

White, C. (1987). Developing information-processing skills through structured activities with a computerized file management program. *Journal of Educational Computing Research, 3,* 355–375.

White, S. (1988). Computers in social studies classrooms. *ERIC Digest,* EDO-SO-88-5. Bloomington, IN: Clearinghouse for Social Studies/Social Science Education.

CHAPTER 9

OVERVIEW

When you hear the word *evaluation*, what do you first think of? You may think of one or more of the following: grades, passing or failing, tests. If you did, you are not unusual. Many people associate evaluation with nervousness, threat, and fear. However, evaluation should be seen in a positive light because of the important role it plays in helping students learn—by enabling adults to meet student needs. Your response to the question above may be a positive one. If it is, it will be somewhat easier for you to construct a view of social studies evaluation as a means of helping students learn. If it is negative, use this chapter to find ways evaluation can be made less threatening and more helpful to both students and teachers.

This chapter discusses the evaluation process in social studies and the types of assessment that can be used in the process. The emphasis is on utilizing a wide range of assessments. This range is important. Evaluation that recognizes students' developmental needs and that also recognizes that social studies involves working with processes, concepts, generalizations, values, and attitudes helps teachers plan lessons that promote meaningful learning and measures progress for a wider range of attainments. This chapter also discusses ways to remove stress and potential bias in evaluation to help get more accurate assessments of student learning.

Evaluating and Meeting Student Needs in Social Studies

OBJECTIVES

1. Describe the purpose of evaluation.
2. Differentiate informal evaluation from formal evaluation.
3. Describe how the progress of culturally diverse students with limited English proficiency can be evaluated.
4. Discuss how the progress of nonreaders can be evaluated.
5. Identify appropriate means for evaluating the progress of students in crisis.
6. Identify different disabilities students might have and suggest possible means for evaluating the progress of these students.
7. Explain actions teachers can take to obtain more valid measures of the knowledge of students from various ethnic backgrounds or students with learning disabilities.

WHAT IS EVALUATION?

Evaluation is defined, in this book, as the process of using information to make judgments about how effectively a program meets the needs of students. The evaluation process should tell us: what students' needs are, how well we have met those needs, and what we can change so that we will be better able to meet their needs. Evaluation in social studies looks particularly at students' understanding of their social world. The evaluation process in social studies should:

1. have a specific purpose
2. measure what it intends to measure (have validity)
3. be appropriate to lesson, unit, and course objectives
4. match students' characteristics
5. be continuous as students work toward mastering objectives (Sunal, 1990)

The evaluation process should be used to provide information with which the teacher can more effectively plan instruction for individuals and groups. It should also be used to collect information so that communication with parents can be based on documentation of students' work and how they do it.

Each evaluation serves one of two general purposes, formative and summative evaluation. Formative evaluation checks on how well students are doing while an activity or a unit is in progress. Formative evaluation tells a teacher whether students are accomplishing the objectives they are working toward or whether they need more review or application activities.

Formative evaluation begins with involving students in an exploration activity that diagnoses their prior learning. Sometimes a pretest is used to make such a diagnosis. Based on the students' exploration activities and/or a pretest, the teacher decides whether the next set of activities in a lesson is appropriate. Changes are made if it is evident students already know the ideas or skills that were to be taught. Changes are also made if students appear to have a lower level of knowledge or skills than anticipated. As the lesson progresses, teachers use practice activities to decide whether students are ready to move forward or if they need more explanations or even reteaching. Formative evaluation is used in units as well as in lessons. Within units it is used to decide whether students are ready for the material in a specific part of the unit. Throughout the year, teachers also use formative evaluation to determine whether students are ready for new units and when they have accomplished meaningful learning of the content of the current unit.

In summative evaluation, students' progress is examined at the end of an activity, unit, or other part of the curriculum. Summative evaluation is used to determine the level at which students have learned the processes and/or content on which they have been working. The summative evaluation helps the teacher decide whether students are ready to move on to the next part of the curriculum.

The evaluation process is accomplished through assessment. Assessment is the process of observing, recording, and otherwise documenting the work students do and *how* they do it. Evaluation is the process of interpreting that evidence and making judgements and decisions based on the assessment (Finkelstein, 1991).

PRINCIPLES THAT GUIDE EVALUATION AND ASSESSMENT

Appropriate evaluation involves regular and periodic assessments of each student in a wide variety of circumstances. These circumstances should represent the range of social studies activities the student is involved in. The assessments made of the student should rely on demonstrated performance during real activities, not only on skills testing. What students can do independently and what they can demonstrate with assistance both need to be assessed. When teachers assess what the student can do with assistance, they are examining the direction of growth of the student. Assessment utilizes a wide array of tools and a variety of processes. Among these are artwork, stories and informational writings, games, taped reading, systematic observation, records of conversations with parents, the student, and others, summaries of student progress as individuals and in groups, and teacher-made and other tests (Finkelstein, 1991).

The evaluation process should include self-evaluation by students. The student is ultimately responsible for learning. To make decisions that facilitate their own learning, students need to be aware of their strengths and weaknesses through self-evaluation. Decisions regarding how best to develop their abilities can be made once some skill in appropriate and accurate self-evaluation has been developed.

Evaluation and the assessment that supports it are essential components of the teacher's role. Students and parents are also a part of evaluation and assessment. The evaluation of assessment information should involve teachers, parents, and students. Both the evaluation process and the assessment procedures it uses should support a parent's relationship with the student and respect the language and culture of the family. Discussion of the information should lead to the development of a plan of action that will support the continued growth of the student's abilities. A regular process for information sharing between teachers, parents, and students about growth and development and school performance must be established. Letter or numerical grades alone are not enough of a report to parents. It is important to replace or accompany such information with more meaningful, descriptive information in narrative form. An example of a progress report form incorporating the principles that guide assessment and evaluation appears in Table 9–1 (Finkelstein, 1991). Overall, the evaluation process and the assessment procedures must support students' development and learning. They should not threaten students' feelings of self-esteem (Finkelstein, 1991).

Table 9–1

Progress Report Form: Social Studies

	Amount of Progress	Teacher Comments
	Low ⟷ High	

1. Concept understanding as evidenced in:
  a. writing
  b. speaking
  c. graphic expression
2. Problem-solving ability as evidenced in:
  a. participation in discussions
  b. participation in activities
  c. willingness to take risks
  d. suggesting unique solutions
  e. focused thinking
  f. seeing through problems to a solution
  g. making appropriate responses
3. Thinking-skill development as evidenced in:
  a. exhibiting creativity
  b. exhibiting logical thought processes
  c. grasping main idea
  d. vocabulary		

Source: Adapted from J. Finkelstein, "Appropriate assessment practices for early childhood/elementary social studies." Paper presented at the annual meeting of the National Council for the Social Studies, 1991, Washington, D.C.

TYPES OF ASSESSMENT USED IN THE EVALUATION PROCESS

The evaluation process can use informal or formal assessment. Formal means of evaluation include teacher-made and standardized tests. These tests can use multiple-choice items, matching items, true/false items, fill-in-the-blank items, or short essays. With students in the early elementary grades, formal tests are difficult to construct and are not widely used. Informal means of evaluation include observation, interviews, the collection of work samples, diaries and logs, quality circles, group self-evaluation, and performance testing. Informal and formal assessments are used in evaluating skills, content, and the affective area (see Table 9–2). Both informal and formal assessment can also be conducted using computers and are often written into software programs.

PRETESTING

It is important to utilize some form of pretesting before instruction. Pretesting can be done informally or formally. It helps the teacher determine what skills and/or ideas the students are bringing to a lesson with them. Both the general level of understanding among a group of students and individual levels of understanding can be determined through pretesting. Without pretesting, teachers are instructing blindly without knowing where students need help and where they already have appropriate understanding. Pretesting should occur in a situation similar to that which will be utilized to help students invent the skill or idea being taught. It is best accomplished as part of the exploration phase of a lesson, when students are confronted with an activity that requires them to use the skill or idea with some understanding.

INFORMAL EVALUATION

Informal evaluation involves collecting information in a structured environment without direct testing (see Table 9–2). In this type of evaluation, the teacher carefully selects the assessment used. The assessment situation is well organized but tailored to the individual student. Events occurring during such assessments are typically not highly structured nor easily predictable.

Table 9–2

Types of Assessment Used to Evaluate Objectives

	TYPE OF OBJECTIVE		
Type of Assessment	*Content*	*Process*	*Affective*
Formal			
Multiple choice	X		
Matching	X		
True/false	X		
Fill in blanks	X		
Short essay	X	X	X
Informal			
Observation			
Anecdotal records	X	X	X
Checklists	X	X	X
Interviews	X	X	X
Work samples	X	X	X
Portfolios	X	X	X
Diaries/logs	X	X	X
Group discussions	X	X	X
Quality circles	X	X	X
Role plays	X	X	X
Performance testing	X	X	X
Computer assisted	X	X	X

Note: The X indicates types of objectives that can be evaluated using each form of assessment.

OBSERVATION

Observation is probably used for informal evaluation more than any other type of assessment (Boehm & Weinberg, 1987). Teachers make observations of their students throughout the day for very short time periods, often less than a minute. Much of this spontaneous observation is not recorded. The teacher uses it for formative evaluation, to determine how an activity is going, or how a particular student is responding to an activity.

More structured observation happens when a teacher systematically observes a student at regular repeated intervals. The teacher sets up a schedule for observations. The schedule should be appropriate to the type of observation being made. If the focus is on a behavior that the teacher thinks may occur frequently, such as leaving the room to go to the bathroom, the teacher may note whether the student is present every 15 minutes or half hour. If the behavior is likely to occur at certain times of the day or during certain parts of a lesson, such as during a transition from one part of an activity to another part, the teacher may make systematic observations every 30 seconds or 60 seconds during this part of the lesson. In developing an observation schedule, the teacher should clearly identify what the purpose of the observation is. The schedule must be set up so that it will help the teacher make the desired observations. A schedule that requires too many observations is not realistic in terms of the time a teacher has available for observation; a schedule that results in too few observations prevents the teacher from obtaining the information needed to evaluate the student appropriately. The development of appropriate observation schedules takes expertise, which is acquired by trying out schedules and determining whether they result in the information needed.

Systematic observation is recorded as it is done. Classrooms are busy places, with lots of interruptions. If an observation is not recorded immediately it is likely that it will not be remembered accurately. A single incident that is outstanding in some way, although it is not typical of the student's behavior, is sooner remembered.

ANECDOTAL RECORDS

One method of recording observations is the anecdotal record. It lists the student's name, the date, the time of day a behavior occurred, and a description of the behavior observed. In describing the observed behavior, the teacher tries to be objective and does not draw any conclusions. (See Table 9–3 for an example of an anecdotal record.) Teachers can record anecdotes of any type of behavior. A series of anecdotal records, for example, can focus on behaviors that demonstrate cooperation, questioning, arguing, or decision making.

CHECKLISTS

Checklists often guide observations. These are lists of behaviors of interest to the teacher. They guide the observation because they enable the teacher to collect specific pieces of information. The teacher can observe more students when a check-

Table 9–3

A Teacher's Anecdotal Record

RECORD 1

Name: *Mikal*	Date/Time: *2/16*	*11:35*

Event:

Eduardo sat down with Angela and Mikal at their table. Angela said "OK, what do you want to do on this job we've got?" Eduardo said, "I'm good at making models, let's make a model of this place, the Parthenon." Mikal said, "That's crazy. It's too much work." Eduardo replied, "It won't be bad. I know how to do stuff like this and it'll be fun. Angela is a good drawer so she can make a drawing we can work from and she can do the background. You can build it with me and all of us can look up how big it was and other stuff we gotta know about it." Angela said, "Sounds good. Let's get started." Mikal said nothing for about thirty seconds, then said, "No, I never did a model and I don't want to do something I never did before. I like to do stuff I already did." Then Mikal got up and walked off and sat down with Tonya and Jeff and asked them what they were going to do for their job.

RECORD 2

Name: *Mikal*	Date/Time: *2/17*	*11:10*

Event:

Eduardo walked over to Mikal who was sitting alone, and said, "Yo, Mikal! Hey, you'd like to do a model once you got started on it. Come on over and Angela can show you the drawing she made. You could help us decide how much to do. Angela is fighting with me over it. She wants it to be really fancy. Maybe you could settle our fight." Mikal said, "I told you I didn't like to do stuff I don't know nothing about." Eduardo said, "OK, OK, I said you'd like it, but, well, so what else do you want to do?" Mikal said, "I thought we could do a play. But we don't have enough people. Costumes would be a pain to do. We would have to have some kind of background. OK. Let me see what Angela did, maybe I could try it." Both boys went over to where Angela was sitting and she explained her ideas.

list is used because the observation is usually shorter and less intensive. An example of a checklist appears in Table 9–4.

DIFFICULTIES WITH USING SYSTEMATIC OBSERVATION

In a typical class of twenty or more students, it is often difficult for a teacher to use checklists and anecdotal records systematically. When a teacher is actively involved with students, it is not always possible to mentally stop and make a careful observation of a student. With careful planning, a teacher can identify times when it is likely that systematic observation can be carried out. One such time is during individual study or practice sessions, when a teacher can move freely among students. Such observations should be designed to require little time. A checklist will be helpful. Checklists are also very useful with small groups of students as they are working. If used immediately following work with a group, they

Table 9–4

Sample Economics Education Checklist for the Study of Wants and Needs

ACTIVITY: STUDENT:	Glenn	Dick	Terry	Francine	Mimi
Needs					
1. Identifies food as a need	X	X	X	X	X
2. Identifies shelter as a need	X	X	X	X	X
Wants					
3. Identifies a television set as a want	X		X		
4. Identifies roller skates as a want	X	X	X	X	X
5. Prioritizes wants	X	X	X	X	X
6. Develops a time line for obtaining the item prioritized as #1 on the wants list	X	X	X	X	

are more accurate and can be completed rapidly. Anecdotal records often are best used with a student about whom the teacher has concerns. They enable the teacher to get a picture of the behavior of a single student or of a few students once several systematic observations of behavior have been made.

All observers should try to be aware of personal biases they have. Each of us has different levels of tolerance for various situations. We need to be aware of our attitudes toward distracting behaviors and what we consider to be "good" manners. Such student behaviors as repetitive question asking, very fast responses, or very slow responses may affect our ratings of students. A "violent outburst" of anger to one observer might be seen as "fairly normal for a student of this age" by another observer (Good & Brophy, 1990). Bias can be related to the observer's sex, race, age, cultural or ethnic identity, or theoretical perspective (behaviorist, Piagetian, etc.). The bias the observer has can put a student's actions in a favorable light or an unfavorable one dependent on the student's sex, race, or other characteristics (Boehm & Weinberg, 1987). Bias can also be introduced into an observation when the student is aware of being observed. Such awareness often results in a change of behavior. Finally, bias can be introduced by the type of observation procedure used. For example, a checklist may not match the purpose of the observation. Or the observation procedure may be too complicated, which can introduce error into the observation.

INTERVIEWS

Another structured evaluation form is the interview. The most common interview usually involves one student talking with one adult. The interviewer should have a list of prepared questions or topics to guide the interview. If the interviewer follows the list, the required information will be collected. In Table 9–5 an example

Table 9–5

Interview Guide on Hausa Culture

Interviewer: (Introduces the student to what will follow.) "We've been exploring Hausa culture in West Africa. Since everybody has been following up different parts of Hausa culture, I wanted to talk to you about what you have found out."

1. "What part of the culture did you decide to explore?"
2. "Can you tell me what you think is the most interesting thing you have found out?"
3. "Do you think this is really important for everyone to know, or is it something that is interesting but not something everyone should know? Why?"
4. "What are three things you have found out that you should share with everyone in this class because you think everyone should know them? Why?"
5. "If we think about these three important things, do you think we will decide that they are not very different from what we have here in our culture, or will we decide that they are really different? Why?"

of an interview guide is given. The interviewer should not comment or offer information unless it is necessary to restate or otherwise clarify a question. The interviewer's primary role is that of listener. Student responses should be recorded either in writing, on a tape recording, or on a checklist. Since interviews often provide a lot of information, it is easy to forget some of it if it is not recorded quickly. The recording method should not be threatening to the student. A tape-recorded interview might be played back to the student a couple of times during the interview. If a student is nervous or does not feel like talking, it is best to stop and try again at another time. For some topics, having younger students draw a response or act it out may serve as a method of getting longer responses and therefore more data. Because interviews often provide lots of information, the adult should review notes of the interview, organize, and summarize them soon after they are completed. Delay makes summarization a huge task and often introduces errors.

WORK SAMPLES

Student work samples collected on a regular basis enable a teacher to look for changes in the amount and kind of information or detail expressed, attitudes expressed, vocabulary, concept development or restructuring and general ability to express ideas (see Table 9–6). Samples can include products from a variety of assignments such as artwork, language experience stories, poems, paragraphs, practice work, and summary reports. Very young students often do not want the teacher to keep their work; they want to take it home. When this happens the teacher may want to make photocopies. Or the teacher might ask students to place work samples in a student-decorated special folder that is given to parents periodically. Many teachers have students make a booklet during social studies units that records and reflects the students' progress in learning about the topic. Work samples can give teachers a wide variety of information. It is helpful to focus examination of work

Table 9–6

Student Work Samples

PROJECT:

WORK SAMPLE 1

I like to work with my hands. I don't know what I can do as a job when I am grown up. I don't think I need to graduate high school. My Pop didn't graduate high school. He has a good job. He works on trucks for a long distance driving company. He is always working. He never gets laid off. We always got lots of food and a roof over our heads. I have toys and games I want. My Pop wants me to graduate high school but I don't know if it's important.

WORK SAMPLE 2

The trip to the vo tech school was interesting. I really liked the Autocad classes. I guess the other kind of drafting is old. The new stuff on computer looks great. I guess I need to know some stuff, some math and stuff to be really good on the Autocad. My Pop said I should take Autocad because that is where jobs will be when I am grown up. I also liked the Xerox repairman. I never thought about jobs like that or repairing computers. I like to work with my hands and that's the kind of jobs that there should be lots of when I'm grown up. Those men that repair computers and Xerox machines said I will need to graduate high school. I guess maybe the old days when you could get a job if you were good with your hands but didn't graduate high school are gone.

WORK SAMPLE 3

I am writing this on the word processor. I really like to use it because my handwriting is lousy and what I write looks a lot better when it's printed out. Also, I should know how to use word processors and other kinds of computers because if you look around you lots of people use them in all kinds of jobs. I went to the car parts store with my Pop on Saturday and they had a computer there. It had all the parts in it, how many they had, and their price. The man said he was surprised a kid like me was so interested in how they had their information laid out on the screen. He said, when I get in high school, to look him up because he likes to hire kids who know something about computers to work for him part time. I'm beginning to get a pretty big list of classes I want to take because I should know this stuff and it's fun besides. They will keep me busy. I probably have got more classes I want to take than I can fit in my high school schedule. I guess it might not be so hard to fill it up and before I know it I will graduate high school.

samples by listing specific items of interest before examining the samples. A teacher might be interested, for example, in focusing on a student's knowledge of map skills or in identifying the attitudes a student seems to hold in regard to an issue.

PORTFOLIOS

An increasingly popular method of evaluating older students is through the use of a portfolio. Students develop their own portfolios. They select the samples of their work on which they will be evaluated and present it. A portfolio contains a variety of works to demonstrate the range of knowledge and skills (see Fig. 9–1). Typically students select samples of what they believe to be their best work. Teachers of younger students can incorporate this form of evaluation by providing stu-

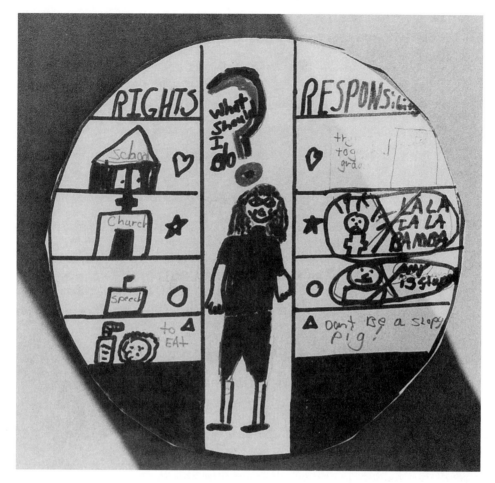

Figure 9–1   A student's drawing can be part of a portfolio.

dents with opportunities to select products from some of the assignments to be included in the portfolio. Or teachers can provide young students with a list of required types of assignments to be included.

DIARIES AND LOGS

Students often have had experience in keeping diaries and logs, particularly if they have been taught with the whole language approach. Individual diaries can be used in which a student is asked to write about social studies. Leading questions can be provided such as:
• What did you like best in social studies today?
• What did you like least in social studies today?
• What do you think was the most important thing you learned?

- What confused you or bored you?
- What else do you want to mention?

Students can write in their diaries daily, weekly, or at other intervals. They should be encouraged, but not required, to respond to all the questions. Responses not directly relating to the questions, but relating to social studies, should also be encouraged. Length of response should not be important. A log is similar to a diary but is usually a form that students fill out (see Figure 9–2). A log can be kept on a daily basis or less frequently. It is an effective way for students to sum up what they liked or did not like about a lesson or a unit and what they learned or did not learn.

Groups can use both diaries and logs to keep track of their work. These formats can help members evaluate how well their planning process went, how well their plans worked out, and what they will do next. Diaries and logs can serve as the basis for discussion in class when students use them as notes for evaluating their own work and the social studies program.

It is important to remember that students often use diaries, and sometimes logs, to express very private feelings. When encouraging students to use diaries and logs to evaluate work in a group or in other ways in which the content of the writing becomes public, it is important to use caution, since students should not feel their privacy is being violated. If the diary or log is going to be read by the teacher, or shared in any other way, students should be aware of this before they are encouraged to write in it. The teacher should request permission before reading students' entries aloud.

QUALITY CIRCLES

Quality circles provide an opportunity for groups to evaluate activities they have been involved in and to plan future work. Four or five students might use notes from diaries and logs to evaluate their activities and identify what might be the most successful means to use in accomplishing their objectives for future work. The groups need questions to guide their evaluation and planning. These might include:

- What do we do well?
- What are our weaknesses?
- When do we have problems? or When don't we work well together?
- What can we do to solve these problems?
- What can each one of us do to improve?

GROUP SELF-EVALUATION

Evaluation should always be a part of group work. Students can use a checklist and group discussion to evaluate work periods, group cooperation, data sources, study skills, and information-gathering activities (see Table 9–7) as well as the progress of their plan. Teachers should provide sets of questions to guide the group in evaluating itself or to help an individual student evaluate her own work

Name: _____ Date: _____

What I liked best in social studies this week:
_____

What I liked least in social studies this week:
_____

The most important thing I learned in social studies this week:
_____

Something else I would like to say:
_____
_____
_____

Name: _____ Date: _____

I liked: 😊
_____
_____

I didn't like: ☹️
_____
_____

The most special: 😌
_____
_____

My own idea: 😊
_____
_____
_____

Figure 9–2   Written and drawn social studies logs.

and the group's work (see Tables 9–7 and 9–8). The teacher should encourage students to summarize and, as appropriate, review planned strategies and the time line for carrying out work. As students identify things they have done well and identify problems, they should also suggest and record ways of correcting their problems. These should be discussed with the teacher. Any recommendations

Table 9–7

Sample Group Discussion Checklist

TOPIC:

STUDENT:	Eric	Melba	Patrice
1. Has materials prepared for discussion Notes:	X	X	X
2. Participates appropriately in discussion Notes:	X	X	
3. Demonstrates leadership Notes:	X	X	X
4. Contributes to assignment of tasks Notes:	X	X	X
5. Contributes to planning for next activity Notes:		X	X

Table 9–8

Questions for Evaluating and Guiding Group and Independent Study

SUGGESTED QUESTIONS FOR SELF-EVALUATION OF GROUP WORK

1. Did the group get to work promptly?
2. Did we understand our task?
3. Did everyone in the group have the opportunity to share their opinions and ideas?
4. Did everyone participate?
5. Did we wander off the topic at hand to other things?
6. Did we offer facts and experiences to help in solving problems?
7. Were disagreements settled through compromise with the agreement of all of us?
8. Did we seek help from each other when needed?
9. Did we listen to each other?
10. Did we seek clarification from the teacher only when we didn't understand or could not solve the problem on our own?

SUGGESTIONS FOR AN INDIVIDUAL'S SELF-EVALUATION OF THE GROUP AND OF THE INDIVIDUAL'S OWN PARTICIPATION IN THE GROUP

1. Did you have enough chance to express your ideas and information about the topic?
2. Were you happy during the group work?
3. What would have made you happier during the group work?
4. Did anyone seem to do most of the group's work?
5. Who in the group listens to you?
6. Who in the group doesn't listen to you?
7. Did anything bother you during the discussions? If so, what was it?
8. What should the group do to improve its functioning?
9. Considering your abilities, assigned tasks, effort, and contributions, what grade do you think you should receive?
10. Use the criteria in #9 and grade each member of your group.

should be listed and saved. The next time the class works on a similar project, the teacher should review these points as a reminder to the students of the desired behaviors they need to use to continue being successful or to improve upon their skills. With very young students the teacher may want to lead such evaluations with the entire class. Older and more experienced students may perform such evaluations in small groups. The cooperative learning strategies discussed in chapter 7 utilize group evaluation as part of the teaching/learning process. Group self-evaluation is important in cooperative learning but can also be used in classrooms that do not utilize these strategies.

PERFORMANCE TESTING

In performance testing, students are asked to perform a skill they have learned or to apply a concept in a new situation (see chapter 3). A performance test occurs, for example, when a student is asked to identify cardinal directions when standing in the school cafeteria after having practiced identifying them outside.

A lesson, or a series of activities within a lesson or set of lessons, may serve as an evaluation. The student performance being evaluated may be the ability to participate in a group discussion, to plan out the steps needed to complete a project, to list materials needed for an activity, to make decisions regarding which of several activities has first priority and must be finished first, to formulate hypotheses that can be tested, or to organize data collected using a charting format, etc. Since many social studies activities cannot be completed without students' applying learned skills and knowledge, the successful completion of social studies lessons and projects can serve as a form of evaluation. Among the specific tasks and projects that have this possibility are role playing, writing assignments, simulations, displays, and models. In addition to grading the products of a lesson, each student can also be given a set of questions requiring a description of the skills and steps used in completing the project.

FORMAL EVALUATION

TEACHER-MADE TESTS

Evaluation using teacher-made tests was introduced in chapter 3. Production and/or recognition items were discussed. Teacher-made tests can be performance assessment tests that are either manipulative or paper and pencil. When paper-and-pencil tests are constructed, multiple-choice, matching, true-and-false, fill-in-the-blanks, or short essay items can be used. With very young students, a version of the short essay test can be given by asking students to dictate language experience stories related to social studies activities they have been involved in. Primary-grade students often can write and illustrate short essays related to social studies content. The other types of items must be carefully constructed and can focus on either production or recognition. Useful resources for information on constructing test items are Good and Brophy (1990), *Educational Psychology*

How is this activity involving these students in performance testing?

(4th ed.) and Thorndike and Hagen (1991), *Measurement and Evaluation in Psychology and Education* (5th ed.).

All test items should be written to reflect the objectives of the units and lessons. Questions for knowledge objectives are the easiest to construct. Testing process skill objectives requires that new data be provided for the student to use in answering the question. It is possible to measure attitudes, but giving grades for attitudes in a nation that supports freedom of thought is not appropriate. It should be noted that many value and moral objectives will be shared in a society and that, through discussion, students will tend to come to common answers. Tolerance for the validity of different points of view should be underlined. As part of the discussion, the teacher should ask probing questions concerning why students believe as they do. The purpose of such questioning is to assist students in identifying logical consequences and illogical statements and to help students determine what the world would be like if everyone behaved in this way.

In designing a teacher-made test that accurately assesses whether students have learned what was taught, it is important to carry out several tasks. The teacher must have clear, written objectives for a unit before beginning the unit. The objectives should be matched to the content of the unit's lessons to make certain that each objective is actually addressed in the unit. These objectives are rewritten if they change as the lessons are taught. Then, before writing test items, the teacher prioritizes the objectives, deciding which are the focus of the unit and which are of less weight in it. Those objectives that are most heavily focused on should be more strongly represented in the test. Finally, the teacher decides what type or combination of types of questions will be used in the test and writes the test items. Guidelines for writing appropriate social studies essay and objective test items follow.

Essay Questions. Guidelines for writing social studies essay questions are:
- Decide what process skills you want students to use before you write any questions.
- Write essay questions with clear tasks. (For example, have students describe steps in completing an activity.)
- Write essay questions that require more than repeating information.
- Use only a few questions, and make sure they require answers that are not lengthy.
- Make sure the questions vary in difficulty.
- Give clear directions. (Students should know whether an answer should be in outline form or paragraphs, its point value on the test, and what criteria will be used to evaluate answers.) (Good & Brophy, 1990)

Objective Test Questions. Social studies objective test questions should ask students to respond to important content. Guidelines for such objective questions are:
- The question must present a problem.
- The question should be as short as possible.
- Answer choices should be short.
- The question should use the negative infrequently and make it noticeable by underlining the *not* when it is used.
- There should be only one correct or clearly best answer.
- All answer choices should be plausible.
- A particular response should not be longer than the others since this suggests it is the answer. (Good & Brophy, 1990)

STANDARDIZED TESTS

Many general achievement tests contain social studies items. Examples of such tests are the Iowa Every-Pupil Test of Basic Skills, the Metropolitan Achievement Tests, the Tests of Basic Experiences—Social Studies, the Stanford Achievement Test, and the SRA Achievement Series. The Primary Social Studies Test (Grades 1–3) is a standardized test that has been developed just for social studies. The Buros *Mental Measurement Yearbook,* found in college and university libraries, describes these and other tests. The *Social Studies Evaluation Sourcebook* (Superka, Vigliani, & Hedstrom,1978) is another source of information about tests.

Teachers can use standardized tests to compare a student's performance with the performance of other students who are the same age. Such a comparison is part of norm-referenced testing. These tests are standardized or normed on a sample of students representing the total population of students in the country.

Some states use tests they have developed to match statewide objectives or learning outcomes for social studies. These are criterion-referenced tests. They test students' learning against a criterion, the statewide objectives for social studies. These are standardized on the student population in that state.

Criterion-referenced tests designed to measure the specific curriculum taught should result in a better evaluation of what students have learned than would a norm-referenced test, which is likely to test material not taught. Unfortunately, some tests ask students factual questions that depend on simple memorization of what might be minor content. Teachers need to examine the content of the questions on both norm-referenced and criterion-referenced standardized tests to determine whether the content that was taught is being tested and whether the test items are measuring meaningful learning. In some states, the test used may contain very few, if any, social studies questions. Typically these tests most heavily examine learning in language arts and reading, have a secondary focus on mathematics and spend the least time on social studies and science. This test is of little help in evaluating students' social studies learning. This type of test is also dangerous because it tends to lead teachers away from placing importance on appropriate and comprehensive evaluation of social studies learning. Teachers need to understand the problems that result from standardized testing and its limitations. If standardized tests are used, they should be just one component of a more comprehensive program of assessment and evaluation.

It is interesting to note that California is eliminating use of its California Achievement Tests. Instead, two to three students will be randomly selected out of a classroom, interviewed, and given tasks to accomplish over a half-day period. The interviews and tasks will focus on thinking skills. This will allow for a form of evaluation that is informal in approach yet has some statewide standards. It will reduce the stress that students often feel when everyone is tested at the same time on a test that obviously is different from teacher-made tests.

Standardized tests are typically given late in the school year as a form of summative evaluation. They summarize student achievement and are often used in planning a student's placement in the next school year. These tests may be used to evaluate how well a school has taught social studies in comparison to other schools in the school system or state.

COMPUTER-ASSISTED EVALUATION

Computers can assist in evaluation by:

1. directly testing students
2. involving them in simulations that require them to use problem-solving skills, decision-making skills, and knowledge
3. setting up a situation that students can explore and then react to later

Some software programs such as *World Atlas Action* by DLM Software incorporate elements that enable teachers to write their own questions to assess student learning as a result of program activities or to write questions in addition to those available with the program. This software also provides a summary of student responses for teacher use. Not all software has this flexibility, but many have sets of questions that may be appropriate for evaluating a particular student or group of students. Another type of software that may be used in evaluation is that represented by *On The Playground* by Tom Snyder Productions. This program is used by a group of students. The students set up criteria that they will use to make decisions in a problem setting determined by the computer. After working through the problem situation, the students, with the help of the program, decide how well they adhered to the criteria they had set up. Some software such as Test Generator 3.2 by COMpress and Test Maker by Bertamax are designed to be used for writing objective tests. As teachers explore available software they should consider its use in evaluation as well as its ability to meet the needs of individual students and of the class as a whole.

EVALUATING THE ACCOMPLISHMENT OF AFFECTIVE OBJECTIVES

Important affective objectives in social studies education include the development of interests in particular topics, attitudes toward individuals and groups, and values. Interests are preferences for particular activities (Nunnally, 1967). Attitudes concern feelings about specific people, organizations, social institutions, government agencies, and so on (Eichelberger, 1989). Attitudes are generally categorized as negative or positive. Values deal with preference for "life goals" and "ways of life." The social studies values are often encountered in studying issues relating to economics, politics and government, morality, and religion (Eichelberger, 1989). Long-lasting beliefs or a preference for a capitalistic economic system versus socialism are values, preferences, or judgments. Moral values are those that consider right versus wrong actions. For example, a person may hold the moral value that honesty in government is essential.

Affective objectives are frequently measured by using one of three paper-and-pencil self-reporting formats. One of these formats is the self report, in which the student responds to statements such as the following:

"Television commercials are a positive force in United States society today."

"I strongly agree."   "I agree."   "I'm not sure."   "I disagree."   "I strongly disagree."

This statement relates directly to a person's attitude toward television commercials. A first criterion for developing such a statement is to write it so that it relates directly to the particular attitude, interest, or value that is being assessed. A second criterion is that the statement must differentiate among the levels of interest, attitude, or value that various people might have. Several statements can be given to students in this format, enabling the teacher to evaluate whether an affective objective has been achieved. A second self-report format asks students to complete a sentence such as

"I like television commercials that. . . ."

This format results in a wider range of answers but also limits to just a few the number of statements that can be used. A third format includes asking students to prioritize choices or alternatives by rank ordering several items, by positioning them on a continuum, or by choosing between either-or positions.

Additional methods using quite different formats to determine whether an affective objective has been accomplished include observing of students; reviewing diaries and logs; using values clarification strategies (discussed in chapter 10); and setting up discussions, group work situations, and role plays.

IMPACT OF MULTICULTURAL FACTORS AND LIMITED ENGLISH PROFICIENCY ON EVALUATION

Students who are culturally diverse and/or limited English speakers need teachers who hold high expectations for their success and who serve as their advocates. When teachers analyze an individual's problems, they need to avoid blaming the student; instead they must consider some of the social, political, and economic variables that can affect the student's progress in social studies. Learning about students' cultural backgrounds can result in a better evaluation of student performance, instructional methods, and curriculum (see also chapter 14).

North American students bring to the classroom richly diverse cultural backgrounds. Each teacher brings to the classroom a personal background that is likely to be somewhat different from that of the students. The teacher's personal background influences both expectations and evaluation of student performance and behavior. Students bring their culture to school with them. Teachers need to avoid evaluating the culture instead of the student. Standardized tests typically reflect the mainstream culture. Teacher-made tests will reflect the teacher's culture, which is often the mainstream culture. As a result, formal evaluations do not appropriately evaluate all students. Informal evaluation measures can more appropriately evaluate students with differing cultural backgrounds—but may also show biases.

As students are evaluated it is important to understand their different cultural backgrounds. Some cultures place more emphasis on working as part of a group and some place more value on being the most successful member of a group. In some cultures there is more concern with social development than with academic performance. Some cultures value behavior that is quiet and unquestioning while others value curiosity and talkativeness. Some prefer assertiveness and even boastfulness while others look down on these traits. Some value seatwork and some value active interchanges between students. Of course, every member of a cultural group will not display the same characteristics nor hold the same values. To assume that this is true is a form of stereotyping. However, each culture does have dominant values. Teachers should try to get to know each of their students well.

Part of getting to know your students includes learning about the dominant values of the culture they represent. When a society includes many different cultural groups, it is likely that a teacher will have students whose cultural background differs from that of the teacher. Teachers need to visit libraries, talk to school district personnel, read local newspapers, and actively search out sources that will provide information on the dominant values of the cultures their students represent. This will enable the teacher to provide evaluation techniques that better assure an accurate measure of what the student has learned in class. Students need to learn to function in the dominant culture as well as in their own. Accurate evaluation helps a teacher identify which skills a student needs to develop in order to accomplish this task.

Cultural traits combined with limited English proficiency can have strongly negative consequences for students in school. There is evidence that students with limited English proficiency are often placed at the wrong grade level. Olsen (1988) reports that 40 percent of the immigrant students he surveyed believed they were placed at the wrong grade level. Such placements are often based solely on age and English proficiency. Language minority students are often misplaced because, on average, they require five to seven years to approach grade norms in English academic skills, yet show peer-appropriate second language conversational skills within about two years of arrival. Their teachers may advance them on the basis of their interactional skills in English rather than their ability to handle specific academic coursework successfully (Scarcella, 1990, p. 147).

Research studies with students who have limited English proficiency and with culturally diverse students for whom English is their native language suggests that they should be tested in multiple settings, since they often behave differently in various settings or with different partners (Scarcella, 1990; Olsen, 1988). Observational evaluation is important. Students can be observed both in the classroom and on the playground or in the lunchroom. Teachers should give them an opportunity to be evaluated through observation while they are involved in group assignments, group projects, and individual work. Performance, nonverbal tests, and tests involving mostly numbers need a minimum of verbal skills and may reflect these students' social studies learnings better than verbal tests.

Many times these students will need to be taught to be testwise. First, many may not realize that tests are an important part of their evaluation. Second, they need to be taught test-taking skills, such as how to cope with a timed standardized test and how to fill in blanks on an answer sheet. While these are skills all students need to learn, it can be expected that many language minority students and culturally diverse students have a cultural background that has not prepared them to understand either the role of testing or the behaviors it requires.

Sometimes direct question/answer paper-and-pen questions get little information from African-American students because these students associate hostility with direct questions (Gay & Abrahams, 1983). Another type of problem arises when students come across a typographical or other error in a test. Language minority students are often confused and leave this part of the test blank while many American students would quickly ask the teacher about it. The language minority student is often so unsure of what is appropriate in the testing situation that it does not occur to him or her to ask the teacher about an error found in a test. These students usually need information about the types of behaviors expected during tests. They often find explicit instruction, models, and practice tests helpful.

Timed tests often cause students anxiety. Many African-American and Hispanic students reportedly score poorly on timed essay exams because they have little experience with strict time limitations (Scarcella, 1990). Some specific test formats, such as multiple-choice tests, may temporarily confuse students even when they have been given instructions explaining what multiple-choice questions require (Scarcella, 1990). To avoid these problems teachers should allow students extra time, should familiarize them with the test formats they will encounter in their class, and should allow them to take practice exams.

Teachers need to be aware of bias in the vocabulary and pictures used in assessment procedures. Immigrant students are unlikely to be familiar with historical events and people in the United States such as Thanksgiving, Daniel Boone, pioneers, and astronauts. They are also unlikely to be familiar with vocabulary words relating to:

- some occupations, such as baking (since ovens may not be used in their first culture)
- vehicles (trains and garbage trucks may be unfamiliar to them)
- sports (they may never have seen hockey or surfing)
- musical instruments (e.g., guitar, drums, accordion, or harmonica)
- nursery rhymes (Twinkle, Twinkle Little Star)
- children's stories (*Cinderella, The Three Bears*) (Cheng, 1987)

Pictures used in assessment procedures can also be misunderstood. Cargill (1987) reports that a picture of a child smiling is often interpreted by Asian students as a child being embarrassed, confused, or even angry while teachers in the United States interpret it as a child being happy (p. 1).

Teachers may also misinterpret behaviors expressed by students during interviews. For example, most Asians nod their heads during an interview, giving the impression that they clearly understand what is being said. This is a gesture of courtesy and may not indicate that the individual actually understands what is being said (Cheng, 1987, p. 120). When using an interview, a teacher needs to check frequently to see that the student understands the questions and to provide examples. Teachers also need to encourage feedback from students, keep the environment relaxed, nonthreatening and comfortable, and avoid eye contact if the student's culture views it as threatening (Scarcella, 1990, p. 153).

Oral presentations, including show-and-tell sharing by very young students and the more formal oral reports of older students, often limit some students. These students come from homes where the conversational structure may be quite different from the tight and explicit oral presentation used in the white, middle-class culture and expected in classrooms. For example, African-American students may relate topics loosely, as they would in their own homes (Michaels, 1981). Their presentation may move off on tangents and seem to be disorganized, yet the teacher will find that the topic is addressed if careful attention is given to what the student is saying. Students, especially those from diverse cultural backgrounds, need specific information about teacher expectations and grading criteria. The teacher should provide models of successful oral presentations they are required to make and opportunities for students to practice in a nonthreatening environment before giving their formal presentation.

Writing skills are taught to be used in content areas like the social studies, so teachers need to pay attention to them. Students with limited English proficiency and/or culturally diverse backgrounds should be encouraged to write. Often their writing skills are weak. Teachers should not overlook providing writing opportunities if writing skills are to improve. A solution that seems to work well is to give two grades—one for content and the other for writing skills.

The teacher needs to consider many factors, and to use a wide range of strategies, if culturally diverse and/or limited English speaking students are to be appropriately evaluated. Ongoing evaluation is important with these students if they are to be full participants in the social studies program. Their full participation, in turn, will enrich the program as these students add new elements to it from their heritage. It is also important if the social studies program is to help them succeed in the dominant culture so that they can earn a living and have access to the opportunities afforded by our economic and political system.

EVALUATING NONREADERS

Many of the considerations suggested in reference to students with limited English proficiency are appropriate for evaluating nonreaders. These students have even greater limitations because they cannot read written material, nor can they respond in writing. Many will respond well to tape-recorded questions and situations. They can listen to a question or a situation and tape their response. This works particularly well with older students who often like responding via a machine—it can be private, and it makes them feel like they are in command of the situation.

Many means of informal evaluation are also appropriate for nonreading students. These include interviews, group discussion, role plays, drawings, quality circles, performance testing, tape-recorded diaries, checklists, and anecdotal records.

EVALUATING STUDENTS IN CRISIS

Students who are in crisis situations, experiencing a serious illness, dealing with loss from a death or a divorce in their family, suffering from the effects of having a parent out of work for a long time, or experiencing emotional stress or physical abuse often respond best to informal evaluation methods. Formal testing often increases the stress in these students' lives. The time limits, answer sheets where circles are filled in with a pencil, and stilted language in questions are examples of characteristics often found in formal testing that are likely to induce stress. Informal evaluation methods are less likely to place additional stress on students. These methods can be more easily modified to deal with a withdrawn student and with one who is acting aggressively. As efforts are made to relieve stress and to help students cope, students will gradually adjust and begin to display age-appropriate behaviors again. Continual evaluation in a variety of formats helps teachers provide support to the student when it is needed. Teachers need to maintain individual contact with each student and as much as possible with each student's family in order to be aware of a potential crisis. Students do not always share these crises, so that a teacher who does not make an effort to build good communication with both students and their families may not be aware of the difficulties a student is facing.

EVALUATING STUDENTS WITH DISABILITIES

Students with many different types of disabilities will be participating in the social studies program. An excellent discussion of possible disabling conditions and of adapting curriculum and evaluation procedures for various conditions is given by Cook, Tessier, and Armbruster (1987). Mainstreaming disabled students in social studies programs has been discussed by Herlihy and Herlihy (*Mainstreaming the Social Studies*, Washington, D.C.: National Council for the Social Studies,1980). This book is a good resource for ideas on adapting the social studies program to students with special needs and on evaluating their progress in achieving social studies objectives. Many students with disabilities do well in the regular social studies program and need only minimal changes in the evaluation procedures used. Hearing- or speech-impaired students can often draw or write out responses to questions if they have difficulty with oral communication. A visually-impaired student will often be able to respond verbally to questions or to a tape-recorded evaluation measure.

It is important to remember that students often expend extra energy in overcoming limitations imposed by their disabling condition. They tire more quickly than do most students because they put in this extra effort. Evaluation methods must take the fatigue factor into account, as well as the shorter attention spans that result from fatigue. It can also be expected that, like any other student, these students may become nervous, highly active, or grouchy as they tire. Informal evaluation methods often more easily take into account the special needs and quicker fatigue probability of disabled students. When formal evaluation methods are used they should be used in shorter periods that are spread out over a longer than usual time. Standardized tests unfortunately do not often provide extra time or make other accommodations in their testing procedures for students with diagnosed disabilities. Teachers should check with developers or with those in charge of the testing program in their school district to find out whether extra time can be given to these students.

The regular classroom teacher needs to work closely with special education personnel to evaluate student progress and to adapt evaluation procedures and materials to student needs. All students receiving special education services in the United States will have an Individualized Educational Program (IEP). The IEP includes:

- an evaluation of the student's present level of achievement
- long- and short-range goals for the student
- specific services that will be provided for the student
- information concerning the student's level of participation in the regular school program
- a timetable for reevaluating the student's progress

Specific social studies goals are not always addressed in IEPs. If not, the goals that are given in each student's IEP must be considered and social studies objectives related to these goals developed. Reference texts such as those cited above by Herlihy and Herlihy (1980) and Cook, Tessier, and Armbruster (1987) should be helpful in this process. An overview of the types of disabling conditions and their implications for evaluation follows.

MENTAL RETARDATION

Students with some mental retardation usually are more immature than their peers. They lag behind in development, have a shorter attention span than their peers, become frustrated with a task more quickly, have poorer language skills, form friendships with younger children, and are less socially able than their peers. When assessed, these students need shorter tasks where they work with many concrete examples. Computer software provides opportunities for these students to be involved in drill and practice activities at their own pace. Their progress as they use such programs can be monitored and used in evaluation. Research studies have indicated that these students do not use computers as much as do gifted students, yet they benefit from such opportunities. Talking about what they are doing and how they did something is important. Evaluation should not rely on their verbal, reading, and writing skills. It should focus on their use of a skill or concept in a new situation. For example, if a student with mental retardation has been involved in activities that teach the concept of an assembly line through making and packaging chocolate chip cookies for sale in the school cafeteria, the student might be asked to plan an assembly line for making another product, such as pizza.

VISUAL IMPAIRMENT

Students with major visual impairments are usually identified before they come into the classroom. Students with minor visual impairments, for example nearsightedness, may not have been identified or may develop the impairment during the school year. A student who shows little interest in an event across the street from the school may be seeing just a blur. A student who squints a lot, rubs his eyes, tilts his head to one side, complains of headaches or nausea after close work, or has poor eye–hand coordination should be referred for vision testing. Those visually impaired students whose eyesight cannot be corrected to nearly normal with eyeglasses or other techniques do need some special arrangements.

Arrange the classroom so that the visually impaired student does not easily bump into things. Accompany written directions with verbal instruction. Use maps and globes with raised contours and other learning aids with surfaces that can be felt. Visually impaired students should have individual student atlases or maps in front of them rather than having to view things on a distant wall map. The visually impaired student can benefit from working in pairs and small teams with normally sighted students. Rotate leadership so that the visually impaired student has opportunities to work in a variety of roles. Praise and reinforcement are important. Independence must be fostered through making reasonable demands on the student. For example, if students are asked to describe areas shown on a map, the visually impaired student should work with a raised-contour map, or with a map produced by his or her team where yarn is glued to a flat map creating a raised outline of the map's features. Evaluation can utilize information about the student's progress acquired through tape recordings made by the student, teacher observation of the student at work, student constructions, and project work and cooperative efforts between the student and other members of a team.

HEARING IMPAIRMENT

Students with hearing impairments may also have language development delay as a result of their disabling condition. Hearing impairment is a condition that is not always quickly identified. It is sometimes confused with mental retardation because of the language delay that may be involved. A student with a hearing impairment may not speak clearly and may have a reduced vocabulary compared to his peers because he is not hearing some sounds. Testing for hearing impairment should be considered if a student has poor speech, speaks very loudly or very softly, or is reluctant to speak. It is also a possibility if a student does not respond when spoken to or says "what?" or turns his or her head toward the speaker, looks intently at the speaker's face, or has a short attention span when spoken to but works well at visual and tactile tasks. Students who complain of earaches or pain in the head around the ear or down the neck may also have hearing impairment.

Seat the student so that others' faces are visible. Use many visuals such as overhead transparencies. Sign language should also be used if the student understands it. Make sure both you and the students speak clearly in a normal voice. Exaggerated or overly slow speech will be hard for the hearing-impaired student to understand. Identify key words and phrases in activities and write them on the chalkboard or overhead transparencies. Point to the word when you refer to it. List student responses on the board so students answer questions. Have students work in pairs or small teams and take turns being the leader. Activities using concrete materials are important because they present opportunities for the student to learn new vocabulary and to interact verbally with others. Even seriously hearing impaired students will often have some residual hearing and will be aware of some sounds. They will also feel sound as vibrations—perhaps you have noticed being able to feel music or crowd noise vibrating right through your bones. When evaluating the hearing-impaired student, focus on visual formats and do not depend heavily on specialized vocabulary since hearing-impaired students may acquire it more slowly than will other students. These students can often communicate their progress very clearly through drawings, journals, letters, mimes, projects, and constructions. Computer programs are also good ways to keep a record of their progress.

PHYSICAL DISABILITIES

The range of physical disabilities is wide. Most involve some impairment of motor skills. Structure evaluation and teaching tasks to deemphasize motor skills. If motor skills are involved, sequence tasks in short steps. Verbal assessments often work well. Working with partners or in small teams is also helpful to the student with a physical disability. Independence should also be encouraged. Microcomputers can often be used with such students in evaluation. Word processing, for example, may be much easier than writing with pen or pencil.

SPEECH PROBLEMS/LANGUAGE DEVELOPMENT DELAY

These disabilities are sometimes found in connection with other problems, such as hearing impairment. Students with these problems are usually identified at an early age. Speech/language therapists will recommend procedures the teacher can use. Use clear, normal speech and listen attentively when the student speaks. Small-group activity and opportunities to demonstrate leadership abilities are also important for these students. Emphasize visual techniques in evaluation procedures such as artwork, logs, and computer programs.

BEHAVIOR DISORDERS

In comparison with their peers, students with behavior disorders are usually much more withdrawn or much more aggressive. The disorder may have a physical cause, such as nervousness resulting from an allergy or it may be psychological, such as a reaction to a divorce in the family. Consider the student's behavior in relation to his or her peers and cultural background. In some neighborhoods, the culture may promote more-assertive or more-passive behavior than the teacher is used to. If the student is very different from his or her peers, and you are concerned with extreme aspects of the student's behavior, refer the student to special education personnel for help in determining the cause of the behaviors and in deciding on the teaching and evaluation procedures that will be appropriate. Expect the student with behavior disorders to have a shorter attention span than his or her peers, a lower threshold of frustration, and a greater need for reinforcement, reward, emotional support, and patience. Informal evaluation methods and/or short, carefully sequenced tasks will work best with these students. Teacher observation is often very useful for assessing the progress of these students. Creative activities that the student can complete at his or her own pace can be an effective assessment technique. These activities enable a teacher to determine what the student finds interesting, how the student perceives the idea, and how well the student can plan and carry out an activity of personal interest.

LEARNING DISABILITIES

Learning disabilities vary greatly. Special education personnel will have to identify the best learning and evaluation procedures to use with a particular student. Emotional support is important because these students are often frustrated by their disability. Because many young children will mature out of their disability, they should be given time—not pressured but helped to develop self-assuredness and confidence.

EVALUATING GIFTED STUDENTS

Curiosity and creativity are characteristics of many gifted students. Often, these students will give a creative, perhaps unexpected response to an assessment. On standardized tests, and some teacher-made tests, these creative responses are marked wrong. In interviews, these students often deviate from questions with creative answers, or they may delve more deeply than do other students. Informal evaluation should indicate gifted students' level of development and pace of growth. These students need encouragement, but their creativity and curiosity may be exhausting to teachers. When evaluating these students, make certain to consider novel responses adequately.

A Practice Activity

Your students have been working on a unit focusing on global interdependence. They have carried out research to identify major producers and users of iron, coal, copper, silver, aluminum, gold, and tungsten. Their research was carried out in groups, with each group responsible for a different mineral. Within the groups, two students were responsible for identifying the major producers of the mineral they were studying and two were responsible for identifying the major users. The students have found that a major producer of a mineral is not necessarily a major user. As a result, major producers and users are interdependent. You are considering how to evaluate.

What is the most important objective of the lesson that you will need to evaluate?

· If you asked each group to produce a world map showing the flow of minerals from users to producers, would this be satisfactory? If not, what would be a more appropriate means of evaluation?

· If you have a student with limited English proficiency in your room, will this means of evaluation be appropriate and satisfactory for evaluating this student? If not, how can you change the evaluation so it will be satisfactory?

· If you also have a student with a visual impairment, will the means of evaluation you have identified after considering the needs of the student with limited English proficiency be satisfactory for the visually impaired student? If not, how can you change the evaluation you have planned so it will be satisfactory?

· If you also have a student in crisis because of the recent divorce of his or her parents, will the evaluation you have planned up to this point be satisfactory? If not, how can you change the evaluation so it will be satisfactory?

☞ *As you can see, it is difficult to evaluate every student in a class appropriately with one evaluation strategy. However, when a teacher has a wide repertoire of evaluation strategies and tries to consider the needs of all of his or her students, it is likely that much of the time each student will be evaluated with an appropriate strategy.*

SUMMARY

Each student is special. Those with disabilities, those who are gifted, those who have a cultural background different from the dominant culture, and those in crisis situations are more like other students than they are different from them. As students are evaluated, they must be approached in terms of their similarity to other students even when they have special needs that must be considered. All students have needs special to themselves but for some, the needs are greater than for others. In spite of greater needs, a student should be treated first as a student and second as a student with special needs.

Evaluation is a positive process helping teachers structure the learning environment to meet students' needs as they work with the social studies program. For a social studies program to be effective, evaluation begins with determining students' abilities as well as their limitations. Teachers must take the time to learn about the students they teach. They must realize that their students' physical, emotional, and cultural needs must be addressed to help them get the most they can from school and to receive a fair measuring and recognition of their accomplishments. Both informal and formal methods need to be used to gain a fair and complete measure of the success all the students have had in attaining the social studies objectives set for them. Most often, teachers using a range of evaluation strategies will find that they are able to evaluate their students appropriately.

REFERENCES

Boehm, A. & Weinberg, R. (1987). *The classroom observer,* (2nd ed.). New York: Teachers College Press.

Cargill, C. (1987). Cultural bias in testing ESL. *A TESOL professional anthology: Culture* (C. Cargill, ed.). Lincolnwood, IL: National Textbook Co., 1–7.

Cheng, L. (1987). *Assessing Asian language performance.* Rockville, MD: Aspen Publishers.

Cook, R., Tessier, A., & Armbruster, V. (1987). *Adapting early childhood curricula for children with special needs.* Columbus, OH: Merrill.

Eichelberger, R. (1989). *Disciplined inquiry: Understanding and doing educational research.* New York: Longman.

Finkelstein, J. (1991). Appropriate assessment practices for early childhood/elementary social studies. Paper presented at the annual meeting of the National Council for the Social Studies, Washington, D.C.

Gay, G. & Abrahams, R. (1983). Does the pot melt, boil or brew? Black children and white assessment procedures. *Journal of School Psychology, 21*(4), 330–340.

Good, T. & Brophy, J. (1990). *Educational psychology* (4th ed.). New York: Longman.

Herlihy, J. & Herlihy, M. (eds.). (1980). *Mainstreaming in the social studies.* Washington, DC: National Council for the Social Studies.

Michaels, S. (1981). Sharing time: Children's narrative styles and differential access to literacy. *Language in Society, 11,* 423–443.

Nunnally, J. (1967). *Psychometric theory.* New York: McGraw-Hill.

Olsen, L. (1988). *Crossing the schoolhouse border: Immigrant students and the California public schools.* San Francisco, CA: University of California, Berkeley.

Scarcella, R. (1990). *Teaching language to minority students in the multicultural classroom.* Englewood Cliffs, NJ: Prentice-Hall.

Sunal, C. (1990). *Early childhood social studies.* Columbus, OH: Merrill.

Superka, D., Vigliani, A., & Hedstrom, J. (1978). *Social studies evaluation sourcebook.* Boulder, CO: Social Science Education Consortium.

Thorndike, R. & Hagen, E. (1991). *Measurement and evaluation in psychology and education* (5th ed.). New York: Wiley.

CHAPTER 10

OVERVIEW

In social studies, psychology works toward the goal of understanding and accepting our individuality. Sociology focuses on helping us understand our social nature and the social groups we form with others. Research in psychology helps students develop positive self-image and self-confidence, to better accept and understand themselves and to learn to accept and relate to others. This understanding enables us to live with others as social beings (Pagano, 1978). The development of the attitudes and values integral to each person's personality supports the goals of individual and social development.

Social studies programs work to develop citizenship. As they do so, the self-development of the individual and the development of each person's ability to relate to others in the society are basic elements. The development of attitudes and values that support responsible citizenship include both character education and education promoting the development of ethical behavior. These two areas are related, although different. Character education refers to helping students build a set of values and attitudes that enables them to be responsible, active citizens. The development of ethical behavior refers to helping students make decisions to behave in ways that reflect a system of ethics focused on what is best for all people.

Various aspects of the social studies curriculum related to psychology, sociology, and values education continue to be controversial. The disagreement is over what to teach and how to teach it. This controversy can be expected to continue since a democratic society encourages a variety of opinions and the public discussion of those opinions. This chapter describes research and teaching practice related to psychology, sociology, and values education. Where controversy exists, this chapter attempts to present a variety of viewpoints and does not claim to present a final answer.

Psychology, Sociology, and Values Education

OBJECTIVES

1. Describe how the classroom environment and the curriculum can indicate the level of the teacher's respect for students.

2. Describe some areas that affect the development of self-concept and how teachers can work positively with students in each area.

3. Identify three aspects of morality.

4. Describe two moral development theories.

5. Identify two means by which teachers can facilitate students' moral behavior.

6. Describe values clarification, value analysis, and teaching a specific value.

7. Describe attitudes important to learning social studies and to being a citizen in a democracy.

8. Describe a lesson that works with an area of psychology, sociology, or values education and incorporates exploration, invention, and expansion.

RESPECT FOR STUDENTS AND FOR ONESELF AS A TEACHER

THE CLASSROOM ENVIRONMENT

Think about classrooms you have seen. Can you remember one that seemed to convey a respect for students through its layout? If you can remember such a classroom, think about what characteristics caused you to identify it. Can you remember a classroom whose layout conveyed limited or little respect for students? If so, what characteristics caused you to remember it?

Students get some sense of how much respect a teacher has for them with their first step into a classroom. The layout of a classroom suggests whether the teacher will encourage informal, frequent communication between students and between students and the teacher. A teacher who encourages discussion and cooperation by sitting students next to one another and by setting up areas where small groups can work demonstrates respect for students' ability to work with others and to exercise control of both their behavior and their learning. Within such an environment, it soon becomes evident that the teacher views himself as a learner enthusiastically exploring new ideas and new information along with his students. A teacher's respect for students means that he does not expect them to always know something that has been taught nor does he penalize them for making a mistake. In such a classroom, the learning cycle in Table 10–1 can be used effectively. Students should have enough confidence and respect for each other and themselves to observe others' behavior carefully, to discuss it, and to draw implications for successful future cooperative activity.

Table 10–1

LEARNING CYCLE: Psychology

Theme: Psychology (For Third Grade)

OBJECTIVES	PROCEDURES	EVALUATIONS
	Materials: For each pair of students, provide 2 shoeboxes; one pair of scissors; one glue bottle and glue stick; 10 sheets each of red, pink, and white construction paper; one large, red, lacy paper heart; a set of marking pens; 5 small valentine stickers; one vial of glitter; 1 response sheet for each student; 1 checklist for each student.	
	Exploration	
Students will construct a Valentine's Day mailbox using a given set of materials.	Provide pairs of students with a set of materials for making mailboxes to be used on Valentine's Day for collecting valentines. Put all extra materials away so that they are not visible or available to the students. Give each pair of students time to use the materials to make their valentine mailboxes. As they	Student completion of mailbox.

OBJECTIVES	PROCEDURES	EVALUATIONS
	are working, have two other students record what strategies are being used by the pair as they are working. Observations should be recorded every five minutes on the checklist.	

OBJECTIVES	PROCEDURES	EVALUATIONS
	Invention	
Students will express an awareness of problems arising from a scarcity of materials.	When all pairs of students have had time to make their mailboxes, ask students to record any problems they encountered on question 1 of the response sheet. Then discuss the activity and problems they encountered in it.	Appropriateness of student response to question 1 of the response sheet.
Students will state at least one solution to the problem of scarcity.	Have students fill in question 2 of the response sheet. Ask students to look at copies of the observation checklists and to summarize them. Lead a discussion in which they identify how the problem of scarcity was solved. Ask: "How did you define each category on the checklist?" Have students discuss examples of each category. These might include examples such as: a) sharing; b) arguing/grabbing; c) being sneaky.	Appropriateness of student response to question 2 of the response sheet.
	The discussion might include questions such as: "Which pairs of students seemed to have had little trouble in coping with the scarcity of materials?" "Which strategies did they use?" "Who felt angry or frustrated?" "What was happening?" "What happens when we talk together to try to figure out how to share the materials when we don't have enough of everything?" Write out the process as described by the students.	Record student participation on a checklist.
Students will define *sharing*.	Have students define *sharing* on their response sheets. Then have them contribute to a whole group definition. Write out their definition on the chalkboard.	Appropriateness of student response to question 3 of the response sheet.
Students will define *negotiation*.	Introduce the term *negotiation*. Have the students define negotiation using the process they described earlier on their response sheets. Have them contribute to a whole group definition. Write the definition developed by the students on the chalkboard. Have students copy it down in their notebooks.	Appropriateness of student response to question 4 of the response sheet.
Students will describe how negotiation and sharing can solve a problem of scarcity of materials.	Discuss the advantages of sharing and negotiation in a situation where there is a scarcity of materials. Ask students to fill in question 5 of their response sheets.	Appropriateness of student response to question 5 of the response sheet.

(Cont.)

OBJECTIVES	PROCEDURES	EVALUATIONS
Students will apply sharing and negotiation in solving a problem involving scarcity.	***Expansion*** Give pairs of students materials to decorate the covers of folders their work is kept in, making sure that a scarcity of some materials exists. Tell students that a scarcity of materials exists and ask them to remember the discussion of sharing and negotiation. Encourage them to use the positive strategies discussed in this situation. After students have finished decorating their notebook covers, discuss how successful their efforts at sharing and negotiation were. Ask students to draw a picture of two people building something together. Then ask them to write a short narrative describing the scene.	Observe students' behaviors in sharing and negotiating for scarce supplies. Evaluate drawing and narrative for accuracy in illustrating sharing and negotiating.

CHECKLIST

Pair number: ***Observer:***

Observe the pair of workers once every 5 minutes, and record in a sentence or two the way they are behaving and working.

OBSERVATION 1 Time: _____

OBSERVATION 2 Time: _____

OBSERVATION 3 Time: _____

OBSERVATION 4 Time: _____

OBSERVATION 5 Time: _____

OBSERVATION 6 Time: _____

RESPONSE SHEET

Name:

1. What was the main problem you had in using the materials you were given?

2. What was one way of solving this problem?

3. What does *sharing* mean?

4. What does *negotiation* mean?

5. How can sharing and negotiation help solve the problem you had with the mailbox materials?

CURRICULUM

Acceptance of, and respect for, students is also communicated through the curriculum. This happens when:

- students have some responsibility for actively contributing ideas and materials used in the curriculum
- they are involved in discussions that demonstrate a respect for their opinions
- they help make decisions relating to the curriculum

Involving family members in the classroom supports the curriculum used by the teacher and conveys a respect for the students. It is unlikely that the teacher can provide all the material on which a rich experience base can be built (Sunal, 1986). Family members can be heavily involved in the curriculum. For example:

> A group of fifth graders became interested in the traditional culture of the people living in the Appalachian Mountains. Courtney's father came to class and brought slides of his childhood home in Tennessee. He showed them a slide of a panel that could be opened in the kitchen revealing the original log walls of what was first a cabin and was later covered over with wood planks and expanded into a

The curriculum is enriched when students are encouraged to bring in materials associated with their ethnic heritage.

large farmhouse. He also played a dulcimer for them and helped each student try to play it. Finally, he told them some traditional Appalachian Mountain ghost stories. Courtney's teacher had never been to Tennessee, had never before played a dulcimer, nor had he heard the ghost stories.

Involving Courtney's father resulted in both students and teacher learning new things. The curriculum was enriched, communicating the teacher's respect for the knowledge and attitudes of the students' families. Respecting what parents can bring to the classroom indicates acceptance of them and respect for their children.

Involving family members in the curriculum incorporates the student's culture and is a foundation for multicultural education. Each culture can give us different perspectives on social issues, on life, and on the curriculum. As students experience a wider range of cultures, they are likely to overcome some of their prejudices (see also chapter 14). Curriculum that gives students interpersonal problems to work with, as demonstrated in the learning cycle in Table 10–1, can be responsive to student needs and can recognize student abilities. The classroom layout, the curriculum, and the involvement of students' families can all demonstrate respect for students.

SOME AREAS AFFECTING THE DEVELOPMENT OF SELF-CONCEPT

An individual's self-concept is the complex product of all of life's experiences. It is affected by the cultures of the home and of the school. During the elementary and middle school years students are developing a sense of independence, and learning to cope with feelings of jealousy, fear, and aggression, and are forming friendships (Perry & Bussey, 1984).

INDEPENDENCE

Consider the sample learning cycle in Table 10–1.

Time for Reflection: What Do <u>YOU</u> Think?

· How do you think student independence could be fostered during the invention phase?

· How might the activities during the invention phase cause a need in students to be dependent?

Elementary and middle school students do act independently. However, they also are dependent on adults at times (Sears, 1963). As they develop cognitively and socially, students become better able to plan solutions to problems and to understand the social environment. As a result they are more and more able to be independent.

Becoming ever more independent is part of the maturation process. Students usually try to be independent when they find an opportunity to do so. Positive attempts at independence are usually rewarded by teachers. Sometimes students' attempts result in unsafe or disruptive behavior, which teachers try to control. When students' independent attempts do not work, teachers are usually expected to help them out (Maccoby and Masters, 1970). Adults should help, but only after they are sure a real attempt has been made to accomplish the task. Help given too quickly enforces dependency, frustration, and sometimes aggression or withdrawal.

Students become independent when they are expected to be responsible (Quilty, 1975). For example, putting materials away after finishing with them and keeping things in one's own locker demonstrate responsibility. Expectations of responsibility should be accompanied by reasons, as in this example, "The scissors and stapler you need are on that shelf. It's nice that the last person who used them returned them to where they belong, because now they are easy for everyone to find when they need them." Students may work responsibly on a task but they usually do not work in the same ways that adults do. They often start, then stop and attend to something else, then come back to what they were working on, and so on. Efforts at responsibility should be recognized and rewarded. Independence and responsibility depend on one another. A student who is not expected to be responsible is not likely to be thought of as capable of independent behaviors. Students from various cultural backgrounds can be expected to display independence and responsibility differently. For example, students from Asian backgrounds often assume responsibility for tasks and carry them out well but may not be as likely to organize others to do a task unless the teacher indicates permission to do so (Scarcella, 1990). These students are demonstrating respect for the teacher in a manner approved by their culture. Teachers help students develop independence by:

1. planning carefully
2. anticipating difficulties
3. giving clear directions
4. providing outlines of suggested procedures

Expecting and encouraging responsibility and independent behavior shows respect for students as individuals who are in the process of growing up.

JEALOUSY

In the sample learning cycle in Table 10–1, how much potential for jealousy would there be in using this invention activity with first graders? with fourth graders? Jealousy is a natural feeling resulting partly from egocentrism, especially in younger students who sometimes find it hard to accept another student's being the center of attention even for a short while (Ginsburg & Opper, 1979). As students mature, their egocentrism and the occasional jealousy it causes weaken. Even though jealousy is normal in students, it threatens their self-respect. Usually, jealousy means a person is uncertain of the affection of another person in the presence of a third party. This uncertainty lessens self-respect.

Jealousy is expressed by students in several ways, including aggression, immature behavior, and boasting. When a student is displaying any of these behaviors much more frequently than is common among his or her peers there may be cause for concern. Using peers for comparison is important because some behaviors are more common among some groups of people than among others.

Teaching that encourages students to discuss concerns and to analyze their behavior, as suggested in the sample learning cycle (Table 10–1), assists students in learning to cope with feelings of jealousy. Contests between students resulting in winners and losers foster jealousy and reduce self-respect (French, Brownell, Graziano, & Hartup, 1977). Instead, an emphasis should be placed on each student's doing as well as possible. A related problem is identifying one student as a model and saying the others should emulate this model. While a teacher cannot avoid all situations that produce some jealous feelings, it is important to recognize potentially negative situations so efforts can be made to reduce their effects on students. It is also very important to find a wide variety of positive behaviors and types of accomplishments to recognize in students.

Students should have opportunities to examine situations whose development and outcome may have been influenced by jealousy. Historical situations as well as recent events can be examined. For example, how much did jealousy influence racist attitudes toward Jackie Robinson? Was Caucasian control of major league baseball being jealously guarded? What is meant by "jealously" guarded? In another type of situation, students might discuss "How jealous are Americans of Japanese success in business?" Do jealous feelings prevent us from logically viewing and dealing with Japanese businesses? Teachers can also find many opportunities to discuss jealousy in children's literature. Were Cinderella's sisters jealous of her beauty? Was this why they were mean to her? After reading *Vilma Martinez* (by C. Codye, Raintree Publishers, 1990), students might discuss whether others' jealous feelings might have affected events in her life and her accomplishments as a leading Hispanic-American activist. Consideration of emotions such as jealousy should be a part of the social studies program at all grade levels. Students' own feelings, situations that develop in the classroom, children's literature and historical and current events all reflect emotions and offer a beginning point for a discussion.

FEARS

Some limited fear is part of life. It is reasonable to be a bit fearful and therefore more cautious when walking down the streets of many large cities late at night, for example. Students often have fears that are not reasonable and they need to learn to understand and overcome them during the elementary and middle school years. Very young children develop fears frequently between ages 2 through 5. As their ability to make mature interpretations of observations and events develops, fears weaken and students become more realistic.

Student fears are not overcome quickly. It is important to remember that the student thinks the fear is reasonable because his thinking processes are immature. It is also important to remember that students usually grow out of their fears as they mature.

Time for Reflection: What Do <u>YOU</u> Think?

· What is a fear you remember having?

· Can you remember gradually experiencing this fear less and less?

· Can you think of anything that helped reduce the fear?

Any fear takes a long time to overcome. However, every young child develops some fears. It is important not to promote any fear. One negative activity is to use a threat to enforce discipline, such as "Eat your food or the police officer will make you eat it." Such comments can help create fears. Teachers must also avoid passing their own fears on to their students. Students are quite sensitive to adult emotions. A real effort to withstand fear will lessen the chance of the student's acquiring it. The student is likely to be more impressed by the adult's effort than by the adult's fear. When students are distressed it is important to acknowledge that distress. Not doing so can result in building a fear in students, since the teacher's avoidance might be interpreted as fear.

Fear is often expressed so strongly that the adult cannot help but be aware of it. The best approach is to listen to the student, discuss the fear, and show sympathy for the student's feelings (Maxim, 1989). The fear will not be talked away but the student will know that fear has been recognized as real and upsetting. Activities where students describe situations in which they feel fear and how they try to cope with the fear can be helpful. These activities might focus on trying to help the student invent strategies that are successful in helping them recognize and cope with their fear. Use of a learning cycle focusing on one or more fears students may have can be used as opportunities arise or may be planned in advance by the teacher.

Students during the middle school years often develop fears that are related to the social situations they find themselves in—situations that are becoming more and more an area of concern and great interest to them. Students near, or just into, adolescence often fear ridicule. They worry when placed in a situation where the potential for ridicule seems great to them. For example, when they are asked to make an oral presentation before a class many young teens will be nervous, shaky, and may freeze entirely, unable to remember a word of what they wanted to say. Younger students are typically less inhibited and easily overcome mistakes they make. The growing pressure young teens feel in social situations and the fear of ridicule cause the inhibitions and worry they exhibit. Teachers need to help students develop confidence. This is often done through teaching techniques such as looking just over the heads of listeners at the wall behind them. Since young teens often compare themselves with the polished presentations they see in videos and commercials, it is important to discuss the bloopers that professional actors make and to encourage them to watch a program that features such bloopers. Once they recognize that the professional presentations they see are the result of many retakes and of much editing as well as of years of professional training, they may be able to readjust their expectations of themselves and their peers more realistically.

Teachers of young teens need to think about the causes of the fears they see exhibited by their students. Some will be related to the changing social situations involving peers that students are learning to cope with. Some will be due to abuse or other out-of-school situations that may be severely stressful. Some will be due to a feeling that they are different and therefore not acceptable to others because they represent a minority cultural background in their class. Teachers have a limited ability to help reduce fears generated by many of the situations young teens are in. So it is important to work to reduce fears when possible. It is also important to be aware of whom to contact for assistance when a student is involved in a situation where the teacher can offer only very limited help.

The student who seems to have no fears may be an unusual student—as is the student who has many fears. As always, a student's peers are a good index of what is to be expected, because culture influences the fears a student has.

Fear that may be shared by several students should be examined. How fearful were they during a recent weather event—a tornado, a warning of a tornado, a severe rainstorm with lots of thunder and lightning, a blizzard? How did others react to this same event? How fearful are they of a serial killer whose killings are described on television frequently? How fearful are they of gang killings? of killings by one student in order to take another student's new, expensive shoes? of getting caught in between two older adolescents shooting at each other because of an insult? How fearful are they of getting AIDS?

Students should also have an opportunity to discuss stories in which an individual deals with fear. *Island of the Blue Dolphins* (by S. O'Dell, Houghton Mifflin, 1960) offers opportunities to discuss the fears of a young Indian girl surviving alone on a Pacific island for years. *The Planet of Junior Brown* (by V. Hamilton, Macmillan, 1971) describes the fears felt by people living in the inner city. *Downwind* (by L. Moeri, Dutton, 1984) describes an accident at a nuclear plant and the fear of many people as they try to flee. For very young students, books such as *Will I Have a Friend?* (by M. Cohen, Macmillan, 1967) and *Timothy Goes to School* (by R. Wells, Dial, 1983) engage students in considering others' fears and how they cope with them.

Many historical situations involved fear. Students might consider how fearful a slave using the underground railway felt. They might talk about possible events that might have caused fear among the members of the Lewis and Clark expedition. What fears did people who moved from the mountains of Kentucky, Tennessee, and West Virginia have as they began life in large northern cities? Was President Reagan afraid of the Soviet Union (now the Commonwealth of Independent States) when he called it the "evil empire?"

Fear is sometimes justified. It is something felt by an individual and sometimes by a group of people. Fear has been present in the past and it is with us now. Students should be encouraged to examine situations from the past as well as situations in the present and situations in literature to determine what role fear has played.

AGGRESSIVE FEELINGS

What situation(s) cause you to feel aggressive? Do you view yourself as more, less, or about as aggressive as the average person? Some students are consistently more or less aggressive than the average student. Their aggression is part of their personality. Situations, however, also create many aggressive feelings. Some students become aggressive when frustrated. They usually have not been strongly reinforced for reacting to frustration by sharing, cooperating, talking, and other prosocial behavior (Patterson, 1976). These students often associate with other aggressive students (Perry & Bussey, 1984). Families who use erratic physical punishment often have aggressive children. These students believe the only reason not to be aggressive is to avoid getting caught and punished. Punishment often pushes them into further aggression. Aggressive models in real life and in the media teach aggressive behaviors. Some students come from cultural backgrounds which encourage higher or lower levels of aggression than are typical among most students. As they mature, students learn that society views aggression as more justified in some circumstances and less justified in others. Most students also learn to feel guilty when they are aggressive in situations their society views as not justifying aggression. As a result, they are more likely to avoid aggression as they get older (Perry & Bussey, 1984).

Aggression can be reduced. One way to reduce it is to eliminate situations that promote aggression. These include frustrating situations and aggressive media programs. Another way to reduce it is to teach students that aggression does not reward them, for example, by using timeout procedures. Teaching students how to resolve conflicts and interact positively with others helps. Finally, helping students learn how to monitor and control their own behavior is important. These strategies should help students realize that less aggressive behavior results in more attention, affection, and approval (Perry & Bussey, 1984). Cooperative learning is one means of accomplishing much of the learning needed by students if aggression is to be reduced (see chapter 7).

Students should examine aggression as it is displayed in current events. One country fights with another; who is the aggressor here? In another country there is a guerrilla movement. Who is the aggressor there? A traveler is attacked on a subway train. Who is the aggressor? Historical events can also be examined in discussions of aggression. Were the thirteen colonies an aggressor when they declared independence from England? How did the Choctaw Indians first react to the aggression from settlers as they took over their land and began to farm it?

Children's literature can be used to explore aggression. *The Runner* (by C. Voight, Atheneum, 1985) offers an opportunity to talk about aggression and conflict in a family. *A December Tale* (by M. Sachs, Doubleday, 1976) focuses on child abuse. *Cider Days* (by M. Stolz, Harper & Row, 1978) describes conflict and aggression in school caused by racial bias. Aggression is a part of students' lives. It is a part of adults' lives on an individual basis and between nations. Students need to recognize it, discuss it, and learn strategies for reducing it.

FRIENDSHIP

Throughout childhood, students add to the number of acquaintances they have and develop some close friendships. At different ages, students expect somewhat different things from friends and so the character of friendships changes a bit over the years.

There is evidence that students usually are closest to others who are similar in age, race, sex, interests, degree of sociability, and values (Singleton & Asher, 1979). Through the early elementary school years students prefer a friend who is easily accessible, has nice toys, and plays easily. There is a preference for someone who quickly rewards attempts at friendliness (Perry & Bussey, 1984). During the middle of the elementary school years, shared values become important. Mu-

Friendships are often built when students work together at enjoyable tasks.

tual acceptance, admiration, and loyalty are important. Friends are supposed to help each other and to be satisfied by the amount of help they receive (Perry & Bussey, 1984). Beginning during middle school, students really start to care about what happens to a friend. They stress mutual understanding and closeness but still expect their friends to be useful to them (Reisman & Shorr, 1978).

Students who can make and keep friends are skillful at initiating interactions with their peers, maintaining ongoing interactions, and resolving interpersonal conflicts. These skills are developed through four primary strategies that teachers can help students develop:

- greeting another student directly ("Hi! What's your name?")
- asking appropriate questions ("What's your favorite TV show?")
- giving information ("I like to play checkers.")
- trying to include the new friend in their activities ("Do you want to play tag at recess?")

Students also need to know that it is important to keep trying even when rejected. Teachers should recognize that the willingness to keep trying depends on self-confidence. So teachers need to work to build each student's self-confidence. Media, particularly interactive computer programs, should be considered as aids in helping students develop skills in making and keeping friends. One example of a computer program that can be used in the primary grades is *On the Playground* produced by Tom Snyder Productions. This program is designed to be used on one computer with the whole class. The program sets up a situation where a new student has arrived and the other students must decide whether to spend their recess time getting to know the new student and involving him in their games. The program branches so that as various choices are made, different events occur, based on students' choices. Discussion between class members is encouraged as consequences are projected, and analyses of the results of various strategies for handling the situation are encountered. Students can see how various decisions lead to different results.

Once a friendship has begun, some skills are needed to continue it. Among these skills are:

- rewarding a friend by smiling at him or her
- imitating the friend's actions
- paying attention to the friend
- approving of what the friend does
- complying with the friend's wishes
- sharing things with the friend
- communicating well
- being a good listener
- giving information needed by the listener
- judging your own actions on whether you have shown or not shown respect for others' rights and welfare (Hartup, Glazer, & Charlesworth, 1967; Perry & Bussey, 1984)

Teachers can effectively coach students in social skills that will help them begin and continue satisfying friendships. Coaching involves telling or showing students how to use a specific social skill. This includes giving students opportunities to practice the skill and giving feedback with suggestions for improving the use of the skill. Among the skills that have been effectively taught are asking questions, learning to give positive reinforcement to others (such as smiles), making good eye contact, speaking clearly, and taking turns (Perry & Bussey, 1984).

Friendship can be examined through discussing current events and historical situations. News reports often talk about the friendship between the United States and the United Kingdom, or about new friendship between the United States and another country. How is such friendship different from and similar to the friendship between two students? At one time the United States has been both a friend and an enemy of Germany. Relationships between individual people sometimes also undergo great change. Is it a similar process? What have been some of the causes of the change in relationship between the United States and Germany? What is meant when the media report that someone got a city building contract because he was the friend of the mayor? What is meant when someone says he has a friend at city hall who is going to fix his traffic ticket? Does real friendship mean you do illegal things for your friends? Henry Ford and Thomas Edison were close friends. What was the basis for their friendship?

Many books discuss friendship between children and young adolescents. *Jennifer, Hecate, Macbeth, William McKinley, and Me, Elizabeth* (by E. L. Konigsburg, Atheneum, 1976) is one such book for older students. *Louie* (E. J. Keats, Greenwillow, 1975) is a book for younger children that describes how a shy boy makes friends. The actions of friends in such stories can be examined and compared to those of the students. They can decide if and why they would want the characters in the book as friends.

Friends and friendship are always a matter of interest and sometimes of concern to students. Exploring what friendship means and how it develops and grows should be a part of the social studies curriculum throughout the school years.

SELF-ESTEEM

Self-esteem and self-concept are closely connected. If a person is pleased with his self-concept he will have high self-esteem. If the person's self-concept is negative, he will have low self-esteem. Coopersmith (1967) conducted longitudinal research that indicated that most students have formed a stable sense of self-esteem by the middle school years. Self-esteem appears to be related to social behavior. Students with high self-esteem participate more frequently in discussions and other activities rather than being passive listeners (Coopersmith, 1967). They express their opinions and approach new tasks with self-confidence, are less likely to conform to peer pressure, make friends easily, and are not preoccupied with personal problems. These positive characteristics are thought to be the result of high self-esteem based on a positive self-concept. It is possible, however, that the reverse might occur. High self-esteem could be the result of these positive characteristics rather than the cause of them. In either case, teachers need to work to foster a positive self-concept in each student and to indicate respect and appreciation for each student's abilities and cultural background.

VALUES AND MORAL EDUCATION

Our values are an important part of our self-concept. Values are decisions about the worth of something based on a standard we have set (Sunal, 1990). When an individual decides something has value, he decides it is worthwhile. The standards we set in determining value are morals. Morals are our judgments of rightness and wrongness. Something that is judged as right will be valued.

THREE ASPECTS OF MORALITY

Morality has three aspects:

1. moral reasoning
2. self-evaluation
3. conscious resistance to deviant thinking and behavior

The specific situation often affects each person's reaction in each of these aspects of morality. For example, a student may feel guilt in one setting but not in another. Evidence also suggests that growth in moral reasoning is aided by finding that others have different perspectives in morality that conflict with one's own perspectives (Perry & Bussey, 1984). Finally, some evidence indicates that moral judgments are multidimensional social decisions (Bandura, 1977). Moral judgments depend on synthesizing several varieties of social information to arrive at conceptions of appropriate and inappropriate behavior (Bandura, 1977).

Self-evaluation has been studied by Hoffman (1977), who views guilt as empathic distress accompanied by the belief that you are responsible for someone else's distress. Parents' and teachers' use of explanations and inductive reasoning helps children learn to accept responsibility for their misbehavior. In inductive reasoning, an individual becomes familiar with examples and nonexamples of something and then uses them to develop a concept or generalization. For example, Bandura (1977) suggests that children develop personal standards of appropriate conduct, and that they learn to guide their behavior by rewarding and punishing themselves for attaining or falling short of goals they have set for themselves.

When children are tempted to do something they are not supposed to do, the likelihood of succumbing to temptation depends on the following:
• child-rearing and school experiences
• understanding of the deviation
• situational factors

Children whose parents and teachers firmly and consistently insist that they learn and practice habits of self-regulation, who justify their disciplinary action with inductive reasoning, who are warm and communicative, who avoid the use of unnecessarily harsh discipline, and who are models of self-controlled behavior are most likely to display desirable conduct when away from adults. Children who think of themselves as internally motivated to behave morally, who anticipate blaming themselves for deviating, who expect pride for good behavior, who know how to talk themselves out of deviating, and who know how to avoid thinking about forbidden activities are better able to resist temptations than children lacking these qualities. A student might, for example, notice a brightly colored, fancy new pencil, one that is considered the latest thing in pencils, on the desk of another student at a time when nobody else is in that part of the classroom. Since this student's mother doesn't buy her something just because it is a fad and would only buy her the usual yellow pencils, the student is tempted. She could take the pencil, hide it, and use it out of class, so nobody would know she took it. It isn't really expensive so its owner wouldn't make a fuss about it for very long. However, this student realizes that she would be afraid to use the pencil because others might decide she stole it. She also knows she would feel guilty and wouldn't want to look the owner in the face. She decides that the guilt she would feel isn't worth it. She knows she would be ashamed of herself. So she quickly moves away from the area and puts the temptation well away from her. The particular situation and the mood a person is in when faced with temptations also influence the likelihood for resisting temptation (Perry & Bussey, 1984).

MORAL DEVELOPMENT THEORIES

Moral development has been described by Jean Piaget and Lawrence Kohlberg. Some disagreement exists about how accurately their theories predict moral development, but a number of the implications of their theories should be considered in social studies education. Piaget found that children's conception of rules seemed to occur in three stages (Ginsburg & Opper, 1979).

1. The egocentric stage (about ages 4 to 7). Children do not knowingly follow rules; they decide what is right and wrong on the basis of what adults permit or forbid them to do.
2. The incipient cooperation stage (about age 7 to about age 10 or 11). Children are more social and cooperative as they demonstrate an understanding that rules are made to help solve interpersonal conflicts.
3. The real cooperation stage (beginning at about age 11 or 12). Children are able to develop appropriate rules and understand why rules are needed.

Kohlberg (1969) tested individuals from a variety of cultures and economic levels, finding similarities in development. Building on Piaget's work, he outlined his ideas as follows:

1. Cognitive development is the major factor in social behavior. As cognitive development occurs, understanding of morally appropriate behavior and the reasons for that behavior also occurs.
2. Cognitive and social development occur in stages. Each new stage is qualitatively different from the one that preceded it.
3. Maturational factors and the continuing restructuring of behavior through experience and maturation result in the requirement that no new stage may be achieved unless all preceding ones have been attained.

Kohlberg developed a Moral Judgment Scale that is used to determine which of six stages a person is in (see Table 10–2). A Stage 1 person obeys because he does not want to be punished for not obeying. A Stage 1 person might suggest, for example, that you should not steal something because you might get caught and go to jail. A Stage 4 person believes in maintaining authority and in conforming to accepted law and order. He might say that no matter how good the result and no matter what the reason, if you steal you have violated laws protecting someone else's property. A Stage 6 person has individual principles of conscience that are always acted upon regardless of the popular norm of behavior. This person would believe that stealing is usually wrong. When a person's life depends on something that is obtainable only by stealing, however, then stealing is right, and the person is wrong who does not value life highly enough to steal what is needed to maintain it.

Kohlberg combined the stages to form three levels of moral development, each of which contains two stages. Level 1 is preconventional behavior, with Stages 1 and 2. Here, reasoning is selfish, and the individual considers his own desires and not what is good for society. Level 2 is conventional behavior and contains Stages 3 and 4. Reasoning focuses on what is accepted by society and on conforming to social expectations. Level 3 involves postconventional behavior and includes Stages 5 and 6. Reasoning becomes unselfish and goes beyond what is considered conventional by society. It focuses on what is best in principle for all people, not just those in one's own society.

Table 10–2

Kohlberg's Stages of Moral Development

LEVEL 1: PRECONVENTIONAL

Moral reasoning is related to the immediate consequences of actions and to the power of those in authority over an individual.

Stage 1: Obedience to power—"Daddy says I have to do this." Seeking rewards and avoiding punishment—"Will Mommy send me to my room for doing this?"

Stage 2: Satisfying your own needs—"What will I get out of this?"

LEVEL 2: CONVENTIONAL

Moral reasoning begins to involve a consideration of others, especially family and peers, and a desire to maintain the existing social order.

Stage 3: Approval of others—"What would my friends think if I did this?"

Stage 4: Law and order—"Is this the best thing for my society?" "Does my society say I can do this?"

LEVEL 3: POSTCONVENTIONAL

Moral reasoning involves making decisions based on universal principles, not on the needs of any one person or society.

Stage 5: Good of society—"If this law isn't really good for society, it can be changed." "You should do what you feel is right unless the majority of people have democratically agreed on something else."

Stage 6: Good of all people—"Is this really the best for people in general, even though it will mean a sacrifice for me?" "My society isn't going to benefit from this, but it is the right thing to do because it will mean greater equality among all people on Earth in the long run."

OVERALL CHARACTERISTICS

In these stages, two characteristics are evident:
1. The decisions people make through their moral reasoning move from selfish to unselfish decisions.
2. The decisions people make require them to decide what is right in a given situation. In making this decision, people may decide on the basis of selfish or unselfish reasoning, depending on the stage they are in.

Kohlberg's Moral Judgment Scale determines the stage a person is in by presenting him with a dilemma that has many solutions. Each solution is different and represents the moral basis a person used to decide what the dilemma's solution should be. An example of one of Kohlberg's dilemmas is:

> In Europe, a woman was near death from cancer. One drug might save her, a form of radium, that a druggist in the same town had recently discovered. The druggist was charging $2,000, which was 10 times what the drug cost him to make. The sick woman's husband, Heinz, went to everyone he knew to borrow the money, but he could only get together about half of what the drug cost. He told the druggist that his wife was dying and asked the druggist to sell it cheaper or let him pay later. The druggist refused. The husband became desperate and broke into the store to steal the drug for his wife. Should the husband have done that? Why or why not?

Kohlberg's theory has implications for teaching. Students cannot be expected to understand adult explanations of right and wrong because they do not have the cognitive ability to do so. Students are likely to be motivated by whether an action brings them reward or punishment rather than by whether it is right or wrong. Students will mature and begin to understand "why" if explanations are given. Eventually they will develop their own set of moral standards and values. To do so they will need to know and judge others' values and actions. Students need experience in situations requiring reflection and decision making to make logical–moral decisions.

Five guidelines have been used in developing teaching materials to stimulate students' movement to higher stages in moral development:

1. Genuine moral issues must be considered by students.
   They should be issues students are really concerned about.
   The teacher should not show any preferences for how these issues are re-solved.
2. Moral and social conflict must be experienced during the discussion of the dilemma.
   The dilemma should not be one on which everybody would quickly agree to a resolution.
3. Students need to practice applying what they are currently able to do to new problems.
   The teacher should not try to rush them into the next higher stage.
4. Students need to be exposed to peers who are in the next higher stage of development.
   Teachers should mix students in groups.
5. Students need to be confronted with their own inconsistencies over time.
   They should be asked to reflect on why they are making specific moral decisions. (Beyer, 1974)

Teachers should supply the basic data needed in a dilemma, remain neutral, and facilitate discussion of varying viewpoints in an open, nonthreatening atmosphere. Dilemmas often present themselves as events that occur in the classroom or are reported in the news media. Teachers should take advantage of these events. An example of such an event is a natural disaster occurring in a nation with which our country has serious political disagreements. Should we offer help? How much help should we offer? What kind of help should we offer? What should we do if some or any of our help is refused? Should we send help through a third country?

Teaching that focuses on a dilemma should utilize a learning cycle similar to that used with generalizations. Students are confronted with the dilemma during the exploration. During the invention they are asked to state the problem the dilemma brings up. Then they are asked to state a tentative position on the problem. During the discussion, the rationale for their positions is explored. Finally, a decision is made on whether or not to stay with the tentative position. During the expansion students might try to develop a scenario describing what happens as a result of the various decisions they have made. Or they might consider a dilemma presenting a similar problem.

Judgment has been found to become increasingly abstract up to around age 16 (Kohlberg, 1969), indicating that Kohlberg's insistence is accurate that cognition cannot be separated from moral development. It has been found, however, that an individual may seem to operate at two or more stages, according to which dilemma he is given. Kurtines and Greif (1974) suggest that Kohlberg's Moral Judgment Scale has problems: Many of the details of administration are left to the examiner, intuitive scoring methods are used, and reliability is uncertain because a person's score may fluctuate widely over a short period of time. They suggest that the instrument for identifying a person's stage of moral development may be the problem more than the theory itself. Since moral development comes through practice making and examining moral questions rather than through testing, teachers should concern themselves with providing students with lesson experiences in which they actively confront moral issues rather than trying to determine students' particular stages of moral development.

FACILITATING MORAL BEHAVIOR

Research indicates developmental changes in the moral judgments children can make. It is not clear, however, whether the development of moral conduct matches that of moral judgments. Does our ability to recognize what is morally best translate into action? Social rules and expectancies become part of social actions quite early in life. Qualitative shifts in cognitive development occur and follow predictable sequences. Teachers can facilitate students' internalization of moral behavior and decision making by using inductive reasoning with students and by verbally attributing prosocial motivation to students.

Even though research results are not clear, teachers can expect that students' cognitive developmental level will influence their ability to understand reasons for moral actions and for rules. Students will continue to need guidance, but it should be guidance resting on logical, prosocial reasons for acting in particular ways in a given situation. Finally, students must not be punished when they cannot understand that an action is wrong or inappropriate. Explanations and inductive reasoning will do them more good, as will the adult's understanding and appreciation of students development.

TEACHING APPROACHES IN VALUES EDUCATION

Three approaches have played important and often controversial roles in values education in recent years. These are values clarification, value analysis, and teaching a specific value. Each requires preparation and thought if it is to be used appropriately and effectively for the purposes for which it was designed.

VALUES CLARIFICATION

Values clarification is a teaching approach that developed in recent decades, along with the development of teaching approaches focusing on moral reasoning. In this approach, the emphasis is on the process of thinking about what is valued more than on the specific values themselves. The values-clarification approach is used to help students decide what they really think is important, what value they personally put on something. For example, the teacher may help the student explore just how trustworthy he or she really is and what they mean by being trustworthy. Would they keep a friend's secret when another friend is curious? Would they keep silent when the teacher is threatening to punish someone else for damaging a computer disk and they know their friend did it but have promised to keep it a secret? Is helping someone with math problems they find difficult without being asked for help part of being a trustworthy friend? Is refusing to listen to gossip about a friend part of being trustworthy?

Teachers often take advantage of events to involve students in values clarification. For example, a student might say "Anybody who burns the flag or does something like that should get out of this country. Love it or leave it." The teacher would respond with a series of questions that would encourage the student to explore the feelings that led to this statement. The teacher tries to remain neutral and serves as a facilitator of the student's own exploration of his feelings. The teacher does not try to instill a particular value in the students. Instead the teacher is recognizing that the student lives in a complex society where many different values are displayed by people. Students may not be sure what values they do hold, nor why they hold them. The teacher is trying to help students decide what they value and what is worth valuing (Raths, Harmin, & Simon, 1978, p. 10).

A seven-step process occurs in the values clarification process (Raths, Harmin, & Simon, 1978, pp. 63–65) as outlined in Table 10–3. This process takes place during the invention phase of a learning cycle. In the exploration phase, a situation occurs or is structured by the teacher, that offers an opportunity for values clarification. During the expansion, the teacher engages students in values clarification in a situation that is similar but has some distinct differences from the original problem. The process outlined in the seven steps is more of an orientation than a required strategy. Teachers adapt it to their students as needed. They may use it with the whole class, a small group, or a single student.

Table 10–3
The Values Clarification Process

1. Choosing freely
"Where do you suppose you first got that idea?" or "Are you the only one among your friends who feels this way?"

2. Choosing from alternatives
"What reasons do you have for your choice?" or "How long did you think about this problem before you decided?"

3. Choosing after thoughtful consideration
"What would happen if this were implemented? If another choice was implemented?" or "What is good about this choice? What could be good about the other choices?"

4. Prizing and being happy with the choice
"Are you happy about feeling this way?" or "Why is this important to you?"

5. Prizing and willing to affirm the choice publicly
"Would you be willing to tell the class how you feel?" or "Should someone who feels like you stand up in public and tell people how he or she feels?"

6. Acting on the choice
"What will you do about your choice? What will you do next?" or "Are you interested in joining this group of people who think the same as you do about this?"

7. Acting repeatedly in some pattern of life
"Have you done anything about it? Will you do it again?" or "Should you try to get other people interested in this?"

Adapted from L. Raths, M. Harmin, and S. Shore, 1978, pp. 63–65.

Often a teacher will use a clarifying response (Raths et al., 1978) with a student to help the student begin to become aware of and think about what he is thinking and feeling. The following exchange between a teacher and a student illustrates a teacher using clarifying responses.

Mr. Dolan: *You don't seem to be saying much in your group.*

Tasha: *Nope, I'm not.*

Mr. Dolan: *How is everything going?*

Tasha: *Everything's OK, no problems.*

Mr. Dolan: *You aren't having any problems.*

Tasha: *Everybody's OK in my group. I can talk if I want to.*

Mr. Dolan: *You aren't having any problems with the others in your group?*

Tasha: *Nope, they're OK. What we're doing is OK, too.*

Mr. Dolan: *What the group is doing seems OK to you.*

Tasha: *Yeah, I just don't feel like doing anything with them now.*

Mr. Dolan: *Think about what your group is doing and if there is anything you would like to do. Let's talk tomorrow if there is something you would like to do.*

The teacher has tried to remain neutral. Tasha hasn't been criticized or evaluated. The teacher is not trying to tell Tasha what she should be doing. He is trying to help Tasha think about what is keeping her from participating in her group. He is also encouraging her to consider what she might want to do. Clarifying responses that are often helpful to students include:

- Is this important to you?
- Are you happy about that?
- Did you think of other things you could do?
- Would you really do that or are you just talking? (Raths et al., 1978, pp. 59–63)

Clarifying responses are used extensively in the seven-step process outlined in Table 10–3.

There are several ways to carry out values clarification. Paper-and-pencil questionnaires can be used. These involve students in rank-ordering alternatives, in responding to a forced-choice set of statements, in using a checklist, or in indicating their position on a continuum.

In rank ordering, students are given a list of statements or items to order. The ordering can be from most to least important, most to least useful, most to least desirable, or any of a variety of other categories. For example, students could rank-order qualities they think are important in a good friend. Consider the example in Table 10–4. The rank orderings arrived at by the students should be discussed by the class after they are done.

A forced-choice activity makes students choose between two or more choices in responding to a statement. An example is given in Table 10–5. Students should mark their choices. Young children may be asked to choose between drawings of

Table 10–4

Sample Rank-Ordering Form

What Is Important in a Friend?

In class, everyone listed those qualities they thought were important in a friend. These are the qualities that were listed:

Has ideas for games	Likes things I like
Is happy	Listens to me
Does the same things as me	Agrees with me
Shares	Does what I say
Dresses like me	Tells me what he or she finds out

Which of these qualities do you think are the most important in a friend? Write them down. First write down the most important quality, then the next most important quality, and so on until you get to the least important quality.

Most Important Quality in a Friend: _____

_____

_____

_____

_____

_____

_____

_____

_____

Least Important Quality in a Friend: _____

situations, or they can raise their hands to register their choice as the teacher reads the items aloud. Afterwards, the teacher can tally the choices or students can do it as a group. As student choices are discussed, the teacher uses clarifying questions such as those in Table 10–3 to help the students probe the reasoning for their responses.

When a checklist is used, students are first presented with a statement, situation, or story that involves valuing. Then they are asked to check off those adjectives from a list of positive and negative adjectives that describe how they feel about the statement, situation, or story. Table 10–6 is an example of using a checklist in values clarification. Student responses on the checklist are used as the focus of a discussion that follows.

Table 10–5

Example of a Forced-Choice Questionnaire

People have ideas about what makes a good friend. Some people's ideas about which qualities a good friend has are given below. Do the following:
* Read each idea.
* If you agree with the idea circle **Agree.**
* If you disagree with the idea circle **Disagree.**

What Makes a Good Friend?

Agree	Disagree	1. A good friend smiles at you a lot.
Agree	Disagree	2. A good friend likes the same clothes you like.
Agree	Disagree	3. A good friend has ideas for things to do together.
Agree	Disagree	4. A good friend likes to do the same things you do.
Agree	Disagree	5. A good friend shares things with you.
Agree	Disagree	6. A good friend likes things you like.
Agree	Disagree	7. A good friend listens to you.
Agree	Disagree	8. A good friend does what you say.
Agree	Disagree	9. A good friend agrees with you.
Agree	Disagree	10. A good friend takes the blame when something goes wrong.

Table 10–6

Sample Checklist

What Is a Friend?

A group of students surveyed all the students in their school. Their survey was on the topic of "What is a friend?" After they put all their information together, they decided on the following description:

> A friend is someone who is just like you. A friend dresses like you, likes the same jokes, talks like you, and likes to play the same games. A friend never disagrees with you. A friend always lets you have first choice and shares everything. A friend never gossips about you and stands up for you to everybody else. A friend will lie about something if it will get you in trouble to tell the truth. A friend will never get mad at you.

What do you think about this description? Put a checkmark below beside each word that tells what you think about this description.

I think the description is:

_____ Helpful	_____ Silly	_____ Thoughtful
_____ Bad	_____ Impossible	_____ Important
_____ Wise	_____ Unimportant	_____ Good
_____ Strong	_____ Useful	_____ Weak
_____ Honest	_____ Tough	_____ Fair
_____ Mean	_____ Unfair	_____ Accurate

Table 10–7

Example of a Continuum

What qualities do you think a friend should have? Some choices are listed below. For each choice circle the quality you think is most important. You can circle the middle if you think this is best. Or you can circle between the middle and the quality if you think this best describes friendship qualities.

1. Always Shares				Never Shares
1	2	3	4	5
2. Always Listens				Never Listens
1	2	3	4	5
3. Always Imitates What I Do			Never Imitates What I Do	
1	2	3	4	5
4. Likes To Do What I Do			Doesn't Like To Do What I Do	
1	2	3	4	5
5. Dresses Just Like Me			Dresses Very Differently From Me	
1	2	3	4	5

A continuum allows students to indicate what they think within a range of possible responses (see Table 10–7). A continuum is more abstract than are the other paper-and-pencil formats. Students have to choose from the multiple alternatives represented by each continuum. Therefore, continuums are best used with students in upper elementary and middle school grades. Students' responses on the continuums can be tallied and discussed in class.

This process focuses on students' exploring their feelings. It does not emphasize thinking about how the choice fits into larger social problems or the effects such a decision would have if many people were to make it. The emphasis is on the personal, with less stress on wider implications. The continuum approach has been criticized because of its:

1. focus
2. broad interpretation of what a value is
3. lack of attention to what cognitive structures are needed for this type of questioning to help students successfully clarify their values (Fraenkel, 1977)

Values clarification generally focuses on a specific situation. Thus it can be criticized for promoting ethics that are limited or tied to a specific situation. The approach has been criticized for implying that a person's actions are governed by the situation, by what is practical now, rather than by moral principles that should apply in all situations. This criticism is leveled at the approach because the seven-step process does not ask students to justify their decisions. They could be learning that one viewpoint is as good as another no matter what the situation is. To some extent, it might also be criticized as amoral. Issues of privacy are raised when students are encouraged to state their beliefs publicly. The strategies used sometimes place teachers in the role of a psychological therapist, a role for which they have not been trained. The values-clarification approach has been strongly criticized. Public furor is sometimes created when it appears that the approach is being used. An overview of strategies for involving students in values clarification has been given above. Teachers should carefully study the approach to ensure that they are using it properly if they decide to include it in their teaching methods.

VALUE ANALYSIS

Value analysis involves strategies to help students think in an organized, logical manner about:

- their values
- why they make specific choices
- what the consequences of having a particular value are
- how a value may conflict with other people's values (Banks & Clegg, 1979; Taba, Durkin, Fraenkel, & McNaughton, 1971)

The five skills in Table 10–8 have been identified as important in analyzing values (Fraenkel, 1977).

Value analysis can occur at almost any time. The exploration phase of the learning cycle can involve either a situation planned by the teacher or can take advantage of an ongoing event. The value analysis occurs during the invention phase. During the expansion phase, values in a similar situation might be analyzed, or the same situation might be reanalyzed and the value(s) in it reconsid-

Table 10–8

Value Analysis Skills

1. Identifying values

Students identify the values people seem to have in a situation they are given to explore.

2. Comparing and contrasting values

Students identify and compare a person's values in different situations or the values of different people in the same situation.

3. Exploring feelings

Students come to understand the emotions or feelings associated with values as they talk about their own feelings, identify with others' feelings, and explore situations in which they find new feelings are aroused.

4. Analyzing value judgments

Students provide evidence supporting or refuting a value judgment.

5. Analyzing value conflicts

Students are confronted with a dilemma and determine what the conflicts are, what alternatives exist, what the consequences of each alternative might be, what the best alternative might be, and why it might be the best alternative.

Source: Adapted from J. Fraenkel, 1977.

ered. Sometimes a story from children's literature might lead to value analysis. For example, in the story of *Goldilocks and the Three Bears,* Goldilocks goes into someone else's house, eats their food, breaks their furniture, and sleeps in their beds. What values was Goldilocks displaying? Why did she do what she did? What were the results? Did what she valued conflict with what the bear family valued? Students' skills in value analysis can be built using a sequence suggested by Banks & Clegg (1979, p. 32). In an analysis of the story of *Goldilocks and the Three Bears,* the sequence suggested in Table 10–9 might occur.

Table 10–9

Value Analysis Sequence

1. What is the value problem?

Students should decide whether it is right for Goldilocks to be in the bears' house.

2. What is occurring that might involve values?

Students may decide that Goldilocks is eating food other people have made and sleeping in their beds without their permission and that she did break their furniture.

3. What does Goldilocks' behavior tell us about what she values? What does the bears' behavior tell us about what they value?

Students might decide Goldilocks values her own needs above all else. They might decide the bears value their right to privacy more than Goldilocks' right to satisfy her needs.

4. How do these values differ or conflict?

Students may decide that Goldilocks' and the bears' values are in conflict. The bears cannot have their privacy if Goldilocks feels the only way she can satisfy her needs is to enter their home immediately and not wait until they get home.

5. What are the sources of the values expressed?

Students may decide that Goldilocks learned at home that she doesn't have to wait to satisfy her needs. The bears may live in a community that regards the right to privacy as important.

6. What other values could be expressed? What alternatives are there?

Students may decide that Goldilocks could respect the right to privacy of the bears and wait until they got home to ask them to share their food and a place to sleep. Or, the bears could expect Goldilocks to come into their home and they would be upset if she didn't make herself comfortable in their home.

7. What are the consequences if various choices are made?

Students may decide that the consequences of Goldilocks' present choice is that the bears find their food eaten and their furniture broken. Also, the bears chase Goldilocks away. Making another choice, Goldilocks might have waited until the bears came home and asked them for help. Then they might have invited her into their house and shared what she needed with her. Or, maybe Goldilocks would have looked like a tasty morsel to the bears and they might have eaten her!

8. What choice do you make?

Students may decide that Goldilocks should wait until the bears get home and ask for their help.

9. Why did you make this choice and what will its consequences be?

Students may decide that Goldilocks should wait until the bears get home and ask for their help because she wasn't dying of hunger and should have had some respect for the bears' privacy. They might also decide that the consequences will be good; everyone will share and be happy.

Value analysis using the sequence in Table 10–9 can become a part of the teacher's repertoire of instructional strategies. When a situation arises requiring value analysis, the teacher can lead a discussion following this sequence. Older students can eventually learn to apply the sequence to situations where a value conflict occurs.

Situations where value analysis is helpful often occur. Children's literature presents many such opportunities. Legal cases also present such opportunities (Naylor & Diem, 1987, p. 367). Other sources of situations where value analysis may well occur are classroom incidents, personal incidents students recall, current events, and historical events. Some computer software such as *Taking Responsibility* (Tom Snyder Productions) offers opportunities to analyze values in a situation that is hypothetical, in this instance a situation in which two students have sneaked back into their classroom during recess and accidentally broken an item belonging to their teacher.

Time for Reflection: What Do <u>YOU</u> Think?

· Consider the sources of situations for value analysis and suggest one that you might use with a sixth grade class.

· What values do you think were in conflict in this situation?

The values-analysis approach has been criticized as too logical in attempting to analyze what is affective. Certain values, particularly religious values, must be taken on faith and cannot be logically analyzed. Value analysis may not always be appropriate but it gives students a means by which they can analyze social issues and problems. It is also helpful in personal decision making. These situations are all important in the social studies curriculum.

TEACHING A SPECIFIC VALUE

During the 1980s another approach to moral education evolved. This approach focused on teaching and modeling a specific value, such as honesty. Both values clarification and moral reasoning focus on the processes of reasoning and selecting values. Teaching a specific value focuses on behavior that demonstrates the value (Lopach & Luckowski, 1989; Parker, 1988; Wright, 1988). In this approach the exploration involves preparing a situation in which the value can be demonstrated. For example, a student can role play a situation such as returning to its owner money he has found. During the invention the value is modeled, described, and discussed. The teacher might have students read and analyze stories in which honesty is demonstrated. The value is demonstrated by students during the expansion. The students may devise their own role plays that demonstrate honesty.

The questions raised by this approach include "What values will be selected for the content of moral education?" and "Who will select them?" Advocates appear to believe that it is impossible to have a value-neutral education and that it is possible to agree on a common set of core values to be taught. There is an emphasis on promoting cohesion across all groups in our society by promoting a common set of core values. Others are concerned about whether teachers will be expected to indoctrinate students with a set of values selected by an elite group. Some curriculum guides, particularly the California Framework for History/Social Science, stress values.

The three approaches discussed here indicate the range of purposes that exists in values education. This is an area that is basic to social studies curriculum and to all of education. Yet it is an area having no clear specifications. Researchers and curriculum developers have put a great deal of effort into developing and testing the approaches described. Each has something to offer teachers and students. However, each must be approached with thought and attention to how it is carried out and why it is being used.

ATTITUDES

Attitudes are a mental set toward taking some action based on the desirability of anticipated consequences. The anticipated consequences may be thought to be desirable, creating a positive attitude toward the action. Or they may seem to be undesirable, resulting in a negative attitude towards the action.

Social studies is concerned with social attitudes and also with attitudes towards social studies and the social sciences. Attitudes exist when a behavior is displayed as a regular pattern in a range of similar situations. They limit or facilitate the application of skills and ideas. For example, if a student is not willing to try to understand an argument or an explanation, it does not matter that he is capable of understanding.

Attitudes are learned from experience, developing gradually as a result of encouragement and example. Prosocial attitudes are encouraged by taking the perspective of others, through empathy and role taking. Learning to take the perspective of others increases students' ability to set moral standards and use them to make mature value decisions (Selman, 1976). Taking the perspective of others involves knowing what others want, feel, and believe. This is not enough, however, to make students behave considerately. Teachers need to call attention to, and explain, other people's perspectives if students are to learn to be sensitive to these perspectives (Bearison & Cassel, 1975).

Empathy involves reacting to another person's situation or display of emotion with the same emotion the other is experiencing. A student who feels happy when another student feels happy is responding empathically. Role taking involves accurately understanding what another is feeling, thinking, or perceiving, but it does not necessarily involve actually feeling the same way as another person (Perry & Bussey, 1984, p. 256). A student who realizes another student feels happy but who does not himself feel happy is involved in role taking. Both empathy and role taking are other-oriented capacities and contribute to prosocial behavior. In elementary and middle school students, empathy is associated with a willingness to help others who are having problems, including people who seem to be lonely and people who have had accidents and may be hurt (Weissbrod, 1976). Empathy develops when students are involved repeatedly in experiences where they both have the same emotion, such as happiness. Teachers using small-group activities increase the likelihood that students will experience the same emotion as a result of the activity they are jointly involved in. A student's empathic responding can be strengthened if, when disciplining the student for causing another's distress, teachers draw the student's attention to the other's distress while at the same time scolding the student (Maccoby, 1980). Teachers can also do this by encouraging the class to acknowledge the happiness or pride of fellow students in various accomplishments. Role taking can be strengthened by providing students with opportunities to practice the behaviors desired. For example, students who were involved in skits where they acted out how each of several story characters was feeling were later found to be more likely to share with a needy other (Iannotti, 1978).

As generalized aspects of behavior, attitudes cannot be taught in the way that specific facts and skills can be. Teachers need to be aware of the potential influence of the attitudes they model as important persons in their students' lives. Teachers need to address attitudes students have, discussing them in an open manner while avoiding indoctrination into the teacher's attitudes. There is evidence that an attitude has been learned when teachers see in their students a new willingness to take (or refrain from) an action based on the learner's:

- concept of what the action is
- predictions as to the desirable or undesirable effects of taking (or not taking) the action (Seiger-Ehrenberg, 1991, p. 292)

DEVELOPMENT OF ATTITUDES THAT PROMOTE MEANINGFUL LEARNING IN SOCIAL STUDIES

Attitudes are affective responses that reflect our feelings and personal likes and dislikes. The development of attitudes that promote meaningful learning is a fundamental role of the social studies curriculum (see Table 10–10).

CURIOSITY

A curious student wants to know, try a new experience, explore, and find out about things around him or her. This is an attitude that promotes all kinds of learning.

Curiosity often appears in the form of questioning. Inviting students to ask questions is one way of showing that curiosity is valued. Asking students to verbalize their questions too early can create problems, however. Something new may elicit questions that are no more than expressions of interest. For example, when looking at a picture of a bullfight in Chile, a student may ask, "Why are there more

Table 10–10

Attitudes of Value in Learning Social Studies

1. Curiosity
   a. questioning
   b. wanting to know

2. Respect for evidence
   a. open-mindedness
   b. perseverance
   c. desire to know the evidence behind statements
   d. willingness to consider conflicting evidence

3. Flexibility
   a. willingness to reconsider ideas
   b. recognition that ideas are tentative

4. Critical thinking
   a. willingness to consider methods
   b. wanting to improve on past ideas and performance

5. Responsibility to people and the environment

horses with men riding them than there are bulls in the ring?" A student needs time to take in what is there and relate it in his mind to what is already known. Then he will be ready to ask the questions that help him make sense of it. After having some time to examine the bullfight picture and think about it, the student may ask "Why do these people think it is fun to kill a bull?" or "Do animals die often in the kinds of races we have, like horse races or dog races?"

Young children and those with a limited attention span may get no further than asking the superficial question that expresses interest before they turn to another topic. Questioning brings satisfaction if it helps them share their pleasure and excitement with others. Teachers should welcome and provide opportunities to ask questions in order to promote curiosity. Satisfaction resulting from expressing curiosity helps students gradually sustain interest for longer periods and ask more thoughtful questions relating what the student knows to the new experience.

Curiosity is a wanting to know rather than a flow of questions. Wanting to know stimulates effort to find out, perhaps by investigation, using a library or making a special visit. One of the goals of the exploration phase of the learning cycle is to create curiosity.

RESPECT FOR EVIDENCE

Open-Mindedness. Social studies is concerned with the social world. To examine the social world and to make decisions about it, evidence must be gathered and used to develop and test ideas. Students and teachers must be open to seeking and hearing various views and to examining problems before they can make meaningful generalizations. A social theory is not useful until it has been shown to fit evidence or make sense of what is known. The use of evidence is central to social studies activity of students, citizens and social scientists.

Students show they know that an unsupported statement is not necessarily to be believed when they ask "How do you know that's true?" or when they say "Prove it." Adults often expect students to accept statements because of the authority of their position. This may reduce the students' desire to ask for evidence. If a teacher appears to accept statements without evidence or offers no evidence for a statement, the attitude that evidence is not necessary is transmitted. Asking for evidence and reasons is essential in social studies education, especially in a democracy.

Perseverance. To obtain really convincing evidence often takes perseverance. Sometimes it seems impossible to gather evidence for something, yet when the student keeps on trying, it becomes possible. Perseverance does not mean keeping on trying if something is not working. It does mean being willing to try again, learning from earlier difficulties, and changing your ideas as a result of what has been learned. Teachers should provide students with some social studies assignments that require seeking out information rather than just accepting the most easily available information.

Willingness to Consider Conflicting Evidence. It is not easy to extend a respect for evidence to situations where other evidence or other ideas may conflict with what you think you already know. A respect for evidence involves the willingness to do this. Students are more likely to be willing to consider conflicting evidence —even if it leads to mistakes—if their teacher accepts the mistakes and rewards the students' effort.

RESERVING JUDGMENT

A respect for evidence requires reserving judgment. An individual does not make a judgment until an effort has been made to find out whether there is conflicting information, and such information is willingly considered and is used in making a decision. Students find this a difficult process which does not result in immediate satisfaction. Instead, there is a period of uncertainty and of mental challenge before a judgment occurs.

FLEXIBILITY

Mental flexibility relates to the products of social studies activities in a manner similar to the way respect for evidence relates to the processes occurring in social studies activity. The concepts and generalizations that we form when trying to understand the social world change as experience adds more evidence to develop or contradict them. Such changes are most rapid in children's early years since their limited experience means their first ideas are often quite different from what they need to understand. Unless there is flexibility, each experience that conflicts with existing ideas causes confusion and creates a rival idea instead of modifying and developing an existing one.

Flexibility and a recognition that conclusions are always tentative is important in social studies. We never can have all the evidence, so there is no certainty that our ideas can be absolutely correct. Elementary and middle school students may not be able to understand the tentativeness of ideas, but teachers need to promote attitudes that will enable them to eventually develop this understanding. One way of doing this is to preface conclusions with a statement like "As far as we can see. . . ." It also helps to talk with students from time to time about how their ideas have changed and about how they used to think.

CRITICAL THINKING

Both before and after arriving at a conclusion, students need to be willing to consider the process they followed in reaching the conclusion. Are their methods logical? Are they making unwarranted assumptions? Are they skipping a necessary step? A willingness to consider those methods used helps students evaluate the methods they use, discover problem areas, and reflect on how they might do things differently. Wanting to improve on the ideas they have and on the processes they use to come to conclusions is an important attitude in students. Such a desire to improve leads to a willingness to consider the processes followed in reaching conclusions. It makes students more willing to identify problems and to seek alternatives.

Robert Ennis (1991, p. 68) provides a working definition. "Critical thinking is reasonable, reflective thinking that is focused on deciding what to believe or do." It requires us to be disposed toward: seeking a clear statement of a question, seeking reasons, trying to be well informed, using credible sources, taking into account the whole situation, trying to keep with the main point and the original question, being open-minded, reserving judgment, persevering, being willing to consider conflicting evidence, being flexible, and being curious. These dispositions are accompanied by abilities that are constructed over time. Teachers can have an important role in helping their students construct these abilities. Ennis (1991, p. 68–71) identifies five major abilities:

1. clarification (focusing on a question, analyzing arguments, asking/answering clarification questions)
2. support (judging credibility of sources, making observations)
3. inference
4. advanced clarification (defining terms and judging definitions, then identifying assumptions)
5. strategy and tactics (deciding on an action and carrying it out)

RESPONSIBILITY TO OTHERS AND THEIR CULTURE

In social studies, students are encouraged to investigate and explore their social environment in order to understand it and to develop skills for further understanding. Such investigation and exploration should involve an attitude of respect for others and the environment and a willingness to care appropriately for the people and things in the environment. Growth in inquiry skills should be accompanied by a development of sensitivity and responsibility toward the social and physical environment.

A sense of responsibility toward someone or something is more likely to occur when a person has had experience with that person or thing or knows something about him, her, or it. For example, a person who has painted walls in a house and understands the effort that goes into this task is likely to take more care of the walls than someone who has not been so involved. Knowledge and experience help, although they are not enough to create the attitude.

Many of the concepts relating to responsibility for and sensitivity to people and the environment are complex (interdependence, for example) and sometimes controversial (the use of nuclear power), but it is still possible to begin the development of attitudes toward people by example and rules of conduct. Rules that teachers and students have agreed on help establish a pattern of response, but only when students begin to act responsibly (e.g., not taking others' pencils or destroying others' property). The way to accomplish this is to gradually hand over to the students the responsibility for making decisions about how they should behave.

The development of these attitudes is important not only in learning social studies but also in becoming a responsible citizen in a democracy. With them, students can begin to perceive social studies as a search for knowledge and understanding.

Time for Reflection: What Do YOU Think?

Describe an activity that a teacher can do in each part of a learning cycle to promote a student's self-concept, identity, or acquisition of a value.

· Grade Level

· Objective

· Exploration Activity

· Invention Activity

· Expansion Activity

SUMMARY

Personal and social development occur because of maturation and also because of experience. Teachers can provide experiences that will encourage students' development, help them cope with difficulties they encounter, develop morals and values, and develop attitudes that are prosocial and conducive to learning. Both adults and students' peers have some effect on students' development. The teacher is a powerful person in a student's life and must work to ensure that his or her effect is a positive one for the student as an individual and as a participating citizen in a democracy. The area of psychology and values education is one that is generally acknowledged to be part of the school's curriculum. However, it is an area requiring sensitivity to the needs and cultural background of each student. It is an area where each student will have different needs and where each of these needs has a strong impact on the student. Because of the needs each student has and because of the differences between students there has been controversy over how this psychology and values education is taught. Moral reasoning and values clarification are two areas that have generated a lot of this controversy. Much of the controversy is due first to the recognition that psychology and values education are both important and sensitive issues, and second to conflicting ideas on how to teach them well. The controversy often involves people's basic beliefs about morality and students' relationships with each other. Since this is an area in which issues have not been resolved, we most likely will continue to see debate.

REFERENCES

Bandura, A. (1977). *Social learning theory.* Englewood Cliffs, NJ: Prentice-Hall.

Banks, J. & Clegg, A. (1979). *Teaching strategies for the social studies: Inquiry, valuing and decision making* (2nd ed.). Reading, MA: Addison-Wesley.

Bearison, D. & Cassel, T. (1975). Cognitive decentration and social codes: Communication effectiveness in young children from differing family contexts. *Developmental Psychology, 1,* 29–36.

Beyer, B. (1974). *Ethnicity in America.* Pittsburgh: Social Studies Curriculum Center, Carnegie Mellon University.

Coopersmith, S. (1967). *The antecedents of self-esteem.* San Francisco: W. H. Freeman.

Ennis, R. (1991). Goals for a critical thinking curriculum. In A. Costa (ed.), *Developing minds: A resource book for teaching thinking.* Revised edition, Vol. 1, Alexandria, VA: Association for Supervision & Curriculum Development.

Fraenkel, J. (1977). *How to teach about values: An analytic approach.* Englewood Cliffs, NJ: Prentice-Hall.

French, D., Brownell, C., Graziano, W., & Hartup, W. (1977). Effects of cooperative, competitive, and individualistic sets on performance in children's groups. *Journal of Experimental Child Psychology, 24,* 1–10.

Ginsburg, H. & Opper, S. (1979). *Piaget's theory of intellectual development* (2nd ed.). Englewood Cliffs, NJ: Prentice-Hall.

Hartup, W., Glazer, J., & Charlesworth, R. (1987). Peer reinforcement and sociometric status. *Child Development, 38*(1017–1024).

Hoffman, M. (1977). Moral internalization: Current theory and research. In L. Berkowitz (ed.), *Advances in experimental social psychology* (Vol. 10, pp. 86–127). New York: Academic Press.

Iannotti, R. (1978). Effect of role-taking experiences on role-taking, empathy, altruism, and aggression. *Developmental Psychology, 14*, 119–124.

Kohlberg, L. (1969). Stage and sequence: The cognitive developmental approach to socialization. In D. Goslin (ed.), *Handbook of socialization theory and research* (pp. 118–140). Chicago: Rand McNally.

Kurtines, W. & Greif, E. (1974). The development of moral thought: Review and evaluation of Kohlberg's approach. *Psychological Bulletin, 81*, 453–470.

Lopach, J. & Luckowski, J. (March, 1989). The rediscovery of memory in teaching democratic values. *Social Education*, 183–187.

Maccoby, E. (1980). *Social development: Psychological growth and the parent–child relationship.* New York: Harcourt Brace Jovanovich.

Maccoby, E. & Masters, J. (1970). Attachment and dependency. In P. Mussen (ed.), *Carmichael's manual of child psychology* (3rd ed., Book 2). New York: Wiley.

MacDonald, N. & Silverman, I. (1978). Smiling and laughter in infants as a function of level of arousal and cognitive evaluation. *Developmental Psychology, 14*, 235–241.

Maxim, G. (1989). *The very young: Guiding children from infancy through the early years.* Columbus, OH: Merrill.

McGhee, P. (1976). Children's appreciation of humor: A test of the cognitive congruency principle. *Child Development, 45*, 552–556.

Naylor, D. & Diem, R. (1987). *Elementary and middle school social studies.* New York: Random House.

Pagano, A. (1978). Children learning and using social studies content. In A. Pagano (ed.), *Social studies in early childhood: An interactionist point of view* (pp. 82–94). Washington, DC: National Council for the Social Studies.

Parker, W. (1988). Why ethics in citizenship education? *Social Studies and the Young Learner, 1*, 3–5.

Patterson, G. (1976). The aggressive child: Victim and architect of a coercive system. In L. Hamerlyck, L. Handy, & E. Mash (eds.), *Behavior modification and families. 1. Theory and research* (pp. 267–316). New York: Brunner-Mazel.

Perry, D. G. & Bussey, K. (1984). *Social development.* Englewood Cliffs, NJ: Prentice-Hall.

Piaget, J. (1951). *Play, dreams, and imitation in children.* (C. Gattegno & F. Hodgson, Trans.). New York: Norton.

Piaget, J. (1954). *The construction of reality in the child.* (R. Cook, Trans.). New York: Basic Books.

Quilty, R. (1975). Imitation as a dyadic interchange pattern. *Scandinavian Journal of Psychology, 16*, 223–239.

Raths, L., Harmin, M., & Simon, S. (1978). *Values and teaching* (2nd ed.). Columbus, OH: Merrill.

Reisman, J. & Shor, S. (1978). Friendship claims and expectations among children and adults. *Child Development, 49*, 913–916.

Rest, J. (1983). Morality. In J. Flavell & E. Markham (eds.), *Carmichael's manual of child psychology* (4th ed.). New York: Wiley.

Scarcella, R. (1980). *Teaching language minority students in the multicultural classroom.* Englewood Cliffs, NJ: Prentice-Hall.

Sears, R. (1963). Dependency motivation. In M.R. Jones (ed.), *Nebraska symposium on motivation. 2.* Lincoln, NE: University of Nebraska Press.

Seiger-Ehrenberg, S. (1991). Concept development. In A. Costa (ed.), *Developing minds: A resource book for teaching thinking.* Revised edition, Vol. 1, Alexandria, VA: Association for Supervision and Curriculum Development, 290–294.

Selman, R. (1976). Social-cognitive understanding: A guide to educational and clinical practice. In T. Lickona (ed.), *Moral development and behavior: Theory, research, and social issues.* New York: Holt, Rinehart & Winston, 299–316.

Singleton, L. & Asher, S. (1979). Racial integration and children's peer preferences: An investigation of developmental and cohort differences. *Child Development, 50*, 936–941.

Smilansky, S. (1968). *The effects of sociodramatic play on disadvantaged preschool children.* New York: Wiley.

Sunal, C. (1986). Parent involvement in social studies programs. In V. Atwood (ed.), *Elementary school social studies: Research as a guide to practice.* Washington, DC: National Council for the Social Studies.

Sunal, C. (1990). *Early childhood social studies.* Columbus, OH: Merrill.

Taba, H., Durkin, M., Fraenkel, J., & McNaughton, A. (1971). *A teacher's handbook to elementary social studies* (2nd ed.). Reading, MA: Addison-Wesley.

Walker, L. (1983). Sex differences in the development of moral reasoning: A critical review. *Child Development, 54,* 1103–41.

Weissbrod, C. (1976). Noncontingent warmth induction, cognitive styles, and children's imitative donation and rescue effort behaviors. *Journal of Personality and Social Psychology, 34,* 274–281.

Wright, I. (Fall, 1988). Citizenship education and decision making. *International Journal of Social Education,* 55–62.

CHAPTER 11

OVERVIEW

When you hear the word "geography" do you think of the question "Where is it located?" Locating places on a map or globe is the task that most Americans associate with studying geography. Geographers do much more than locate places. In this chapter you will learn how to sequence and teach the many skills used by geographers, especially the unique set of skills associated with mapping and map reading. You will become acquainted with the important concepts and generalizations of geography as applied to local, national, and global regions. Suggestions are offered on how to sequence the skills and concepts associated with the five themes of geography throughout the elementary and middle school social studies curriculum.

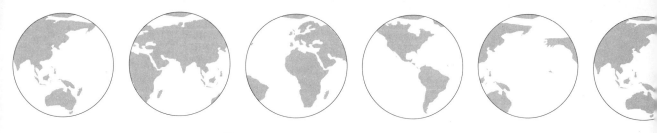

Geographic Education

OBJECTIVES

1. Identify each of the five themes of geography.
2. Explain how the five themes of geography are used in the social studies curriculum to teach geography.
3. Identify activities that help students to describe the three-dimensional characteristics of the world and translate them into the two-dimensional map.
4. Explain the advantages of using the globe with students.
5. Identify the key concepts and skills needed to use maps.

DEFINING GEOGRAPHY

Time for Reflection: What Do <u>YOU</u> Think?

Which of the following questions are geographic questions?

1. What religion calls its place of worship a mosque?
2. Where are the tropical rain forests of the world?
3. What is a good agricultural product to raise in a rocky and mountainous area?
4. How is a business district different from the residential area of a city?
5. How are the Rocky Mountains different from the Appalachian Mountains?
6. What routes did people take to get to California during the Gold Rush?
7. Where do our fresh fruits and vegetables come from during December and January?
8. Why do African fishermen paint brightly colored designs on their boats?
9. Why do the Egyptians build their homes in the desert instead of on the flood plain?
10. Should our state legislature pass a law prohibiting sanitary land-fills from receiving waste from other states?

Everyone wants to know what is happening around them. Because of this curiosity everyone, even the very young child, has a little bit of the geographer in them. Geographers have developed their search for knowledge about the world into a discipline that stresses both
• knowledge about the world
• a systematic approach to gaining and interpreting that knowledge.
Geographers begin their study by asking "where?" but spend the vast majority of their time investigating the question, "Why is this where it is?"

Geographers are unique because they apply their efforts to understanding both the physical and cultural characteristics of the world. They approach their study through the perspective that location is an important characteristic of everything on earth. They believe that through the study of locations and their relationships to each other, geographers can help explain the dynamics of the world. For that reason geographers look more for similarities than for differences. When they do encounter a unique difference, they seek to learn why this is different from what they expected.

Geographers believe that their goal of understanding how all of the parts of the world are globally interrelated is very important for today's citizens. They point out that there are not only global systems in nature such as winds and currents but that many cultural systems such as communications and transportation are also global in nature. For this reason geography helps us understand our own nation and our interdependence with other people throughout the world. When examining these worldwide geographic distributions, geographers address many of the issues and concerns of the curriculum movement in global education.

Both the elementary and middle school social studies and natural science curriculums contain many elements of geography. When these elements are taught as individual facts in isolation from one another they fail to be remembered and do little to help citizens make wise decisions about how they should interact with the natural and cultural world. In 1984 the members of the National Council for Geographic Education and the Association of American Geographers issued *Guidelines for Geographic Education: Elementary and Secondary Schools*, their recommendations for improving geographic education in the United States. These guidelines organize all the elements of geography under five themes, which can be more easily remembered and used than could all the separate elements.

■ THE FIVE THEMES OF GEOGRAPHY

Professional geographers recommend the use of five organizing concepts or themes for schools:
* location
* place
* relationships within places
* movement
* regions

Each of these themes can be understood at different levels of concreteness and abstraction, and so the five themes can be used at all grade levels. Geographers recommend that the youngest students consider the environments they know and can explore through their own observation and interactions. As students acquire more skills, they use more indirect sources of data. As a result, they expand their knowledge about the world and their definition of each theme to include new examples and new relations or generalizations about the themes.

THEME 1—LOCATION: POSITION ON THE EARTH'S SURFACE

The importance of location is the fundamental assumption of geography. Sometimes we need to know an absolute or exact location, such as in which room in the school will we find the fourth grade. At other times we can be satisfied with a more general or relative locational description, for example, "Much of the world's oil is found around the Persian Gulf." Some of the activities that fall into the location theme are learning to locate places

- in the community
- on the earth
- on a map or a globe.

THEME 2—PLACE: NATURAL AND CULTURAL CHARACTERISTICS

This theme is descriptive of both the natural and human features of the landscape. Learning concepts that describe different features such as mountains, plains, capital cities, and the developing world are a part of the place theme. Students gather data and answer questions to help them describe places. Such questions might include:

- What is the lay of the land?
- How much water is present at this place?
- Does the water usually come from the atmosphere as rain or snow or from a stream or body of water?
- Are there lots of wild animals living in the area?
- Do plants dominate the landscape or is the land largely bare?
- Are there many people in this place?
- Have the people done much to change the appearance of the area?

THEME 3—RELATIONSHIPS WITHIN PLACES: HUMANS AND ENVIRONMENTS

The natural environment tends to limit what people can do in a place. However, throughout history people have been quite clever in dealing with these limitations. In dry areas where there was not enough water to grow needed food, people found ways to bring water to where it was needed. Today people in dry places with advanced transportation systems do not worry about growing their food; they use their transportation facilities to import the food. The learning cycle in this chapter uses the theme of relationships within places (see Table 11–1).

Table 11–1

A GEOGRAPHY LEARNING CYCLE: People and the Environment

Geographic Theme: Relationships within Places—Humans and Environments

(For Primary and Intermediate Grade Levels)

OBJECTIVES	PROCEDURES	EVALUATIONS
	Exploration	
Students will suggest what the word "environment" means to them.	While the students are out of the room rearrange the desks, turn off the lights, start a tape of soft music and spray the room with a flower-scented room freshener. If the students do not notice the changes when they return to the room, ask them how the	Students' participation in making suggestions on paper.

room has changed. Ask for their reactions to the changes: "Do you like these changes in the environment?" Ask: "What do you think of when you hear the word environment?" Record each response on a slip of paper and place it on the bulletin board.

Invention

Students will classify elements of the environment into those created by people.

Students will identify changes in environments and suggest if the changes were caused by nature or people.

Students will judge changes in the environment as positive or negative and give reasons for their judgments.

Over several days' time, have students work in small groups to classify sets of pictures and locate pictures that illustrate various aspects and ideas about the natural and human environments and change.

The following are appropriate tasks: Identify natural and human impacts or changes, identify scenes similar and different from their own area, examine pictures from other nations and classify them, and decide if the changes they observe are positive or negative. Have students record their classification titles and decisions regarding positive or negative changes. (Note: The content of the pictures given to the group will guide their classification possibilities.)

Each day the groups should share the ways they classified the picture and discuss their findings and conclusions. At the end of their daily discussions they reorganize the bulletin board by moving, removing, or adding new words, pictures, and conclusions.

Record of decision regarding positive or negative changes.

Record of classification schemes prepared by each group.

Expansion

Students will plan for and change the environment of their classroom.

Display a list of occupations including doctor, clerk, janitor, lumberjack, architect, farmer, and gardener. Ask the students, "Do any of these people have jobs that cause them to change the environment as they work?"

Ask the students for suggestions regarding how they could change the environment in their classroom. Have each student develop a plan for changes in the classroom. Through discussion arrive at a consensus regarding how the classroom will be changed. Record these decisions on a classroom map.

Have the students change the room to reflect a holiday, new season, or topic being studied.

Additional actions might include taking part in a clean-up campaign or researching laws concerning the environment.

Individual and final classroom changes to map and action taken in making those changes.

THEME 4—MOVEMENT: HUMANS INTERACTING ON THE EARTH

People do not remain in one place nor do they only use resources from the place where they live. While this has been true throughout all of recorded history, it is more apparent in the modern world. With an ever-increasing technology, the interactions of people will probably continue to increase. The movement of ideas and products affects not only places of origin and destination but also places along the way. Raw materials are extracted, new products are grown or produced in factories, transportation centers are expanded or established. Ideas such as preservation, conservation, and democracy are being heard and attempted in new places. People not only travel to other nations to visit, but people in a wide range of occupations often spend part of their working lives in other nations. There are also systematic movements among the natural forces of the earth. For example, currents carry warm and cold water to new locations; they also carry pollution created by people to new locations throughout the globe. Global problems are concerns of geographers as they study movements between places and regions.

THEME 5—REGIONS: HOW THEY FORM AND CHANGE

It is difficult to conceive of the scale of the entire world, so geographers frequently divide it into regions to conduct their studies. After studying many regions, geographers begin to get a picture of how the entire world works as they investigate the interactions of regions. Since the criteria for establishing a region is determined by the person doing the study, a region can be as small as the individual classroom, school, neighborhood, or community with which very young students are familiar and in which they can observe and investigate. As students develop their understanding of the five themes of geography and develop their skills, they can begin to study the larger and more formal regions that are defined by physical and topographic features or political control. Those regions, such as the Middle East and the Far East, which are defined by the interaction of many complex features are appropriate for study by students who have well-developed concrete reasoning schemata or are formal thinkers.

GEOGRAPHIC LEARNING

Stoltzman (1990) explains that geographically literate citizens are aware of:
- what is happening in the world
- why it is happening
- how it impacts other people throughout the world as well as themselves

Therefore, geography is good citizenship education.

In reviews of research on geographic learning both the teams of Rice and Cobb (1978) and Buggy and Kracht (1988) concluded that elementary students do have the abilities to learn geographic skills. They also concluded that carefully planned instruction at the primary and elementary grades is effective in increasing both geographic knowledge and skills.

A 1988 survey of the Council of Chief State School Officers of states and territories reported that 93 percent of their schools planned to increase emphasis on geography at the elementary level within the next five years. Geographers are working with teachers in the schools through the State Geographic Alliance System. Most states have such alliance efforts. In addition, the National Council for Geographic Education has increased its efforts in working with the schools and has produced many new publications and studies to help teachers.

WHAT WERE YOUR RESPONSES TO THE TEN QUESTIONS ?

Now that you have learned more about the definitions of geography, examine your responses to the series of questions at the beginning of this chapter in Time for Reflection: What Do <u>YOU</u> Think? (p. 256). Eight of the ten questions are geographic in nature (2, 3, 4, 5, 6, 7, 9, and 10). Questions one and eight are more representative of questions that an anthropologist would ask.

SEQUENCING CONCEPTS IN GEOGRAPHIC EDUCATION

In the traditional elementary and middle school social studies curriculum, place names, locations, recognition of physical landforms, and map and globe skills have been the geographic content stressed. Textbooks have introduced geography in grades 1 and 2 and emphasized it in grades 3 and 4. In the third grade text, rural and urban communities have been examined, while fourth grade books have tended to emphasize climatic and physical regions of the world.

Textbooks have emphasized the place theme by discussing concepts such as mountain, river, plain, continent, equator, suburb, community, transportation, and lake (Haas, 1991). The location theme has been emphasized through map exercises that have students locate places and symbols and identify directions on maps of classrooms and familiar locations such as shopping centers. Scale has been introduced in grade 3 and grid systems in grade 4 (Haas, 1989). Thus the elementary social studies curriculum has tended to continue to teach the stereotypical view of geography as a study of locations.

A major problem of emphasizing only the location and place themes is that their study becomes one of trying to commit isolated information to memory. Pigozzi (1990) concludes that the most important reason for learning geography is its usefulness, which is made clear through the relationship and movement themes. It is only through learning all of the themes that students can combine a sufficient number of appropriate concepts to form generalizations in geography. Table 11–2 shows a number of geographic concepts and relates them to the appropriate themes of geography. The generalizations students make can be tested by examining similar types of data from another region.

All five themes of geography must be stressed at all grade levels. This is possible since geographers do study the world by dividing it into small regions. Very young students learn geography through personal interaction with their own environments. They observe their surroundings in the school, on short walks or field

Table 11–2

The Five Themes of Geography and Related Concepts

LOCATION	PLACE	RELATIONSHIP	MOVEMENT	REGION
absolute	environment	attitude toward	migration	nation
grid system	landform	adaptations	diffusion	physical
map/globe	climate	inventions	barriers	cultural
legend/key	land use	technology	systems	community
relative	vegetation	pollution	currents	states
directions	elevation	changes	wind	Middle East
distance	population density	industry	transport	Europe
scale	rural/urban	deforestation	communicate	historical
equator	buildings	conservation	causes	district

trips, and record their information in simple essays, drawings, and maps. When making their maps and drawings, students decide what things they observed that are important to include and what symbols to use. Sequence, approximate size, and locations relative to one another are the characteristics of the spatial skills on the maps of students at the K–2 level. They compare their personal observations with similar information indirectly gathered through pictures and stories about other regions of their community, state, nation, or other nations. By identifying similarities and differences, they refine and elaborate their concept definitions. The learning cycle approach to structuring lessons provides the student with time and opportunity not only to be exposed to knowledge but also to examine concepts and their relationships and to test and refine their conclusions and generalizations.

Since learning cycles are not complete until the students relate concepts to each other and to new situations, organizing lessons into learning cycles requires careful inclusion of related concepts. The knowledge is presented in a connected way so that students are assisted in organizing the knowledge for more systematic storage in their memories. Superordinate concepts should be stressed. For example, when students learn about rivers they do not stop with the idea that rivers are moving bodies of water. Instead they learn that rivers are a unique type of body of water that moves through a channel from a source, to its mouth. Along its course the river may form a flood plain and a delta. Students learn that waters of the rivers don't just move over the earth but that they change the earth as they move and that the appearance of the water also changes. Sometimes rivers take away the earth and at other times they create new landforms. Sometimes a river is peaceful and helpful to people while at other times and places it can be dangerous and destructive. The number of generalizations, the degree of complexity, and the depth of the evaluation of how people should act toward rivers are determined in the learning cycle by the level of development of the student's knowledge and skills.

Young students can examine pictures of rivers and their landforms. They might decide if the scene is peaceful or dangerous. Students who can gather data from maps might also examine national or world maps and discover the sources of large rivers and follow the course of the rivers. They might also identify the cities that are located along the river's course and relate their sizes to the distance between the cities. Still older students who can understand the relationship among incline, speed, and runoff might predict where dangerous situations might develop along the course of a river. These students might also evaluate the cost of controlling a river or learn how laws restricting the use of land help reduce such costs.

In planning a geography learning cycle, the teacher should keep in mind the experiences, skills, and interests of the students as well as the five themes of geography. The teacher must decide what is important and useful for students to learn. A first grade teacher in an area where flood watches are common might include a discussion of flood watches and how to respond to them, while a first grade teacher in another region might dismiss the idea as unimportant and irrelevant for first graders.

As students develop their skills, they can begin to study more complex regions and issues. It is the complexity of the region that makes it more difficult to understand—not its distance from the student as the expanding horizons curriculum assumes. There is a difference between actual geographical distance and psychological distance. What is understandable is directly related to common experience and empathy. Therefore, it is possible for young students to be interested in and to learn accurate and legitimate information about areas of the world that are far away from them in geographical distance. It is particularly important with young students to

- give students enough accurate information
- have students look for similarities
- link these with familiar concepts
- help students imagine how the people in another place would feel or respond.

For example, young students who learn about Mexican students celebrating a holiday with a piñata should be led to see that the Mexican children get presents and candy just like they do on special days such as birthdays, Easter, Hanukkah, or Christmas.

Geographic knowledge at all grade levels should include a consideration of all of the five themes of geography and should stress the concepts related to each theme. Table 11–3 describes student activities appropriate to each of the five themes. Some of the activities are more appropriate for the primary level (K–3), intermediate level (3–5), or middle grade level (6–8). As you read through the list, try to assign an appropriate grade level to each activity. Among the list are four activities that might be appropriately presented to all three levels of students by changing the examples or region of study.

DEVELOPING SPATIAL CONCEPTS

It is not until after the age of 11 or 12 that students develop an understanding of the reference systems that enable them to locate items in their correct positions and at correct distances from one another. This means that students in grades K–5 will understand space in a way different from that of the geographer, and that

Table 11–3

Sample Student Activities for the Five Themes of Geography

THEME	INITIAL INSTRUCTION (GRADE LEVELS)	CONTINUED USE (GRADE LEVELS)
Location: Position on the Earth's Surface		
learning to read maps and globes	K–2	3–8
plotting a route for a field trip	K–2	3–8
gathering data from a map to write a report	4–6	6–8
learning about day/night	K–2	3–8
Place: Natural and Cultural Characteristics		
planning a trip to a place	K–2	3–8
comparing charts of pictures for similarities and differences	K–2	3–8
making or reading graphs of climate	4–5	6–8
identifying nations from clues	4–5	6–8
Relationships within Places: Humans and Environment		
discussing the causes and solutions to problems of endangered species	4–5	6–8
determining ways weather has influenced their behavior and that of people in another location	K–2	3–8
comparing graphs of population density and elevation	6–8	
reading about earthquakes, tornadoes, floods, etc.	3	4–8
Movement: Humans Interacting on the Earth		
locating cities or nations where class families have lived	K–2	3–8
locating where their food was grown	1–3	4–8
tracing the path of a product from its origins to you	3	4–8
keeping track of the places they hear about on the news	3	4–8
Regions: How They Form and Change		
listing the differences in parts of their city	1–2	3–8
identifying boundaries for states and nations	3	4–8
dividing their school into areas where certain activities happen	K–2	3–4
doing an extended study of Latin America or the Old West	5	6–8

even older students may have difficulty understanding the world as it is spatially presented on maps. This does not mean that maps should not be used or map conventions taught prior to the 5th grade, but it does mean that the types of maps used will be different. It also means that the types of information included on a student's map or observed by a student on an adult's map will probably be interpreted differently by the student and the adult.

Geographers have studied how students learn about maps. After an extensive review of such research studies, Rushdoony (1968) made recommendations about instructing students in map and globe use beginning with 4-year-olds in the preschool.

A person begins to develop his or her spatial understanding in the first few months of life. Early development of spatial understanding is greatly influenced by the egocentric nature of the learner. At first children view things from their own perspective. Later they come to recognize that there are multiple perspectives from various locations. Last, they are able to use an abstract reference system to locate items in relationship to one another. The three types of space that children come to understand are:

- topological
- projective
- Euclidean

TOPOLOGICAL SPACE

Topological space is the first type of space that students come to understand. Preschool children have mastered some of its elements. Topological perceptions include:

- proximity or near-byness
- separation
- order
- enclosure
- continuity (Holloway, 1967)

The concept of "stands for" or "symbol" is also understood by very young children. Therefore, they can identify simple symbols on maps and locate them in order. They can differentiate shapes and be taught to place labels on them.

When very young students make their maps they are usually linear and are closer to pictures. This is because items are shown visually and not from the perspective usually used in maps, that of directly above. Things are shown as connected but distance is not correctly shown nor is direction.

Elements of topological space continue to dominate mapping efforts until the onset of concrete operations at about age 7 (Downs et al., 1988). The child's concept of form will be more accurate than that of distance. Several researchers report that they have been successful in teaching students between ages 4 and 7 elements reflective of topological space that appear on maps (Savage and Bacon, 1969; Atkins, 1981; Downs et al., 1988). However, all report variation in success within the class and greater success when concrete items and terms are used.

PROJECTIVE SPACE

Beginning in the preoperational stage (approximately ages 4–7), students start to understand elements of projective space. This enables them to see that items appear different from various distances and angles. These new understandings enable them to develop the idea that "locations are related to other places." This leads to a better understanding of distance and direction. Their maps become roughly accurate (Catling, 1978). These changes in a student's understanding of space take place between the ages of 7 and 11.

EUCLIDEAN SPACE

As students become formal operational (between ages 12 and 16) and increase their knowledge of concepts and language, they relate locations correctly to one another simultaneously (Holloway, 1967). Direction and distance become accurate and are measured in relationship to such abstract coordinates as the prime meridian, the equator, and the poles.

LEARNING MAP AND GLOBE SKILLS

Maps and globes are important tools for geographers because they provide a convenient way to organize data by location. By their very nature maps and globes are quite different from the real world. They are not a picture of the world but an interpretation of the map maker. They contain only that information that the map maker considers important to include for the purpose of the map. Therefore, one of the most crucial elements of a map is the title of the map. The title tells the reader what major idea is shown on the map. Maps can show a wide variety of information—from the way to a friend's house to the location of volcanoes throughout the world.

One of the best ways for students to learn the definition of a map is to make their own maps (see Figure 11–1). In so doing, they encounter and solve the same kinds of problems professional map makers encounter. Mapping the classroom, the schoolyard, or the route taken on a neighborhood walk is an excellent choice for primary grade students. Such mapping may begin by making three-dimensional models in a sandbox, on a table, or on the floor with blocks, milk cartons, or plastic models. Older students might map their individual routes to school or their rooms at home before studying about continents and nations. Students should also have the opportunity to examine a variety of maps made by cartographers so that they can compare and judge their own ideas against those of professionals. Such an activity is appropriate for students of all ages. The teacher will be able to infer the spatial skills a student understands from the maps that student makes.

While globes and maps have been relatively expensive and were fragile in the past, today they are more durable and are made from a variety of materials at greatly reduced costs. Schools can now afford to have several globes so that small groups of students can explore and mark on a globe rather than gaze at it from afar. Maps, too, are being made of new materials that are cheaper and more durable, making it possible for each student or pair of students to have an atlas or placemat-like map before them. Such instructional materials provide students with a more active involvement in learning.

Figure 11–1 Children can construct a more thorough understanding of maps and of their community by making their own maps.

Put a globe where young students can get to it, and you will see how they are drawn to explore its wonders and to ask questions. It is this model of the earth that should be studied before maps are introduced. There are several reasons for introducing globes before maps. First, a globe is more concrete and realistic than a map. Second, students are familiar with models because of their toys. Third, while maps may include more specific information, all of the information that is used in reading a map is available on the globe, and the globe presents the information more accurately. The shape, location, relative location, distance, and size are all more accurate on the globe than they can ever be on a map. Because of their two-dimensional nature, maps show distances and shapes inaccurately. Map users see misinformation that can lead to misconceptions. Misconceptions not only impede a student's ability to answer geographical questions correctly, but they often remain even after instruction tries to correct them. For instance, many American children believe that Alaska and Hawaii are islands located just a little west of California and Mexico or in the Gulf of Mexico. It is the visual impact of the larger items on a map that helps create and maintain such misconceptions.

Reading a map or globe requires knowledge concerning the four superordinate concepts of:

- symbols
- directions
- distance
- grid systems

and the conventions of their presentation on globes and maps. Like most concepts, each of these can be understood at a variety of levels of abstraction. It is also possible to use these concepts correctly on a map without thoroughly understanding them—just as it is possible to drive a car without understanding how its various systems work. However, understanding does account for greater success in use and especially in knowing *when* maps can be most effectively used. Each of these concepts must be introduced, practiced, and refined by the student throughout the elementary and middle school grades.

Very young students can begin to learn from and about globes and maps. The first maps should be of familiar locations and should use few symbols. In sixth grade textbooks, publishers provide students with the various types of maps found in most commercial atlases. However, students at this age are just beginning to develop their understanding of the abstract Euclidean space that these maps use, and they are just starting to read locations, distance, and elevations with exact measurement. The use of topographic maps and symbols can be introduced as students increase their understanding of Euclidean space and think more in abstract terms.

Geographers divide map and globe work into three types of skills:
- map making
- map reading
- interpretation

The interpretation of data on maps is related to the complexity of the question being asked and to the data that students can read and understand from the map. Even young students should be encouraged to make inferences and to interpret data from a map based on their mastery of spatial concepts. Only older students can be asked to begin making inferences from data shown on two or more maps.

SYMBOLS

The idea that something represents or stands for another thing is learned in the preoperational stage, usually around ages 5 to 7. Globes and maps are themselves symbols and they make extensive use of symbols. There are two types of geographic symbols:
- point symbols
- area symbols

Point symbols are used to denote those locations that cover small areas, which would appear as a point on small-scale map or globe. The simplest point symbols to identify are called pictorial symbols because they appear similar to a picture of the real item. Maps for the beginner use a few pictorial or semipictorial symbols. The increased details of pictorial symbols require lots of space. As map makers include greater amounts of information on a map, they simplify the symbols that make them abstract.

Area symbols are those that are used to show things that cover acres or square miles of land. Shading and colors are area symbols, and they are very abstract. There are few universal symbols on maps and globes, partly because there are so

Figure 11–2 In one class, each student contributed to the legend for a map by drawing one of its symbols on a card.

many things that might appear on a map. Even the meaning of a color may change from map to map.

Maps have legends or keys to specify the meaning of symbols used on a particular map (see Figure 11–2). Students must learn the habit of using the legend to be able to read maps. Symbol is the first of the superordinate concepts related to maps that students come to understand.

DIRECTION

Directions are learned initially in relationship to oneself and then in relationship to other objects. Pointing to and describing where things are in relationship to the self, to other people, and to objects is the beginning of directional activities. Students in the early primary grades have these capabilities. Knowing left from right is important for learning map directions since east is 90 degrees right of north and west is 90 degrees left of north. Students should be taken outside to learn to locate north. Then they should face north and locate east and west by raising their arms. Students should be told south is to their backs when they are pointing east with their right hands. The walls in the classroom should then be labeled with the correct directions. Items outside and inside can then be located in relation to the cardinal direction from the student and from other objects. When maps and globes are introduced, they should be oriented correctly toward the north, and students should be encouraged to trace directions with their fingers over the surface of the globe or map. Students in the early primary grades can memorize directions on a map and give correct answers, but this does not mean that they understand directions.

DISTANCE

Correct measurement of distance on a map using a scale requires accurate use of mathematics skills, an understanding of proportionality, and the ability to divide quickly. A student must also be able to conserve distance or recognize paths of the same length. Distance does not mean only a straight line measure; it is also the key to the correct size and shape of an area. Therefore, exact measures of distances should not be attempted until students are in the intermediate grades. However, relative distances can be considered in the primary grades. Near, farther away, and farthest can be introduced.

Because the globe provides a more accurate presentation of distances in all directions than does a world map, measurement of world distances should be done first on the globe. Pieces of string can be stretched over a globe between two points to get a relative measure of distances between places (see Figure 11–3). The pieces of string can be compared to see which is longer. As the string is laid on the globe, the student can also observe the directions of the path one would travel to get between the points. Students can be asked to decide what means of travel they would use to get from one place to the other. When actual measures in miles are needed, a string or strip of paper is placed between the points and then moved to the scale where the distance is read by placing the paper or string next to the scale.

GRID SYSTEMS

The grid system is the most complex of the four superordinate concepts. It is a way of finding location. The idea is that a vertical line and a horizontal line will intersect at only one place. To use a grid system, the student needs to understand this principle and to practice locating the correct intersections. Grid systems are first taught by using a system similar to that used in locating a seat in an auditorium with numbers for the rows and letters for the seats. When transferred to a map, letters are placed along the horizontal axis and numbers along the vertical axis. Road maps of individual states usually include this type of a grid system. Such a grid system gives an approximate location. The grid system can also be introduced with a dot-to-dot game concept. Children's names can be used to identify the individual lines (both vertical and horizontal). Then, they can identify the

Figure 11–3   Young children measure distances between places on a globe using pieces of yarn.

points where their lines intersect with other students' in the class (where does Mary's line cross Cindy's?). Exact locations are given by the system of latitude and longitude. Each line of latitude and longitude is identified by a number and a direction. Since every line of latitude or longitude is not on a map, locating places by latitude and longitude requires the ability to sequence numbers in relationship to the rectangular grid. It also requires the ability to estimate. Directions on a map must also be understood.

In addition to symbols, directions, distance, and grid systems, students must understand what is shown on a map. This also requires an understanding of physical concepts such as mountains, lakes, and rivers, and of cultural concepts such as cities, buildings, and bridges. A student who really understands maps should be able to visualize the landscape shown on the map. He or she should be able to correctly match a map with photographs and aerial photographs of places shown on the map.

READING AND MAPS

Reading words on a map is different from reading words in a story. Except for the title of the map, words on a map are labels for specific locations. Words may be placed in very different ways on a map. Reading left to right is not always

Using a map to plan a route for a field trip can be fun.

the standard convention on a map. Sometimes the words are written at odd angles. Map makers spread the label out to cover the areas being designated. Many words are spread out much wider than the normal reading eye span. This is particularly true on wall maps. The style of print is often used as a symbol. More important features will have fonts that make them more visible. The same type of font will be used to designate all of the same type of feature or type of region. The teacher needs to assist students in discovering the ways words appear on a map.

The following instructional activities help students construct map and globe concepts and provide practice using the skills needed to read and interpret data from maps and globes.

1. Students arrange a box of crayons, pencil, book, and scissors on their desktops and draw a map illustrating the arrangement. They remove the items and give them along with their map to a partner. The partner then uses the map to place the items on his desktop. The map drawer checks to see if the arrangement is correct.
2. Younger students make "Me Maps." A tracing is made around the body and the children use the agreed upon symbols to draw on their eyes, nose, heart, knees, ears, mouth, waist, and elbows in the correct locations.

3. Students follow a map to go on treasure hunts within the school or on the school grounds. The maps may be drawn by the teacher or other students.

4. Students map their classroom or school grounds selecting what information to include and the symbols to use. They then place each symbol in the appropriate location. Actual measurement of distance can be used if the students have such skills.

5. Students make maps illustrating the route they take to school. Older students also write directions to their homes, which classmates trace on a map.

6. When taking a field trip, students use a city or state map to plan the routes to and from their destinations. Older students can measure the distance involved and try to locate the shortest route. They may also write out a set of directions for the trip.

7. Students plan trips to visit famous cities and landmarks. They compute the distance traveled.

8. Using an atlas, students trace the courses of major rivers from their sources to their mouths. They tell the directions the rivers flow and the elevations of the sources and they identify landmarks along the rivers' courses.

9. Students use the gazetteer to find the latitude and longitude of cities they hear or read about and locate them on the map.

10. Using the equator, prime meridian, and other selected meridians and parallels as a guide to location, students make freehand drawings of regions or the world.

SUMMARY

Geographers have long recommended that map skills be taught beginning in the primary grades through the use of developmentally appropriate activities. They see drawing maps, reading maps, and making inferences and comparisons as techniques to help students develop their thinking skills and knowledge of geography (Winston, 1984). The emphasis in the elementary grades on learning map skills has helped give students and teachers the impression that location is geography. By introducing a definition of geography containing the five themes that can be taught at all grade levels, geographers believe that students will better understand the world in which they live.

REFERENCES

Atkins, C. (1981). Introducing basic map and globe concepts to young children. *Journal of Geography, 80*, 228–232.

Buggey, J. & Kracht, J. (1985). Geographic learning. *Elementary school social studies: Research as a guide to practice.* Bulletin 79, V. Atwood, (ed.). Washington, DC: National Council for the Social Studies.

Catling, S. (1978). The child's spatial conception and geographic education. *Journal of Geography, 77*, 24–28.

Council of Chief State School Officers. (1988). *Geography education and the state.* Washington, DC: Council of Chief State School Officers.

Downs, R., Liben, L., & Daggs, D. (1988). On education and geographers: The role of cognitive development theory in geographic education. *The Annals of the Association of American Geographers, 78,* 680–700.

Haas, M. (1989). Teaching geography in the elementary school. Bloomington, IN: Clearinghouse for Social Studies/Social Science Education. ERIC Digest EDO-SO-89-6.

Haas, M. (1991). An analysis of the social science and history concepts in elementary social studies textbooks grades 1–4. *Theory and Research in Social Education, 19,* 211–220.

Holloway, G. (1967). *An introduction to the child's conception of space.* New York: Humanities Press.

Joint Committee on Geographic Education of the National Council for Geographic Education and the Association of American Geographers (1984). *Guidelines for geographic education: Elementary and secondary schools.* Washington, DC: The Association of American Geographers. ED 252 453.

Meyer, J. (1973). Map skills instruction and the child's developing cognitive abilities. *The Journal of Geography. 72,* 29–35.

Pigozzi, B. (1990). *A view of geography and elementary education* (Elementary Subjects Center Series No. 18). East Lansing: Michigan State University, Institute for Research on Teaching, Center for the Learning and Teaching of Elementary Subjects.

Rice, M. & Cobb, R. (1978). *What can children learn in geography?: A review of the research.* Boulder, CO: Social Science Education Consortium. ED 166 088.

Rushdoony, H. (1968). A child's ability to read maps: Summary of the research. *The Journal of Geography, 67,* 213–218.

Savage, T. & Bacon, P. (1969). Teaching symbolic map skills with primary grade children. *The Journal of Geography, 68,* 326–332.

Stoltzman, J. (1990). *Geography education for citizenship.* Bloomington, IN: ERIC Clearinghouse for Social Studies/Social Science Education.

Winston, B. (1984). *Map and globe skills: K–8 teaching guide.* Indiana, PA: National Council for Geographic Education.

CHAPTER 12

OVERVIEW

Everyone needs to know about their past. This chapter is concerned with how we learn about our past and how that past can be made meaningful to us as individuals and as citizens of an increasingly interdependent world. The study of history can be personal and exciting, but more often it is seen by school children as remote and uninteresting. Students have difficulty giving reasons for studying history, as it does not seem to serve a utilitarian need. In this chapter several reasons for studying history will be investigated. A variety of ways to help students gather data about history will be suggested. The chapter will also consider how to help students begin to examine history in order to identify the contributions it makes to their lives and their future.

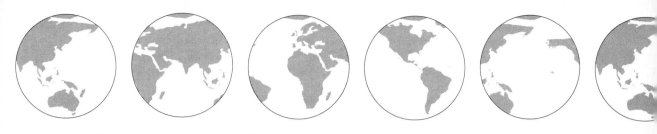

History Education

OBJECTIVES

1. Differentiate between the definition of history given by the scholar and that used in the schools.
2. Identify four goals for the study of history.
3. Explain why studying different topics in history is suggested for elementary and middle school students.
4. Describe how time lines are used to assist in developing an understanding of time.
5. Explain how the learning cycle approach to teaching is appropriate to the needs of students in studying history.
6. Identify the various resources that should be used in teaching history to students and explain the contribution each makes to the development of historical understanding.
7. Explain the importance of teaching students to think critically about historical events and people.

DEFINITION OF HISTORY

Think for a moment about your experiences in the study of history, then do the activity below.

Time for Reflection: What Do <u>YOU</u> Think?

- Identify at least six things that define, for you, the study of history.

- Examine your list. What appears to dominate? Is it predominately a list of people, events, and dates? Did you include references to a method of study? Does your idea of history seek to give a meaning to what is going on in the world? Is your idea of history dominated by the dead and the nonrelevant? Or is your idea of history one of a continuous process of providing meaning that helps you understand today's world and gives you a glimpse into the future? Do you see history as providing you with a set of true relationships that explain the past, the present and the future?

- Discuss your answers with friends. Do they see history as you do?

- Can you offer an explanation for differences or for the lack of differences?

History means different things to different individuals. Even historians do not agree on a single definition of history or what constitutes an appropriate historical problem for investigation. This is one of the major problems facing the teaching of history at all levels. However, historians generally agree on three important aspects. History is **a chronological study** that **interprets and gives meaning to events** and **applies systematic methods to discover the truth.**

Unlike the social scientist, the historian cannot rely on observations and experiments to gain facts. The historian has only what has been left and preserved to provide hints as to what may have taken place. Like the detective, the historian must conduct an exhaustive search to find many clues. Discoveries are most likely just clues, not complete records. They reflect the perspectives and memories of their preservers. Therefore, the historian interprets the evidence, deciding on the degree of its importance and its accuracy. The ability to place times and events in chronological order is important in establishing cause-and-effect relationships. Historians not only examine the motives and actions of people but often apply principles from science to help them interpret the evidence. Working in history requires the scholarly values of logic and persistence. When the answer is found the task is still not completed; the results must be communicated to others or the knowledge may be lost forever.

HISTORY IN SCHOOLS

History plays an important role in the social studies curriculum. American history is the most common single course among the states' social studies curriculum requirements. State histories are also among the most frequent requirements.

Historians have played a major role in all of the national commissions and committees that have addressed both history and social studies from 1892 until 1989 (Hertzberg, 1989). History is one of the specifically identified subjects in goal 3 of the National Goals for Education (1990) that will help prepare students for "responsible citizenship, further learning, and productive employment in our modern economy." The statement goes on to say that "All students will be knowledgeable about the diverse cultural heritage of this nation and about the world community." (United States Department of Education, 1990, pp. 5–6.)

Two important dimensions of citizenship education in a democracy have been identified by Engle and Ochoa (1988). Socialization is the process whereby a child comes to accept and support his or her culture. This provides for the continuity of the society. For a democracy to continue to reflect the will of its people, Engle and Ochoa suggest that its citizens must also experience the forces of counter-socialization. Such forces require people to examine their personal and social beliefs and to analyze the problems of their nation and their world. Counter-socialization activities require views to be supported with reason and evidence. Such behaviors are needed from citizens in a democracy who have the job of deciding which ideas, institutions, programs, and behaviors should continue, should be changed, or should be abolished. Clearly, the study of history provides the opportunity for both socialization and counter-socialization experiences. Engle and Ochoa suggest that very young children should receive instruction that is largely socialization, but that some counter-socialization instruction is appropriate in the later elementary grades. The learning cycle, "The First Thanksgiving in the United States," is an example of how history helps socialize students (see Table 12–1).

The role of the study of history in the schools has been predominately that of socializing the young into the American democratic tradition and preparing them to be citizens. Much study has been devoted to learning about the origins of the nation and its struggles to grow physically, politically, and economically. Famous people and events have tended to dominate the study of history. Perhaps your definition of history greatly reflects this traditional approach to history. In recent years social and ethnic groups have argued for the addition of new important events and a wider range of people in an attempt to present a more accurate interpretation of the nation and the world.

Table 12–1

HISTORY LEARNING CYCLE:
The First Thanksgiving in the United States

History Theme: First Thanksgiving (For Primary and Intermediate Grade Levels)

OBJECTIVES	PROCEDURES	EVALUATIONS
	Exploration	
Students identify the tasks people must do when they move.	Ask: "How many of you have ever moved?" Divide class into groups of 4. Each group is to pretend it is a family and make a list of things they must do because they will be moving in a month or two. Consider how you will get to your destination, where you will stay when you arrive, what you will take with you. Have groups share their lists and record a composite on the board. Discuss tasks with which the children in the family might help. As a homework assignment: from your own things select those that you would take if you were moving, but everything you take must fit into one large brown grocery sack. Bring a list of these items to class tomorrow.	Students working together in groups make logical choices. Note participation (checklist may be used).
	Invention	
Students express their awareness of the difficulties of moving and make decisions based on personal priorities. Students compare physical differences in moving today and in 1620.	Children share their lists and discuss the reasons for their selections. Discuss: "What was the first thing they selected?" "What did you want to take that you had to leave behind?" "Would you have made the same selection if you knew there were no stores in the place you were going to?" Discuss any changes they would make. This was the problem the Pilgrims had. Trace route of Pilgrims on map or globe. The trip took 66 days. Show sheet 3 from *Coming to America* kit*, how the Mayflower was loaded with people and supplies. Discuss how the trip of the Pilgrims was different from traveling today. Record differences on board. "Do you think the Pilgrims had as much difficulty deciding what to take as you did?"	Students' feelings and concerns. Record participation on a checklist.

Checklist of students' participation in recording differences on board. |
| Students identify items Pilgrims might have brought with them based on what students recognize as their needs and space. | Ask students to make a list of what they think the Pilgrims brought with them. Classify the items. Did students mention tools, household items, arms, clothing, and food? Examine sheets 4 and 5 for ideas. Compare these ideas of scholars to students' list. No one really knows for certain what the Pilgrims brought with them. | Students' listening and classifying. |
| Students work in small groups to gather data from books about | Students work in small groups using books about Pilgrims and Thanksgiving to find answers to assigned questions. Give each group different questions from categories such as: reasons for leaving | Appropriateness of answers to questions. |

| Pilgrims and Thanksgiving. | England, problems on ship, surviving/living in Massachusetts, celebrating first Thanksgiving. Groups report their research to the class and discuss why Pilgrims felt they should celebrate. | |
| Students draw conclusions regarding how contemporary and Pilgrim Thanksgivings are similar and different. | Compare our modern-day celebration of Thanksgiving with the first Thanksgiving by listing similarities and differences on the board. Write two summary statements together, one for similarities and one for differences. | Students share ideas, recorded on participation checklist. |

Expansion

| Students compare celebrations of the harvest in Korea, the Philippines, and the United States by identifying similarities and differences. | Recall reasons for Thanksgiving and when it is celebrated. Ask: "Do you think only Americans celebrate a Thanksgiving?" "Why?" "Why not?" Provide short readings on Chusongnal in Korea and Pista Ng Aniham in the Philippines. Ask students to identify at least 3 similarities with the way the Pilgrims celebrated. Identify at least one idea from each celebration that you find interesting and different from our Thanksgiving. Tell why you selected it. Discuss: "Why do farmers throughout the world celebrate at the end of the harvest?" Today, few Americans are farmers but we still celebrate Thanksgiving. "Why do you think we continue to celebrate Thanksgiving?" | Students give accurate comparisons and show interest, as recorded on a checklist. |

*Coming to America *kit. Chicago: National Livestock and Meat Board.*

The most recent assessment of students' knowledge of United States history by The National Assessment of Educational Progress in 1988 measured what students in grades 4, 8, and 12 had learned along a continuum of four levels of proficiency:

- *Level 200:* Knows simple historical fact
- *Level 250:* Knows beginning historical information and has rudimentary interpretive skills
- *Level 300:* Understands basic historical terms and relationships
- *Level 350:* Interprets historical information and ideas

The questions were written to reflect three areas believed to be critical in studying American history: chronology, context, and reasoning skills.

At the fourth grade, about three-quarters of the students performed at or above the lowest level (200) of proficiency while only sixteen percent reached or exceeded Level 250. Their knowledge of history consisted largely of facts that can be learned from everyday experience. Fourth graders could give reasons that specific national holidays were celebrated, could identify national symbols, and could match accomplishments with names of key people.

The eighth graders displayed a surface understanding of information but little in-depth knowledge. Two-thirds performed at or above Level 250, but only thirteen percent performed at or above Level 300. Their understanding of history was limited to knowing details and terms. They had difficulty in seeing relationships between events.

Among the high school seniors, 89 percent achieved at Level 200 and 46 percent at Level 300 but only 5 percent showed proficiency at Level 350.

Students at all grade levels had some knowledge of United States history. Their knowledge and understanding appeared to increase with age. However, the majority of high school seniors lacked the higher levels of skills necessary to see relationships and interpret information and ideas.

Students in the study were questioned concerning what history they had studied and the methods they used in studying. Among the fourth graders, 83 percent reported studying a variety of history topics to varying degrees. The greatest emphasis was on the Native Americans, Pilgrims, and American colonies. Ninety-five percent of the eighth graders reported that they had studied United States history in grades 5, 6, 7, or 8. Half indicated that they had not studied the period from 1945 to the present while the highest numbers of responses indicated they had studied the period of time through the end of the Civil War. Ninety-five percent of the seniors reported having studied United States history during their high school careers. Those whose study lasted a year or more performed better that those reporting less time in studying United States history. Clearly, the study showed that students were capable of learning history when given the opportunity. The most frequently used methods reported were reading and memorizing textbook material rather than analyzing sources and documents and interpreting their meaning.

BENEFITS OF STUDYING HISTORY

In response to concerns over what they saw as an inadequate quantity and quality of history teaching in American elementary and secondary schools, the Bradley Commission on History in the Schools was formed in 1987. Their final report has been endorsed by the major national organizations of historians and history teachers. The Bradley Commission says that the study of history is "vital for all citizens in a democracy, because it provides the only avenue we have to reach an understanding of ourselves and of our society, in relation to the human condition over time, and of how some things change and others continue." (Bradley Commission, 1988, p. 5). The benefits can be grouped into three categories.

- *First,* personal benefits lie in helping individuals attain their identity by finding their own place in the history of the world.
- *Second,* the study of history helps individuals better understand and study the other humanities.
- *Third,* unifying citizens into communities is done through creating a national identity.

People learn the growth and development of a set of common beliefs and actions that enables them to function as a group with common aims. The intellectual skills used and promoted by the systematic study of history help all people develop intellectually.

The Bradley Commission refers to these intellectual skills as the "habits of the mind." The commission goes on to say that the principal aim of the study of history is the development of the perspectives and modes of thoughtful judgment associated with the study of history. Table 12–2 lists the perspective and the particular modes of thought that historians use in making their critical judgments and interpretations of people, institutions, and events. The modes of thoughtful judgment are similar to the tasks of critical thinking that go into making a decision, whereas the perspectives are more similar to conclusions about the world from the study of history. Thus, historians view the benefits of studying history first from a personal perspective, while the creators of the school curriculum tend to see the benefits of studying history primarily as its contribution to a sense of community and national unity.

Time for Reflection: What Do YOU Think?

- Look at Table 12–2. Rank the six statements in the Perspectives column from most important to least important in contributing to a sense of community and national unity in the United States.

- Now look at the Modes of Thoughtful Judgment column. Which of these statements must be performed to reach the conclusion in your first ranked perspective? Your second, etc.? Rank the Perspectives again but with the individual's personal learning and needs as the consideration. What major differences do you notice in the rankings? Are the same modes of thought still the most important with your new ranking?

- Discuss your ranking with your classmates. Your rankings and matches may vary. Try to identify reasons for this.

Table 12–2
Habits of the Mind Associated with History

PERSPECTIVES	MODES OF THOUGHTFUL JUDGMENT
Understanding the past is significant to individual and society	Distinguish between significant and inconsequential
Comprehend the diversity of cultures and shared humanity	Develop historical empathy
Comprehend the interplay of change and continuity	Identify causal factors
Accept uncertainties of life	Determine consequences
Consider conclusions and generalizations as tentative	Identify multiple causation
Read widely and critically	Evaluate ethics and character
	Explain role of geography and time
	Identify facts, assertions, inferences, and evidence

In creating a curriculum, educators must establish goals and rank them according to the knowledge, skills, and attitudes to be learned. By doing this exercise and sharing it with others, you have encountered some of the problems of establishing a curriculum in history. Did you agree with your classmates? Did you have any difficulty understanding what the historians were trying to say? Do you think that the historians would understand your views? At one time curriculum decisions were made by politicians, scholars, and administrators. Teachers' organizations struggled for a long time to obtain entrance into this process. This exercise has been simplified by reducing the number of viewpoints to only two. After compromises are made and the goals accepted by all, the next part of the problem is placing learning goals into an appropriate order for teaching and assigning them to grade levels. Teachers and researchers have important roles in this process.

CHILDREN AND THE LEARNING OF HISTORY

While children may not be able to understand history as completely as the historian does, they are able to deal with some aspects of the study of history just as they deal with certain aspects of mathematics, science, music, art, and the social sciences. Many educators and historians advocate the early teaching of history and suggest specific content and ways to improve students' poor knowledge of history. Few, however, investigate what kind of history students know or how children actually learn history. In the following section, research findings and the guidelines suggested for the curriculum are discussed.

HISTORY AS A DISCIPLINE

Piaget explains that children learn about their world and its working by interacting with people and things. He found that children up to the age of 7 or 8 tended to confuse the age of something with its size (Piaget, 1969). However, they did understand that birth order determines the age of people and that this age difference remains constant through time.

A preoperational child's ability to understand time is closely related to intellectual tasks of centration and reversibility (Sunal, 1990). The tendency to center attention on only a part of an event prohibits the ability to see relationships within an event. The inability to reverse the thinking process keeps a child from correctly sequencing events and prohibits seeing causes and effects. These difficulties should no longer be of great concern once the students are at the concrete operational stage, which includes the majority of students in grades 3 through 8.

STUDENTS' AND HISTORIANS' UNDERSTANDING OF TIME

In summarizing the research on students' understanding of time, Zaccaria (1978) found that the ability to think formally about time as measured by Piaget's testing procedures develops during the middle to late teens. This was much later than formal reasoning for other disciplines. The characteristics of time investigated were largely those of physical time, order, succession, and velocity associated with science. Many question whether these characteristics of time are the same as the time that the historian uses. Zaccaria developed a table identifying four different uses of time. In it he showed that an understanding of time begins during the first year and continues to maturity. Zaccaria's four uses of time include:

* a past time that is remembered and related to present actions
* the use of time as a frame for marking activities
* a time in the future that can be modified by acting now
* time relating to the skills used in history or the interest in history

Accordingly, an understanding of various uses of time are present in such comments as: "This morning in school," "When I was younger," "This week," "Study time," "Next month," and "Time marches on." In their research, Levstik and Pappas (1987) found that students in grades 2, 4, and 6 associated history and chronology by placing events into time spans ranging in complexity from "long ago" to "the time of the Incas" and the "American Revolution." These various uses or schema of time tend to remain a part of the adult's concept of time.

Time for the historian is most important in establishing the sequence of events needed to validate a cause-and-effect relationship. Time is also important in the recognition of examples of such historical concepts as change and continuity.

OTHER ASPECTS OF THE STUDY OF HISTORY

Four purposes of teaching history in the elementary school are identified by Hoge and Crump (1988, p. 14):

* to make the past seem real
* to build insights into present circumstances and events
* to develop a love and respect for history learning, including an understanding of its limitations
* to help students recognize their own relationship to history

These goals are different from, but related to, those of the professional historian. Table 12–3 identifies sample concepts associated with each of the goals that identify the professional's study of history. These help show when various aspects of history can be, and are being, taught in the curriculum. An examination of the time-related concepts illustrates that time as the historian uses it includes culturally and formally defined concepts such as "generation" and "Victorian Era" that are learned through an instructional process. Table 12–3 identifies many other concepts related to the study of history. Some are a part of a child's socialization into the American culture. Others are terms that are historians' interpretations of events. Young students are exposed to these terms, which are frequently found in textbooks. A clear understanding of a number of specific

Table 12–3

Goals and Sample Concepts in Learning History

TIME	METHODS	INTERPRETATION	SOCIALIZATION AND VALUES
Chronology	Evidence	Tradition	Heritage
Cause and Effect	Objectivity	Ideology	Holidays
Continuity	Bias	Historigraphy	Founders
Change	Primary Data	Nationalism	Hero/Heroine
Generation	Secondary Data	Evolution	Human Rights
Decade	Alternatives	Relationship	Constitution
Century		Revolution	Declaration of Independence
Past		Leadership	Freedom
Present		Civilization	Individuality
Future		Barbarian	Justice
Time periods:		Contribution	Responsibility
Middle Ages			Compromise
Civil War			Decision Making

concepts and the application of thinking skills are important to the historical method. Since it is generally believed that learning in all disciplines begins before the onset of formal operations, the understanding of history should be increased through early attempts to teach these concepts and to practice the skills used by the historian.

In their extensive review of research on the teaching of history, Downey and Levstik (1991) conclude that "there is no evidence that delaying instruction in history is developmentally appropriate . . . global-stage theory appears to have limited explanatory power in historical thinking" (p. 407). They point to the new findings of domain-specific cognitive researchers that suggest students know more about time and history and use it in more mature thinking when they have an adequate knowledge background. They conclude that such findings support an early and in-depth introduction to the study of history in the curriculum.

Using familiar experiences and events as an entrance into the study of history and examining the history of current issues are recommended approaches for the teaching of history to elementary students. In-depth learning is encouraged to provide a context in which inferences and relationships can be made. These recommendations come from both supporters of the developmental psychology and the socialization rationales for the study of history. The present expanding-horizons curriculum provides many opportunities for examining familiar aspects of history through artifacts, personal observation, stories, biographies, pictures, and field trips.

PERSONAL IDENTITY AND SOCIALIZATION

Others claim that for the vast majority of people, the study of history is more associated with the development of one's identity. In their view, the study of history has more benefits for affective learning than for cognition and logic. Kieran

Egan (1979) presents a theory of educational development that he believes combines the ideas of several developmental psychologists with the educational process. Many see his ideas as particularly helpful for the teaching of history. His theory assumes that the motivation for learning is an attempt to understand one's own place in the world. This requires recognition of both the cognitive and affective abilities and needs of the individual. He also draws upon the social sciences to provide perspectives on how societies through time have educated their citizens.

Egan identifies four stages (explained below). All continue to be a part of the mature thinker's perspective of society. The development of each new stage depends upon a full development of the previous stages. At each stage the learner needs a satisfying interpretation or story that enables him or her to explain what is happening or what has happened. Egan uses the story analogy because, like a story, the interpretation has:
- a *beginning* that sets expectations
- a *set of events* that develops an explanation
- a *conclusion* that the learner accepts or believes

The events and conclusions are not always logical in the scientific sense. However, the acceptance of the conclusion reduces tensions and allows the individual to continue on to new problems.

Egan bases his four stages on the emotional needs of the individual.
- *Mythic Stage:* begins about age 4 or 5 and lasts until age 9 or 10
- *Romantic Stage:* begins at 8 or 9 and lasts until age 14 or 15
- *Philosophic Stage:* begins about age 14 or 15 and lasts until age 19 or 20
- *Ironic Stage:* begins about age 19 or 20 and continues through adulthood

Egan sees each of the stages beginning quite suddenly with the learner accepting a new interpretation of the world. As the individual continues to study, he or she gathers more and more information that must be placed into the interpretation. So it slowly undergoes modifications until suddenly the old interpretation no longer works, and a new stage and its interpretation emerge.

Because we are concerned with students between the ages of 5 and 14, we will elaborate on the characteristics of lessons for the mythic and romantic stages only. Common characteristics of these lessons are:
- the selection of the topic to study
- the close link to affective needs, including the development of values and morals
- the role of in-depth study and research

At the mythic stage, students have no sense of the reality of the world. They control and understand their world through their wishes and wants. Lessons at the mythic stage have four characteristics that help students understand the meaning of events and why things are as they are.

1. Presentations are made in a story format, which begins by setting expectations or establishing a problem to solve.
2. A child's understanding is linked to his/her emotions and morals. Love, hate, fear, joy, good, and bad are used to create interest and motivate learning.
3. Two clear-cut and personalized forces or actions are examined.

4. The conclusion is a single absolute answer that explains why things are as they are.

Application of these guidelines would involve young students in learning the story of Frederick Douglass, for example, as a struggle to learn to read and to gain personal freedom. Students would learn that, as a young house slave in Maryland, Frederick quickly learned the fundamentals of reading from his mistress. When her husband forbade her to continue teaching Frederick, claiming that it made him discontented, the young boy secretly found ways to have things read to him. He then studied the words and sentences to master his skills in reading. Through this experience, Douglass began to realize the advantages freedom provides people. On his second attempt, he was able to escape to the North. He became one of the most famous abolitionists, speaking and writing on the importance of freedom and rights for slaves and also for women. On a speaking tour to England in the 1840s, Douglass earned enough money to purchase his freedom. He founded *The North Star* newspaper in Washington, D.C. So clear and descriptive were his words that they are quoted today to help us understand the importance of freedom to all people.

The onset of the romantic stage is a recognition that the world is autonomous and separate from the child's control. The world is viewed as a complex and confusing place. During this stage students begin to learn the rules of the world, including causality and the logical interactions of the physical and social worlds. At the end of the stage students understand what is real and possible and have established their own identity. Egan believes that the student attains success in the romantic stage by first examining the extremes and gradually over time determining the reality. Students begin by associating with the most powerful, noble, and courageous. The difference in the lessons of the romantic stage from those of the mythic stage is that the topics meet the new emotional needs of the students:

- Presentations are made in a story format, which begins by creating expectations or a problem to solve.
- Students are engaged with an in-depth study to determine the real relationships in the physical and social world.
- Examination is done of only two forces or actions at a time.
- Formation of a realistic conclusion explaining why things are as they are is encouraged.

Egan suggests the best topics for study are people and places different from the student's everyday world and those for which many details can be learned. Through examining these many details, students learn the reality of relationships. Egan says that it might be possible that students could become very interested in the lives of their grandparents, but he believes that the ancient Egyptians may be as good a choice, if not better. Both topics can include lessons in which the relationships of people and events can be identified and explained. Students can learn how the Egyptians used the Nile and why such a wealthy civilization developed there. They can also learn how the lives of their grandparents were different from their own and how their grandparents solved their everyday problems.

Piaget and other cognitive psychologists and Egan and his supporters differ on what they believe to be the motivation of the learner. The cognitive psychologist's view is that the learner stands apart from the world, logically and scientifically examining it. Egan sees the learner as emotionally involved and in need of knowledge to feel in control of his or her own life. They tend to disagree on what are the best topics for the study of history. They do agree on the need for in-depth examinations of topics and on the need of the learner to reach conclusions.

The learning cycle approach to history lessons helps assure that teachers will provide time for a more in-depth study and will encourage the drawing and applying of conclusions. It is an answer to the common criticism of traditional history lessons as being a superficial coverage of too much material.

A Practice Activity

Test your understanding of the goals of history education and the application of the learning theories on the following short descriptions of history lessons. Which theorist's views, Piaget's or Egan's, best justify the lesson and which goal of history learning is being stressed in each description? Refer to the text and to Table 12–2 for assistance.

1. Primary students examine and play with colonial toys. They compare them with their own toys by identifying their common characteristics and they learn their proper names.

2. First grade children study the origin of Thanksgiving and the sacrifices and struggles the Pilgrims made in leaving England and settling in Massachusetts. The learning cycle in Table 12–1 further illustrates these lessons.

3. Fourth grade students interview people who attended and taught in their school when it was first built. They identify changes in the physical facilities and the curriculum that have taken place over the years. They make a time capsule representing a typical week in their school year and place it in the library to be opened in 25 years.

4. The sixth grade students study the Middle Ages and learn about the work and entertainment of both the nobles and the peasants. They examine art books and construct model markets, homes, and castles. They read the story of Robin Hood and others about knights, kings, and queens. Each student researches an individual who lived during the Middle Ages and makes an oral report. They are surprised to learn that some of their characters are related or are members of the same community. Each community group then uses the Timeliner Software program to make a time line illustrating the accomplishments and conflicts of their community,

including at least one contribution from each of their reports. They send letters to these communities to inquire about the area today.

5. Small groups of eighth grade students are given different sets of diary entries and letters written during the Civil War. Each group examines their data and writes a short paragraph describing how the people during that time felt about the Civil War. When they compare their paragraphs, they are surprised to find that their conclusions are not in agreement. A discussion follows in which proof is demanded for certain conclusions. In the end they decide that none of their paragraphs is accurate enough by itself and that writing accurate history is much harder than they ever thought.

6. When a third grade class starts talking about the new television season, Ms. Marlow asks them what they think people did for home entertainment before television. The students speculate and then decide to ask their grandparents or older neighbors. They decide to ask each person the five W questions: who, what, when, where, and why. The survey identifies radio as the important source of entertainment. Bobby says he doesn't understand this because all he hears on the radio is music and a little news. Ms. Marlow plays several tapes of old-time popular radio shows. The students look forward to hearing the tapes of the Lone Ranger, Green Hornet, and Fibber McGee and Molly. The owner of the local radio station visits the classroom and shows pictures of old radios and radio stars. He brings along two recordings, one that includes Edison's first recording and another that includes news reports on important events of the twentieth century. The children compare the technical quality, physical appearance of the equipment, and the broadcaster's presentations with what they hear on radio and television today. They summarize what they learned by writing a radio program. In their program they include samples of the kinds of programs, sound effects, commercials, and news programs they studied. They also tell of the inventions and changes in technology that influenced radio and how this has changed people's knowledge of the world.

Discuss your responses with your classmates. You should find each of the goals of history and each stage of both theorists present at least once in the ideas described. Following are some suggested answers.

SUGGESTED ANSWERS

☞ *More than one goal of teaching history might be found in a lesson.*

Lesson 1: *Cognitive theorists, especially Piaget, use something from the child's environment. The lesson stresses methods of observation and com-*

parison and the time concept of change. Depending upon the toys, it is possible that continuity might also be discussed.

Lesson 2: *This lesson definitely stresses Egan's view of the mythic stage. Since holidays are a part of the child's experience, Piaget's theory would also support this lesson. The goal of the lesson is socialization, since it is teaching the meaning of a holiday and stressing socially approved values. In reading the learning cycle you will notice an emphasis on additional values, particularly rational decision making and methods of using primary data and secondary data.*

Lesson 3: *This lesson uses the student's school environment; Piaget's theory is incorporated. The methods of studying history are stressed. Perhaps some interpretation would be used in selecting the items for the time capsule.*

Lesson 4: *This lesson reflects the ideas of Egan concerning lessons for the romantic stage. The students should acquire a sense of the Middle Ages. Additionally, time emphasis comes through the concepts of chronology and change.*

Lesson 5: *This lesson has a strong cognitive development emphasis using the historical goal of methods by examining primary data and detecting bias. It would be expected that the values of liberty, freedom, individualism, and justice would also be stressed. Depending on the actual data, the student might also make personal interpretations or conclusions.*

Lesson 6: *This lesson also places much emphasis on methods of gathering data. It is strongly supported by cognitive theorists and it does use the familiar concept of entertainment. Time concepts of change and continuity are present. Egan would like the great amount of detail these lessons provide for the student.*

USING TIME LINES IN THE STUDY OF HISTORY

The concept of time is very abstract. Time lines are concrete devices commonly used to assist students in understanding time-related concepts. Physically making a time line is only part of the instructional process. Questions and exercises using the time line are essential if students are to discover the meaning imbedded within the time line.

While the primary emphasis on the calendar in kindergarten might appear to be the recognition of numbers and counting, the calendar helps mark the passage of time and the important changes that occur with the passage of time. Recording changes in the weather and seasons and recognizing holidays and birthdays are beginning points for the study of time in history. As time passes, certain things change and others remain the same, illustrating continuity. Students need to recognize these and mark regularities in the passage of time. Appropriate questions related to the calendar include the order in which things were done during the day and the recall of past activities. Such questions help young children mark the orderly passage of time.

The first time lines that students make are concerned only with the correct ordering of events. A clothesline on which items are attached with clothespins makes a good time line. Students can also attach pictures together in chronological order on a bulletin board to form a mural. Place time lines where they can be easily seen and reached for use.

Complete time lines not only order events but also order them over the uniform passage of time. Placing events along the time line requires the ability to add and subtract. When long periods of time are considered, multiplication and division are needed. Neatly placing drawings or pictures on a time line and labeling events with words are physically difficult tasks. Younger students need large pieces of paper and small timespans.

Along the time line equal timespans are marked. This can be done with the help of colors and knots. As students progress through the grades, longer timespans are studied. A century is a very abstract concept. Large timespans need to be divided into more understandable divisions. A decade is the entire lifetime of fourth and fifth graders. A generation, twenty years, is a time period that is understandable and helpful.

When considering events over a longer period of time, students should be asked questions linking the passage of time to generations to assist them in their understanding. Such questions include:

- How many generations passed between the events (the Civil War and the Spanish-American War)?
- If the father fought in the Civil War, who was more likely to have fought in the Spanish-American War, the son or the grandson?
- Were there many people still alive who had firsthand experience with the war and its aftermath or is their understanding based on secondary sources?
- Have there been any important events that might change the probabilities of what events are likely to happen to people in a war or because of a war at this time?

Thinking about cause-and-effect relationships and hypothetical predictions can be stimulated by removing and moving events along the time line and asking:

- What events might not have happened if the compass had not been invented at this time but 200 years later?
- Rearrange the events on the time line and ask whether the new arrangement is a possibility.
- If this event were removed from or added to the time line what others events might also be removed or added?

RESOURCES FOR TEACHING HISTORY

School systems provide teachers with textbooks for their students. When teaching children about history, educators need to use a variety of resources in addition to textbooks. Some of the students do not have reading skills or powerful enough language skills to understand what is written or spoken. Additional resources provide opportunities to learn history through a greater variety of learning skills.

Part of learning history is learning how the historian gets and processes information. Historians use many resources. No one resource should dominate the study of history. Each must be evaluated for its usefulness, accuracy, and limitations. Some resources are readily available in every community while others can be fairly easily obtained through inquiries to the right places.

LOCATING AND USING HISTORICAL RESOURCES

- Ask for help. People are very willing to help if they are asked nicely for specific things.
- Thank people who have offered help. Have your class write a letter and include some of the things they learned as a way of reviewing and illustrating their attention and learning.
- Prepare students in advance for any type of special behavior needed in encountering resources.
- Make students aware of their learning objectives in advance before the experience and excitement of encountering the resource distracts their attention.
- Prepare data collection sheets for use during the experience with the resource.
- Provide additional adults to help small groups and to assure physical safety.
- Use topics from social history to add a multicultural dimension to the study of history.

PEOPLE AS RESOURCES

History is a part of everyone's life. People in your community have lived through some of the most amazing events in the history of the world and can provide a wealth of information on social history. Through examining the similarities and differences in lifestyles, impacts, and responses of the various racial, ethnic, and social groups in your community to specific events, a multicultural dimension is added to the study of history (Singer, 1992). While some can give you firsthand experience, others can lead you to those people or tell you about them because they remember what others have told them. Begin by talking to the family members or neighbors of your students. Have students write letters to local history buffs, leaders of business and civic organizations, or the local newspaper asking for specific information or for the answers to questions.

Some teachers have had great success in dealing with senior citizens' groups or nursing home residents while others have worked well with collectors or craft makers. Not all people may want to visit a class, but many will be happy to receive one or two students. Even young students should be prepared with a written list of meaningful questions to ask. Tape recording presentations is a help in getting information correct, but permission must be obtained before recording. For longer units of study, it is often nice to have one or two individuals who work well with the age group and visit several times as the study progresses.

ARTIFACTS AND MUSEUMS

Museums are an important source of artifacts—but so are attics, basements, and antique stores. Larger museums often make reproductions available at reasonable prices. One or two carefully selected artifacts can provide many opportunities for young children to use their observation and thinking skills. Interesting questions and discussions that lead to forming hypotheses and investigations can be initiated by examining artifacts. Sturdy and inexpensive artifacts or reproductions provide a highly concrete experience for the study of history. Examining the materials, craftsmanship, and workings of artifacts reveals much about the values and lifestyle of both maker and user. Artifacts provide the opportunity to examine such concepts as change and continuity.

A trip to a museum or restoration is often reported as a positive memory of the study of history. Even small local museums may have some very different or unusual things that students have never seen. Sometimes the observer is surprised to find displayed things they see everyday and never think to be of value or related to history. Because museums display collections, they are often appreciated by the middle grade students who delight in collecting and learning all about their own collections. Many museums and restorations provide active programs especially for students that allow them to handle things, take part in live demonstrations, or remain several days to live and work in another time period. Whatever the type of experience available at a museum or restoration, a student will learn best if the opportunity for pre- and post-visit instruction is provided. Teachers should contact the facility well in advance of the visit. Many museums have planned activities or reading lists to assist the teacher in preparing for the visit. They may also provide special guides or programs for student groups.

THE COMMUNITY AS A RESOURCE

State and local history is often included in the elementary and middle school curriculum. These studies provide the opportunity to gather data firsthand as a historian might and to process it into meaningful conclusions and displays. Third grade teacher Caroline Donnan (1988) explains that she was able to meet all of the social studies skill objectives through a third grade study of the local community.

Cemeteries are often the locations of commemorative monuments to events or people (see Figure 12–1). A trip to the cemetery can help teach young students about the life cycle and about how and why people are remembered. It also requires the display of respectful behavior. Older students can look more closely at the tombstones and discover changes in lifespans and the reduction of infant and child mortality. Rubbings can be made or epitaphs copied to provide information.

Figure 12–1   **This artifact, Frankie's tombstone, could lead students to an interesting investigation.**

Cemeteries include the remains of the rich, poor, famous, and commoner. Oftentimes, ethnic, religious, or racial groups are buried in separate cemeteries or sections. Examining these can raise a number of interesting questions:

- Why would a family allow their son to be buried with other soldiers rather than in the family plot?
- Why are people of one religion all buried together?
- Do grave sites all look alike?
- How many generations of a family are buried in one plot? What might this tell you about the family?

Figure 12–2 What can this old gristmill tell students about the history of their community?

The architecture of your community illustrates the origins of ethnic groups, changes in preferences, and the wealth of each owner. It also indicates the technology and materials available to the builders (see Figure 12–2). The names of streets reflect their functions and the people and places admired by the citizens. Changes in transportation are reflected in houses that once were carriage houses or in the disappearance of trees and front lawns as streets were widened for automobile traffic and garages were added. Some buildings have been used for a variety of purposes and some are no longer in use. Speculation and investigation of their future usage are worthy activities.

Many communities have special memorials, statues, and buildings. These acknowledge important people, businesses, and events of local concern. They often link the community to the national and world events students read about in textbooks.

DOCUMENTS AS RESOURCES

Perhaps you associate documents with treaties and laws. Every American should be aware of what is in such important statements as the Declaration of Independence, the Constitution, and the Emancipation Proclamation. Many textbooks include reproductions of such major documents. For this discussion, documents are defined as the official or public records of events in the lives of individuals, businesses, communities and institutions. Historians examine many documents. Not all documents are as difficult to read and understand as the Constitution. Locally, documents often can be obtained through government offices, individual businesses and organizations, and local museums. Families may also have deeds, wills, and certificates to share. A number of state historical societies have packets of documents especially for the use of teachers. The National Archives has also prepared kits. Original documents are often handwritten and difficult to read. Most educational packets of documents also include printed copies of the document so that it is much easier to use for detailed analysis.

Questions to be answered when examining documents include those that aid in gathering information and those that aid in interpretation and establishing meaning. Data-gathering questions include:

- Who wrote or signed the document?
- When and why was it written?
- What does the document say?
- What values are expressed in the document?
- Does the document include any words that indicate bias or prejudice?
- Does the document order action? By whom? To whom?
- Is the document sworn to or legally binding?

Questions that assist in establishing meaning and interpretation include:

- What things happened as a result of the issuing of the document?
- Does the information in the document agree with other resources?
- Is this document likely to be more accurate than data in another source?
- Why might this document have been preserved?
- What specific truth or conclusion does this document help me arrive at?

DIARIES, LETTERS, AND PICTURES AS RESOURCES

Diaries, letters, and pictures are also primary sources of data. Some books are available that contain such resources on specific events and time periods. Local families and museums may also have such items that could be copied to share. Estate and garage sales are good sources of old pictures.

Since these primary sources are all likely to contain some interpretation, questions concerning the author's or photographer's credentials and views must be asked:

- Who wrote the material or took the picture and for what reasons?
- How likely was the author to know the facts and to make accurate conclusions?
- Does the author/photographer have a reason to support one view or another?
- Are there any facts present or does the writer present only conclusions?
- What other sources agree with the facts or views presented?
- What words might indicate a bias or lack of objectivity?
- What does this document help me understand?

Teachers Leah Moulton and Corrine Tevis (1991) found the local museum a great source of historical pictures of their community. On the back of each picture, they copied and then covered the museum's description. As their second graders examined the pictures they identified the first thing they noticed, two things they might not see at the location today, and they gave each picture a title. Following the class discussion, the descriptive paragraphs were uncovered and read aloud.

Table 12–4 is a complete learning cycle in one lesson designed for grades 5 to 8. The skills of gathering and interpreting the data for signs of change and continuity are the emphasis of the lesson. The procedures involve providing each pair of students with a copy of the photographs (shown on pp. 300–301) and a set of guiding questions written by the teacher for these specific pictures. The copies of the 1906 picture were made from a photograph of the original taken with a 35 mm camera. The questions begin with an easily attainable but challenging task to motivate the students to examine the pictures in detail. The modern picture is provided as current data to assist students in making the comparisons.

Table 12–4

HISTORY LEARNING CYCLE: Data Gathering From Pictures

History Theme: Historical Methods

(For Intermediate and Middle School Grade Levels)

OBJECTIVES	PROCEDURES	EVALUATIONS
	Exploration	
Students will describe toys they are familiar with.	Ask: Of all your toys, which is your favorite? Call on several students to share their selection. Ask: Have you ever asked your parents or grandparents what their favorite toys were like? What were the toys? What do you think they would have selected?	Students offer appropriate responses. Record participation on checklist.
	Invention	
Students will gather data from pictures.	Today we are going to work with a partner and compare two pictures of children and their toys. One picture was taken recently and the other about 1906. How many years ago was 1906? Does anyone know an individual that old? How do you think the pictures will compare? Receive a few predictions. Ask for a show of hands of those who agree with each prediction. Assign partners.	Note participation. (A checklist may be used.)

Students will compare two pictures of children and their toys from different time periods by identifying differences and similarities.	Distribute the pictures and questions to consider when comparing the pictures. (Allow about 10 minutes for this activity.)
	1. What is shown in each picture?
	  A. List at least 3 things about the people in each picture.
	  B. Identify at least 10 items shown in each picture.
	2. Where do you think each picture was taken?
	3. Who do you think took each picture? Why?
		Students' notes in response to questions.

4. How are the pictures alike?

5. How are the pictures different?

6. Identify at least three changes that you see illustrated in the pictures.

7. How have the lives of children changed in the years between the time the pictures were taken?

8. What do you think children learned from playing with the toys in the pictures?

9. Which one of the children shown in the two pictures would you most like to be? Give your reasons for the choice.

Students will make conclusions concerning the role toys play in training children for their adult lives.

Ask the students to discuss their findings beginning with questions 4, 5, 6, 7, 8, and 9. Ask: "Do you have any questions about the pictures?" "How many of you think that toys have some purpose other than entertaining children?" "What purposes?"

Students provide correct answers. Record participation on checklist.

Expansion

Students will suggest toys that might have belonged to children in the early 1900s.

Have you seen the commercial on television where the grandfather asks the child to program the VCR? Why might the grandchild be more at ease with such appliances than her grandparents? Discuss: "Do you think boys and girls should be kept from playing with any particular toy?" "Why?" In the 1906 picture most of the toys probably belonged to the girl because very young children didn't have as many toys. When the little boy was as old as his sister, what kind of toys do you think he had? Where could we find out what toys were available for boys around 1906?

Students' answers reflect content of lesson in support of their answers. Record participation on checklist.

Appropriateness of conclusions based on data gathered in surveys as outlined in a report.

BIOGRAPHIES AND HISTORICAL LITERATURE AS RESOURCES

Each year more biographies and narrative books both factual and fictional are becoming available for young readers. *Social Education* publishes annotated lists of new and recommended books related to social studies topics. Many believe that trade books provide a better, or at least an important, source for young people to use in learning history. Engle and Ochoa (1988) say that the humanities are symbiotic partners in citizenship education because the arts express the responses of people and the impact events have on people. The illustrations and engaging language of the humanities are an improvement over dull textbooks. Literature expresses the feelings and emotions of people with which students can identify.

Picture for history learning cycle, Table 12–4.

Stories are not mere entertainment. "They reflect and educate us in important ways of making sense of experience, of investing the world with meaning and of putting world and experience into words" (Egan, 1979, p. 141). Stories also illustrate causal relationships within a context that may be easier for students to recognize than what history books can provide.

The exploration phase of the learning cycle is an excellent place for a story. During the invention phase, narrative histories and biographies both fictional and factual can serve as the sources of data to be analyzed and evaluated. Teachers may read to nonreaders. They may also read to all students from more difficult

Picture for history learning cycle, Table 12–4.

books. One book may be used for all, or students may be allowed to select from a number of books. Not everyone needs to read the exact same book, but all of the books need to be related to the topic of study. The use of multiple books can accommodate different abilities, but authors may present different facts, reach different conclusions, and express various viewpoints and interpretations. The use of multiple books requires students to examine the different opinions just as the historian does.

Successful experiences with the use of narratives and biographies in the study of history in grades 3 through 6 have been examined (Levstik, 1986; Zarnowski,

1990; Drake & Drake, 1990). In each case multiple books were used and the study lasted for a month or more. Although additional research is needed, all of these studies reported that students tended to react strongly to the characters and their situations and that history knowledge was learned.

Among the sixth graders interviewed, Levstik (1986) reports, ". . . children reported overwhelmingly that they loved the opportunity to choose their own books, to explore topics in depth, and to work independently. They talked about being moved, inspired, and angered at times by what they read, and they frequently added that they had learned something they described as the 'truth.' Students also indicated that they read because of the desire to know about something. In examining students' own writing and work on projects done after this study, evidence of the use of advanced literary styles was found."

The meaningful examination and learning of history from trade books is not automatic. The role of the teacher is very important in the student's success. The original selection of books is important. Students' views are colored by the author's interpretation of events and characters (Drake & Drake, 1991). An examination of the biographies students wrote while studying biographies shows that students tended to include more details and reactions concerning the early life of a person and a rather matter-of-fact statement concerning the person's adult accomplishments (Zarnowski, 1990).

Important teacher behaviors that assist students in learning history through literature include:

- selecting resources and helping students obtain additional resources as the study progresses
- organizing formal assignments that require students to manipulate data gathered or to obtain new data related to the study
- providing a reading time each day
- monitoring and providing positive reinforcement for individual and group efforts
- maintaining high standards for class behavior and work
- providing students with the opportunity to share their knowledge with students and those outside their own class
- encouraging students to examine the stories critically for fact, opinion, fiction, and causal relationships

SCOPE AND SEQUENCE FOR TEACHING HISTORY

Opportunities abound for history in the curriculum because there is an element of history in everything that exists or happens. Historians claim that their ideas are often blended with other topics so that teachers and students do not take the time needed to properly encounter history if learning is to take place. The Bradley Commission recommends that the social studies K–6 curriculum should be history based and that there should be no fewer than four years of required history between grades 7 and 12 (Bradley Commission on History in the Schools, 1988 p. 7). They indicate that there are many scopes and sequences that can meet their recommendations. Schools in urban settings might devote a year to the study of the growth and development of cities while those in rural areas might emphasize another topic.

Table 12–5 lists three possible scope and sequence selections of history topics for grades K–8. The Bradley Commission also advocates the use of many re sources, including literature and the arts in the study of history.

Table 12–5

Three Scope and Sequence Suggestions from the Bradley Commission

PATTERN A		PATTERN B		PATTERN C	
Grade	*Topic*	*Grade*	*Topic*	*Grade*	*Topic*
K	Children of Other Lands and Times	K	Learning and Working Now and Long Ago	K	Children's Adventures: Long Ago and Far Away
1	Families Now and Long Ago	1	A Child's Place in Time and Space	1	People Who Made America
2	Local History: Neighborhoods and Communities	2	People Who Make a Difference	2	Traditions, Monuments, and Celebrations
3	Urban History: How Cities Began and Grew	3	Continuity and Change: Local and National History	3	Inventors, Innovators, and Immigrants
4	State History and Geography: Continuity and Change	4	A Changing State	4	Heroes, Folk Tales, and Legends of the World
5	National History and Geography: Exploration to 1865	5	United States History and Geography: Making A New Nation	5	Biographies and Documents in American History
6	World History and Geography: The Growth of Civilization	6	World History and Geography: Ancient Civilizations	6	Biographies and Documents in World History
7	Regional and Neighborhood History and Geography	7	Social Studies Elective: Local History	7	World History and Geography to 1789
8	United States History and Geography	8	United States History and Geography	8	United States History and Geography to 1914

A Practice Activity

Read each of the three sample scope and sequences in Table 12–5 and identify one resource beyond the textbook for each grade and pattern.

Pattern A		*Pattern B*		*Pattern C*	
K	*books*	*K*	*books*	*K*	*books*
1	*books*	*1*	*books*	*1*	*books/people*
2	*people*	*2*	*people*	*2*	*community*
3	*pictures/city*	*3*	*pictures/museum*	*3*	*biography*
4	*pictures*	*4*	*interview/diary*	*4*	*books*
5	*diaries*	*5*	*documents*	*5*	*biography*
6	*documents*	*6*	*pictures*	*6*	*biographies*
7	*pictures*	*7*	*pictures*	*7*	*community*
8	*documents*	*8*	*documents*	*8*	*documents*

SUMMARY

History is an important subject for students to study in grades K–8. Many ways to stimulate and maintain students' interest in the meaningful learning of history are available. Most researchers agree on the need for in-depth study of topics and for the use of multiple resources. There is some controversy over what content and type of history to stress, but there is no shortage of potential content. Our families, the things around us, the issues influencing our lives, and our common heritage of values and beliefs all provide ample content. The data too is present if only we look for it and examine it carefully. The study of history can teach us about the past. It can stimulate us to examine our present behaviors with an eye toward making appropriate changes while maintaining continuity with our worthy past.

REFERENCES

Bradley Commission on History in the Schools. (1988). *Building a history curriculum: Guidelines for teaching history in schools.* Washington, DC: Educational Excellence Network.

Donnan, C. S. (1988). Following our forebears' footsteps: From expedition to understanding. In V. Rogers, A. D. Roberts, & T. P. Weiland (eds.), *Teaching Social Studies: Portraits from the Classroom,* Bulletin 82. Washington, DC: National Council for the Social Studies.

Downey, M. T. & Levstik, L. S. (1991). Teaching and learning history. In J. P. Shaver (ed.), *Handbook of Research on Social Studies Teaching and Learning.* New York: Macmillan Publishing Company.

Drake, J. J. & Drake, F. D. (1990). Using children's literature to teach about the American revolution. *Social Studies and the Young Learner, 3* (2), 6–8.

Egan, K. (1979). *Educational development.* New York: Oxford University Press.

Engle, S. H. & Ochoa, A. S. (1988). *Education for democratic citizenship.* New York: Teachers College Press.

Hertzberg, H. (1989). "History and progressivism: A century of reform proposals." in P. Gagon (ed.), *Historical Literacy.* New York: Macmillan Publishing Company.

Hoge, J. D. & Crump, C. (1988). *Teaching history in the elementary school.* Bloomington, IN: Social Studies Development Center and ERIC Clearinghouse for Social Studies/Social Science Education.

Levstik, L. (1986) The relationship between historical response and narrative in a sixth-grade classroom. *Theory and Research in Social Education, 15*(1), 1–17.

Levstik, L. & Pappas, C. C. (1987). Exploring the development of historical understanding. *Journal of Research and Development in Education, 21,* 1–15.

Moulton, L. & Tevis, C. (1991) Making history come alive: Using historical photos in the classroom. *Social Studies and the Young Learner, 3* (4), 12–14.

National Assessment of Educational Progress. (1990). *The U.S. history report card.* Washington, DC: United States Department of Education.

Piaget, J. (1969). *The child's conception of time.* New York: Basic Books, Inc.

Singer, A. (1992). Multiculturalism and democracy: The promise of multicultural education. *Social Education,* Vol. 56, pp. 83–85.

Sunal, C. S. (1990) *Early childhood social studies.* Columbus, OH: Merrill Publishing Company.

U.S. Department of Education. (1990). *National goals for education.* Washington, DC: U.S. Department of Education.

Zaccaria, M. A. (1978). The development of historical thinking: Implications for the teaching of history. *The History Teacher, 11*(3), 323–340.

Zarnowski, M. (1990). *Learning about biographies.* Washington, DC: National Council for the Social Studies.

CHAPTER 13

OVERVIEW

Economics is something people of all ages encounter every day. Do you remember the first time you heard that you could not have something because there was not enough money or time? Chances are you cannot remember because you were so young. This fact is the basis of economics, and the solutions that people use to get around this fact is the study of economics. This chapter examines ways to help young people understand the role of economics in their lives and in the activities of their community, nation, and world. It also stresses the importance of making rational decisions about the use of our scarce resources.

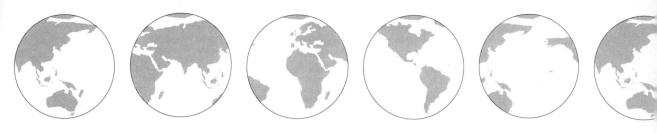

Economic Education

OBJECTIVES

1. Identify the two aspects of the study of economics.
2. List the key concepts for the study of economics and economic decision making.
3. Explain how to use the economic decision model.
4. Explain how economics influences the lives of all people, communities, and nations.
5. Identify ways in which economic education can be integrated into the social studies curriculum through such topics of study as career education, geography, history, community study, and consumer education.
6. Identify common characteristics of successful ways to teach economics to K–8 students.
7. Name potential sources of resources for teaching economics.

INTERVIEW WITH AN AWARD-WINNING TEACHER

The International Paper Company sponsors a national contest to honor teachers for excellence in teaching economics at all levels, kindergarten through college. Nancy Braden has been honored in eight different years for her work with third and fifth grade students. The following is an interview with her concerning her instructional approaches to teaching economics. Ms. Braden teaches at Barling Elementary School in the Fort Smith Arkansas School District.

Interviewer: Nancy, you are one of the most successful teachers of economics to young people in the country. How did you get started teaching economics?

Ms. Braden: I went to a workshop given in my school district by the Arkansas State Council for Economic Education. I anticipated just getting my in-service points, not ever dreaming I'd get interested in it or care anything about it. I planned to be bored for that week. I can't tell you now what was said, but whatever it was, it turned me on, and before it was over, I was planning what I'd do the next year.

Interviewer: I remember your telling me that you didn't remember a lot of what you were told.

Ms. Braden: Not in that one week. No.

Interviewer: Well, I hear your students talking about such complex concepts as aggregate demand, profits, supply and demand. How have you learned all of this information that you now teach?

Ms. Braden: I got the materials they (the Arkansas State Council for Economic Education) had published—the state curriculum guide. I got down and studied it. I was used to preparing my own units because we didn't have any social studies textbooks. I've never been one to use a textbook anyway except as a guide and resource.

Interviewer: You are now teaching social studies in a departmentalized situation. How do you work the economics into your district's curriculum?

Ms. Braden: Well, it just fits in. You couldn't teach social studies without it. There is just no way. All the different areas and people we study from fourth through the sixth grade—all of them can't be understood without economics. You've got to study how the people live, how they meet their basic needs—food, clothing, and shelter. You've got to study what their productive resources are, the natural resources available in the area. You've got to study their economy, their government. You can't study any of this without economics. There is no way to study any social studies without including economics, and I highlight a lot of it. This year we've studied a lot about recycling. We are finding out that it is quite expensive to buy recycled materi-

als, but since our opportunity cost is to ruin our country, we've got to do something. It's going to cost us, so we might as well pay for it now. We saved 26 trees in the last nine weeks of the school year by collecting paper for recycling.

Interviewer: You've mentioned a lot of economic concepts, and I've noticed they are an integral part of your vocabulary. How important is this set of economic concepts to your teaching?

Ms. Braden: Very, very. I've heard other teachers say they've had a hard time getting the concepts across, but I don't find that at all. I call the students "entrepreneurs" and they want to know what I called them. Their parents may not know what the word means, but the students learn its meaning and how to spell it, and they think they are hot stuff. They get excited, and I'm excited. So, I think the kids catch my enthusiasm.

Interviewer: Do you teach the concepts first and then do your study of the problem?

Ms. Braden: I kind of do it all together. When I was teaching in a self-contained room, I mentioned economic concepts in all the subjects. Whenever there is an example of one of the concepts, I make certain that the students call it by the proper economic term. One year a co-worker told me that I was leaving out spelling, English, and math. Well, when we got back the results of the Metropolitan test my students had made a much larger gain in those areas than her students. It wasn't because I had smarter students; it was because they all got turned onto learning by the economics. The classes pull together in the study and it carries over to other work as well. One thing I like is that it works well with all kids, the fast and the slow, and it has meaning for them. When you say something that is going to affect them, they want to know about it.

Interviewer: So you make an extra effort to point out how what you are studying directly or indirectly affects your students and you tend to use an in-depth examination of a particular problem.

Ms. Braden: Yes, usually. This year we did the ecology emphasis. We organized the whole school to put things into the recycle box. They used to pay for the newspapers; they don't now. But we weren't doing it to make money. We were doing it to teach the kids something about the wise use of resources.

Interviewer: What are some of the other topics you've investigated with your classes?

Ms. Braden: "The Economic Impact of Pets" was my favorite. I loved that one. "The Economic Problems of the Local National Park" illustrated many interesting economic decisions. "The Cost of Crime" study started because someone would drop a pencil and another student would take it and use it. Then the students would get into *arguments about to whom the pencil belonged. We talked about taking something that belonged to another. We also studied the interdependence of Barling, the community where our school is located, with Fort Smith.*

Interviewer: *What was your first award-winning study?*

Ms. Braden: *It was called "The Economic Growth of an Industrial Centered Community." It was a study of Fort Smith, Arkansas, where most of the parents work and shop.*

Interviewer: *Sounds like a topic where you would use lots of resource people.*

Ms. Braden: *Oh yes, I used a lot of fathers in that one. I heard that the fathers started calling one another to see if they were being invited to come to the class. I usually have visits from a banker and stockbroker. We've even had the governor. The governor had another appointment and his aides kept trying to get him to leave, but he kept saying, "Just one more question." He was impressed because the students asked him specific questions about his economic policies and programs. Sometimes visiting speakers tell me that they don't think they can get to the low level of the children's understanding, but when they leave they often say that they were afraid they didn't have good enough answers for the students.*

Interviewer: *Well, this school year has just finished. Do you know what you'll study in depth next year?*

Ms. Braden: *I think we will continue with the ecology and recycling study. There were a number of things we didn't have time to investigate this spring.*

Interviewer: *I want to thank you for your time in explaining how you present economics to intermediate students.*

You can read more detailed descriptions of Ms. Braden's award-winning projects and those of other teachers in *The Economic Education Experiences of Enterprising Teachers* published annually by the Joint Council on Economic Education. (See address on p. 334).

DEFINING ECONOMICS

As we have seen with the other disciplines traditionally associated with social studies, the professional in the field and the citizen often have different definitions of the field. There are several different groups of professionals who deal with the economy, and they do not always agree on the goals for economic education. One group is the academics, who look upon economics as a rational study of concepts, their relationships, and the decision-making process. Another group is composed of the business and labor communities, who see economics as related to the importance of work, jobs, and production. Still a third perspective is represented by the consumer advocates, who seek to help individuals learn how to get accurate information to make personal decisions. Certainly individuals have a personal need to know how to make wise economic decisions throughout their lives. Most young children have experienced the pleasures of good economic choices and the disappointments of poor economic choices. Collectively, citizens and various interest groups affect the market and the economic decisions of governments. The emphasis found in the economic curriculum of a particular state or school district tends to reflect the views of the particular group of economic education leaders in the community or state. All of the groups do agree that teaching about economics is important, but what to teach and emphasize and how to instruct students are a source of much controversy.

Economics is based on the realization that people want more than the resources can provide. **Scarcity** is the term economists use to indicate the imbalance of wants and resources. For some, the goal and definition of economic education centers on the analysis of how goods and services get produced and distributed. Others stress examining ways to make the system of production and distribution work better through the formation of governmental and business policies. Perhaps the most inclusive definition is one that defines economics as both a set of knowledge and a way of thinking (Banaszak, 1987). Economics as a body of knowledge includes the concepts, generalizations, and theories developed by people to try to extend their scarce natural, human, and capital resources so that they can fulfill their basic needs and as many of their wants as possible. An important key to the accomplishment of this goal is a systematic way of thinking and making economic decisions.

Since the 1960s the Joint Council on Economic Education (JCEE) and the National Association of Economic Educators (NAEE) have been working together to promote and evaluate economic education in the schools throughout the nation (Armento, 1986). Economists, more than proponents of any of the other disciplines traditionally a part of the social studies, made the decision to make a continuous and long-term commitment to increasing and improving the teaching of economics in the schools. They produced needed guides and instructional materials and evaluated their successes and failures. They also organized their human resources of economists, businesses, and educators through state councils and centers of economic education and raised funds for selected projects. The result was the production of high quality supplemental instructional materials available for K–12 to help teachers instruct students in economics, and these materials apply the results of research into how economics is learned. Today the JCEE and NAEE, as well as state councils on economic education, continue to work to fulfill new needs in economic education and to provide training for both prospective and veteran teachers. You may want to join your state's council or attend some of their training sessions in the future.

Table 13–1

Master Curriculum in Economics:
A Framework for Teaching the Basic Concepts

Fundamental Economic Concepts

1. Scarcity
2. Opportunity Cost and Trade-offs
3. Productivity
4. Economic Systems
5. Economic Institutions and Incentives
6. Exchange, Money, and Interdependence

Microeconomic Concepts

7. Markets and Prices
8. Supply and Demand
9. Competition and Market Structure
10. Income Distribution
11. Market Failures
12. The Role of Government

Macroeconomic Concepts

13. Gross National Product
14. Aggregate Supply
15. Aggregate Demand
16. Unemployment
17. Inflation and Deflation
18. Monetary Policy
19. Fiscal Policy

International Economic Concepts

20. Absolute and Comparative Advantage and Barriers to Trade
21. Balance of Payments and Exchange Rates
22. International Aspects of Growth and Stability

Measurement Concepts and Methods

Tables
Charts and Graphs
Ratios and Percentages
Percentage Changes
Index Numbers
Real vs. Nominal Values
Averages and Distributions Around the Average

Source: Used by permission of the Joint Council on Economic Education.

KEY CONCEPTS IN ECONOMIC EDUCATION

The concepts and values of economics are found not only in the social studies curriculum but also in the high school business curriculum and the hidden curriculum. While there is no formal business curriculum in most elementary and middle schools, many of its goals enter the elementary curriculum through the career education movement. The school and business partnerships also provide a potential for the business perspective on economics to enter the schools. The hidden curriculum reinforces values needed to become a successful worker or consumer by rewarding such specific behaviors as completion of tasks, high standards or merit, deferred gratification, competition, cooperation, and promptness.

The Joint Council on Economic Education identified the concepts that provide the basis for both understanding economics and making reasoned economic decisions. Table 13–1 identifies these concepts and groups them to illustrate important relationships. Table 13–1 does not present a hierarchy of complexity and difficulty. Indeed, the concepts within each of the major divisions vary in their degree of difficulty in the way that they present concrete versus abstract and many versus few examples. The list of concepts is not a comprehensive list of all economics, but rather of the broader organizing concepts. As you read the discussions of these concepts you will be asked to identify additional concepts by filling in the blanks in the text. Your answers will be some of the concepts subsumed by the organizing concepts. Keep in mind that when you teach economics, you will teach the concepts you are identifying and help students relate them to the organizing concepts during the invention phase of the learning cycle.

FUNDAMENTAL ECONOMIC CONCEPTS

The fundamental concepts are necessary to understand all of the various aspects and specializations within the discipline of economics. In your teaching units, you may wish to include only a small part of the field of economics. However, you will always include at least some of the fundamental concepts. These fundamental concepts are the most frequently encountered by most individuals, and you are probably familiar with their meanings even if you do not call them by the term the economist uses.

A Practice Activity

Here is an exercise to see how many fundamental economic concepts you know. Read the following and fill in as many blanks as you can.

Scarcity is present when our wants and resources are not in balance. Sometimes scarcity is just annoying or makes us unhappy, such as when we can't find a parking place or purchase an item we want. At other times our wants include food, clothing, and shelter without which we cannot live. These three wants are often called _____. To fulfill our needs and wants, people work at a variety of _____ producing either _____ such as televisions or performing _____ like cleaning teeth or selling products.

Productive resources are necessary if you are to obtain a product or service. The three types of productive resources are called capital, _____, and _____ resources, since products are made from something, by someone, and with tools. Once a choice is made for the use of a resource, it cannot be used for another purpose at this time or perhaps ever. The most valuable alternative use for the resource is its opportunity cost. Frequently people make trade-offs among their choices to get some of what they want.

Productivity is the amount of output produced per unit of input. Some people are more productive when performing specific tasks than are others. Assembly lines increase _____ because the tasks of production are divided, with each person performing one job in making the product instead of each person making a complete product. This _____ of labor means that workers are interdependent.

Today, the American economy is more highly specialized than it was in the past. Therefore, we use _____ to buy things, or we make exchanges. Not only do individuals and families make purchases but so do other economic institutions such as corporations, governments, and unions. When they find themselves short of money these institutions often borrow money from another economic institution called a _____.

The way in which a society organizes its economic life to deal with its basic economic problems is called its economic system. All economic systems must answer three important questions:

- What to produce?
- How to produce?
- How to distribute the output?

The market economy that dominates in the United States is a decentralized system. The individual decisions of people, businesses, and government as consumers, producers, and investors combine to create the economy. In the world today there is a movement toward more use of the _____ economy and less of economies based upon command decisions by specific people. Still, most nations follow some form of a mixed economic system.

☞ *The concepts that should be used to fill in the blanks are: basic needs, jobs, goods, services, natural, human, productivity, division, money or cash, bank, and market.*

Are you surprised at the amount of economics you know? Did you learn these things formally through schooling? Do you think that elementary and middle school students can learn these things about economics? Research does indicate this to be the case (Schug & Walstad, 1991). Even kindergarten students have been able to master such concepts as scarcity, decision making, production, specializa-

tion, distribution, consumption and saving, supply and demand, business organization, and money and barter (Kourilsky, 1977, p. 183).

MICROECONOMIC CONCEPTS

Microeconomics is the study of individual households, companies, and markets
and how resources and prices combine to distribute wealth and products. The
price of a new car at a given time helps determine the demand for such cars. High
prices may stimulate employers to work overtime to produce more cars. When
there are lots of unsold products, businesses hold sales to stimulate purchases.
The government regulates those businesses that have a monopoly situation to protect the consumers and assure an adequate supply. Even in the United States, our
local, state, and national governments own and operate some special facilities,
such as power production, sanitation, roads, and transportation facilities. Governments regulate taxes to help distribute the burden of paying for public services
fairly among the society. Interest rates, the number of sales, and wages also help
distribute money throughout the economy because of the circular flow of wealth
through the various markets.

MACROECONOMIC CONCEPTS

Macroeconomics is the study of the big picture or the economy as a whole. Macroeconomics provides an overview of the conditions in an entire nation. The Gross
National Product (GNP) is the value of all of the goods and services produced in
a nation for a year. This information provides for comparisons of production
between nations. When the GNP is divided by the population of a nation, the outcome is the GNP per capita. This figure gives an idea of how much money is generated per person. If the GNP per capita is $50, the lives of the people are quite
different from the lives of people living in a nation with a GNP per capita of $2500.
In the nation with the GNP per capita of $2500 the aggregate supply of produced
goods and services is much greater and so also is the aggregate demand for goods
and services. More people are also probably employed.

At various times during the year the same number of people will be unem-
ployed because of temporary changes in the business rate. For example, before
the Christmas holiday more people are working and unemployment is lower because consumers are doing extra purchasing. After Christmas the unemployment
rate is higher because of the cyclical nature of consumer purchasing in the economy.

Inflation occurs when the prices of all goods and services tend to go up in
the nation during the same time period. **Monetary policy** is the regulation of the
amount of money in the nation's economy because of the actions of the Federal
Reserve System in raising and lowering interest rates. Lower interest rates offer
incentives to people to expand and borrow, while higher interest rates tend to encourage investment and savings. **Fiscal policy** is the combined actions of the national government in taxing, spending, and borrowing money, which in effect
adds to or subtracts from the supply of money available to businesses and

individuals. Fiscal and monetary policies are means by which the economy is managed in the United States. Some people and some economists do not think that the national government always manages the economy correctly. These conflicts have the potential of making economics a controversial subject to teach in some communities. These conflicts are often examined in the study of history.

INTERNATIONAL ECONOMIC CONCEPTS

International economics is the study of the economic relationships among nations. Nations have always been interrelated economically, but they are more so today than in the past and will probably become even more so in the future. Nations trade because they have something that other nations want and need or because they want products and resources from other nations. Some nations have an **absolute advantage** because they can provide something that other nations or regions cannot. Other nations can provide a good or service better, faster, or in larger amounts and have what is called a **comparative advantage.** Since foreign-produced goods compete in the market with domestic products, some people want tariffs to stop the import of certain products. However, if nations start erecting trade barriers, international trade slows. This slowdown may affect nations that have not raised their tariffs. Leaders in the United States government stress the need for **free trade** or trade without tariffs to promote the largest amount of sales between nations. Some economists warn that a complete free trade policy may not always be in the best interest of a nation. The study of American history is filled with discussions of international trade issues and their domestic and international consequences.

Nations do not want to buy much more from other nations than they sell. They seek a **balance of payments** between nations. If a nation does not sell about the same amount that it buys, the nation must find the wealth internally to pay for its international purchases. Such actions take away wealth for purchases and investments from the domestic economy.

Nations can always print more money, but that money must be of constant worth or no other nation will want to take it in payment. The **exchange rate** is the price of one nation's money compared with another nation's. Although there are usually small changes from day to day and week to week, nations cooperate to keep the values of their currencies consistent.

The economic conditions within a nation can prompt the movement of both goods and people. Throughout our history, many people have migrated to the United States for economic opportunity. Today people and labor forces still migrate both temporarily and permanently. Such movements are often the source of domestic problems in the nations receiving the immigrants. Since the most educated are often those who migrate, nations whose populations migrate face different types of economic problems prompted by the loss of human resources. Therefore, international economics cannot be totally separated from the other economic concepts discussed above. The learning cycle in this chapter (see Table 13–2) illustrates how the fundamental concept of interdependence is present in microeconomic and international economics.

Table 13–2

ECONOMIC LEARNING CYCLE: Economic Interdependence

*Theme: **Economic Interdependence** (For Middle School)*

OBJECTIVES	PROCEDURES	EVALUATIONS
Students will give examples of situations where they are dependent and independent.	***Exploration*** Discuss the meanings of the words "dependent" and "independent" as the students understand them. Ask them to give examples or role play a situation where they were dependent and one where they were independent. Then ask students to try to describe a situation with two people when both of them are dependent upon each other.	Students offer examples of the dependent and independent situations.
Students will define interdependence.	***Invention*** Tell the following two stories to students: Mrs. Patrick was having a special dinner. She wanted to serve cheesecake with fresh strawberry topping. She went to her favorite fruit and vegetable stand and found bright red strawberries. "This is just what I need," she told the owner. "Don't ever go out of business!" "I won't," replied Mr. Fry, "As long as I have faithful customers like you." The Carmels' baby woke up early in the morning crying. Upon investigation his mother discovered the baby had a temperature. She took the baby to the pediatrician, Dr. Walker, that morning. That evening when Dr. Walker left the office the battery in her car was dead. She called the Carmels' Garage to get the car back in running order. Tell the students: "Let's make a list of the things the two stories have in common." Ask: "Are there any differences?" List these. Ask: "In our stories, what did Mr. Fry do for Mrs. Patrick? Mrs. Patrick for Mr. Fry? The Carmels for Dr. Walker?" etc. Ask whether these are examples of two or more people being dependent upon each other. Discuss. Ask: "Does anyone know the word that describes two or more people being dependent upon each other?" Introduce term "interdependent" if students don't know it. Review the meaning of words with the prefix "inter" such as intercom, intercept, interface, international, interchangeable. Reach a consensus on what the prefix "inter" means. Develop a class	 Record student participation on a checklist.

Table 13–2 (cont.)

OBJECTIVES	PROCEDURES	EVALUATIONS
	definition of "interdependent." Ask students to look at the list of what the two stories have in common. Ask: "What does it take to have an interdependent situation?"	

OBJECTIVES	PROCEDURES	EVALUATIONS
	Expansion Give each student a card with an occupation on it. Students pin on their cards and get into a circle. The student with the term "child" is given a ball of string. As the "child" holds onto the end of the string, he or she passes or tosses the ball to someone with whom a child would be interdependent and explains that choice. As students get the ball of string, they repeat the procedure until all students are holding onto the string. When everyone has had a chance, the teacher asks, "What does this illustrate about interdependence?"	
Students will make conclusions about whether their families are interdependent with other nations based on data collected in surveys.	Ask: "Do you think we are only interdependent with people in our own community?" "Why?" "Could our families be interdependent with people in other areas of the world?" Discuss. Give students the following homework assignment: At home tonight identify three examples each of clothing, food, and appliances that were made in another country. Record the item name and the country where it was made.	
	Students combine their examples and compare the results. All of the nations are located on a world map and a line drawn or piece of string attached from the nation of origin to your city for each different example. Students decide on an appropriate title for this map. Ask: "Can we find alternative sources for each of these products in the United States?" Discuss what would happen if their families stopped buying clothing, food, and appliances from other nations and bought only American products. "Is this possible or do we have to purchase some things from other nations?" "What things and why?" "What would happen if a bad storm destroyed a crop or a big fire destroyed the port and its warehouses in Brazil, Korea, etc.?" "Do you know of any products from our community or state that are sold in other nations?" "How can we find out about this?" Students write letters asking producers where products are sold in the United States and the world.	
	Students should interview produce managers to find out where foods such as tomatoes come from at different times during the year. They might also talk to older people to learn about the types of foods and produce available when they were young. Students should write a three-paragraph report discussing	Appropriateness of conclusions based on data gathered in surveys as outlined in a report.

survey results. Paragraph 1 should discuss the home survey. Paragraph 2 should discuss the produce managers survey. Paragraph 3 should draw conclusions from surveys regarding interdependence. Conclude by discussing the pros and cons of being economically interdependent with people in other areas of the world.

MEASUREMENT CONCEPTS AND METHODS

To help understand and interpret data concerning the economy, economists organize information into tables, charts, and graphs. They also use mathematics to compare numbers and even invent measures to assist in comparing numbers. Young elementary students can begin to use tables, charts, and graphs to help them organize economic information. Middle school students and young teens can also use percentages and averages. In the study of economics more than any of the other social sciences, students are called upon to apply the knowledge and skills they have gained in mathematics to help them understand economic relationships. When the numbers involve money, students often do surprisingly well. However, many important and useful economic concepts do not involve the use of mathematics.

ECONOMIC DECISION-MAKING SKILLS

The fact that people daily encounter scarcity demands that they make choices. Rather than accept the first solution that comes to mind, people are encouraged by economists to make rational decisions that consider the economic long- and short-term consequences. Other social sciences stress rational decision making and reserving judgment. All this means that the decision maker must weigh alternatives and be aware of the "opportunity cost," of what is given up when one alternative is selected. The alternative selected must be considered to give more "benefits" than the opportunity cost. Teaching students to identify alternatives, criteria, and consequences and to select what they see as the best alternative is the essence of teaching decision making.

Preschoolers make decisions, but usually not rational economic decisions. In fact, even adults are guilty of making snap decisions and impulse purchases. The rationale for teaching decision making is not that it will eliminate all poor decisions, but that it will reduce such decisions. Additionally, when students face an important decision these skills will help them take time to carefully identify and weigh alternatives. Students should be helped to see when they need to seek additional information from printed sources or ask for professional advice to help them make decisions. They learn to ask for specific information and evaluate it.

The abstractness in the decision-making process can be made more concrete for students by
- investigating real problems with which the students are familiar
- using a decision-making chart on which alternatives and consequences are recorded and rated.

Table 13–3

Decision-Making Chart

Which three students should represent our class at the program planned for the entire school day of March 3rd?

	ALTERNATIVES			
Student	*Completes Regular Classwork in Advance*	*Has Good Speaking Voice*	*Clearly Understands Ideas in Presentation*	*Will Represent Class Seriously*
Tom	(+)	(+)	(?)	(−)
Mark	(+)	(+)	(+)	(+)
Betty	(−)	(+)	(+)	(+)
Mary	(+)	(−)	(?)	(+)
Carol	(−)	(+)	(+)	(+)
Jerry	(+)	(+)	(+)	(+)
Cynthia	(+)	(+)	(+)	(+)

Table 13–3 shows the type of decision-making chart used in the popular and successful economic video series *Trade-Offs*. The title of the chart is the question to be answered by the decision. Alternatives are listed in the column on the left and the criteria are listed across the top of the chart. Students are first asked to identify the specific criteria for their problem and then offer alternative choices. Sometimes as alternatives are listed or rated, new criteria or alternatives will be discovered and added to the chart. The discussion of the solution is guided by the information written on the chart. The teacher directs the discussion by asking questions about the chart and how various parts of the chart compare. Each alternative and criterion is discussed and given a rating in the box created by the intersection of the appropriate row and column. Symbols such as smiley faces, frowning faces, question marks, pluses, zeros, or minuses are drawn on the chart to conclude the discussion of the alternative and criterion. Rarely will all of the ratings for an alternative contain the positive symbol. The rating process will, however, narrow the list to the better alternatives. Next, students reconsider each of these and decide which they believe will be the best choice for them.

A second and more abstract type of decision-making chart is shown in Table 13–4. In this chart the students are asked to predict long- and short-term consequences. These consequences are also classified as having either positive or negative outcomes. After such information is recorded on the chart, the students then discuss the importance and chance of each consequence happening and make their decision.

Making the final decision is important, as the lesson is not merely an intellectual exercise. Allowing students to make decisions and forcing them to live with the consequences of their choices is an important and realistic learning goal not only for economic education but for social studies. Citizens make many personal decisions which affect the economy through the sales of goods and services. Their votes also influence the way governments both spend and acquire money. Even rationally made decisions may not work out as predicted because some of the criteria involve chance or perhaps not all of the criteria were identified. Nevertheless, the consequences of such decisions cannot be avoided. It is hoped that the cost will not be too great, but perhaps it will be. Teachers should not come to the rescue of poor decisions with an unrealistic save. Instead, they should help students make the best choices and weigh all alternatives. It is correct procedure to ask probing questions designed to stimulate thinking from a particular view and even to suggest some possible alternatives or consequences should students fail to bring them up.

Teachers make many decisions each day; some of these decisions can be made by the students. Many teachers take the time to allow the students to make some individual and classroom decisions. Such a practice helps students recognize their sense of personal control over their lives and the responsibilities they have for both their personal and group behavior. Economic decisions involve the use of scarce resources, and time in the classroom is a scarce commodity, as well as are art supplies, library books, and individual time with the teacher or an adult helper. Teachers need to provide students with the opportunity to make age-appropriate decisions and to practice the decision-making process. Although it takes time to teach decision-making skills, students are then equipped to perform the task in small groups or individually and the teacher can examine students' thought processes with a quick glance at the chart. In the end this often saves teachers time in dealing with poor choices and student conflicts.

Students who make decisions will be more accepting of the decisions of others provided they see the rationality of such decisions. A teacher who follows the policy of encouraging students to make some class decisions may find her own decisions questioned from time to time or may be asked to support her choices or to change them. In this way, the teacher serves as a role model of a rational decision maker and citizen. On some occasions, a teacher might be called upon to remind the student that the decision was not hers, but one made by the school board or legislature.

A Practice Activity

Which of the following decisions would you allow students to make? Be prepared to defend your reasoning to classmates.

1. What refreshments to have for a class party
2. What gifts to make for their parents at Christmas time
3. What assignments to do
4. What game to play at recess
5. What activity to do during free time
6. Where to go on a field trip

7. What books to read
8. What grades students should receive
9. What guest speakers to invite to class
10. How students will be evaluated for grading
11. What projects to make
12. What type of program to present for the PTA
13. How to present the findings of a research project
14. The topic of a special study
15. The date a project or assignment is due

ANSWERS TO THE PRACTICE ACTIVITY

☛ *Author's views on which decisions to allow the students to make are as follows. Several important points must be taken into consideration in making your choices.*

· *The maturity and experiences of the students must influence the decisions. Perhaps you want to specify these before committing to a yes or no.*
· *Remember that the teacher can provide some or all of the alternatives and some of the criteria from which the students may pick. Under the "right" set of controls, you might be willing to say yes to almost all of the situations.*
· *If you voluntarily give responsibilities to students and fail to treat their responses with respect, you will lose the respect of some or all of your students.*
· *Some students might allow personal feelings to cloud their decisions about grades. Individual students view grades as personal rewards and punishments or may see them as a part of their personal identity. Among some ages and cultural groups, the children expect adults to make such important decisions and would not want to grade themselves or others.*
· *You may feel negatively about the questions on evaluations. Evaluation is seen as the responsibility of a teacher. Certainly, you might not want to turn over the entire responsibility for evaluating an activity or project to the students.*
· *Some trade-offs are possible on the issues of evaluation. If specific and uniform criteria for an evaluation are presented and can be applied to a variety of modes of presentation, you might, upon some occasions, allow the students to pick the way they will present their information to you for evaluation. You might also want students to evaluate their work using the criteria and perhaps offer a suggested grade. Such a procedure is not too different from contracting for grades with students. The teacher can make the final grade decision.*
· *In the case of the due date, the teacher in a departmentalized situation may regularly want student input on this topic for a number of very good reasons. You may want to discuss these with your classmates and instructor.*

Table 13–4

Consequences Decision-Making Chart

Should the tariff on Japanese cars be increased?

ALTERNATIVES	CONSEQUENCES	
	Short term	*Long term*
Yes	(+) auto workers pleased, higher employment rate (−) auto agencies carrying Japanese cars angry because sales decline	(+) more United States cars produced (−) price of Japanese cars goes up; Japan raises tariffs on United States goods
No	(+) price of Japanese cars remains same, special sales on United States produced cars (−) United States produces fewer cars, more unemployed autoworkers	(+) United States produces better cars at lower prices through increased productivity and design improvements (−) some United States auto plants close or reduce work hours.

ECONOMIC GOALS AND VALUES

When a decision is made it also requires value choices. The rational decision-making process stresses the values of rational and critical thinking. (See Table 13–4.) The correct decision for an individual or group is based upon their values and morals. Within a society or nation there are some agreed-upon or universally held values, beliefs, and morals. However, not all of the values and beliefs are universal or held in the same order of priority by all people.

Economists do not always agree on the priority of economic values when making decisions and policies. Controversy is present in many economic decisions in both private and public sectors of the economy. To complicate the issue, individuals may actually find their value priorities in conflict when fulfilling their different roles. For example, for consumers the lower price is important, but for union members job security and the unity of action that give unions power are also important. Citizens may want to help protect local jobs, but they also want government services that require increased taxation of individuals and businesses. This is a problem when citizens vote on raising property taxes to pay for school improvements.

The Joint Council on Economic Education has identified seven important goals in the economy that reflect some of the values frequently encountered in economic decision making and policy formation. These are:
• economic freedom
• economic equity
• economic efficiency
• economic security
• full employment
• price stability
• economic growth

Economic freedom is an important characteristic of the market economy. Economic freedom means the opportunity to make your own choices concerning how to use resources and how to obtain additional resources.

Economic equity or fairness to all comes from the realization that there are some differences in the abilities of participants that are beyond their control. Differences such as physical disabilities create unequal opportunities, and policy makers need to take this fact into account to make things equal for all participants. Various groups in society often point out that their needs go unrecognized by the policy makers and that they do not have economic equity. How to maintain equity is one of the most controversial topics.

Economic efficiency as a goal and value has two distinct definitions. One is called technical efficiency and is measured by getting the most output from the least input of resources. Thus, technical efficiency is a reflection of high productivity. The second definition takes a broader view (macroeconomic) and looks at the markets that are affected by the single decision and encourages the choice that is best for all of the markets. The total benefits must exceed the total costs. It is possible for a single person or company to benefit greatly while those choices have sum total effects that hurt many more and cause an overall loss in productivity. Thus, the desire for economic efficiency creates situations in which the individual person or group is forced to place the larger group or society before his or her own good. Teachers are familiar with a similar conflict among students in the elementary classroom as they move from the first level of moral development to the second level.

Economic security is a value that is highly prized by both individuals and society. We make economic decisions based on the probability that we will continue to be healthy, that we will have employment, and that our savings and future will be safe as long as we are willing to work. Those things that disrupt the continued flow of our lives in a negative way are not desirable. Individuals and citizens are often called upon to make decisions that might affect economic security. In the United States we have made available some private and public policies such as Federal Deposit Insurance Corporation, workers' compensation, seniority rights, social security, and unemployment compensation to try to give economic security to people. History is filled with examples of the personal and group conflicts that relate directly to the value of economic security, and such conflicts will continue.

Full employment is the condition that exists when everyone who wants a job has one. While full employment seems desirable, it is probably never possible to attain this goal. There is always some unemployment as people enter the labor market for the first time or decide to move or seek new positions. There is a point where unemployment becomes larger than just these workers and causes undesirable hardships because of the lack of economic security.

Price stability is another value and goal that is desirable but probably never attainable. All prices do not remain the same at all times. The controversy arises among economists and citizens as to when increases and decreases in prices constitute inflation or deflation, which are damaging to the economy. Controversy also arises over managing the economy for price stability.

Economic growth is seen as necessary to continue to provide more products and more jobs for a growing population and for investment and research incentives. Like many of the other goals and values, economic growth is interrelated with factors in a nation's economy and in the international economy. An economy can actually produce more, but the growth may not keep up with increases in the population as a whole or in the work force. Controversy exists as to the best ways to promote economic growth.

Perhaps you do not see how elementary or middle school students would become involved or concerned about some of these goals and values. Can you name some additional value categories or individual values subsumed under the broader headings suggested by the Joint Council on Economic Education and therefore related to the study of economics? Many values such as hard work, accuracy and high standards, honesty, reliability, promptness, cooperation, competition, and social responsibility are promoted by the schools and related to economics. Unfortunately, other negative values are also present and reinforced in the hidden curriculum of the school, society, and the media. The hidden curriculum is what students learn although it is not part of the teacher's stated objectives. Among these negative values are extreme self-interest, immediate gratification, and cheating.

Young people receive mixed messages concerning which values are important. Economic educators claim that by learning economics, rational decision making, and how to examine the rationale for economic values, students will come to see the reasons that they should act in particular ways and adopt desirable values and behaviors. While there is some truth to this claim, perhaps you can identify incidents when knowledge alone did not bring about prosocial behaviors. Additional approaches to helping students develop values are discussed in chapters 10 and 14.

WHAT EXPERIENCE AND RESEARCH SAY ABOUT ECONOMIC EDUCATION

During the 1960s the economists and educators working through the Joint Council on Economic Education developed a systematic plan for working with teachers to improve economic education, including developing a conceptual framework, providing training for teachers, developing instructional materials, and conducting research. By the mid-1970s, economists and educators had reached a four-point consensus concerning what aspects of economics should be taught and how to most effectively accomplish the task. Their consensus illustrates the importance of the role of concepts in the meaningful learning of economics.

- An understanding of basic economic concepts is more important than a heavy dose of factual knowledge.
- Instructional efforts should concentrate on aiding students to achieve a fundamental understanding of a limited set of economic concepts and their relationships.
- Students should be given a conceptual framework to help them organize their understanding of economics, and they should be exposed to a manner of thinking that emphasizes systematic, objective analysis.

- The real personal and social advantages of economic understanding become apparent as individuals achieve competence in applying their knowledge to a wide range of economic issues they themselves confront. (Saunders et al., 1984, p. 2)

SEQUENCING CONCEPTS IN ECONOMIC EDUCATION

The Piagetian style of research in which problems are presented and students are asked to explain what happened has been conducted by economic researchers using economic concepts. Without formal instruction economic reasoning begins to emerge between the ages of five and seven. Concepts with which students have the greatest personal experiences, usually the fundamental or microeconomic concepts such as work, wants, and scarcity, appear to be among the first understood (Armento & Flores, 1986). Two important conclusions come from these studies:

- First, children's economic ideas tend to follow a developmental sequence. Their thinking becomes more abstract and flexible with age.
- Second, although economic thinking shows a gradual improvement with age, mature reasoning appears more quickly for some concepts than for others. (Schug & Walstad, 1991)

With systematic instruction, even kindergarten students can learn economic concepts and economic decision making—weighing alternatives given up against the benefits received (Kourilsky, 1977). (See Figure 13–1.) (Kourilsky's recommended methods of the Kinder-Economy and Mini-Society are discussed in detail on pages 332–333.) Teacher behavior in teaching the concepts of "specialization" (see Figure 13–2) in grades 3–5 was examined by Armento (1977). Student achievement was greater when teachers:

(1) gave more concept definitions and more positive concept examples and reviewed the main ideas of the lesson
(2) used accurate economic conceptual and factual knowledge relevant to the objectives of the lesson
(3) included more of the relevant knowledge generalizations and more of the related concept labels
(4) expressed more enthusiasm and interest in the content of the lesson (Armento & Flores, 1986, p. 98)

The *Trade-Offs* video series for grades 5–8 with its emphasis on examples of economic concepts in the lives of young teens was found to be successful in teaching economic concepts. Students whose teachers had been trained in the use of the materials scored significantly higher than students whose teachers had not received special training (Walstad, 1980; Chizmar & Halsinski, 1983).

Figure 13–1   A classroom store offers lots of opportunities for decision making.

Figure 13–2 This is part of a display of student drawings of specialists.

A Practice Activity

The following are activities that teachers have used to help teach economics. As a practice activity, read each and decide what concept(s) and value(s) are stressed. Indicate what you believe is an appropriate grade level for each activity.

1. Parents visit class and talk about what they do at work.

2. Students research various jobs and learn the types of training the workers must have.

3. Students learn about the newspaper by studying the different jobs and departments at their local paper. They then put out a class newspaper applying their learning.

4. Students analyze advertisements in magazines and television commercials looking for their techniques of appealing to readers and listeners.

5. Students compute the best dollar buys for similar products.

6. Students examine the costs of producing fast foods and compute the price differences in using domestic or imported beef and animal fats versus vegetable oils. They decide which they would use if they ran the restaurant.

7. Students conduct a market survey in school to decide what three booths their class will have at the school fair.

8. Students perform a cost–benefit analysis to determine the best short-term and long-term uses for the tropical rain forests.

9. Students conduct a survey of their families and neighbors to determine where and why people shop for groceries.

10. Students examine safety features on automobiles. They discuss why some are required by law and others are standard features or optional features on particular models. They discuss why all cars are not required to have all of the features.

11. Students examine and map the costs of food and basic services in different states and cities around the country. They attempt to identify reasons for the cost differences.

12. Students investigate the cost of shoplifting to local merchants at the mall. They discover how it affects the prices of products in the stores and the cost of government.

13. Students make a series of simulated life choices about cars, housing, savings, recreation, clothing, etc. They compute the salaries they would need to live the lifestyle they selected and compare it to the types of jobs available.

14. The class starts their own business making and selling a product, which earns $500. They pay expenses and interest and have $325 left. The class decides how this money should be spent or distributed.

15. Students compare the per capita GNP of nations of the world and research the resources and occupations of the people in various countries.

16. Students conduct surveys of their school and homes to determine where and how they might save on the cost of electricity.

17. Students visit a local fast food restaurant or factory and observe the production process. They produce a mural that reflects their observations.

18. Students take orders for Halloween masks of the Teenage Mutant Ninja Turtles and find that they have so many orders that they may not be able to fill them all. They discuss this and decide to use the assembly-line approach to production.

Discuss your answers with your classmates. What determined your placement for grade level? What values were identified the most? Do you think the teachers would encounter complaints from parents or groups for doing such activities? Who might object? For what reasons?

☞ *Here is a suggested range of answers for the practice exercise identifying the grade level, values, and concepts for the 18 activities described. Note that decision making as a value refers to the rational process of making decisions discussed in the chapter and that all of the values in the lessons may not be limited to economic values.*

In answer to the questions about the activities' grade level, values, and concepts the following are suggestions. Those things that should help you select the grade level are the number of examples of the concepts. Gathering data through experience can be at a lower grade than reading or dis-

cussion. Decision making, economic efficiency, and freedom are the most frequently identified values. Probably no one would object to teaching these values. The greatest concern parents might have would be for safety while gathering the data. Children should not be sent house to house seeking data without adult supervision.

SUGGESTED ANSWERS

Activities	Grades	Values	Economic Concepts
1	K–3	economic freedom	work/jobs, manager, goods, services, worker, entrepreneur, assembly line, union
2	3–8	work, deferred rewards, education	laborer, training, manager, profession, trade, union
3	3–8	honesty, work, accuracy	advertisement, specialization, division of labor
4	1–8	decision making, freedom, honesty	propaganda techniques, costs, benefits, choices
5	4–8	decision making, freedom, efficiency	scarcity, comparison shopping, costs
6	4–8	decision making, efficiency	comparative advantage, consequences, price, profit, trade-off, supply, demand, scarcity making efficiency
9	1–8	decision making, freedom	needs, wants, goods, services, consumer, price
10	5–8	decision making, responsibility, freedom, economic security	expenses, profit, trade-off opportunity cost, laws, regulations
11	5–8	efficiency, freedom, price stability	supply, demand, price, production, expenses, productive resources
12	5–8	decision making, honesty, equity, responsibility	choice, expenses, wants, taxes, laws, circular flow, institutions
13	5–8	deferred gratification	wants, savings, choices, opportunity cost, careers, trade-offs
14	3–8	decision making	opportunity cost, savings, interest

Activities	Grades	Values	Economic Concepts
15	7–8	full employment, efficiency	productive resources, GNP, circular flow, supply, demand, economic system
16	1–8	conservation of resources, efficiency, price stability	needs, scarcity, savings, supply, demand
17	K–3	economic efficiency	assembly line, productivity, quality control, specialization
18	3–6	decision making, freedom, economic efficiency	productivity, assembly line, specialization, scarcity, quality control

APPROACHES TO TEACHING ECONOMICS

There is no question that students at all grades, at all ability levels, and from all socioeconomic levels can learn economics. "Although certain instructional approaches, techniques, and strategies have been shown to yield better results than others, comparative studies have concluded that elementary school students can learn economics at some level of understanding through a variety of approaches" (Kourilsky, 1987, p. 200).

THE MINI-SOCIETY AND KINDER-ECONOMY APPROACHES

Economics plays an integral part in all societies, including the one that exists when students interact within the classroom. Students are personally involved in the problems of the class. Involving the students in analyzing and solving these classroom problems is the overall goal of these two programs developed by Marilyn L. Kourilsky, an economic educator at the University of California, Los Angeles. Both programs have been carefully developed and tested to provide a positive educational experience that results in learning important economic concepts (Kourilsky; 1977; 1983). While both programs are for elementary-age students, the kinder-economy is especially designed for students in kindergarten. Each concept is presented in a sequence of three types of lessons.

- First, the students experience the concept in their own classroom society and decide how to solve the situation.
- Second, the teacher helps the students debrief the situation to learn the names, definitions, and relationships between the economic concepts.
- Third, the teacher provides reinforcing activities such as role plays, games, exercise sheets, stories, and art projects for the students to complete.

In beginning the study, the teacher performs two important tasks: arranging the initial scarcity situation in the classroom and leading the students toward reaching their own decision on to how to solve their scarcity problem. Alternatives must be generated, consequences predicted, and a best choice agreed to by the students. The students must come to see that scarcity is frequently present in the classroom society and they must agree that there is a need to systematically try to reduce this problem. The students then set about determining who in the classroom should get the scarce resources. Students usually decide that earning and free choice in spending are the best solutions. Once the decisions concerning the name of the society, the design of the money, and the pay of officers and pay procedures are established, the role of the teacher changes from leader to facilitator.

Instead of the teacher creating the experiences, the students through their interactions create the different problems to be solved. The teacher then encourages the students to examine the alternatives and consequences and to decide on the answer. If students make a poor decision, it will become evident in new problems and can be corrected.

The goal of these programs is to teach economic concepts and the relationships between concepts within society. The teacher must keep these economic goals in mind and not use the mini-society as a form of behavior modification for individual students. The original opportunities to earn money must be activities that all students have an equal opportunity to accomplish so that money gets into the classroom society. From experience it has been observed that $10 or less is ample pay for a regular salary per day. Later, students can be encouraged to come up with creative ways to earn additional money if they wish.

Key to the success of these classroom societies is the teacher's faith in the students to discover the problems and to eventually come to an acceptable decision supported by the class. For example, students may want to open businesses and sell items and services. The problems of where to locate the business and when sales can take place must be solved. Do students need a business license? Can students sell such services as taking tests and doing homework for others?

The teacher as a member of the class has a role similar to that of the students in helping solve the problems. The teacher prods the students to use what they have learned about alternatives and consequences to help solve problems and, if necessary, suggests alternatives and consequences. Teachers also have the additional responsibility of reinforcing the learning through closure activities in the lessons and through reinforcing activities and assignments. The teacher must also be certain to inform the parents of the activities and their goals. Parents must give written permission for students to bring things to school, specifying if they are for use or may be sold or bartered.

The goals of the classroom society programs go beyond the recognition of concepts and require that the students apply and analyze the concepts and make decisions. The students must also learn to live with both the short-term and the long-term consequences of their decisions. Because the kinder-economy and mini-society require a long-term and regular commitment of time during the week to accomplish their goals, the teacher needs to carefully study the available books devoted to the program.

RESOURCES FOR ECONOMIC EDUCATION

Special resources for teaching economics are widely available. In addition to those resources generally available for educators, teachers often employ local resources who are knowledgeable about specific economic issues, as well as recognizing such opportunities as guest speakers and field trips. Teachers also use locally conducted surveys and send out written questionnaires to gather information. All governmental agencies and institutions face economic issues, and some deal directly with regulating various aspects of the economy, collecting taxes, preserving and managing resources on public lands, or regulating product safety and quality. Their printed materials and speakers designed for the general public may be of help in teaching.

Several of the federal reserve banks and the Internal Revenue Service have developed educational materials. Other economic institutions such as trade organizations, private corporations, insurance groups, and financial organizations have materials for use in the schools. Many of these organizations are affiliated with the Joint Council on Economic Education and the various state councils, therefore one way to locate these materials is to contact your state's council on economic education. Your state's department of education should be able to provide you with the appropriate address. They may also provide you with the name of the centers of economic education at colleges and universities in your state. The Joint Council on Economic Education will also be happy to provide you with such information, as well as a catalog of materials they have produced. The address is:

Joint Council on Economic Education
2 Park Avenue
New York, New York 10016
(212) 685-5499

As you know, economics is filled with controversy. Some of the resources will have specific viewpoints. You will want to apply the ideas discussed, evaluate and use sponsored materials, as well as utilize the ideas on the use of the specific methods found in chapter 7.

SUMMARY

The study of economics is integral to the lives of individuals and nations. Economists and economic educators have placed emphasis on research, teacher training, and preparing materials to improve the economic knowledge of all ages. Although a variety of methods are successful in teaching economics, the best approaches place emphasis on the economic concepts and on making rational economic decisions. Many economic concepts are present in the social studies curriculum of both elementary and middle schools. A study of economics for young teens is thought to be especially good because it has the potential to encourage students to make careful career choices and to develop good spending habits.

REFERENCES

Armento, B. J. (1986). Promoting economic literacy. In S. P. Wronski & D. H. Rragaw (Eds.), *Social Studies and Social Sciences: A Fifty-Year Perspective.* Bulletin 78. Washington D. C.: National Council for the Social Studies.

Armento, B. J. & Flores, S. (1986). Learning about the economic world. In V. A. Atwood (Ed.), *Elementary School Social Studies: Research as a Guide to Practice.* Bulletin No. 79. Washington, D.C.: National Council for the Social Studies.

Banaszak, R. A. (1987). *The nature of economic literacy.* Bloomington, IN: Clearinghouse for Social Studies/Social Science Education. ERIC Digest No. 41.

Chizmar, J. F. & Halsinski, R. S. (1983). Performance in the basic economics test (BET) and Trade-Offs. *Journal of Economic Education, 14*(1), 18–29.

Kourilsky, M. L. (1977). The kinder economy: A case study of kindergarten pupils' acquisition of economic concepts. *Elementary School Journal, 77,* 182–191.

Kourilsky, M. L. (1983). *Mini-society experiencing real-world economics in the elementary school classroom.* Menlo Park, CA: Addison-Wesley Publishing Company.

Kourilsky, M. L. (1987). Children's learning of economics: The imperative and the hurdles. *Theory and Research in Social Education, 26,* 198–205.

Saunders, P.; Bach, G. L.; Calderwood, J. D.; and Hansen, W. L. (1984). *Master curriculum guide in economics: A framework for teaching the basic concepts* 2nd ed. New York: Joint Council on Economic Education.

Schug, M. C. & Walstad, W. B. (1991). Teaching and learning economics. In J. P. Shaver (Ed.), *Handbook of Research on Social Studies Teaching and Learning.* New York: Macmillan Publishing Company.

Walstad, W. B. (1980). The impact of trade-offs and teacher training on economic understanding and attitudes. *Journal of Economic Education, 12*(1), 41–48.

CHAPTER 14

OVERVIEW

If someone stopped you and inquired, "Are you a good citizen?" how would you respond? Would you be surprised or insulted by the question? If the person persisted and requested proof, what would be your response? This chapter examines political science and law in light of those concepts that students need to learn to become responsible, participating citizens. It also examines the ways children learn to become active citizens and the roles that the school and teacher play in this process.

Political Science, Civics, and Law Education

OBJECTIVES

1. Explain the importance of knowledge, values, and participation to citizenship.
2. Explain the importance of the individual to democracy.
3. Explain the role of the hidden curriculum in forming students' ideas about power, authority, and governing.
4. Identify political science concepts and values essential to the understanding of democratic government.
5. Explain the multicultural nature of American society and its impact on the democratic tradition of the United States.
6. Identify characteristics of lessons that are helpful in accommodating learning in a multicultural democracy.
7. State a rationale for community participation in elementary and middle school.
8. Give examples of student participation appropriate for elementary and middle school students.
9. List recommended ways to study the law.
10. Explain the role of the media in educating citizens.
11. Identify ways to help children make wise use of the media.
12. Explain why American citizens are interested in issues related to international, global, and peace education.
13. Identify ways in which American citizens are involved in, and become aware of, global issues.

CITIZENSHIP IN A DEMOCRATIC SOCIETY

Being born in the United States or having an American parent makes a child an American citizen. Citizenship is bestowed on an infant and grants the child many rights and privileges. But citizenship is also something that must be learned and then practiced. In its curriculum guidelines, the National Council for the Social Studies declares that "the basic goal of social studies education is to prepare young people to become rational, participating citizens. . . ." (National Council for the Social Studies, 1979, p. 262). Patriotism, or love of country, is an attitude that is established very early in life. Children and adolescents tend to be positive about national symbols, to like and trust their political leaders, and to be highly supportive of their political systems. Researchers have found such positive attitudes even when the students had little understanding of their country or its government (Torney-Purta, 1990). But, are love of country and positive attitudes toward symbols and leaders enough in a democracy?

Time for Reflection: What Do YOU Think?

We assume that citizens are patriotic and loyal to their country and are shocked when we hear the contrary. Patriotism and loyalty involve more than lip service; they require action. Some actions are listed below. Which of these are appropriate ways to participate in our democracy?

pay taxes
volunteer at a hospital
say Pledge of Allegiance
make the vice president the
   butt of a joke
strike and picket
contribute to a political campaign
collect for United Way
serve in military
vote in elections
write letter to members of
   state legislature

serve on a jury
protest against nuclear
   weapons
listen to television news
hold public office
lead a scout troop
sign a petition
help a sick neighbor
know names of his or her
   state's senators
pay bills on time

Discuss your choices with your classmates, keeping in mind that there is not one right answer and that while some perceptions are shared, some opinions will differ. Look again at the list of actions. Which of these might not be considered acceptable in some parts of the world? How is patriotism different from just being a nice person? Is it patriotic to be against a government policy? Look back at your list; which of the items you declared to be participation did you learn to do from your schooling? Which of these did you learn specifically in your social studies class?

Political science is a discipline that studies governments. Political scientists focus their studies on three very different types of questions concerning governing:
- Who has the right and power to govern?
- How do governments organize themselves to make and enforce political decisions?
- How do groups of people influence the political process?

The first question examines historical and philosophical ideas while the second question deals more with the formation of governmental and public policies. The third question addresses politics as it is formally and informally practiced.

All citizens have the need for and the right to services from their governments. Citizens in a democracy have special powers and obligations including:
- bestowing both the power and right to rule on a government of their choice
- selecting those who perform the day-to-day governance
- debating and compromising to instruct the government on the needs of the people and the types of policies desired
- monitoring the actions of governments and keeping informed on issues related to the collective good
- balancing their own self-interest with the collective good

Political scientists believe that the capacity to participate effectively in the politics of a free society requires both knowledge of the political system and a clear understanding of what one is trying to accomplish. This goal is best served if citizens have:

1. an interest in public affairs and a sense of "public regardedness"
2. tolerance and respect for conflicts arising from divergent values and beliefs
3. the ability to examine consequences and to assess the likelihood of alternatives achieving desired goals
4. the ability to assess both long- and short-term consequences (Brody, 1989)

In the United States there has been a widespread acceptance of the centrality of citizenship education in the social studies curriculum. Political scientists, with their emphasis on rational thought and decision making, criticize what is taught in the schools as being a naive, unrealistic, and romanticized image of political life. They say that the ideals of democracy are confused with the realities of politics (Jenness, 1990). The elementary curriculum is singled out for criticism because it tends to fail to recognize the presence of conflict and failure within a democracy. Those determining citizenship education lack agreement on a single focus. Ideas for the appropriate focus span a continuum from stressing patriotism and loyalty through examining and solving social problems to centering on social and governmental criticism.

During the 1970s social studies educators involved with Project SPAN defined the role of the citizen as focusing on relationships between individuals and political entities and on organized efforts to influence public policy (Superka and Hawke, 1982). Since such relationships are found in the neighborhood, community, state, national, and international levels of government, citizenship activities fit into all levels (K–12) of the social studies curriculum. Social studies is primarily responsible for teaching the knowledge, skills, and values needed to understand and participate effectively in the United States political system and to deal responsibly with public issues.

DEVELOPMENT OF POLITICAL AWARENESS IN STUDENTS

Political socialization is one of the major interests of political scientists. Researchers examine two major questions:

- What are the attitudes and knowledge that people have about government?
- What are the sources of this political knowledge and these attitudes?

Concepts from sociology and psychology also enter into the study of political socialization. Political socialization appears to be a developmental process during which three distinct types of political identification processes are experienced: affiliation, knowledge, and participation. Young children develop a basic affiliation and attachment to their political system and its leaders even before they enter school. Older children and young adolescents make gains in their knowledge about the political system. At about age 9 or 10, there appear to be increased abilities to perceive political alternatives and to realize opposing political positions and different interpretations (Torney-Purta, 1991). By the end of the eighth grade (about age 14), students have developed an understanding of the need for consensus and majority rule, but they do not yet seem to recognize the role of debate, disagreement, and conflict in the operation of a democratic political system (Hess & Torney, 1967). The decision to participate in political life is made by young adults. Attitudes during adulthood tend to remain similar to those learned very early in life. If students know the views of their parents, they tend to hold similar views. Schools do impart political knowledge, but parents and the media are seen as greater sources of political knowledge (Hess and Torney, 1967; Torney et al., 1975; Torney, 1991; and Patrick & Hoge, 1991).

CLASSROOM TEACHING METHODS

American students report that reading, discussing, and writing answers to questions were the most frequent activities they were involved in while studying civics (National Assessment of Educational Progress, 1990). An extensive international study of civic education revealed both positive and negative impacts on knowledge and attitudes related to classroom climate and teaching methods. A positive relationship was found between those students ages 14 and 17 who reported their teachers encouraged the expression of opinions in the classroom and higher cognitive test scores on authoritarian attitudes. Students who reported frequently taking part in patriotic rituals tended to be less knowledgeable about government and more authoritarian in their attitudes. The amount of time spent on printed drills and memorization of facts and dates was negatively related to knowledge scores and was positively related to authoritarian attitudes in some of the nations (Torney et al., 1975).

SOCIAL STUDIES CURRICULUM

Perhaps the best answer to the question of what the social studies curriculum teaches about citizenship, government, and law is found in what students learn. The most recent national evaluation of civics knowledge was conducted in 1988 by the National Assessment of Educational Progress (NAEP). Their evaluations are the only nationally representative and continuing assessment of American education. *The Civics Report Card* presents the 1988 achievement from grades 4, 8, and 12. The report says it provides an opportunity to reflect on the extent to which all students are being provided with the kinds of civic learning needed to understand the United States Constitution and the principles that it includes. Four proficiency levels of questions were identified in the test. These allow for comparing the performances of students in subpopulations. The four proficiency levels are:

- *Level 200:* Recognizes the existence of civic life
- *Level 250:* Understands the nature of political institutions and the relationships between citizens and government
- *Level 300:* Understands specific government structures and functions
- *Level 350:* Understands a variety of political institutions and processes

An analysis of the results reveals some positive points concerning civic education in the schools:

- In all grades there was a positive relationship between the level of proficiency and the amount of instruction the students reported having received in social studies, civics, or United States government.
- Seventy-one percent of the fourth graders showed a basic awareness of political vocabulary, institutions, and processes, illustrating a proficiency at Level 200.
- By grade 8, sixty-one percent of the students had Level 250 proficiency.
- At grade 12, fifty percent of the students had detailed knowledge of the major governmental structures and their function indicating a Level 300 proficiency, while only six percent of the twelfth grade students demonstrated proficiency at the most advanced level, Level 350.
- There were no systematic differences in the achievement of students in different regions of the United States.

Disparities in the achievement of subpopulations were of great concern to the evaluators. These include:

1. The greater likelihood of students achieving proficiency at each level if they were from advantaged urban areas and not from disadvantaged urban communities, where students rated lower percentages of proficiency.
2. The significantly lower proficiencies of African-Americans and Hispanic students for all levels of questions in all grades.
3. The inability of the vast majority of both eighth and twelfth graders to describe in writing the responsibilities of the president of the United States.

The National Assessment of Educational Progress report indicates that students' civic understanding increases with age and that the study of civics topics resulted in greater learning.

KEY CONCEPTS AND VALUES IN AMERICAN DEMOCRACY

In some areas of the country, civics courses have been placed at the eighth grade. However, government and civics, while considered important, have also been assigned by the curriculum to the high school grades. Much of the emphasis in civics and government has been placed on preparing the individual to deal with the American government and its agencies and to be future voters. Emphasis has been on the mechanics of government rather than on the concepts of political science. The recommendations from the American Political Science Association for pre-collegiate education do not center on concepts.

Identifying the concepts to teach young students has been left largely to the textbook authors. In the present K–4 textbooks, publishers have included political science concepts, but to a lesser degree than geographic and economic concepts. The most frequently appearing concepts include "law," "president," "government," "citizen," "nation," "rules," "taxes," and "Congress" (Haas, 1991).

The fourth grade students in the NAEP testing (1990) reported studying such topics as community, presidents, laws, and citizens' rights and responsibilities. The eighth grade students in the same testing said that they studied the Constitution, the Bill of Rights, Congress, political parties, elections, voting, and rights and responsibilities of citizens. The treatment of citizenship in elementary textbooks has been criticized for overemphasizing conformity to authority (Engle & Ochoa, 1986; Larkins et al., 1987). Concern of lawyers and educators over the lack of an emphasis on important aspects and concepts related to law and the Constitution prompted the formation of the law-related movement in education during the 1960s (Starr, 1989).

Table 14–1 suggests concepts appropriate for K–8 students that have been derived from the professional literature. Political science concepts are often highly abstract. However, several of the organizing concepts listed in Table 14–1 have examples that are present in any situation where a number of people interact, including the family and the classroom. School is often the first experience in which children interact with a variety of people who judge them on their actions. Schooling requires students to behave in new and different social situations. Lessons on such political concepts as rules, leadership, viewpoints, conflict resolution, and compromise and the relationships among those concepts help students understand their new political situation and provide rationales for desired classroom behaviors. *Socialization* is the name given the process whereby young people learn proper behaviors. Elementary and middle school teachers spend much of their time in socializing their students. When elementary students attend school they must learn to function in a larger and more diverse and pluralistic group than they have previously encountered. In the middle school, students may encounter an even more pluralistic situation.

However, young teens are also engaged in another task with political overtones: identifying the appropriate role of their increasing personal and cognitive

Table 14–1

Essential Concepts and Values in American Democracy

CONCEPTS		VALUES	
power	representative	human dignity	privacy
law/rule	democracy	freedom	respect for the
law making/	leadership	self-discipline	individual
changing	Constitution	democracy	rule of law
authority	Bill of Rights	justice/fairness	diversity
pluralism	due process	social responsibility	honesty
interdependence	compromise	consensus	loyalty
majority	pluralism	equality	international human
minority	decision making	tolerance	rights
conflict	influence		
conflict resolution	government		
viewpoint	nation		

power with that of the larger community in which they are beginning to function more independently. This process is one with characteristics that are counter-socializing, as students challenge the power previously assigned without question to certain people, including parents, teachers, and government officials.

Democracies have faith that their citizens will generally do what is right. An agreement on what is right comes from having common convictions and beliefs. These include the provision for the basic needs of individuals and the respect for the human dignity of individuals. Such ideas are learned through socialization. However, socialization can become conformity for the wrong reasons and to the detriment of the human dignity of some or all of the population. For that reason, citizens must be encouraged to question what is happening and to decide if the consequences are those they consider important and of most worth or value. Appropriate democratic values and beliefs have been identified by the NCSS (1989) and are listed in Table 14–1.

Schools reflect the values of the society. Such values as self-discipline, consensus, equality, tolerance, fairness, loyalty, honesty, and freedom are of great concern in the functioning of all classrooms. The values of a society cannot be imposed on its citizens for long. Citizens must agree on the values and their importance if the society is to function smoothly and its laws are to be readily observed. Elementary and middle school students need to examine the meanings of the values and predict what life would be like if people did not practice these values. In so doing students decide the type of society they want and need and they see the reasons for acting in ways that bring about such a society. Political science's contribution to social studies includes helping students find out how people use their own personal power to make a difference in their lives and the lives of others.

Research on democratic attitudes reports that the classroom climate and the hidden curriculum of the school directly affect students' attitudes. Even if they are not recognized formally in the social studies curriculum, important concepts and values related to politics, law, and political science are being presented indirectly throughout the K–8 curriculum. Formal instruction in democratic citizenship through the social studies curriculum is needed to help students overcome misconceptions and misunderstandings of the democratic philosophy and American government. The learning cycle on the oath of the president (Table 14–2) teaches cognitive knowledge about American government and investigates what Americans value or believe to be important to our democracy.

Table 14–2

LEARNING CYCLE: Presidential Oath

Key Idea: The United States is a nation ruled by a body of laws, not by any one person. (For Middle School and Intermediate)

OBJECTIVES	PROCEDURES	EVALUATIONS
	Exploration	
Students recall and identify different things that the president of the United States of America can and cannot do.	Show several pictures of the president or past presidents of the United States of America. Ask: "What are some of the things the president does?" Then ask, "What do you think the president can't do?" "Would you want to be the president?" "Why?" or "Why not?"	Record students' participation in discussion on a checklist.
	Invention	
Students identify the steps a person follows to become president of the United States of America.	Ask: "What is the process by which a person gets to be president in the United States of America today?" Discuss and help students compile steps in the process. 1. Declare yourself a candidate. 2. Win pledges of votes in primary elections. 3. Be nominated by a political party as their presidential candidate. 4. Campaign for office. 5. Win the election. 6. Prepare to take over and appoint major helpers and advisors. 7. Be inaugurated (officially and formally sworn in by taking the presidential oath).	Checklist recording student participation in discussion.
Students use the presidential oath in determining the relationships of the Constitution to the duties of the president.	Display a picture of the presidential oath-taking. Tell students that all American presidents have taken the same oath. During the campaign, candidates for president promise they will do lots of things. Ask: "What do you want the president to swear to do?" List students' ideas. Ask: "Does anyone know what the actual oath is?" It is written in the Constitution, Article II section 1. "I do solemnly swear (or affirm)	

that I will faithfully execute the office of president of the United States, and will do the best of my ability to preserve, protect, and defend the Constitution of the United States."

Discuss the meaning of the oath: "Are there any words in the oath that you don't understand?" ("Execute" means to carry out, not to kill.) "Does this oath include some or all of our ideas?" "Are you disappointed in what it says?" "Why or why not?" "What appears to be the most important thing in this oath?" (The Constitution—preserving, protecting, and defending it.) "How important is the Constitution to the United States of America?" "Is it more important than the president, Congress, the Supreme Court, and the military forces?" "Why?" "What does the Constitution do for us?" "What does having the president swear to preserve, protect, and defend the Constitution tell us about how our founders and Americans in general view the law?" "What does it say about the importance of particular people or of particular offices or positions?" Ask students, in pairs, to develop a summary statement describing how the United States of America is ruled. They should point out the role of laws as indicated in the lesson's key idea. Share statements. Develop a class statement.

Appropriateness of summary statements describing role of laws and the president.

Expansion

Students predict which other occupations might take an oath to protect and defend the United States Constitution.

Review what was learned about the oath of the president. Examine the following list of occupations and decide for which the person swears an oath: lawyer, council member, judge, teacher, doctor, soldier, governor, mayor, police officer, accountant, senator, member of Congress, citizen, member of the clergy. Ask: "Which of those who take an oath might swear, like the president does, to preserve, protect, and defend the Constitution?" Ask students to list their predictions.

Students' lists of predictions.

Students collect data to determine the accuracy of their predictions.

Check the predictions. In pairs, have students write letters, do library research, or interview people in these occupations. Assign each pair one occupation. Ask about their oaths and how the oath influences what they do when working. Ask students to prepare a summary statement on the occupation for which they collected data. Conclude by discussing the summary statements and the importance of the Constitution to Americans. "Who has responsibilities to preserve, protect, and defend the Constitution?" "Should all Americans take an oath to the Constitution or just some?"

Summary statements prepared by students.

Appropriate topics for additional learning cycles are those related to various aspects of the Constitution or political and legal occupations.

MULTICULTURAL EDUCATION

Multicultural education is a curriculum movement with implications for not only academic disciplines but also for all other aspects of schooling. During the 1960s the term "cultural group" was limited to consideration of ethnic and racial groups. Today it is defined by such additional attributes as religion, sex, and disability. Social studies has the special role of examining the conflicts between the political, social, and economic ideals of democracy and the reality of the lives of individuals. The meaning and history of pluralism in American society are also addressed.

Advocates of multicultural and multiethnic education assume that ethnic diversity is a positive element in a society (Banks & Lynch, 1986; NCSS, 1976). It is a fact that America is and has long been a multicultural society. It is also a fact that practices and laws have often discriminated against various groups in our society. Restrictive immigration laws have been removed and in recent years this has resulted in a new, more diverse wave of immigrants to the United States. By the year 2010, the minority populations of California will be the majority in the state, and at least nine other states can be expected to quickly have a similar demographic composition (Hodgkinson, 1990). The diversity in the origins of America's population is increasing and within the population new groups of people are being formed or recognized for some unique characteristics for the first time. This is bound to have an impact on America economically, socially, and politically.

Being an active participant in American society requires individuals to assume many different roles and often requires the ability to interact with people from diverse backgrounds. Individuals must identify not only with the goals and values of their families but also with those of the nation and a variety of formal institutions. This ability is learned through experience and formal training. It requires social, cognitive, and psychological maturity. The dominant culture of the nation and the cultures of families and friends greatly affect individuals and influence their development.

For most children the school is the first "governmental" institution they encounter. Schools represent the views of the dominant powers in the society. To succeed in school the child must behave in those ways considered "appropriate." An orientation to tasks, scientific logic, individual achievement, and competition traditionally have been rewarded by American schools and society. When children enter school they have already learned a set of the proper behaviors as determined by their family and neighbors. Not all cultural groups value the same ideals or teach children the same set of behaviors. Research has shown that different cultural groups respond differently in school to other children and teachers. They may also learn differently. Some are better at verbal tasks and performing independently from environmental conditions while others are much more aware of and responsive to environmental variables, other people, and nonverbal interactions. Matching the instructional procedures with the learning preferences of the student has implications for the likelihood of their success within school and therefore within the larger society (Gay, 1991). This includes the willingness of students to participate in and feel a part of American society. Democracy requires the informed participation of all people. It also assumes and expects people will function according to a set of common values about other people, personal power, and leadership. As revealed by the National Assessment of Educational Progress testing of the knowledge about law, citizenship, and government, several sub-populations of American youth consistently performed at a significantly lower level of achievement (NAEP, 1990).

Instructional activities that accommodate multiple learning styles and are used throughout the entire school year will help meet the needs of a multicultural society. Similarly, the use of a variety of assessment procedures and techniques matching student learning style preferences (see chapter 9) also recognizes the needs of a multicultural society. Specific instructional procedures that are helpful in promoting multicultural education include those that:

- provide students with continuous opportunities to develop a better sense of self
- help students understand the totality of the experiences of American people and cultural groups
- help students understand that there is always a conflict between ideals and realities in human societies
- explore and clarify alternatives and options within American society
- examine the values, attitudes, and behaviors that support pluralism
- develop decision making and social participation skills
- encourage interpersonal and group interactions
- identify the similarities and differences among the experiences of several groups of people and the conflicts in their perspectives and points of view
- examine the development of the United States for the contributions of all people (NCSS, 1976)

The examination of the meaning and consequences of such concepts as "interdependence," "independence," "prejudice," "racism," "sexism," "stereotypes," "frame of reference," and "justice" confronts important issues faced by a multicultural society as it attempts to overcome conflicts and recognize human dignity. When possible, cross-cultural personal experiences in which students learn about or work with others toward a common goal are helpful. The emphasis of such activities should be to create a "we" perspective or a "cooperative pluralist perspective" rather than to look upon other cultural groups with a "they" orientation (Nakagawa and Pang, 1990). When personal contact is limited or impossible, cooperative group activities and the use of multiculturally oriented materials can describe the lives and present the concerns and feelings of a diversity of ethnic groups. Films, biographies, and literature are especially helpful in portraying the views and feelings of others (Banks, 1981).

LAW-RELATED EDUCATION

The law-related education movement began because of the concern of lawyers and educators over the failure of the traditional textbook approach of civic education to provide a living content and vibrant activities for students (Starr, 1989).

Advocates of law-related education (LRE) often criticize school civics curricula because students are taught the unrealistic perspective of a society that is in harmony and free from conflict. Studying law-related topics provides a more realistic view. Law-related education provides many opportunities to examine the conflict between self-interest and the common good. Legal issues require careful examination of disagreements and conflicts. The resolution of such issues illustrates how society deals with conflicts for the common good and protects dissent through the concepts of individual, minority, and human rights.

Law-related education (LRE) is supported and promoted by the American Bar Association. Often local and state bar associations work with school systems in the training of teachers and by providing guest speakers. Judges, police officers, and lawyers are frequently asked to speak to classes. Field trips to courts to observe the daily meaning of the loss of personal freedom, and to legislative bodies to observe the process of making laws, serve to supply students with information on LRE topics.

Lessons in law-related education stress active student participation in the learning of concepts and the performance of value analysis. Role playing, simulations, mock trials, structured discussion, and analysis of stories containing moral dilemmas or expressing viewpoints are frequently used teaching strategies. Lesson content centers around the need for laws, human and legal rights, individual and civic responsibilities, the processes of the legal system, and the important legal principles and values found in the Constitution and the Bill of Rights. Special projects for intermediate and middle school students have been developed on criminal justice and the judiciary system.

Law-related education seeks to foster growth and development in students of both knowledge and behaviors needed by citizens living in a pluralistic and democratic society. It is recommended that LRE programs be designed to promote growth in several of the LRE learning outcomes listed in Table 14–3 (Anderson, 1980). Table 14–3 also suggests how teachers can evaluate their success in teaching about the law. The desired outcomes of LRE are listed in the right-hand column. The left-hand column lists behaviors and perceptions that are not only the opposite but that reflect a person who is uninformed and lacks both a sense and desire for community. Table 14–3 can be turned into an evaluation instrument by adding a line under each statement where the teacher would mark the classes' or individual student's responses over a period of time. By rewording the statements into sentences and adding a numbered line between the statements, Table 14–3 can be changed into a self-reporting attitudinal measure for older students.

PARTICIPATION

Citizens are expected to participate in their communities. At the beginning of this chapter you were asked to consider whether certain behaviors were those that would be performed by a good citizen. You were also asked to identify those that you learned in social studies classes specifically or in your general schooling. These

Table 14–3

Critical Learning Outcome Continuums in Law-Related Education

Children moved away from:	*Children moved toward:*
perceiving law as restrictive, punitive, immutable, and beyond the control and understanding of the people affected	perceiving law as promotive, facilitative, comprehensive, and alterable
perceiving people as powerless before the law and other socio-civic institutions	perceiving people as having potential to control and contribute to the social order
perceiving issues of right and wrong as incomprehensible to ordinary people	perceiving right and wrong as issues all citizens can and should address
perceiving social issues as unproblematic	perceiving the dilemmas inherent in social issues
being impulsive decision makers and problem solvers who make unreflective commitments	being reflective decision makers and problem solvers who make grounded commitments
being inarticulate about commitments made or positions taken	being able to give reasoned explanations about commitments made and positions taken
being unable to manage conflict in other than a coercive or destructive manner	being socially responsible conflict managers
being uncritically defiant of authority	being critically responsive to legitimate authority
being illiterate about legal issues and the legal system	being knowledgeable about law, the legal system, and related issues
being egocentric, self-centered, and indifferent to others	being empathetic, socially responsible, and considerate of others
being morally immature in responding to ethical problems	being able to make mature judgments in dealing with ethical and moral problems

Source: In Charlotte C. Anderson, "Promoting Responsible Citizenship Through Elementary Law-Related Education," Social Education, 44 *(May 1980). Reprinted with permission of the National Council for the Social Studies.*

are some additional thoughts concerning citizen participation and social studies, providing additional ideas appropriate for use in preparing and involving K–8 students in active participation as citizens.

Before the twentieth century, when fewer people were educated, most of the students were being prepared to become political, economic, and military leaders. The schools specifically taught students to be leaders and stressed the obligations of leadership as an important value. As more and more people came to attend schools, the emphasis shifted. Today participation is being reexamined again because of new changes in society. Educators are giving much thought to the matter of participation. Many believe that the schools can play only a small role in increasing citizenship participation and that many other institutions such as the family, religion, and the media play equal or more important roles. There are a number of very important questions to be examined before involving the schools in participation.

Time for Reflection: What Do YOU Think?

Before reading further, take time to think about your answers to the following questions.

1. Is it enough for a citizen to study the candidates and issues and then vote?

2. Give an example of how or when the average citizen might assume a leadership role?

3. Name three ways citizens of differing interests and abilities might serve their community.

4. What variables can you think of that might help or hinder a citizen's ability to serve his or her community?

5. In what kinds of immediate participation activities can the elementary and middle schools involve their students?

6. What habits related to participating in the community can the elementary and middle schools develop in their students?

Traditionally, citizen participation has been categorized as one of four types of behavior:
- participation in aspects of the electoral process
- participation in grass-root citizen actions
- involvement in providing advice in forming governmental policies and practices
- participation in obligatory activities

More recently, participation has been viewed with a broader sociopolitical definition to include:
- volunteer service through the donation of time and money
- mutual self-help group projects addressing common problems (Langston, 1990)

Figure 14–1 shows that social and political activism or participation is the way people use their personal authority and legitimate power (Procter, 1991). All peo-

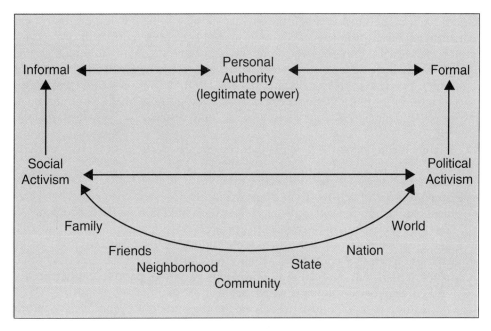

Figure 14–1   **Dimensions of Social and Political Activism**

ple have personal power. Only a few people daily exert political power while many people use their power informally or on a less regular basis. The informal use of power is most likely to be done within the less-formal social institutions such as the family, friends, neighbors, and community-based organizations or clubs. The organized and formal use of power and influence is associated with political institutions beginning at the community level. In today's world many of the issues and concerns of people are not limited by geographical boundaries. The larger the distribution of the issue, the more likely it is that legal and political organizations play a role in the solutions. While political activism receives the greatest amount of publicity, social activism has throughout history responded more quickly to the needs of people, improved the lives of vast numbers of people, and prompted many of the social organizations and much of the social legislation taken for granted today. These and additional important roles are still performed through social action and are of particular importance in a large, diverse democracy such as the United States.

SCHOOL-BASED COMMUNITY SERVICE PROJECTS

Because working people and those with family responsibilities have little extra time, retired people make up a large portion of the volunteers in the United States. Today, citizens who are not educators are greatly concerned with the apparent alienation of youth and various population groups. Many see the volunteer and mutual self-help types of community service as having an important role in correcting societal problems. They seek to involve young people in community service activities. Minnesota and Pennsylvania have included statewide service programs in their schools and other cities and states are considering adding community service to the curriculum (Clark, 1990). Important values underlying these community participation programs include a "passionate commitment to promote reasonableness, tolerance, fairness, and respect. . . ." (Langston, 1990, p. 304).

Claims for the potential benefits that community participation gives students include:
- gaining a sense or a stake in the community
- gaining a sense of self-worth and responsibility
- practicing such important skills as cooperation, decision making, problem solving, and planning or organizing projects
- gaining exposure to positive role models and career possibilities
- increasing a sense of control over their environment
- increasing personal interaction with a wider variety of people of other ages and cultural backgrounds (Procter & Haas, 1990)

In addition to its individual character-building attributes, community service is seen as having the potential to vitalize the education curriculum through experiences relevant to "real life" situations that require the use of social and intellectual skills taught in social studies. Following an extensive survey of community service projects, Procter and Haas (1990) identified six specific types of school-based activities often labeled as community service:

1. Those that use the community as a laboratory in which to practice skills learned in the classroom as a part of the regular curriculum. For example, students might record an oral history of the community and prepare it for use in the school or local library.
2. Special events or co-curricular activities sponsored by the school or a club. Examples would be students taking part in a collection drive for the needy or a disaster relief drive.
3. Service programs that require a minimum number of hours of service for graduation.
4. Specifically designed courses with both classwork and participation components. Examples might include helping organize a recycling center or regularly doing volunteer work at a community center.
5. Programs designed for specific groups of students, such as at-risk or disabled students. An example might include these students using their skills to tutor or read to younger students.
6. Career-oriented programs with emphasis on specific work skills or a professional orientation in which the students work part of the school day.

Because community service opportunities come in a variety of forms requiring different skills and time commitments, there are opportunities for community service at all grade levels. With all types of projects the teacher's role is to assist students in assessing their performance, evaluating their goals, and understand-

Table 14–4

Hierarchy of School-Based Community Service Projects and Their Learning Outcomes

PROJECT TYPE	SKILLS	VALUES	CITIZENSHIP CONCEPTS	GRADE LEVELS	
School Service Project	Identifying needs, Organizing, Group dynamics	Cooperation, Self-esteem, Pride in accomplishment	Participation, Activism	K–12	Basic
Community Service Project	Communication, Critical thinking, Decision making	Respect, Brotherhood, Empathy	Community and democratic values	3–12	
Individual Service Project	Time management, Problem solving, Adaptability, Self-direction	Human dignity, Justice, Responsibility	Appreciation of cultural diversity, Social justice	7–12	Complex

Source: D. R. Procter and M. E. Haas, (1990). A Handbook of School-Based Community Projects for Student Participation ED 216 467. Reprinted with permission of authors.

ing their feelings through thoughtful reflections on their service experience. Participation activities are undertaken by students after careful study and preparation. Students must know why they are involved and how to carry their projects to completion. Teachers and other adults assist students in preparing for such projects.

Table 14–4 illustrates social participation. Three types of community service found in schools today are: school, community, and individual. Social participation is shown on a continuum of possible activities ranging from a one-time activity requiring only a small commitment of time to long-term projects requiring a regular commitment of time and using multiple intellectual and social skills.

School service projects are centered around activities in the school. Tutoring younger students, performing skits to teach safety or health information to other students, making tray decorations for hospital or nursing home patients, and collecting food or blankets for the needy are examples of school service projects. In school service projects teachers provide the students with most of the guidance. Community projects involve students in working with or through governmental and community organizations. Helping on a clean-up drive, planting trees in a park, helping build a children's playground or assisting with a blood drive are all examples of community service projects. The individual service project is one in which the individual assumes the major responsibility in carrying out the service for an extended period of time. Tutoring in an adult literacy program, being a scout leader, and volunteering in a nursing home are all examples of individual service projects. Table 14–4 also shows the skills, values, and citizenship concepts learned or practiced with each type of project and is arranged in a hierarchical order. Individual projects use the skills, values, and knowledge of the other two projects as well as those listed for individual projects. An examination of the social participation presently in the school curriculum indicates that the school and community projects are more predominant in grades K–8 (Procter & Haas, 1990).

STUDYING ISSUES

In the United States, citizens make their wishes known by voting for representatives, by voting directly on issues in referendums, by signing petitions, writing letters, displaying signs, taking part in support rallies, and giving speeches. The rights of freedom of speech, freedom of the press, peaceful assembly, and petitioning the government are guaranteed by the first amendment. Citizens and representatives evaluate the expressions of others. Participation in such activities is expected to reflect evidence of truthfulness and thoughtful consideration of the issues. Provisions are stipulated for legal redress of grievances for untruthful information and malicious intent. Most people will not respect views they consider to be poorly derived. Information and the ability to use it gives a person the power to influence others, to make better decisions, and to exert control in his or her life. To make decisions on political issues, people must be informed. The information and skills learned in school contribute to the goal of informed citizens.

Developing the skills and habit of learning about current issues are important social studies goals (See Figure 14–2). Among the resources for teaching social studies current events are newspapers, magazines, and television programs written for students in grades 1–8.

Media plays a major role in forming public opinion because it controls the knowledge of citizens. Failure to be media-literate is a major obstacle to successful adult civic participation (Nelson, 1990). The newspaper industry has done much to promote the intelligent use of print journalism by making available materials for teachers to use with their students. The fact is that today most people gain their knowledge of current issues and events from the television news. Most people believe that the television presents them with accurate information. Some individuals and groups accuse journalists of being biased while others accuse politicians of controlling or trying to control the media. The United States Communications Act of 1934 requires broadcasters to serve the public interest and provide a broad range of opinions to keep the public informed about all sides of a controversial issue. Since 1968, Action for Children's Television (ACT) has been working for television policies that increase the viewing options for children and young teens, offering, among other listings, public affairs shows and live action dramas (Charren, 1990).

The Children's Television Act of 1990 put a limit on the number of minutes of ads per hour in children's programs and required stations to air educational shows for children as a condition of license renewal. During Operation Desert Storm the major networks produced special programs to answer questions for students about the war. News broadcasts especially designed for students are now becoming available for daily use in the schools. A controversy exists over whether such programs should include commercials. Some states, such as California and New York, have banned those programs that include commercials (Charren, 1990).

Figure 14–2 These students' artwork is one result of their study of issues relating to the management of the world's rain forests.

The major goal of all school news programs is to stimulate students to listen to the news so they include topics of special interest to young people. However, students need to become knowledgeable watchers of television news and documentaries. Few efforts have been made to help students understand how television presents information and what impact this has on the coverage of news issues. Television relies on pictures to present its stories. Television journalists criticize their medium for having scripts so short that they distort the news. Time restrictions prohibit providing a perspective to frame stories and impede providing complete statements of the various views (Trotta, 1991). Students need to become aware of how the various media affect their perception of reality. They also need to learn the skills of critically gaining information through the media. Among these skills are:

- making tentative judgments or deferring judgments until all the necessary facts are available
- recognizing the strengths of each form of media
- recognizing the weaknesses of each form of media
- evaluating the intent of the presentation format
- applying critical thinking skills to the content presented

Teachers can accomplish these objectives through lessons in which students study and use each form of media and compare the various forms of media. Some lesson ideas that accomplish these ends include:

1. Examine the presentation of the same story as it appears in the television news broadcast, the newspaper, and the news magazine and compare how each covers the story. Use a chart with such categories as facts, background explanation, emotional words, opinions or viewpoints, and graphics or pictures.

2. Analyze news stories in the newspaper and on television for their length and content. Discuss the findings and the students' feelings about what they have found.

3. Compare different types of television programs and written articles. Identify what the students like and dislike about the various programs and articles and which are most appropriate in answering various types of questions.

4. Follow a big news story through its development over time. Make lists of the knowledge learned on each day. Ask new questions and form tentative conclusions as the study progresses. When the story is over, review the experience. Identify which of the tentative conclusions were accurate. Identify the most helpful questions asked. Make final conclusions and judgments on how objectively and completely the story was presented.

5. Examine the trade-offs involved in the quality of information and the speed of presenting a story. Decide at what times speed or details are more important.

6. Ask students to generate questions that they still have after reading or hearing a story. Research these questions.

7. Identify the sources of information students have about current events. Interview adults about some very significant event and ask about the ways they got their information.

8. Read biographies or interviews of journalists to discover how they feel about their profession.

9. Interview local journalists about their profession and the problems they encounter.

10. Have the students assume the role of a journalist. Have them write various types of articles and produce their own newspaper or video program. As they encounter the problems of the journalist, discuss these with the students and discuss their feelings about the problems and the solutions used in the class or by the editor.

STUDENT GOVERNMENT

Student participation in the government of their own school through student councils has long been a tradition in the junior high and high schools. Today some schools have also instituted student participation in the lower grades as part of the democratic-schools movement. In schools where such programs are successful the entire school and the principal have a strong commitment to the program. Time, encouragement, and guidance are given to the students to conduct successful experiences. Student government is considered an important learning experience for all of the students and not a popularity contest to select a president or a way to manipulate students.

Students elect representatives who meet regularly and return to meet with their classmates to share concerns and progress. Students identify the problems and needs of the school and are assisted in making the appropriate contacts in the school system and community to carry out their plans successfully. Students carefully research their ideas and develop workable plans. Students then present the plans to classmates, explaining the concerns of the adults and administrators and calling upon fellow students to exhibit the types of behaviors needed to make the program a success. For example, when the students at one school wanted soap in the restrooms, the janitor told them that the soap dispensers would be broken by uncaring students and would only create more problems. The students mounted a campaign to educate their fellow students, pointing out the need for the soap and the necessity for all students to use the dispensers properly. Students also set up a monitoring system to check on student behavior in the restrooms (Sadowsky, 1991). Other schools have made improvements in the safety and physical environments of their schools that have required contacting the proper city officials or raising funds to accomplish their goals. Student government representatives play an important role in welcoming and orienting new students by explaining the school community and its government. Through such a process, students learn how to present their needs in petitions and to address the concerns of public officials in their presentations. They also learn about the responsibilities of citizens to help care for government property and to share its use for the common good.

The democratic classroom is another way of involving students in learning about democracy. The work in such classrooms is designed to have the students practice behaviors that reflect the democratic ideals of rights, responsibilities, and respect for self and others. Democratic classes make use of such techniques as cooperative learning (see chapter 7), the free expression and discussion of ideas, and the involvement of students in making decisions and setting goals (Holmes, 1991). The teacher in such classes does not surrender the teaching of the class to the ideas of the students. Instead, he or she discusses with students the goals of education and the needs of the students to succeed in the class. The teacher models respect for all students and their ideas by inviting them to take part in making age-appropriate decisions. The teacher guides students to consider their needs and the common good through asking questions during the decision-making process and by involving the students in evaluating their choices and revising procedures or instituting new choices as needed. Teachers in democratic classrooms trust their students and allow them to make errors and face the consequences. However, they monitor the classroom activities carefully and encourage the realization and correction of errors before they become big problems.

POLITICAL PARTICIPATION

Some elementary teachers have worked with their students to directly influence the formation of public politics at the local, state, and national levels. The political activities of third grade students at Weber Elementary School in Fairbanks, Alaska, have been featured on television programs in many places including London, England. The students' activities include the selection of a current issue, in-depth study of the facts and claims, the use of communication skills and mathematics skills to gather data and inform citizens and politicians of their findings. Newspaper articles, guest editorials, and letters regularly flow from their classroom throughout Alaska and the continental United States as the students study issues and share their knowledge and views. Not only do the students learn to process gathering information cooperatively but they learn to respond appropriately and usefully in the democratic tradition, explains their teacher, Grace Ann Heacock. "They are being empowered to keep a government of, for, and by the people" (Heacock, 1990, p. 11).

As a result of the active political participation of fifth graders at St. Lawrence School in Fairfield, Connecticut, Public Act 84–56, "Friendship Day," is celebrated on the fourth Sunday in April. Among their activities were lobbying state legislators, testifying on behalf of the bill, and witnessing the signing of the bill into law by the governor (Francis, 1990).

Over several years' time the efforts of the Extended Learning Program at Jackson Elementary School in the Salt Lake School District in Utah have resulted in the cleanup of a hazardous waste site, the passage of two laws, the planting of hundreds of trees, and $10,000 in neighborhood sidewalk improvements. Teacher Barbara Lewis writes: "Solving social problems will bring excitement and suspense into your life" (Lewis, 1991, p. 2). To assist other students, teachers, and interested adults, Lewis has written *The Kids' Guide to Social Action.* Among her advice are ten tips for taking action:

1. Choose a problem.
2. Do your research.
3. Brainstorm possible solutions.
4. Build coalitions of support.
5. Identify your opposition.
6. Advertise.
7. Raise money.
8. Carry out your solution.
9. Evaluate.
10. Don't give up.

Through actively taking part in examining political issues and trying to influence political decisions, the students learn much about the functioning of the government. They also learn important principles concerning the use of power in society and they experience tests of their reasoning skills and values. Such projects are filled with hard work and emotional ups and downs. Not every elementary or middle school teacher will want to use direct political participation with his or her students. However, because of the many options for social action, all teachers can find a form of participation in which to engage their students.

INTERNATIONAL CONCERNS: GLOBAL AND PEACE EDUCATION

Global education is the study of the economic, political, ecological, and technological systems and the problems that extend across national boundaries. The four persistent problems that encompass the entire globe and serve as the focus of global education are:

- peace and security
- national and international development
- environmental problems
- human rights

The five metaconcepts of interdependence, change, culture, scarcity, and conflict are recommended to organize the study of the persistent problems (Kniep, 1989). Throughout all of history, groups of people have been interdependent. In the modern world, interdependence is very great and will likely increase. Governments, corporations, clubs, organizations, states, and individuals are all involved in transnational projects that contribute to global interdependence. Elements of global education are in all the disciplines contributing to social studies content (see the chapters on geography, economics, psychology, and history). Political science, law, and civics are important because many of the actions needed to solve global problems require the cooperation of nations, international organizations, and people living in several nations.

Closely related to global education is the peace-education movement. Prompted by the concerns about nuclear war, peace education today recognizes that removal of nuclear weapons is not enough to stop war. The underlying causes of aggression must be examined and replaced with better ways of preventing conflicts. Peace educators strive to improve human relations between all people and to reduce conflict by promoting increased understanding among people. Peace educators believe that conflicts tend to arise as a result of variations in the distribution of resources and power, giving rise to such emotions as envy and greed. In addition to the interdependence of the economic and natural systems, peace education also looks at the commonality of all peoples and cultures and strongly supports a belief in the universality of human rights. Peace educators seek not only to preserve the world but to preserve it so that all people are safe and secure in body and conscience. They believe that a better world will result when there are better laws and strong national and international governments to enforce the laws.

A Practice Activity

The following are sample activities suggested by global and peace educators for grades K–8. These activities are designed to identify commonalities among people in the problems facing all nations. They encourage cooperation in finding solutions to these problems. As you read the activities, for each activity identify the *academic disciplines* that are closely related to the activity and a *concept* that is necessary to understanding the issue.

1. The students surveyed the national origins of their families and made a map illustrating their findings.
2. Students graphed the number of elephants in the world over the last 100 years. They investigated the reasons for the decline in the elephant population and what is being done to try to stop the decline.
3. Each student researched a nation and wrote illustrated reports to share with classmates.
4. The students read and compared school rules from five different nations.
5. Students read the Universal Declaration of Human Rights and discussed why each right is important. They then discussed whether children might need some additional rights and they wrote their ideas as a Declaration of Rights for Children.
6. Students read about people throughout history who made trips around the world and found that the time to accomplish the trip decreased steadily as technology increased. They then conducted a survey to find out how people think faster transportation and instantaneous communication are changing the world and if people think this is good.
7. Students read newspapers and news magazines to learn about the refugee problem.
8. Students play a variety of games that do not involve competition but that require cooperation to complete.

☞ *Suggested answers to the above questions are:*

Discipline	**Concept**
1. *history/geography*	*immigration*
2. *geography/sociology*	*endangered species, interdependence*
3. *economics/anthropology*	*culture, productive resources*
4. *government/sociology*	*rules, traditions*
5. *philosophy/government*	*rights, human dignity*
6. *history/science*	*technology, interdependence*
7. *sociology/government*	*conflict, self-interest*
8. *sociology*	*cooperation, common good*

There are many interest groups whose concerns fall under the umbrella of global and peace education. There are many special days or weeks throughout the year sponsored by such groups. These groups often supply free educational materials and suggested activities that may be enjoyed by students. The danger is that if such activities are taught in isolation, they will not contribute to meaningful learning. Instead, students may learn only a vague awareness of the issues, may experience despair because they see only a huge problem with no solution, or they may be encouraged to embrace simplistic solutions. Time is needed to devote to in-depth study of the issues raised by global and peace educators. Units that define the problems and investigate subtopics and alternatives are a more appropriate instructional approach for these topics.

SUMMARY

Citizens in a democracy must know the structure and procedures by which their government works and the ideals and values that form the principles of democracy. This includes examining the concerns of others and recognizing that differences and similarities exist within the society. Students need to learn to respect and appreciate the multicultural nature of American society. Today the United States plays a leading role among the nations of the world politically, economically, and scientifically. The lives of American citizens are increasingly more interdependent with those of people all over the world. American citizens, by their participation or lack thereof, are directly and indirectly affecting the lives of people throughout the world. More knowledge about international relations and problems is being emphasized. Calls are coming from many places for youth to play a more active part in their communities. Schools are changing their curricula to increase the participation of their students in various aspects and efforts in their communities. Active participation by citizens is a requirement for democracy to flourish. The schools have long been viewed as a place where students learn the importance of this truth and can acquire and practice the skills of active participation in their society.

REFERENCES

Anderson, C. C. (1980). Promoting responsible citizenship through elementary law-related education. *Social Education, 44,* 383–386.

Banks, J. A. (1981). *Teaching strategies for ethnic studies* (third edition). Boston: Allyn and Bacon, Inc.

Banks, J. A. & Lynch, J. (1986). *Multicultural education in western societies.* New York: Praeger.

Brody, R. A. (1989). Why study politics? In National Commission on Social Studies in the School, *Charting a Course: Social Studies for the 21st Century* (pp. 59–63). Washington, DC: National Council for the Social Studies.

Charren, P. (1990). What's missing in children's TV? *World Monitor, 3*(12), 28–35.

Clark, T. (1990). Participation in democratic citizenship education. *The Social Studies, 81,* 206–209.

Engle, S. H. & Ochoa, A. S. (1988). *Education for democratic citizenship: Decision making in the social studies.* New York: Teachers College Press.

Francis, J. (1990). Hands-On legislation. *Social Studies and the Young Learner, 2*(4), 6–8.

Gay, G. (1991). Culturally diverse students and social studies. In J. P. Shaver (ed.), *Handbook of Research on Social Studies Teaching and Learning* (pp. 144–156). New York: Macmillan Publishing Company.

Haas, M. E. (1991). An analysis of the social science and history concepts in elementary social studies textbooks grades 1–4. *Theory and Research in Social Education, 19,* 211–220.

Heacock, G. (1990). The we-search process. *Social Studies and the Young Learner, 2*(3), 9–11.

Hess, R. & Torney, J. (1967). *The development of political attitudes in children.* Chicago: Adeline.

Hodgkinson, H. (1990). The context of 21st-century civics and citizenship. In W. T. Callahan and R. A. Banaszak (Eds.), *Citizenship for the 21st Century* (pp. 23–31). Bloomington, IN: Social Studies Development Center.

Holmes, E. E. (1991). Democracy in elementary school classes. *Social Education, 55,* 176–178.

Jenness, D. (1990). *Making sense of social studies.* New York: Macmillan Publishing Company.

Kniep, W. M. (1989). Social studies within a global education. *Social Education, 53,* 399–403.

Langston, S. (1990). Citizen participation and citizenship education in the 21st century. In W. T. Callahan, Jr. & Banaszak, R. A. (eds.), *Citizenship for the 21st Century* (pp. 297–310). Bloomington, IN: Social Studies Development Center.

Larkins, G. A.; Hawkins, M. L.; & Gilmore, A. (1987). Trivial and noninformative content of elementary social studies: A review of primary texts in four series. *Theory and Research in Social Education, 14*(4), 299–311.

Lewis, B. A. (1991). *The kid's guide to social action.* Minneapolis: Free Spirit Publishing Inc.

Nakagawa, M. & Pang, V. O. (1990). Cooperative pluralism: Moving from "me" to "we". *Social Studies and the Young Learner. 2*(4), 9–11.

National Assessment of Educational Progress. (1990). *The civics report card.* Washington, DC: U.S. Department of Education.

National Commission on Social Studies in the Schools. (1989). *Charting a course: Social studies for the 21st century* (pp. 59–63). Washington, DC: National Council for the Social Studies.

National Council for the Social Studies. (1976). Curriculum guidelines for multiethnic education. Washington, DC: National Council for the Social Studies.

National Council for the Social Studies. (1979). Revisions of the NCSS social studies curriculum guidelines. *Social Education, 43,* 261–273.

National Council for the Social Studies. (1989). In search of a scope and sequence for social studies report of the task force on scope and sequence. *Social Education, 53,* 376–387.

Nelson, M. (1990). A future for civic education. In W. T. Callahan and R. A. Banaszak (Eds.), *Citizenship for the 21st Century* (pp. 41–57). Bloomington, IN: Social Studies Development Center.

Patrick, J. J. & Hoge, J. D. (1991). Teaching government, civics and law. In J. P. Shaver (Ed.), *Handbook of Research on Social Studies Teaching and Learning* (pp. 427–436). New York: Macmillan Publishing Company.

Procter, D. (1991, November). *Getting your students involved in community service: The sooner the better!* Paper presented at the annual meeting of the National Council for the Social Studies, Washington, D.C.

Procter, D. R. & Haas, M. E. (1990). *A handbook of school-based community projects for student participation.* ED 326 467.

Sadowsky, E. (1991). Democracy in the elementary school: Learning by doing. In J. S. Benninga (Ed.), *Moral, Character, and Civic Education in the Elementary School* (pp. 84–106). New York: Teachers College Press.

Starr, I. (1989). The law studies movement: A brief commentary on its history and rationale. *ATSS/UFT Journal, 44*(1), 5–7.

Superka, D. P. & Hawke, S. D. (1982). Social roles: A focus for social studies in the 1980s. In I. Morrisett (ed.), *Social Studies in the 1980s* (pp. 118–130). Alexandria, VA: Association for Supervision and Curriculum Development.

Torney-Purta, J. (1990). Political Socialization in W. T. Callahan and R. A. Banaszak (Eds.), *Citizenship for the 21st Century* (pp. 171–198). Bloomington, IN: Social Studies Development Center.

Torney-Purta, J. (1991). Cross-national research in social studies. In J. P. Shaver (ed.), *Handbook of Research on Social Studies Teaching and Learning* (pp. 591–601). New York: Macmillan Publishing Company.

Torney-Purta, J., Oppenheim, A. N., & Farnen, R. F. (1975). *Civic education in ten countries: An empirical study.* New York: Wiley.

Trotta, L. (1991). *Fighting for air: In the trenches with television news.* New York: Simon and Schuster.

Index